Ta-daaaah!

Thank you very much for picking up *Haikyu!!* volume 15!! I...think I had something I wanted to write here, but I could also be imagining things. In fact, it's highly possible I was imagining things, so I'll just come up with something better next time.

HARUICHI FURUDATE began his manga career when he was 25 years old with the one-shot *Ousama Kid* (King Kid), which won an honorable mention for the 14th Jump Treasure Newcomer Manga Prize. His first series, *Kiben Gakuha, Yotsuya Sensei no Kaidan* (Philosophy School, Yotsuya Sensei's Ghost Stories), was serialized in Weekly Shonen Jump in 2010. In 2012, he began serializing *Haikyu!!* in Weekly Shonen Jump, where it became his most popular work to date.

HAIKYU!!
VOLUME 15
SHONEN JUMP Manga Edition

Story and Art by
HARUICHI FURUDATE

Translation **1 ADRIENNE BECK**
Touch-Up Art & Lettering **2 ERIKA TERRIQUEZ**
Design **3 YUKIKO WHITLEY**
Editor **4 MARLENE FIRST**

HAIKYU!! © 2012 by Haruichi Furudate
All rights reserved.
First published in Japan in 2012 by SHUEISHA Inc., Tokyo.
English translation rights arranged by SHUEISHA Inc.

The stories, characters and incidents mentioned
in this publication are entirely fictional.

Printed in the U.S.A.

Published by VIZ Media, LLC
P.O. Box 77010
San Francisco, CA 94107

10 9 8 7 6 5 4 3 2 1
First printing, September 2017

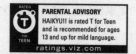

www.shonenjump.com   www.viz.com

SHONEN JUMP MANGA

Go! Go! Let's Go! Date

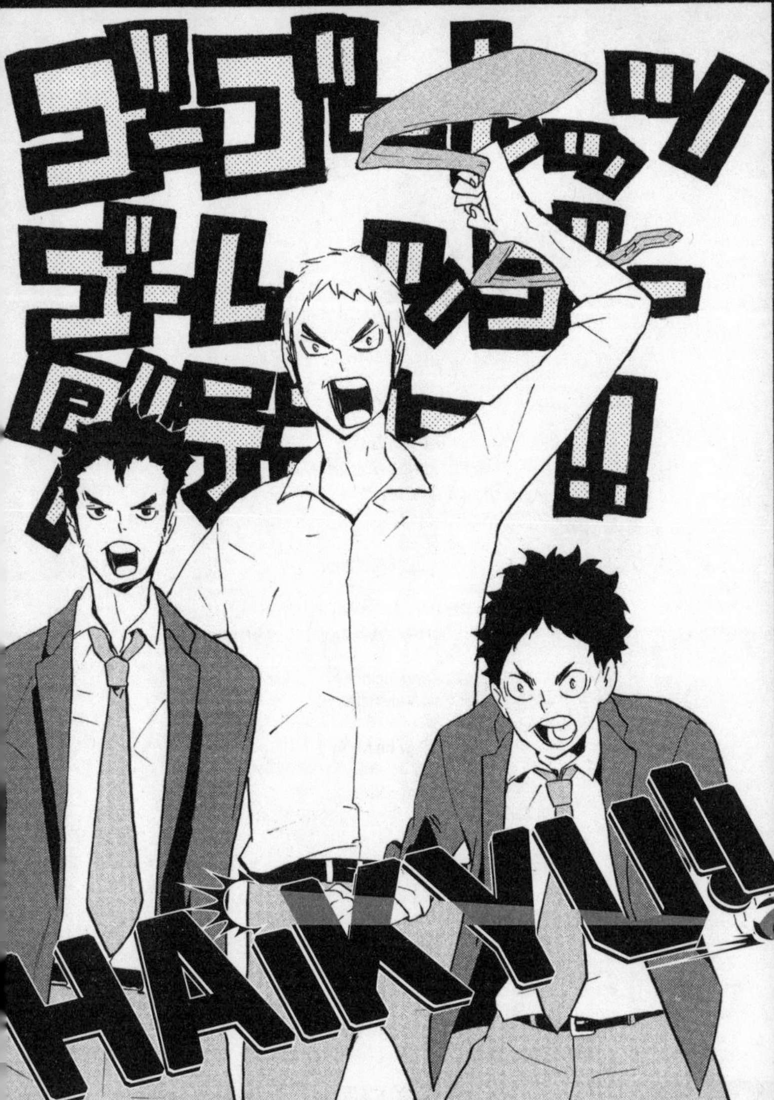

HAIKYU!!

HARUICHI FURUDATE

DESTROYER

15

Karasuno High School Volleyball Club

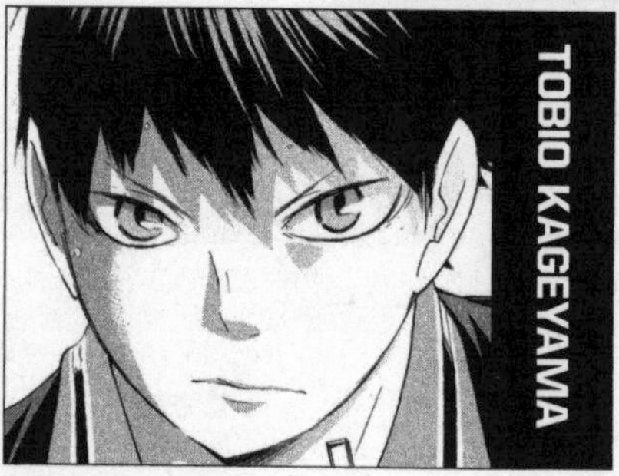
TOBIO KAGEYAMA

1ST YEAR / SETTER

His instincts and athletic talent are so good that he's like a "king" who rules the court. Demanding and egocentric.

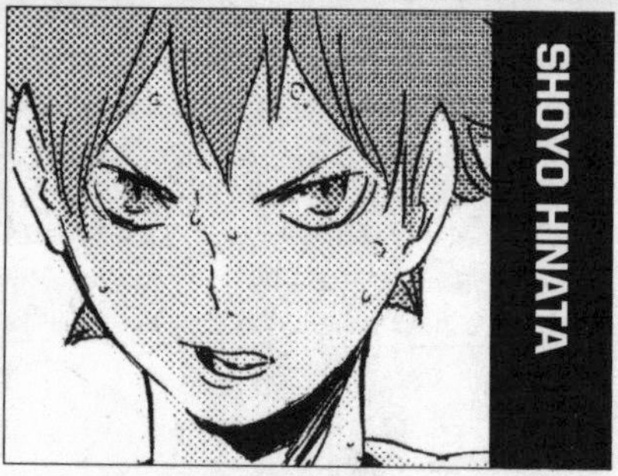
SHOYO HINATA

1ST YEAR / MIDDLE BLOCKER

Even though he doesn't have the best body type for volleyball, he is super athletic. Gets nervous easily.

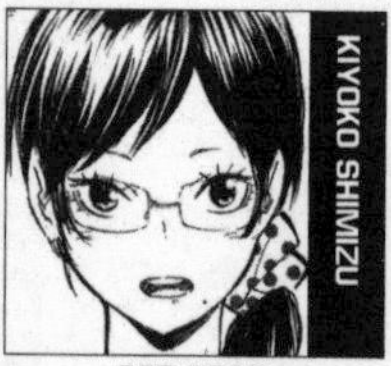
KIYOKO SHIMIZU

3RD YEAR
MANAGER

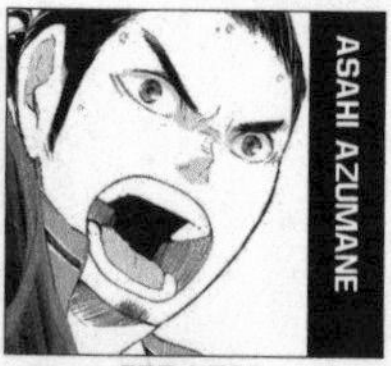
ASAHI AZUMANE

3RD YEAR
WING SPIKER

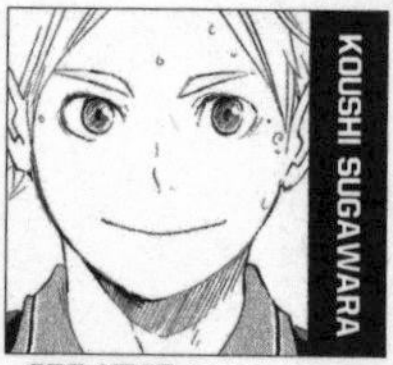
KOUSHI SUGAWARA

3RD YEAR (VICE CAPTAIN)
SETTER

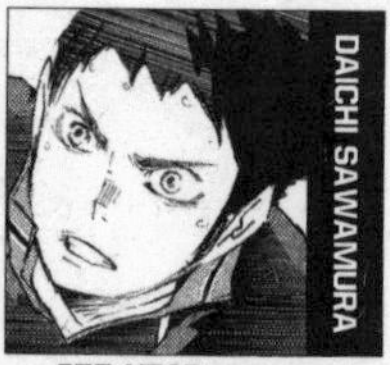
DAICHI SAWAMURA

3RD YEAR (CAPTAIN)
WING SPIKER

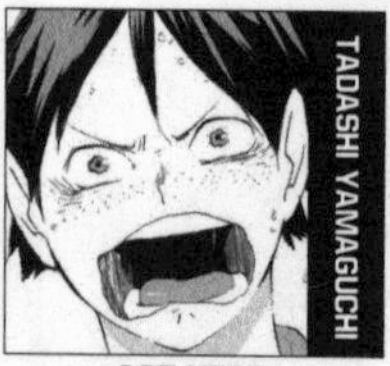
TADASHI YAMAGUCHI

1ST YEAR
MIDDLE BLOCKER

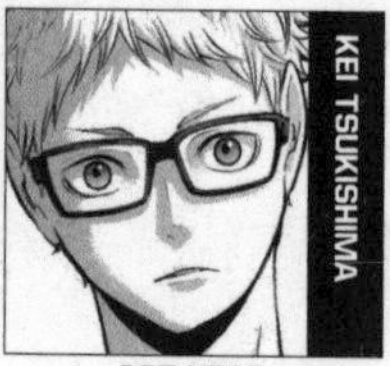
KEI TSUKISHIMA

1ST YEAR
MIDDLE BLOCKER

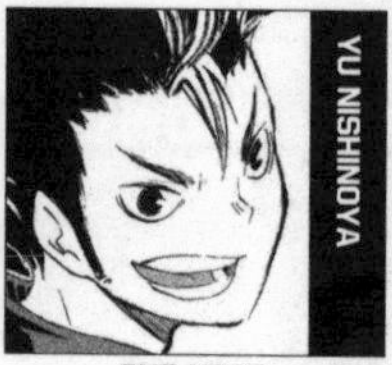
YU NISHINOYA

2ND YEAR
LIBERO

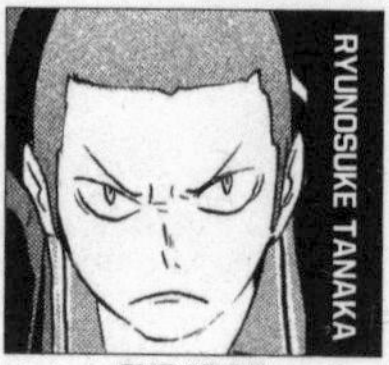
RYUNOSUKE TANAKA

2ND YEAR
WING SPIKER

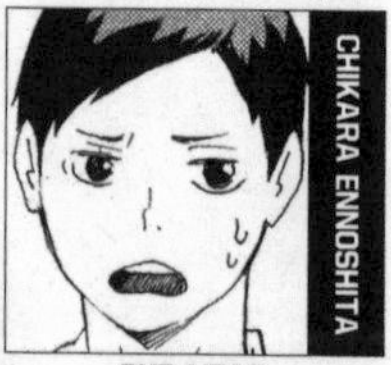
CHIKARA ENNOSHITA

2ND YEAR
WING SPIKER

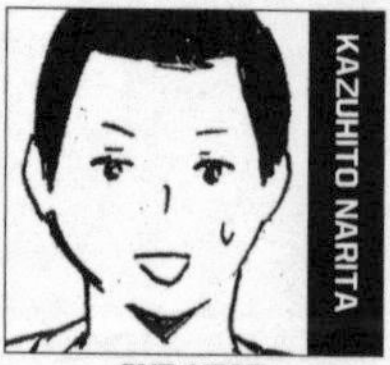
KAZUHITO NARITA

2ND YEAR
MIDDLE BLOCKER

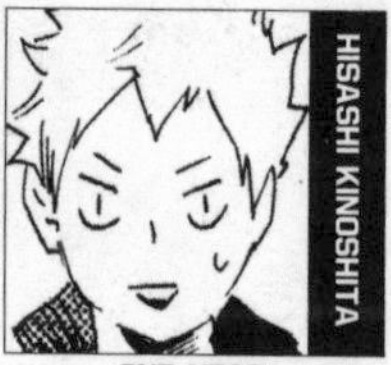
HISASHI KINOSHITA

2ND YEAR
WING SPIKER

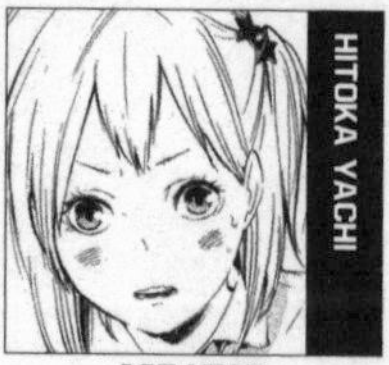
HITOKA YACHI

1ST YEAR
MANAGER

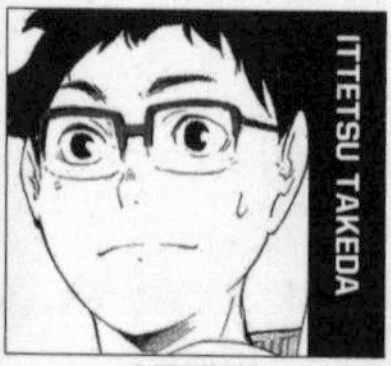
ITTETSU TAKEDA

ADVISER

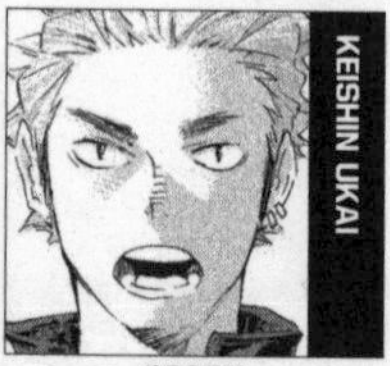
KEISHIN UKAI

COACH

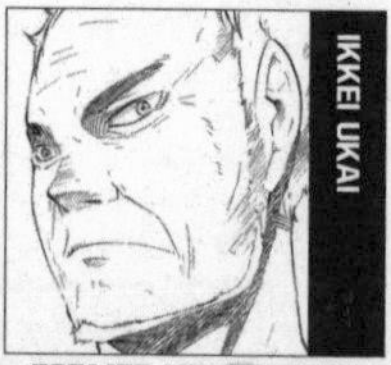
IKKEI UKAI

FORMER HEAD COACH

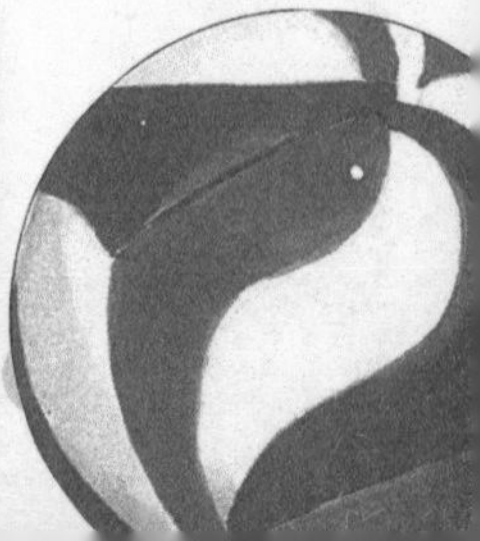

CHARACTERS

MIYAGI PREFECTURE SPRING TOURNAMENT QUALIFIER TOURNAMENT ARC

SHIRATORIZAWA

WAKATOSHI USHIJIMA

3RD YEAR
WING SPIKER

DATE TECH

TAKANOBU AONE

2ND YEAR
MIDDLE BLOCKER

AOBA JOHSAI

TOHRU OIKAWA

3RD YEAR
SETTER

KARASUNO'S MAJOR RIVALS

FUKURODANI (Tokyo)

KOTARO BOKUTO

3RD YEAR
WING SPIKER

NEKOMA (Tokyo)

KENMA KOZUME

2ND YEAR
SETTER

Ever since he saw the legendary player known as "the Little Giant" compete at the national volleyball finals, Shoyo Hinata has been aiming to be the best volleyball player ever! He decides to join the volleyball club at his middle school and gets to play in an official tournament during his third year. His team is crushed by a team led by volleyball prodigy Tobio Kageyama, also known as "the King of the Court." Swearing revenge on Kageyama, Hinata graduates middle school and enters Karasuno High School, the school where the Little Giant played. However, upon joining the club, he finds out that Kageyama is there too! The two of them bicker constantly, but they bring out the best in each other's talents and become a powerful combo! Eliminated from the Inter-High Qualifiers, the Karasuno team sets their sights on the Spring Tournament. They travel to Tokyo for a weeklong training camp with Nekoma and a bunch of other Tokyo powerhouse teams. Later, armed with an arsenal of new weapons, Karasuno heads to the Spring Tournament! Advancing through the prelims and into the quarterfinal round of the qualifiers, Karasuno faces sudden disaster when their captain, Sawamura, gets injured! But his replacement, Ennoshita, steps up admirably and helps lead the team to victory. Karasuno's place in the semifinals is secured, and the question now is who they will face off against next—Aoba Johsai or Date Tech?

HAIKYU!!

15 DESTROYER

CHAPTER 126:
The Third Panel — 007

CHAPTER 127:
Golden Child — 029

CHAPTER 128:
The Wall Will Be Rebuilt — 049

CHAPTER 129:
The New Karasuno — 069

CHAPTER 130:
Overcome — 089

CHAPTER 131:
Aoba Johsai's Gears — 109

CHAPTER 132:
Destroyer — 131

CHAPTER 133:
Setter Battle: Round 2 — 153

CHAPTER 134:
Both Teams — 173

CHAPTER 135:
Slow Starter — 193

Bonus Story — 214

CHAPTER 126: The Third Panel

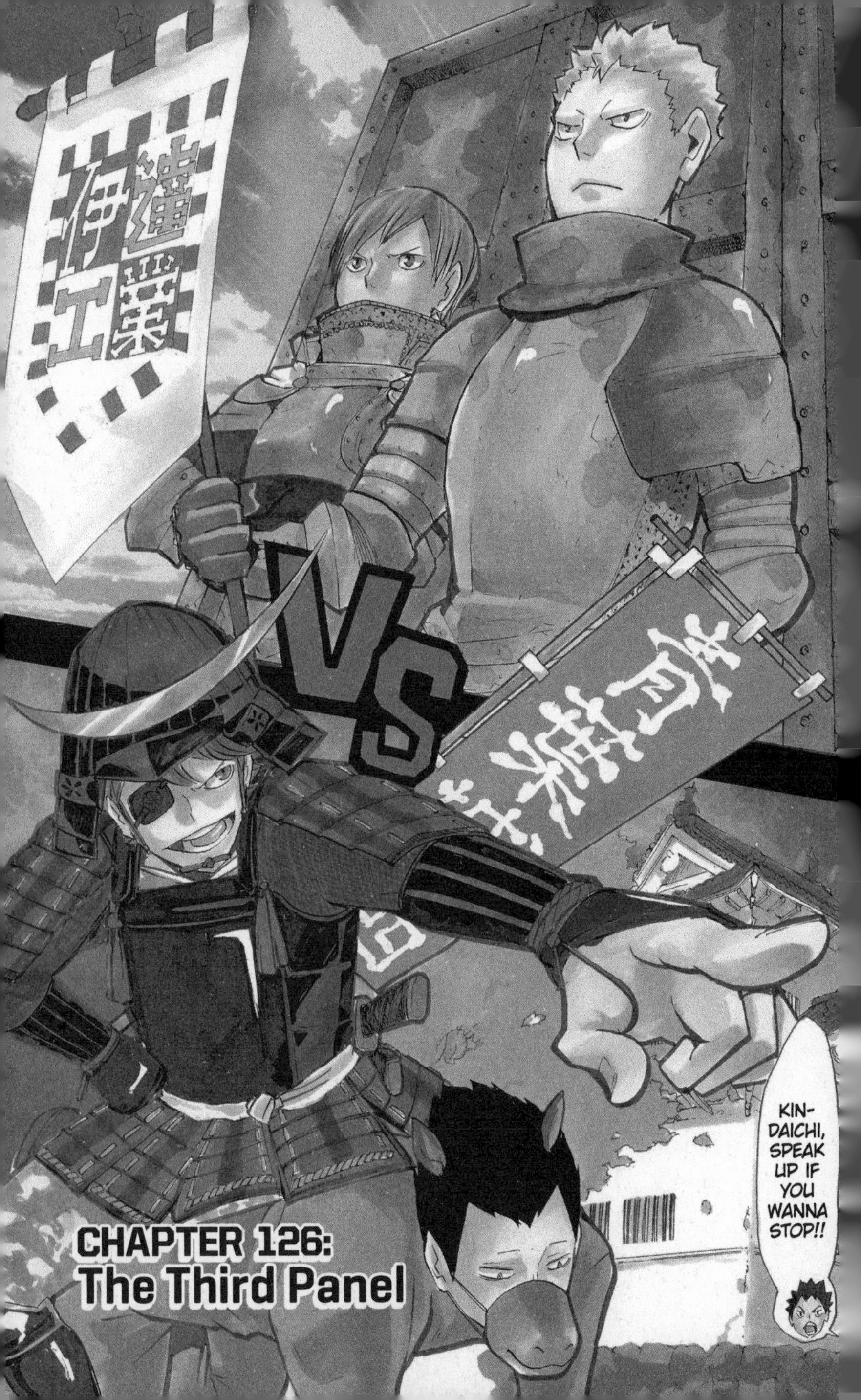
伊達工業
VS
KIN-DAICHI, SPEAK UP IF YOU WANNA STOP!!

HAIKYU!!

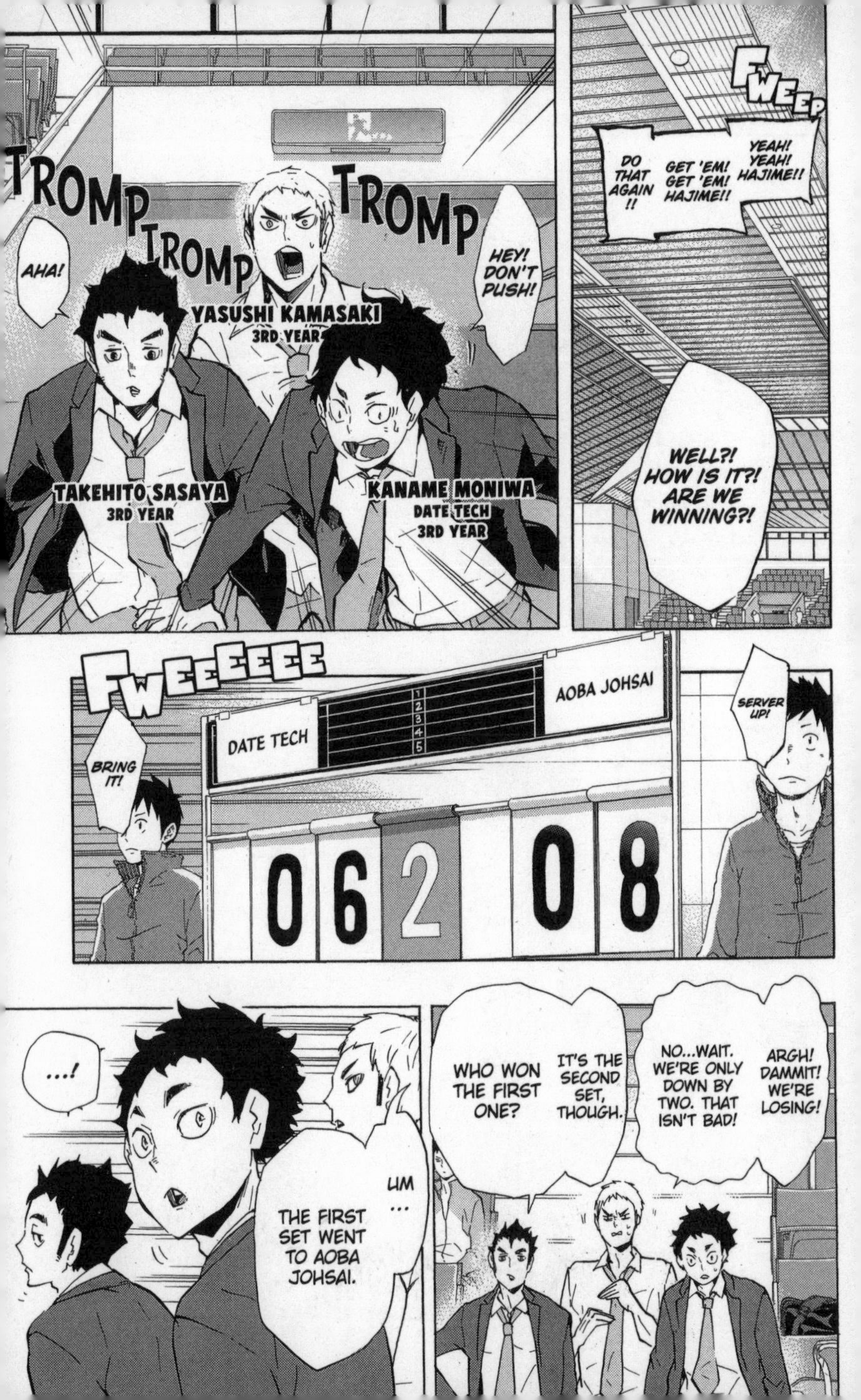
FWEEP
YEAH! YEAH! HAJIME!!
GET 'EM! GET 'EM! HAJIME!!
DO THAT AGAIN !!
WELL?! HOW IS IT?! ARE WE WINNING?!
TROMP
HEY! DON'T PUSH!
TROMP
TROMP
YASUSHI KAMASAKI 3RD YEAR
KANAME MONIWA DATE TECH 3RD YEAR
TAKEHITO SASAYA 3RD YEAR
AHA!
SERVER UP!
FWEEEEEE
AOBA JOHSAI
1 2 3 4 5
DATE TECH
06 2 08
BRING IT!
ARGH! DAMMIT! WE'RE LOSING!
NO...WAIT. WE'RE ONLY DOWN BY TWO. THAT ISN'T BAD!
IT'S THE SECOND SET, THOUGH.
WHO WON THE FIRST ONE?
UM ...
THE FIRST SET WENT TO AOBA JOHSAI.
...!

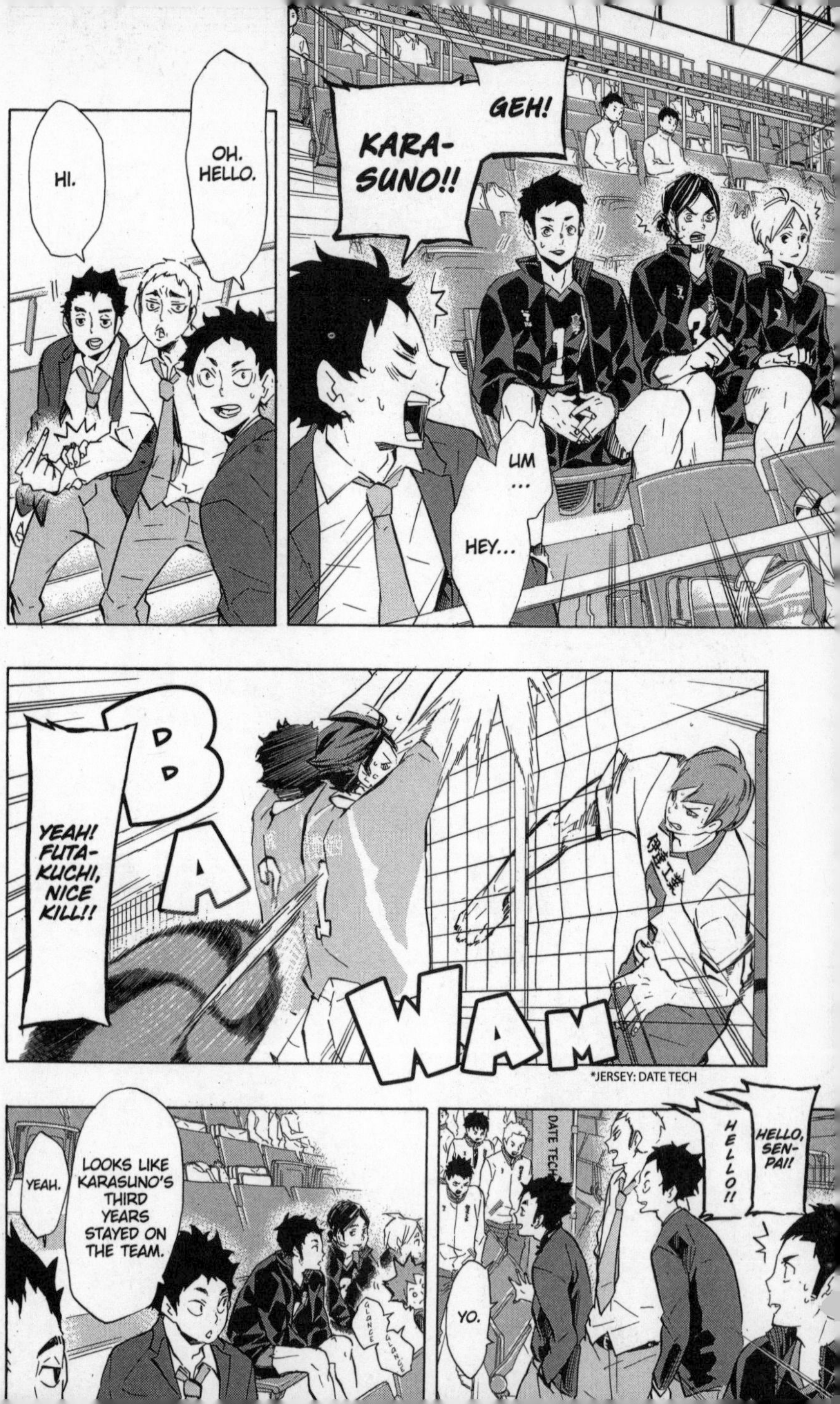
GEH!
KARA-SUNO!!
UM...
HEY...
OH. HELLO.
HI.
BA
WAM
YEAH! FUTA-KUCHI, NICE KILL!!
*JERSEY: DATE TECH
DATE TECH
HELLO, SEN-PAI!
HELLO!!
YO.
LOOKS LIKE KARASUNO'S THIRD YEARS STAYED ON THE TEAM.
YEAH.
GLANCE
GLANCE

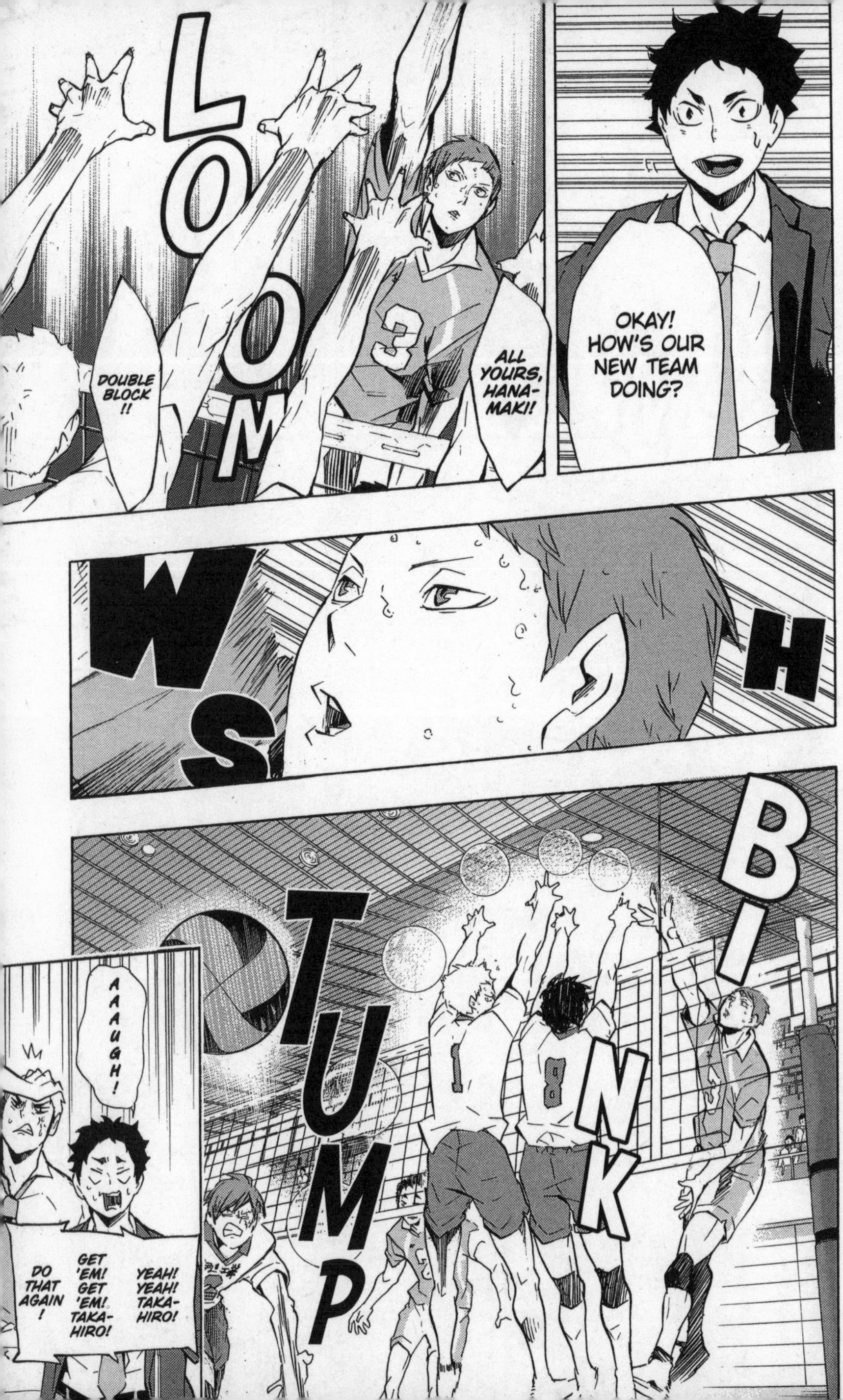
OKAY! HOW'S OUR NEW TEAM DOING?
LOOM
ALL YOURS, HANA-MAKI!
DOUBLE BLOCK !!
WSH
BINK
TUMP
AAAUGH!
YEAH! YEAH! TAKA-HIRO!
GET 'EM! GET 'EM! TAKA-HIRO!
DO THAT AGAIN!

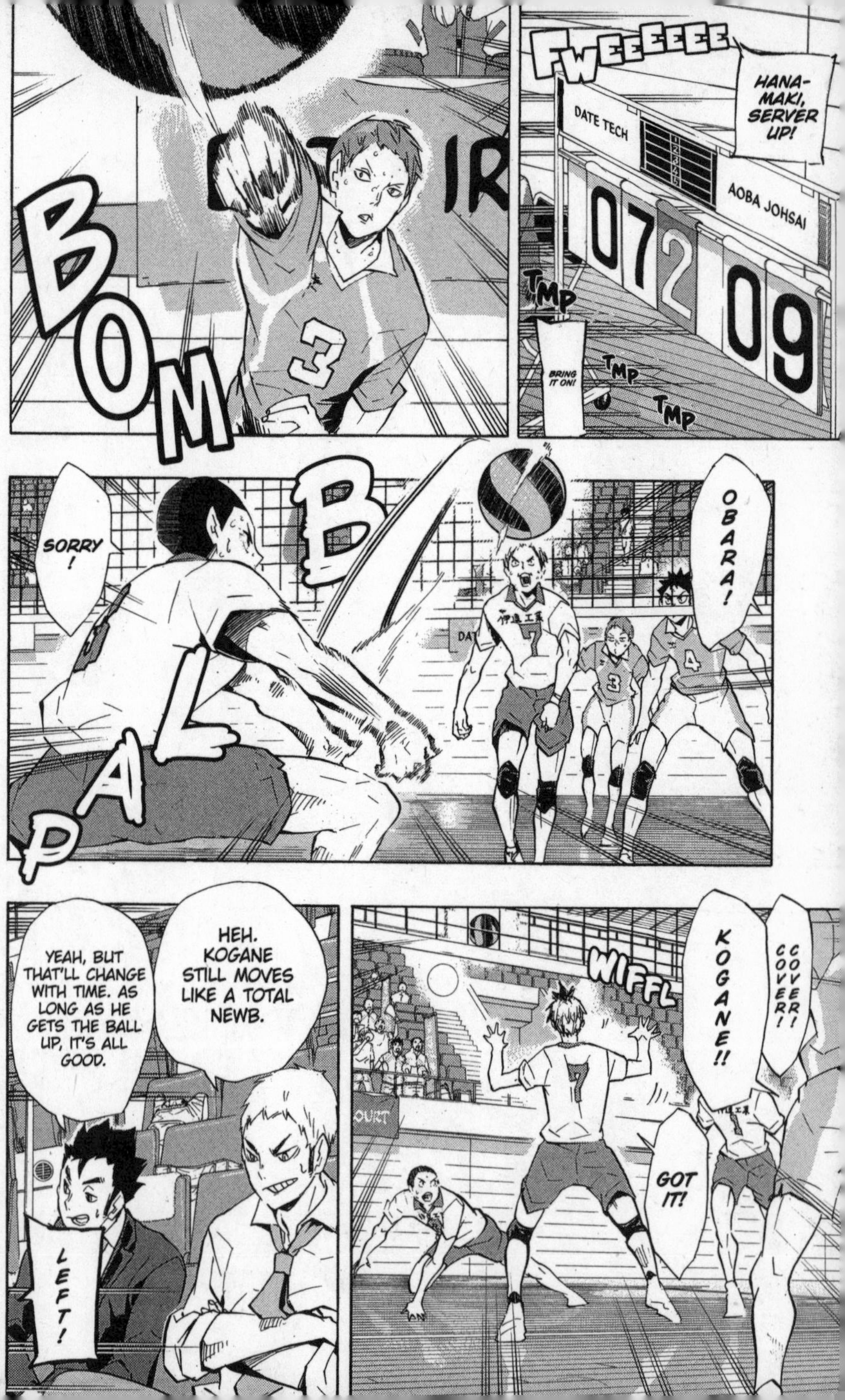
FWEEEEEE
HANA-MAKI, SERVER UP!
DATE TECH
AOBA JOHSAI
07 2 09
TMP
BRING IT ON!
TMP
TMP
BOM
OBARA!
B
SORRY!
PAL
COVER!
COVER!
KOGANE!!
WIFFL
GOT IT!
HEH. KOGANE STILL MOVES LIKE A TOTAL NEWB.
YEAH, BUT THAT'LL CHANGE WITH TIME. AS LONG AS HE GETS THE BALL UP, IT'S ALL GOOD.
LEFT!

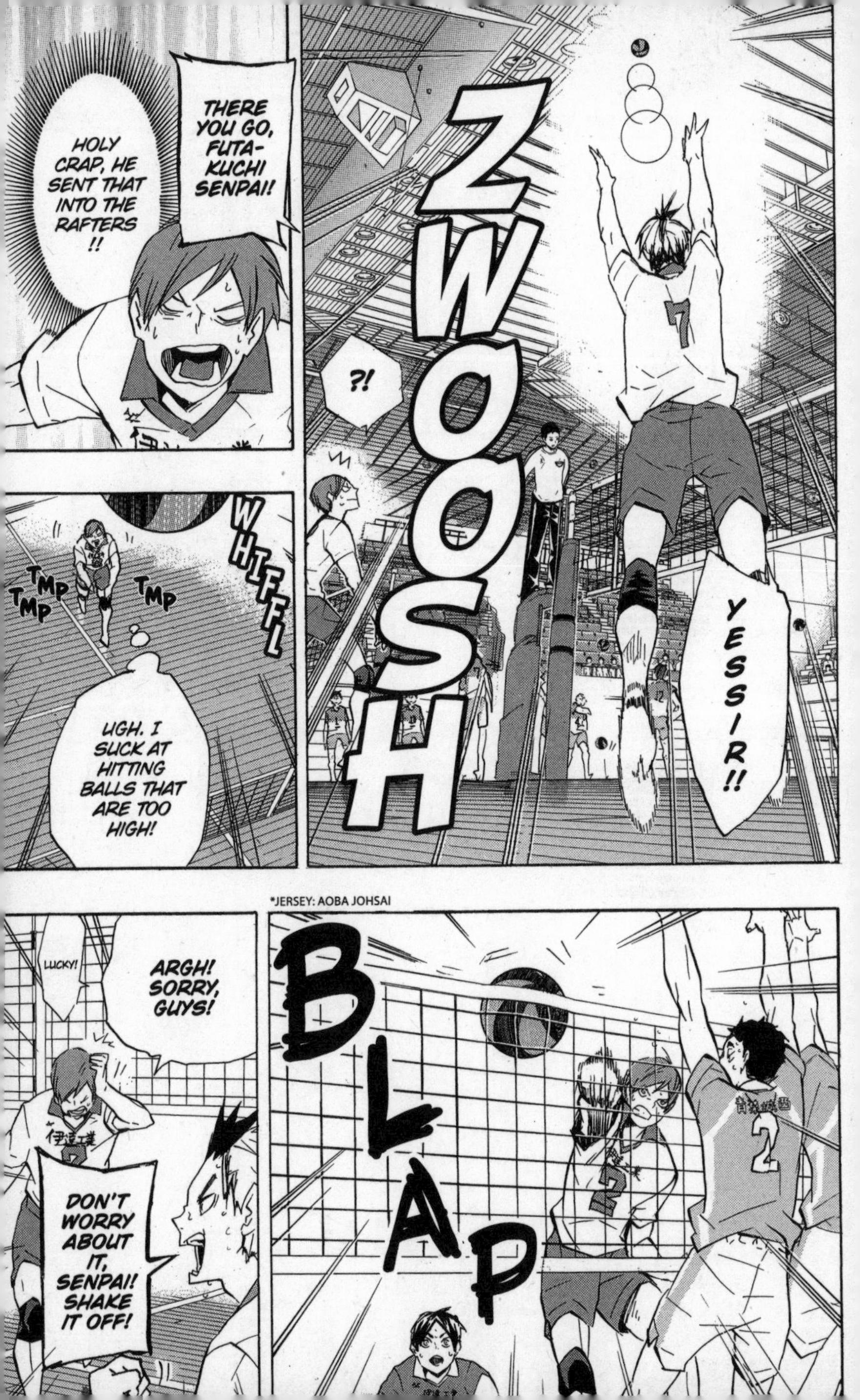
ZWOOSH
?!
YESSIR!!
THERE YOU GO, FUTA-KUCHI SENPAI!
HOLY CRAP, HE SENT THAT INTO THE RAFTERS !!
WHIFFL
TMP TMP
TMP
UGH. I SUCK AT HITTING BALLS THAT ARE TOO HIGH!
*JERSEY: AOBA JOHSAI
BLAP
ARGH! SORRY, GUYS!
LUCKY!
DON'T WORRY ABOUT IT, SENPAI! SHAKE IT OFF!

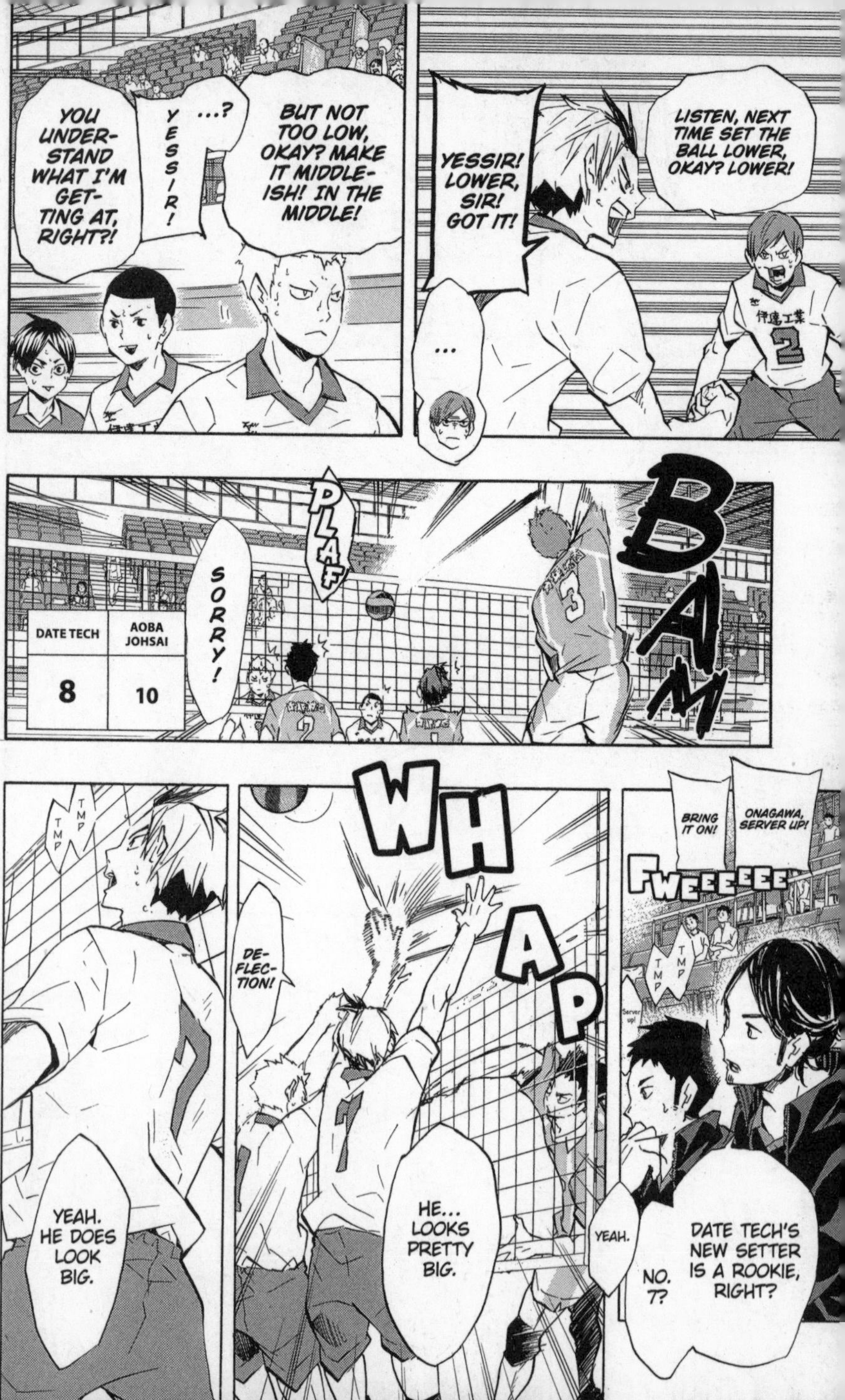
LISTEN, NEXT TIME SET THE BALL LOWER, OKAY? LOWER!
YESSIR! LOWER, SIR! GOT IT!
...
BUT NOT TOO LOW, OKAY? MAKE IT MIDDLE-ISH! IN THE MIDDLE!
...?
YESSIR!
YOU UNDER-STAND WHAT I'M GET-TING AT, RIGHT?!
BAM
PLAF
SORRY!
DATE TECH 8
AOBA JOHSAI 10
ONAGAWA, SERVER UP!
BRING IT ON!
FWEEEEEE
Server up!
TMP TMP
DATE TECH'S NEW SETTER IS A ROOKIE, RIGHT?
NO. 7?
YEAH.
WHAP
DE-FLEC-TION!
HE... LOOKS PRETTY BIG.
TMP TMP
YEAH. HE DOES LOOK BIG.

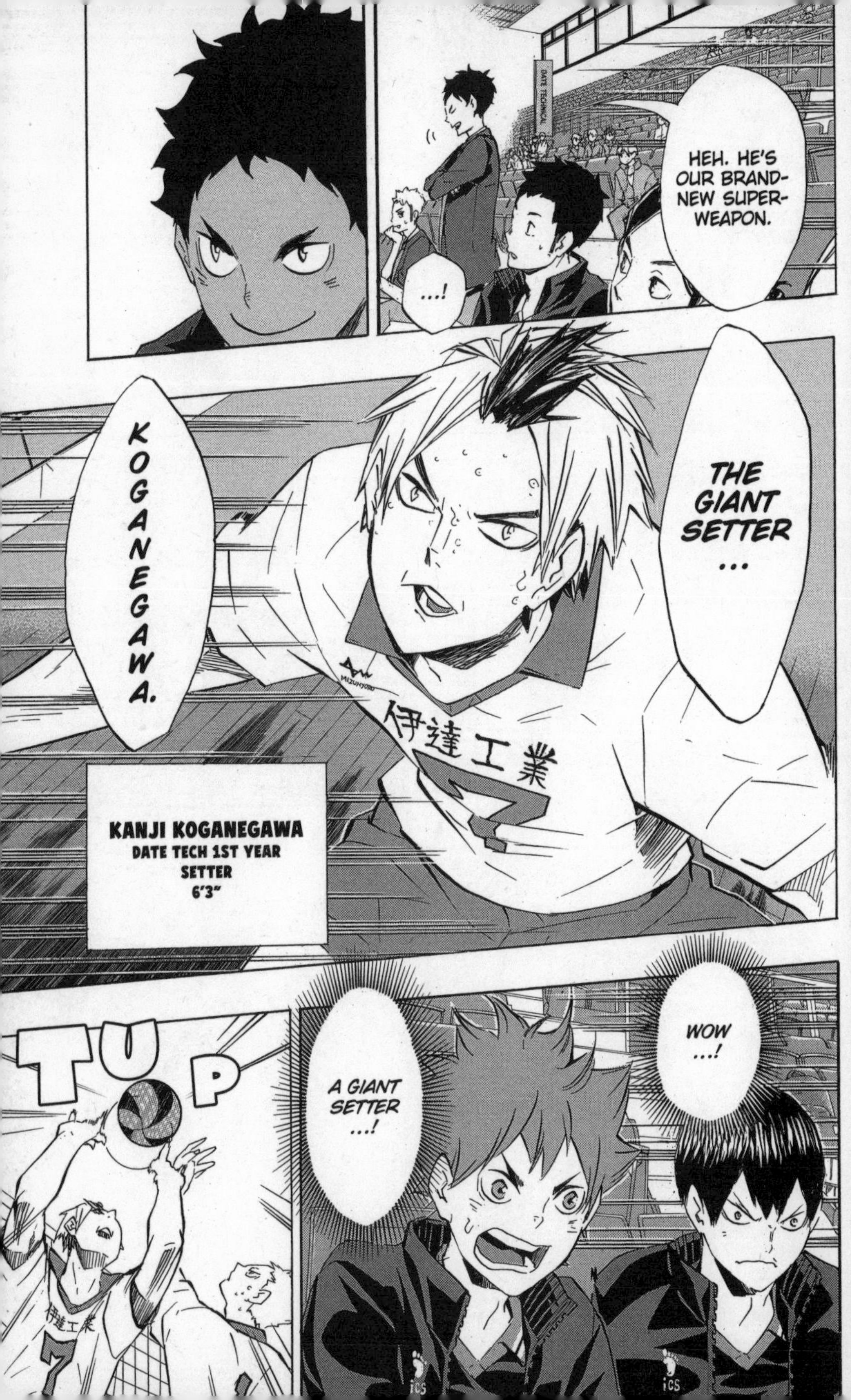
DATE TECHNICAL
HEH. HE'S OUR BRAND-NEW SUPER-WEAPON.
...!
THE GIANT SETTER ...
KOGANEGAWA.
伊達工業
KANJI KOGANEGAWA
DATE TECH 1ST YEAR
SETTER
6'3"
WOW ...!
A GIANT SETTER ...!
TUP

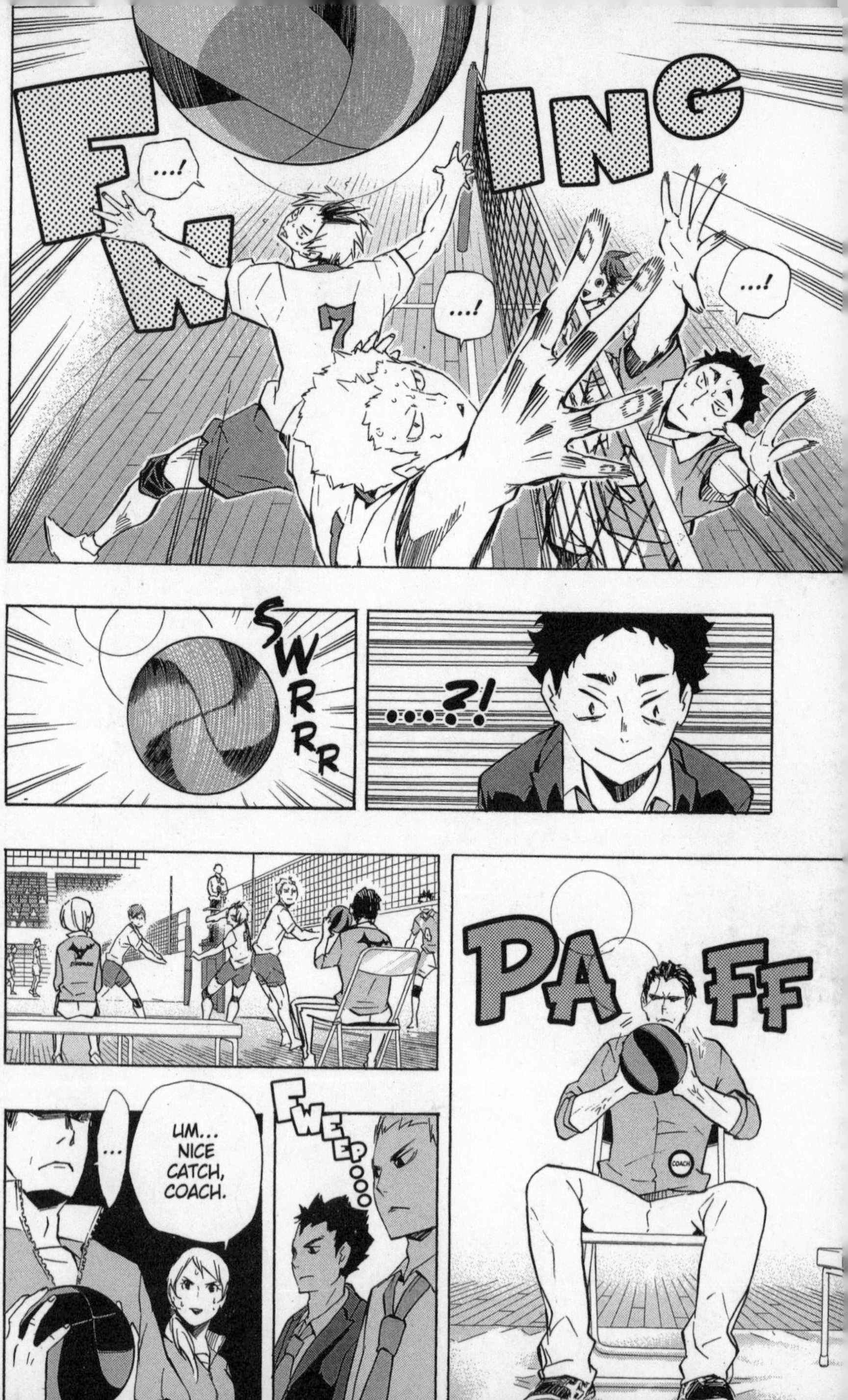
FWING
...!
...!
...!
...?!
SWRRR
PAFF
COACH
FWEEPOOO
UM... NICE CATCH, COACH.
...

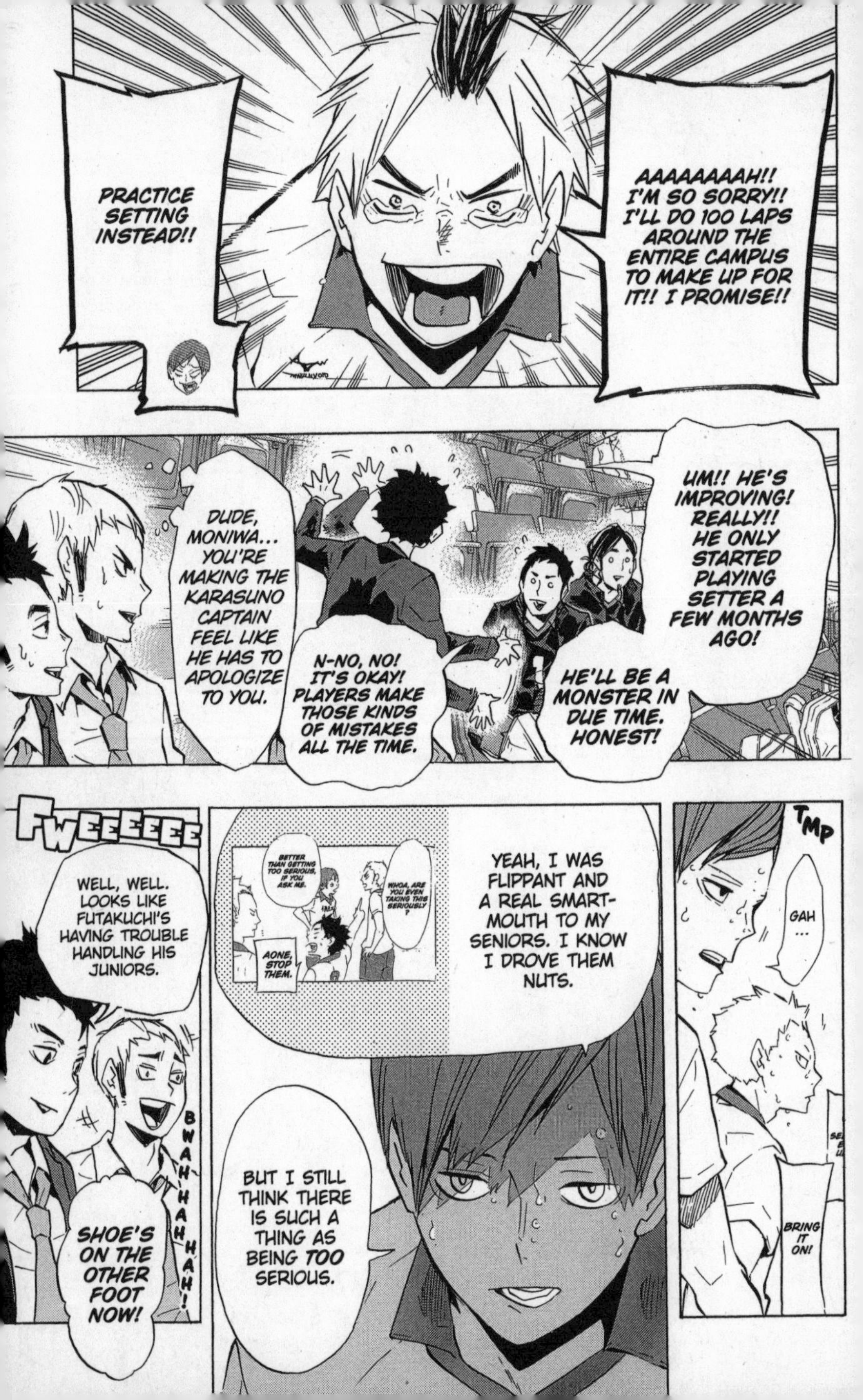
AAAAAAAAH!! I'M SO SORRY!! I'LL DO 100 LAPS AROUND THE ENTIRE CAMPUS TO MAKE UP FOR IT!! I PROMISE!!
PRACTICE SETTING INSTEAD!!
UM!! HE'S IMPROVING! REALLY!! HE ONLY STARTED PLAYING SETTER A FEW MONTHS AGO!
HE'LL BE A MONSTER IN DUE TIME. HONEST!
N-NO, NO! IT'S OKAY! PLAYERS MAKE THOSE KINDS OF MISTAKES ALL THE TIME.
DUDE, MONIWA... YOU'RE MAKING THE KARASUNO CAPTAIN FEEL LIKE HE HAS TO APOLOGIZE TO YOU.
TMP
GAH...
BRING IT ON!
YEAH, I WAS FLIPPANT AND A REAL SMART-MOUTH TO MY SENIORS. I KNOW I DROVE THEM NUTS.
WHOA, ARE YOU EVEN TAKING THIS SERIOUSLY?
BETTER THAN GETTING TOO SERIOUS, IF YOU ASK ME.
AONE, STOP THEM.
BUT I STILL THINK THERE IS SUCH A THING AS BEING TOO SERIOUS.
FWEEEEEE
WELL, WELL. LOOKS LIKE FUTAKUCHI'S HAVING TROUBLE HANDLING HIS JUNIORS.
BWAH HAH HAH HAH!
SHOE'S ON THE OTHER FOOT NOW!

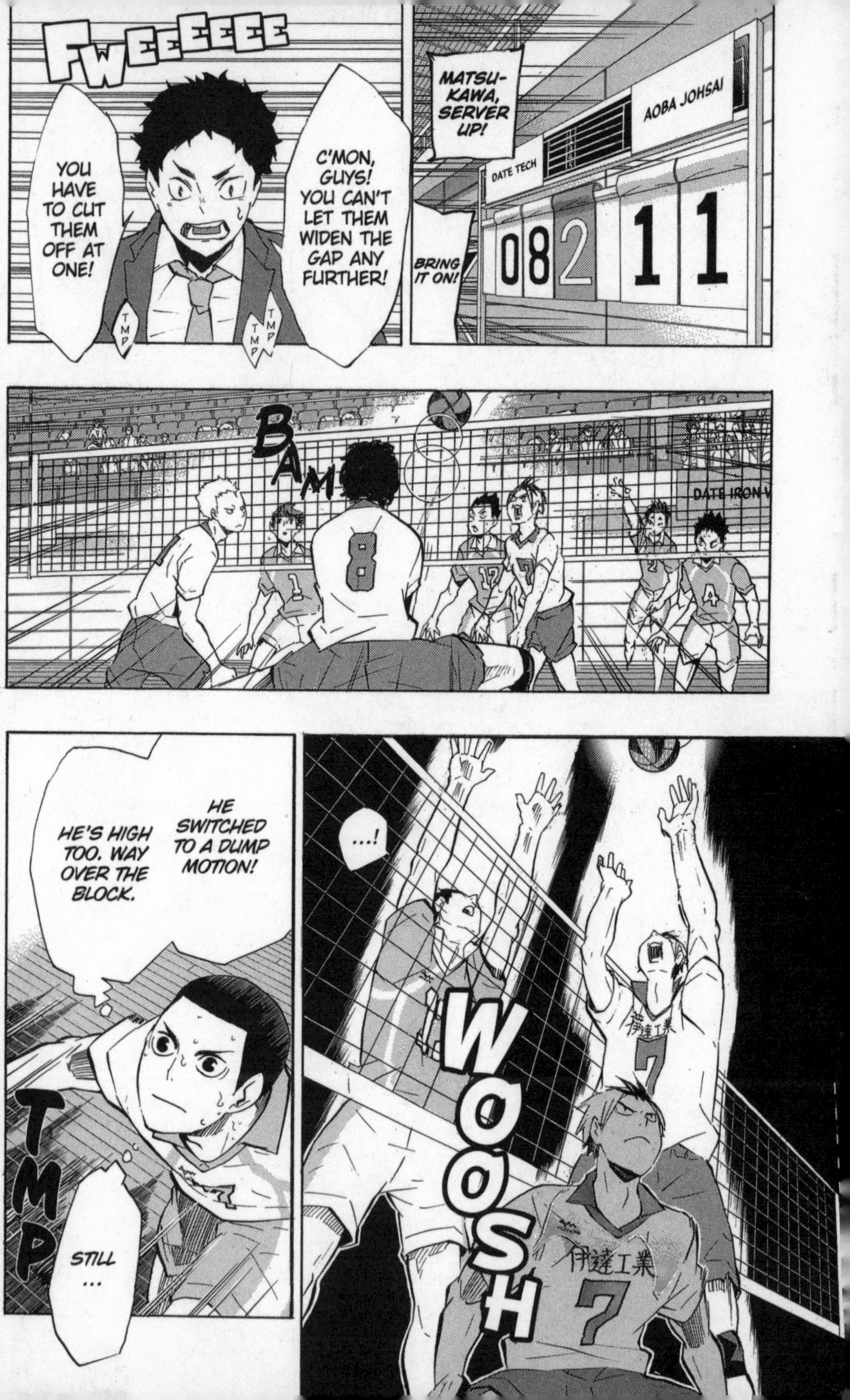
MATSU-KAWA, SERVER UP!
AOBA JOHSAI
DATE TECH
BRING IT ON!
FWEEEEEE
C'MON, GUYS! YOU CAN'T LET THEM WIDEN THE GAP ANY FURTHER!
YOU HAVE TO CUT THEM OFF AT ONE!
TMP TMP TMP
BAM
...!
伊達工業
WOOSH
HE SWITCHED TO A DUMP MOTION!
HE'S HIGH TOO. WAY OVER THE BLOCK.
STILL ...
TMP

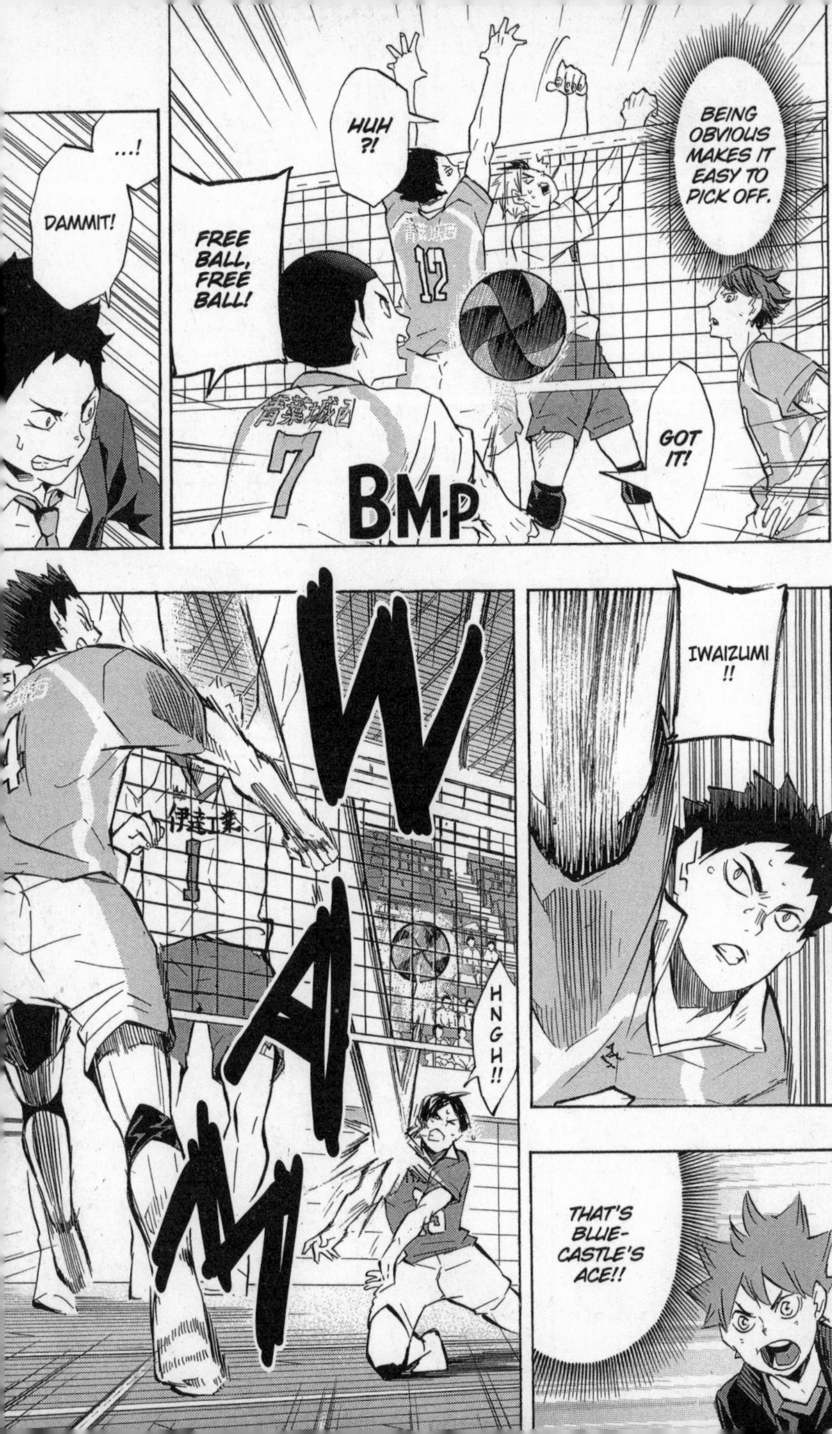
BEING OBVIOUS MAKES IT EASY TO PICK OFF.
HUH?!
FREE BALL, FREE BALL!
GOT IT!
BMP
...!
DAMMIT!
IWAIZUMI!!
THAT'S BLUE-CASTLE'S ACE!!
WAM
HNGH!!

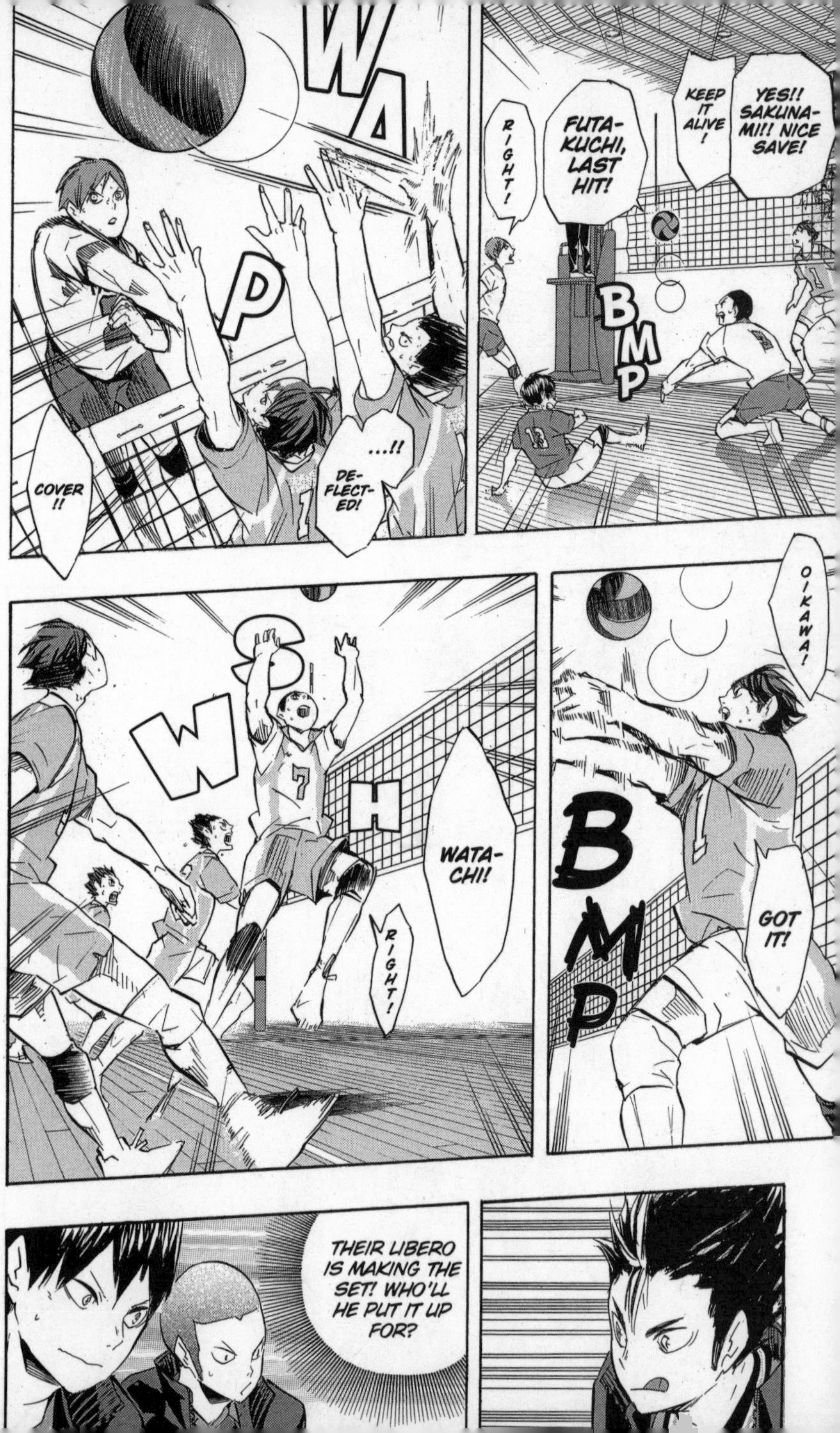
YES!! SAKUNAMI!! NICE SAVE!
KEEP IT ALIVE!
FUTA-KUCHI, LAST HIT!
RIGHT!
BMP
WAP
...!!
DE-FLECT-ED!
COVER!!
OIKAWA!
BMP
GOT IT!
SWH
WATA-CHI!
RIGHT!
THEIR LIBERO IS MAKING THE SET! WHO'LL HE PUT IT UP FOR?

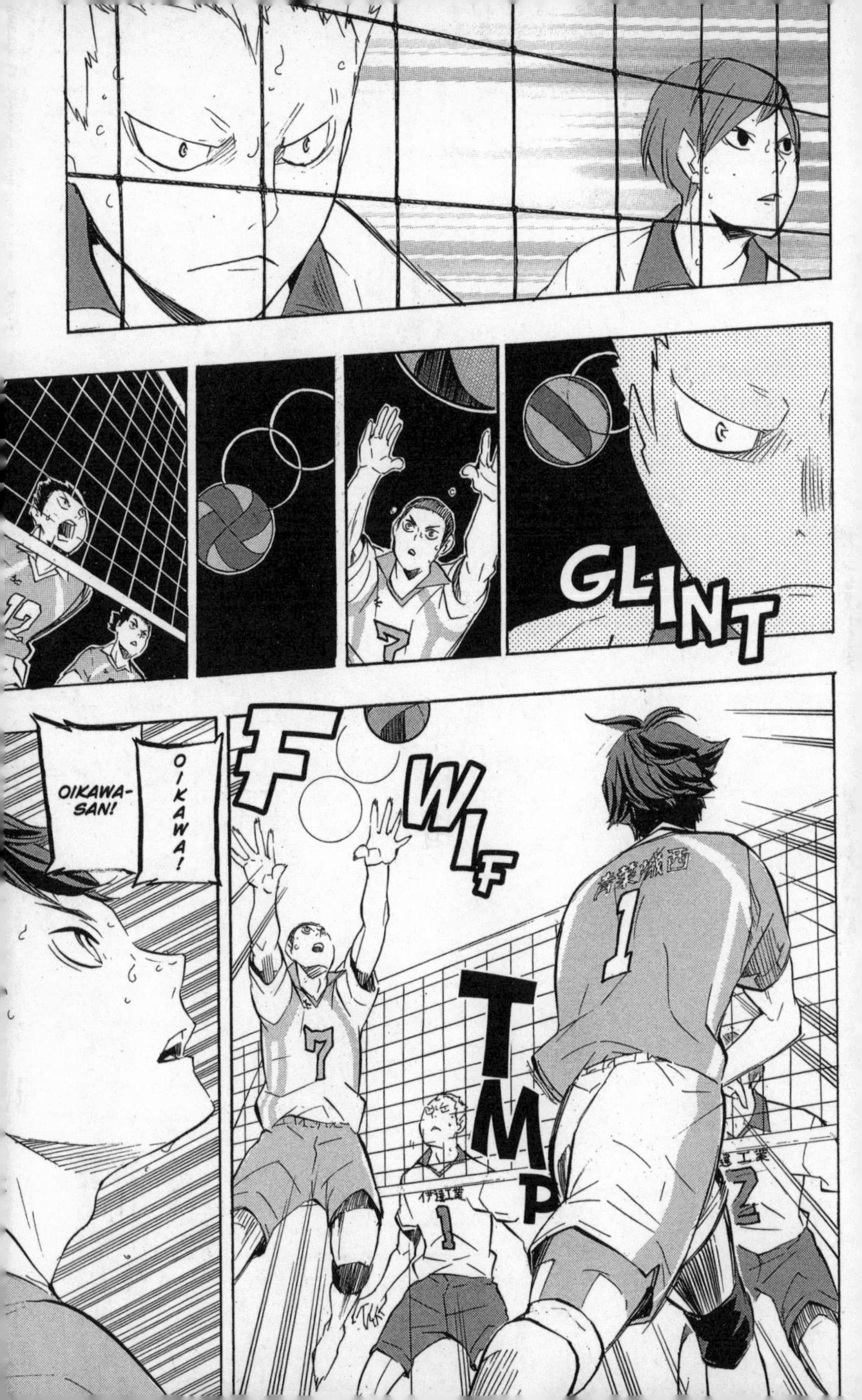
GLINT
FWIF
TMP
OIKAWA!
OIKAWA-SAN!

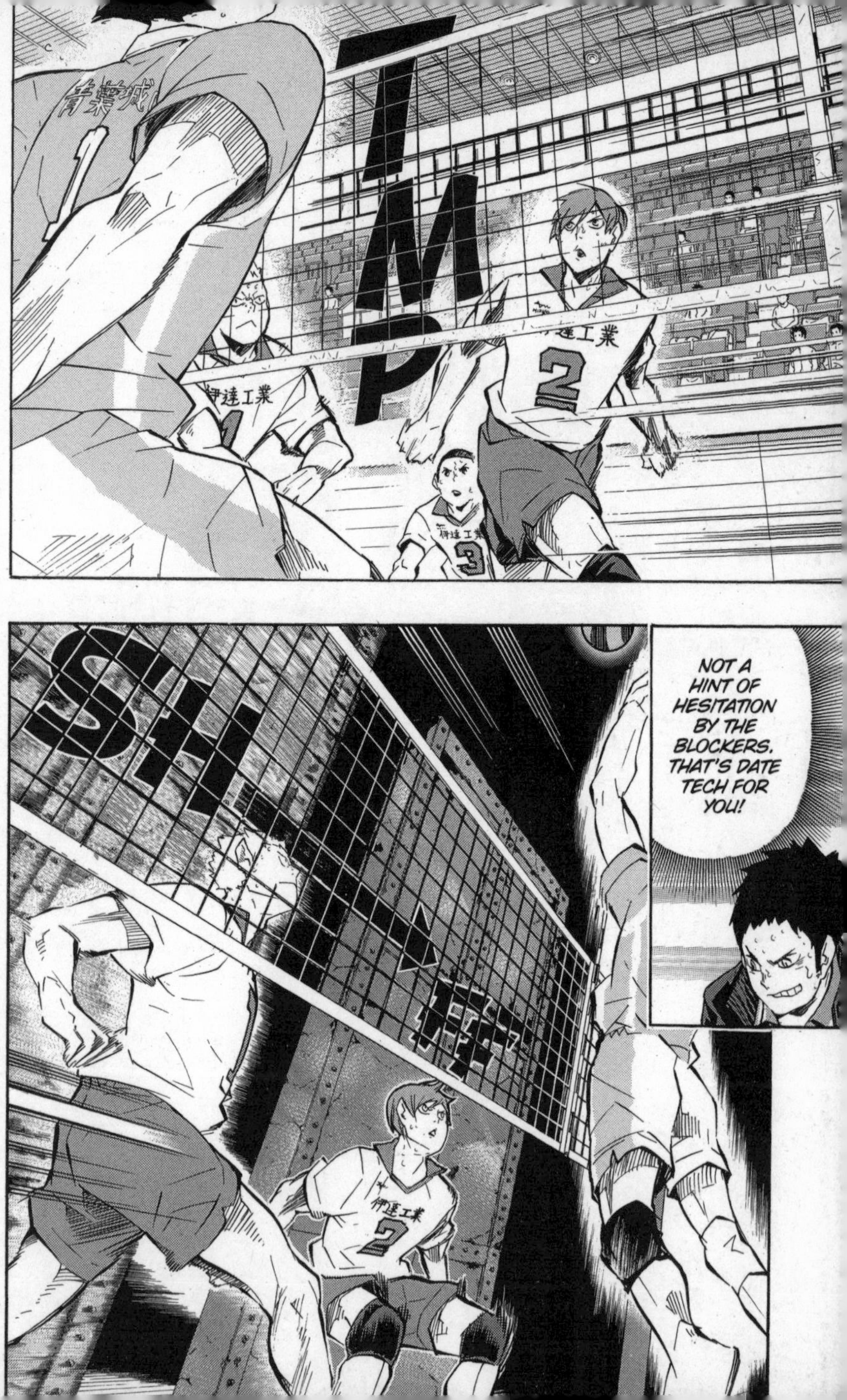
TMP
NOT A HINT OF HESITATION BY THE BLOCKERS. THAT'S DATE TECH FOR YOU!

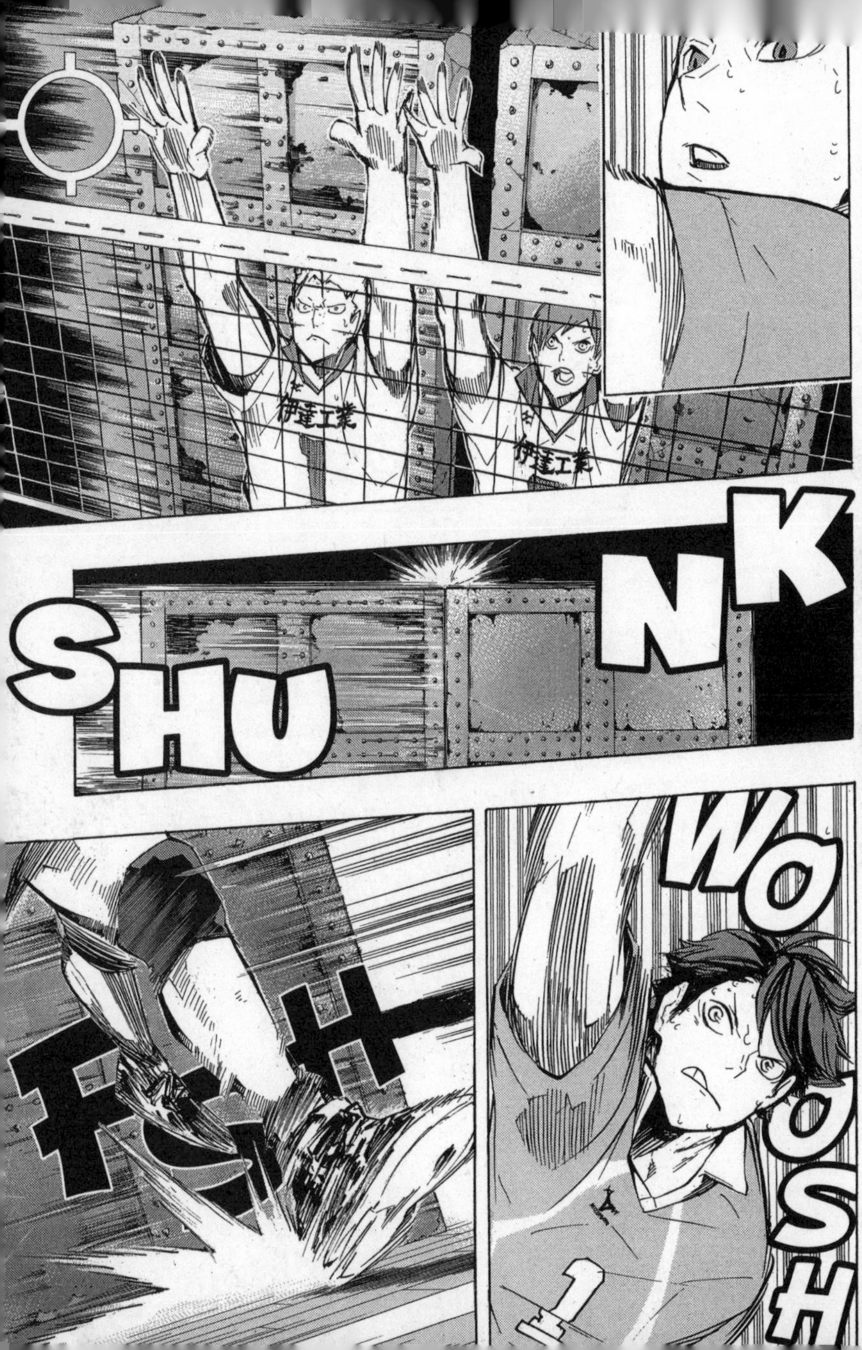
伊達工業
伊達工業
SHUNK
WOOSH

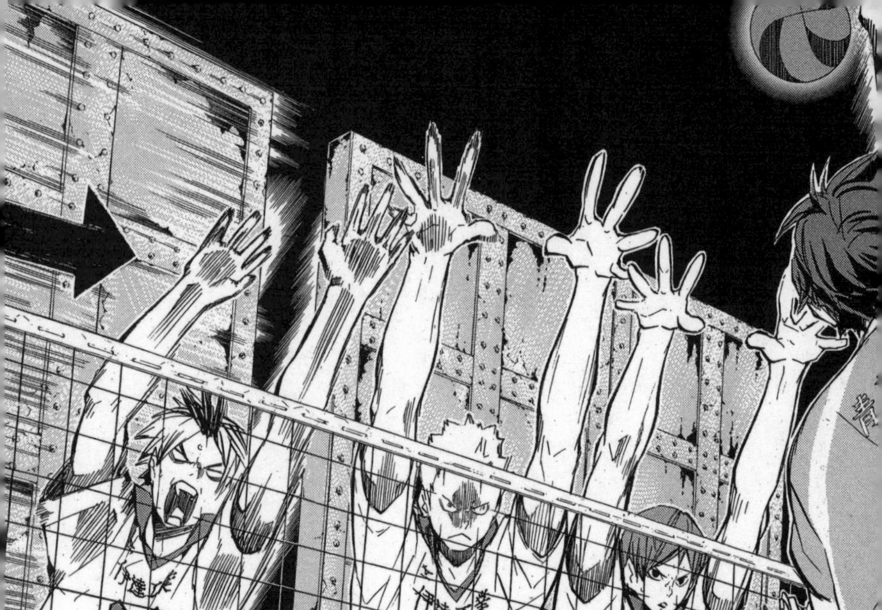

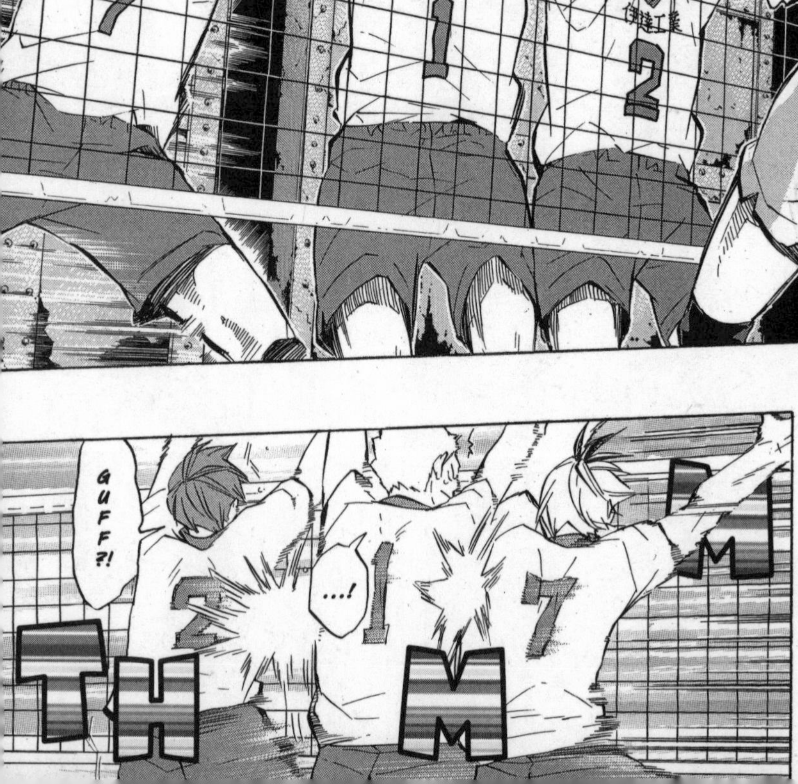

...!
GUFF?!
THMM

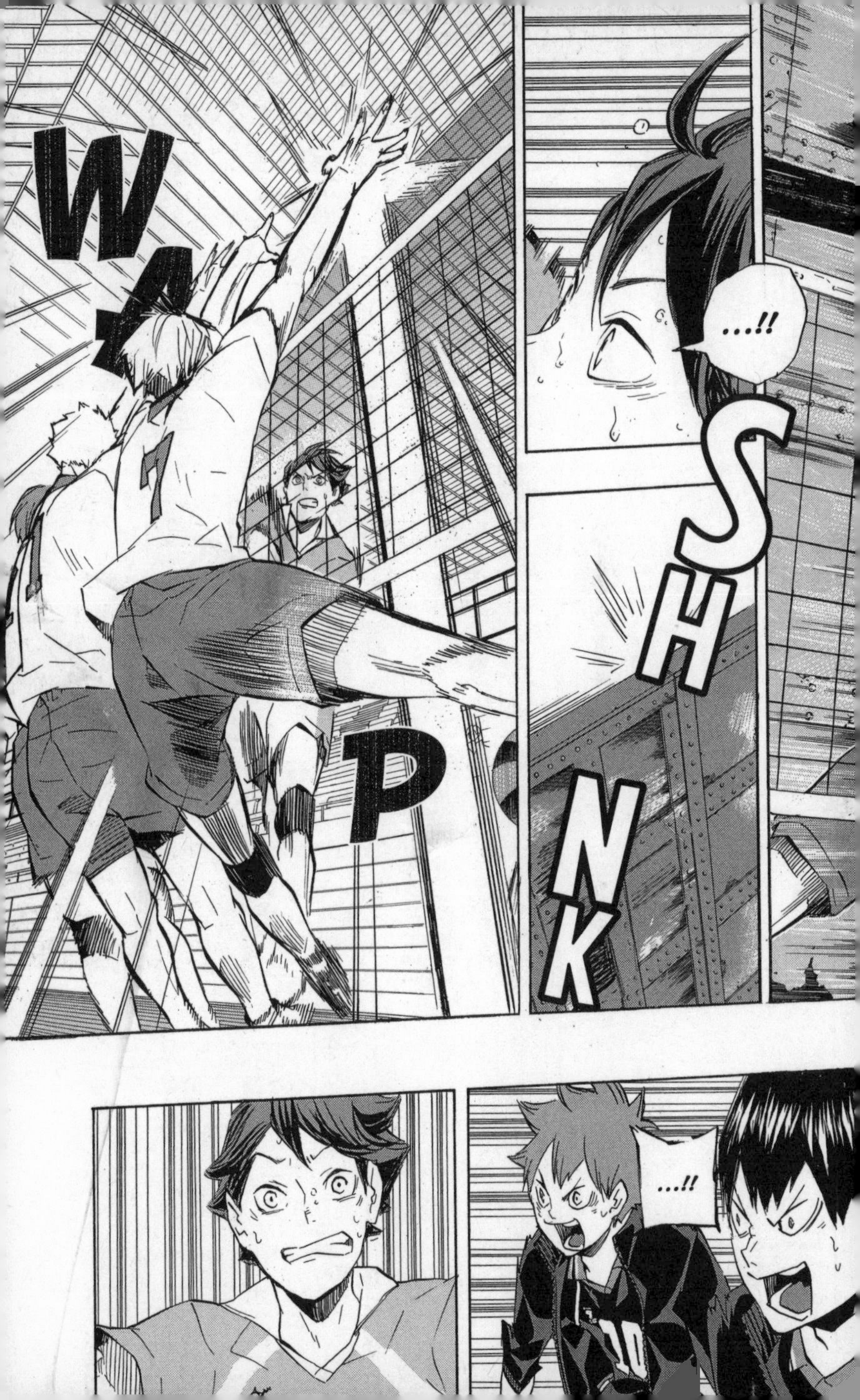
...!!
SHNK
WAP
...!!

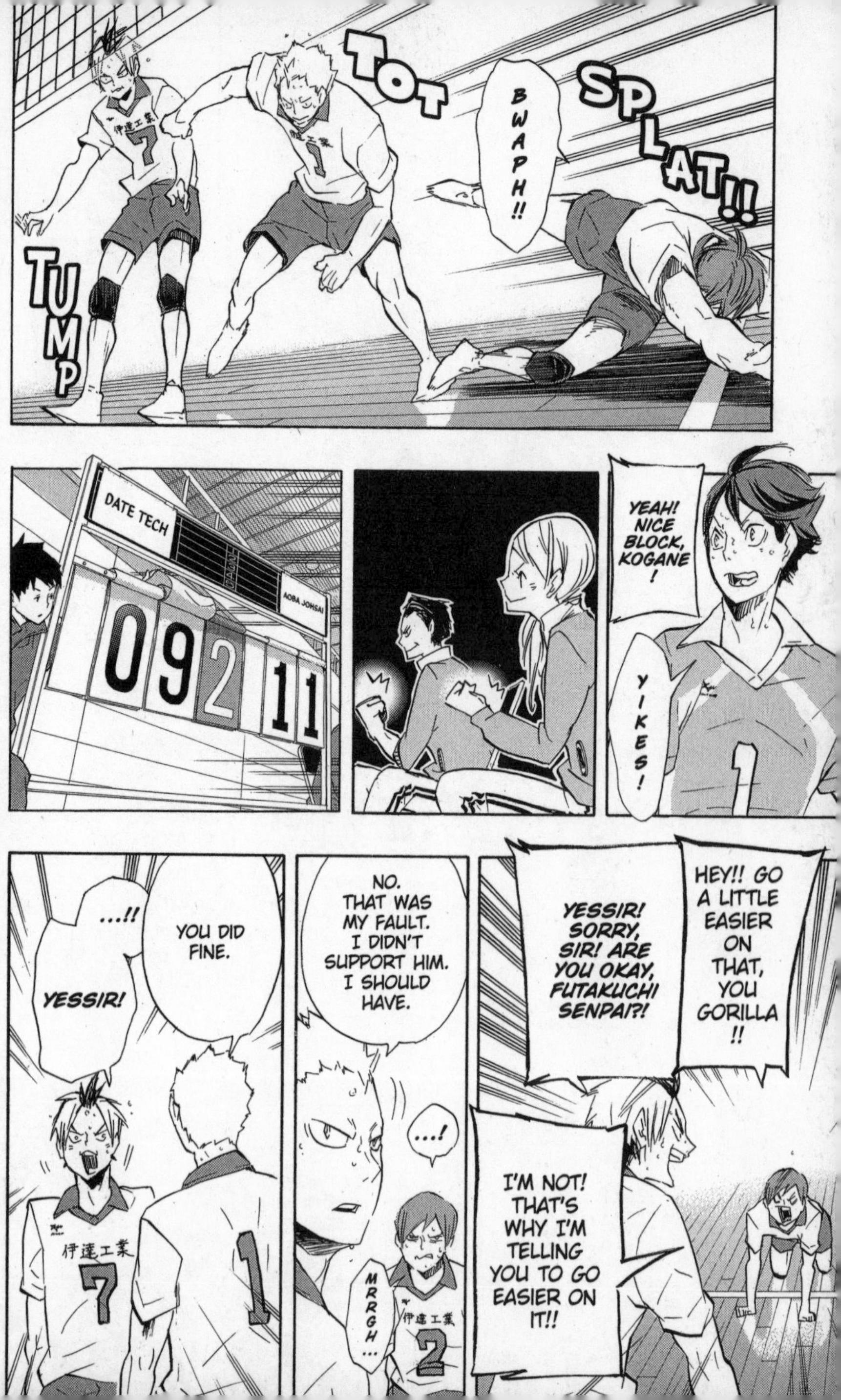
SPLAT!!!
BWAPH!!
TOT
TUMP
YEAH! NICE BLOCK, KOGANE!
YIKES!
DATE TECH
AOBA JOHSAI
09 2 11
HEY!! GO A LITTLE EASIER ON THAT, YOU GORILLA!!
YESSIR! SORRY, SIR! ARE YOU OKAY, FUTAKUCHI SENPAI?!
I'M NOT! THAT'S WHY I'M TELLING YOU TO GO EASIER ON IT!!
NO. THAT WAS MY FAULT. I DIDN'T SUPPORT HIM. I SHOULD HAVE.
...!
MRRGH...
YOU DID FINE.
...!! YESSIR!

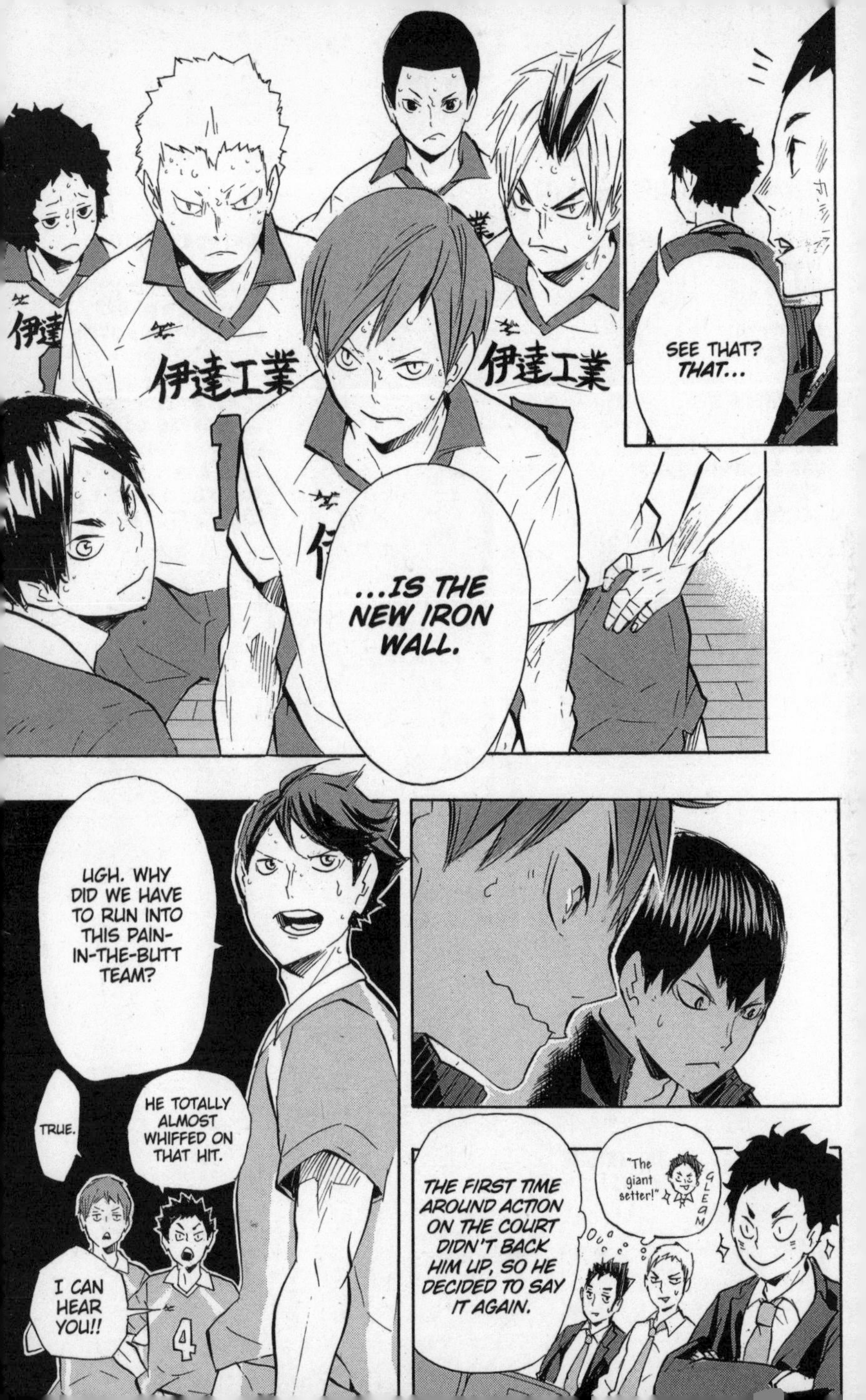

SEE THAT? THAT...
...IS THE NEW IRON WALL.
UGH. WHY DID WE HAVE TO RUN INTO THIS PAIN-IN-THE-BUTT TEAM?
HE TOTALLY ALMOST WHIFFED ON THAT HIT.
TRUE.
I CAN HEAR YOU!!
GLEAM
"The giant setter!"
THE FIRST TIME AROUND ACTION ON THE COURT DIDN'T BACK HIM UP, SO HE DECIDED TO SAY IT AGAIN.

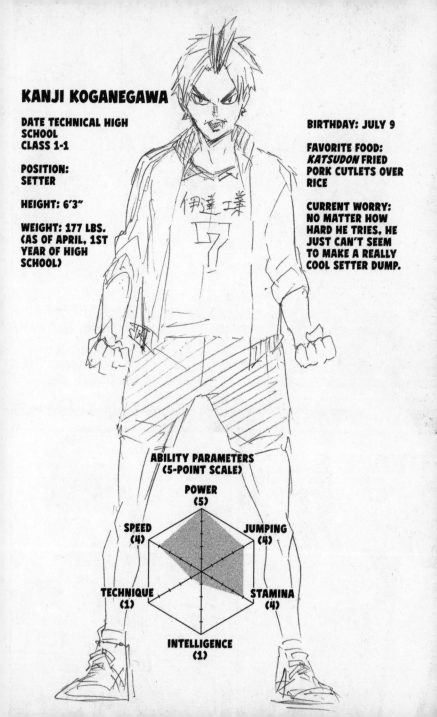

KANJI KOGANEGAWA

DATE TECHNICAL HIGH SCHOOL
CLASS 1-1

POSITION:
SETTER

HEIGHT: 6'3"

WEIGHT: 177 LBS.
(AS OF APRIL, 1ST YEAR OF HIGH SCHOOL)

BIRTHDAY: JULY 9

FAVORITE FOOD:
KATSUDON FRIED PORK CUTLETS OVER RICE

CURRENT WORRY:
NO MATTER HOW HARD HE TRIES, HE JUST CAN'T SEEM TO MAKE A REALLY COOL SETTER DUMP.

ABILITY PARAMETERS
(5-POINT SCALE)

POWER (5)
JUMPING (4)
SPEED (4)
STAMINA (4)
TECHNIQUE (1)
INTELLIGENCE (1)

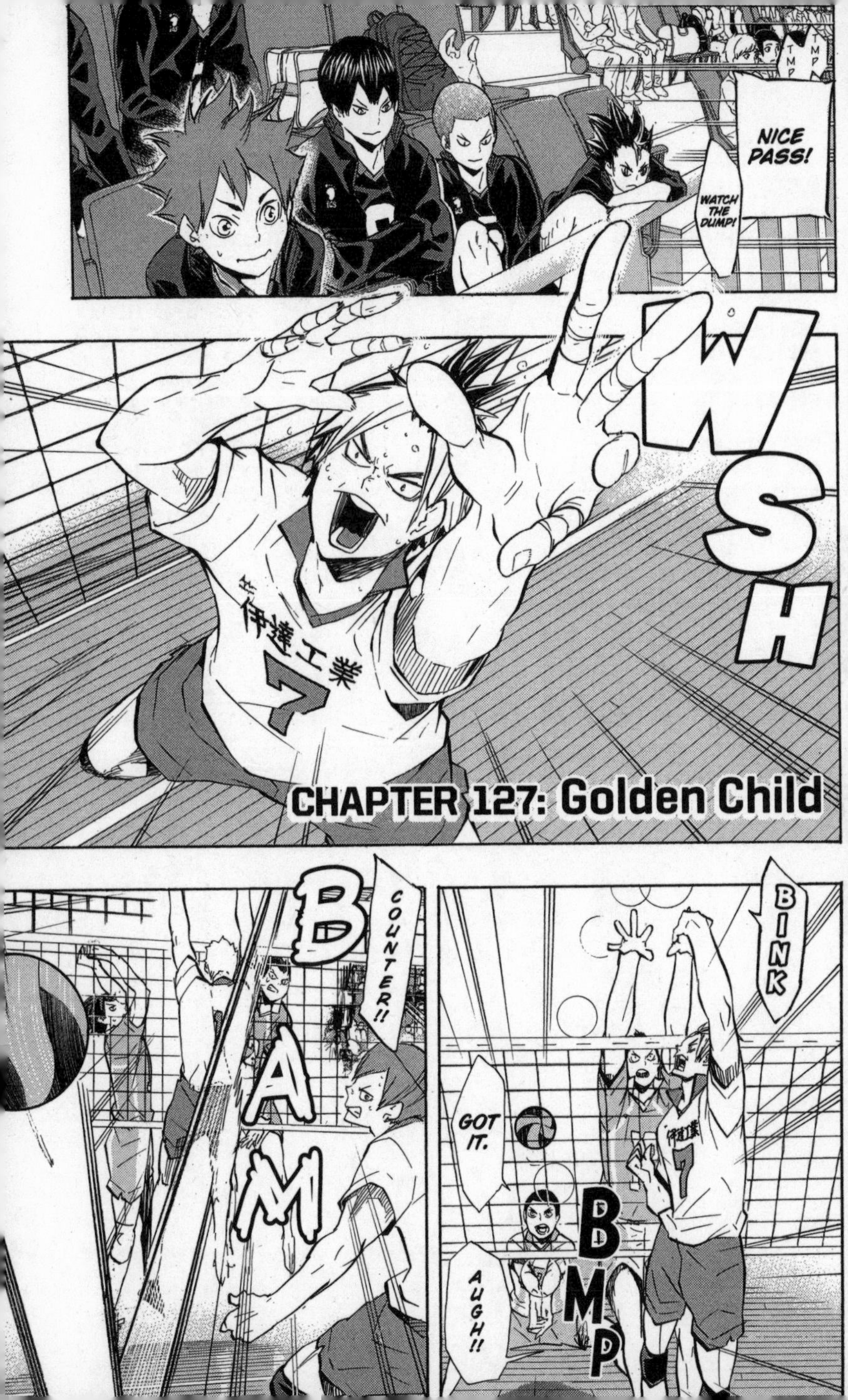
TMP
TMP
NICE PASS!
WATCH THE DUMP!
WSH
CHAPTER 127: Golden Child
BINK
GOT IT.
BUMP
AUGH!!
COUNTER!!
BAM

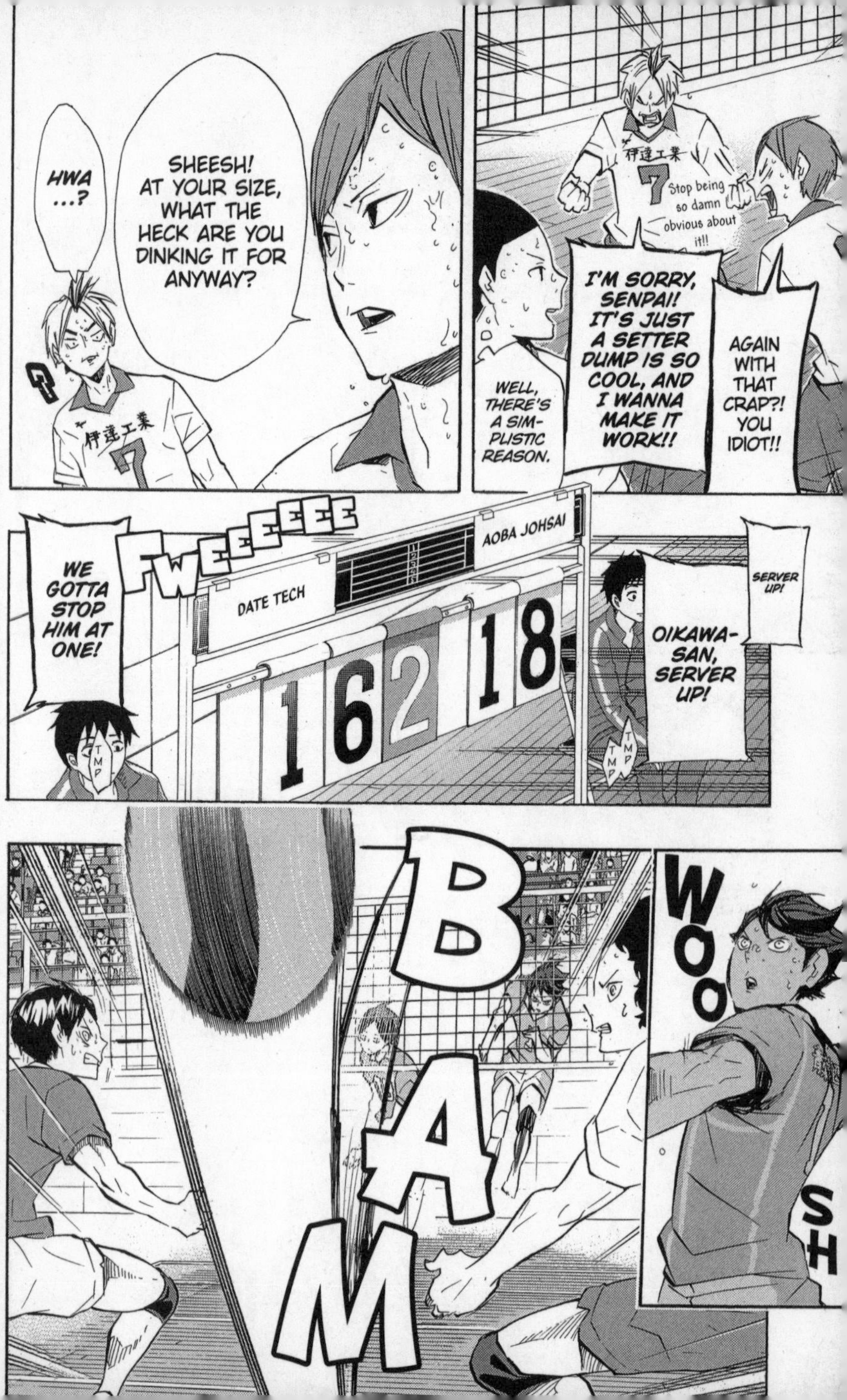
Stop being so damn obvious about it!!
AGAIN WITH THAT CRAP?! YOU IDIOT!!
I'M SORRY, SENPAI! IT'S JUST A SETTER DUMP IS SO COOL, AND I WANNA MAKE IT WORK!!
WELL, THERE'S A SIMPLISTIC REASON.
SHEESH! AT YOUR SIZE, WHAT THE HECK ARE YOU DINKING IT FOR ANYWAY?
HWA ...?
SERVER UP!
OIKAWA-SAN, SERVER UP!
TMP TMP TMP
AOBA JOHSAI
DATE TECH
16 2 18
FWEEEEEE
WE GOTTA STOP HIM AT ONE!
TMP
WOOSH
BAM

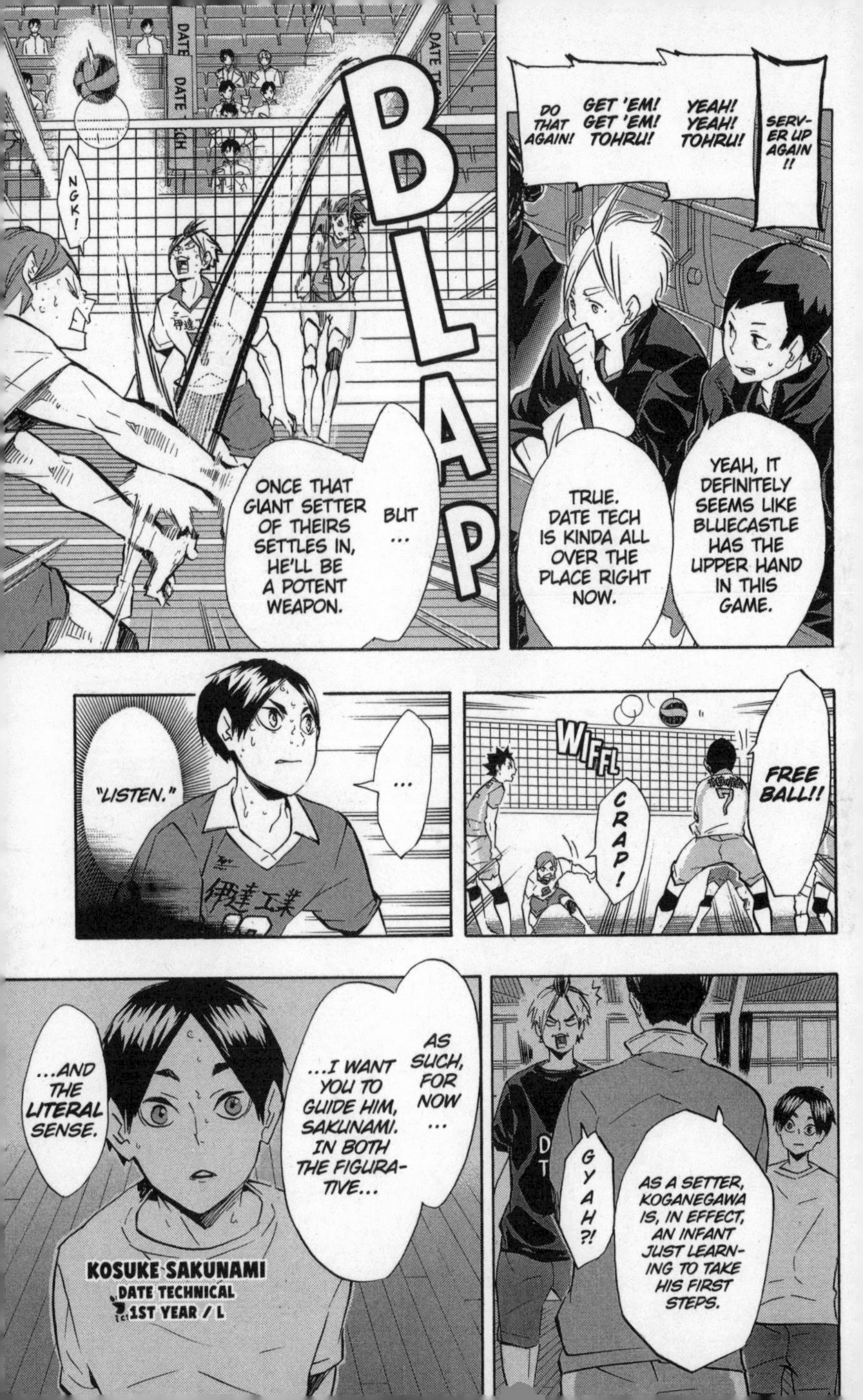
SERVER UP AGAIN!!
YEAH! YEAH! TOHRU!
GET 'EM! GET 'EM! TOHRU!
DO THAT AGAIN!
YEAH, IT DEFINITELY SEEMS LIKE BLUECASTLE HAS THE UPPER HAND IN THIS GAME.
TRUE. DATE TECH IS KINDA ALL OVER THE PLACE RIGHT NOW.
BLAP
BUT ...
ONCE THAT GIANT SETTER OF THEIRS SETTLES IN, HE'LL BE A POTENT WEAPON.
NGK!
WIFFL
FREE BALL!!
CRAP!
...
"LISTEN."
GYAH?!
AS A SETTER, KOGANEGAWA IS, IN EFFECT, AN INFANT JUST LEARNING TO TAKE HIS FIRST STEPS.
AS SUCH, FOR NOW ...
...I WANT YOU TO GUIDE HIM, SAKUNAMI. IN BOTH THE FIGURATIVE...
...AND THE LITERAL SENSE.
KOSUKE SAKUNAMI
DATE TECHNICAL
1ST YEAR / L

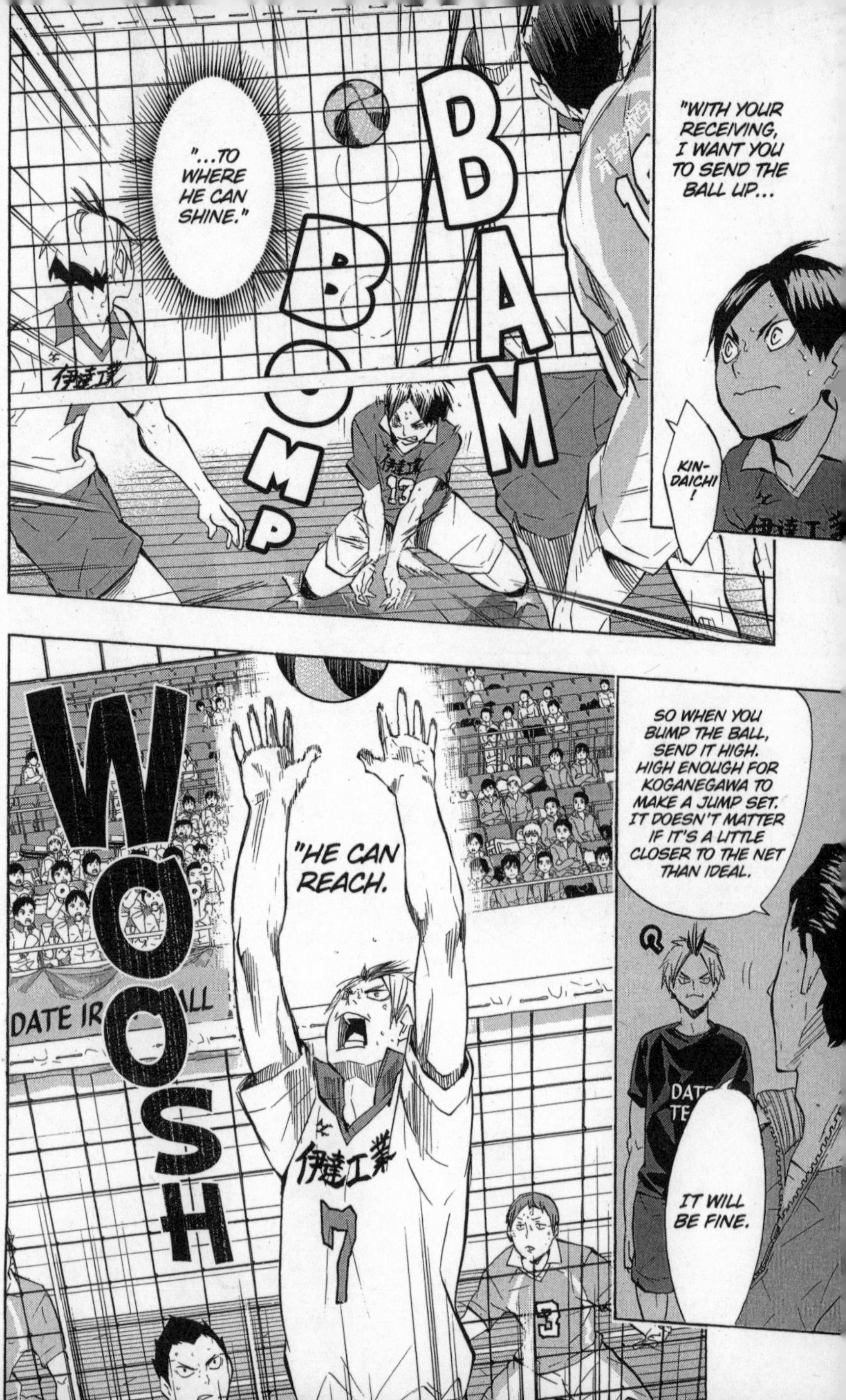
"WITH YOUR RECEIVING, I WANT YOU TO SEND THE BALL UP...
KIN-DAICHI!
"...TO WHERE HE CAN SHINE."
BAM
BOMP
SO WHEN YOU BUMP THE BALL, SEND IT HIGH. HIGH ENOUGH FOR KOGANEGAWA TO MAKE A JUMP SET. IT DOESN'T MATTER IF IT'S A LITTLE CLOSER TO THE NET THAN IDEAL.
IT WILL BE FINE.
"HE CAN REACH.
WOOSH

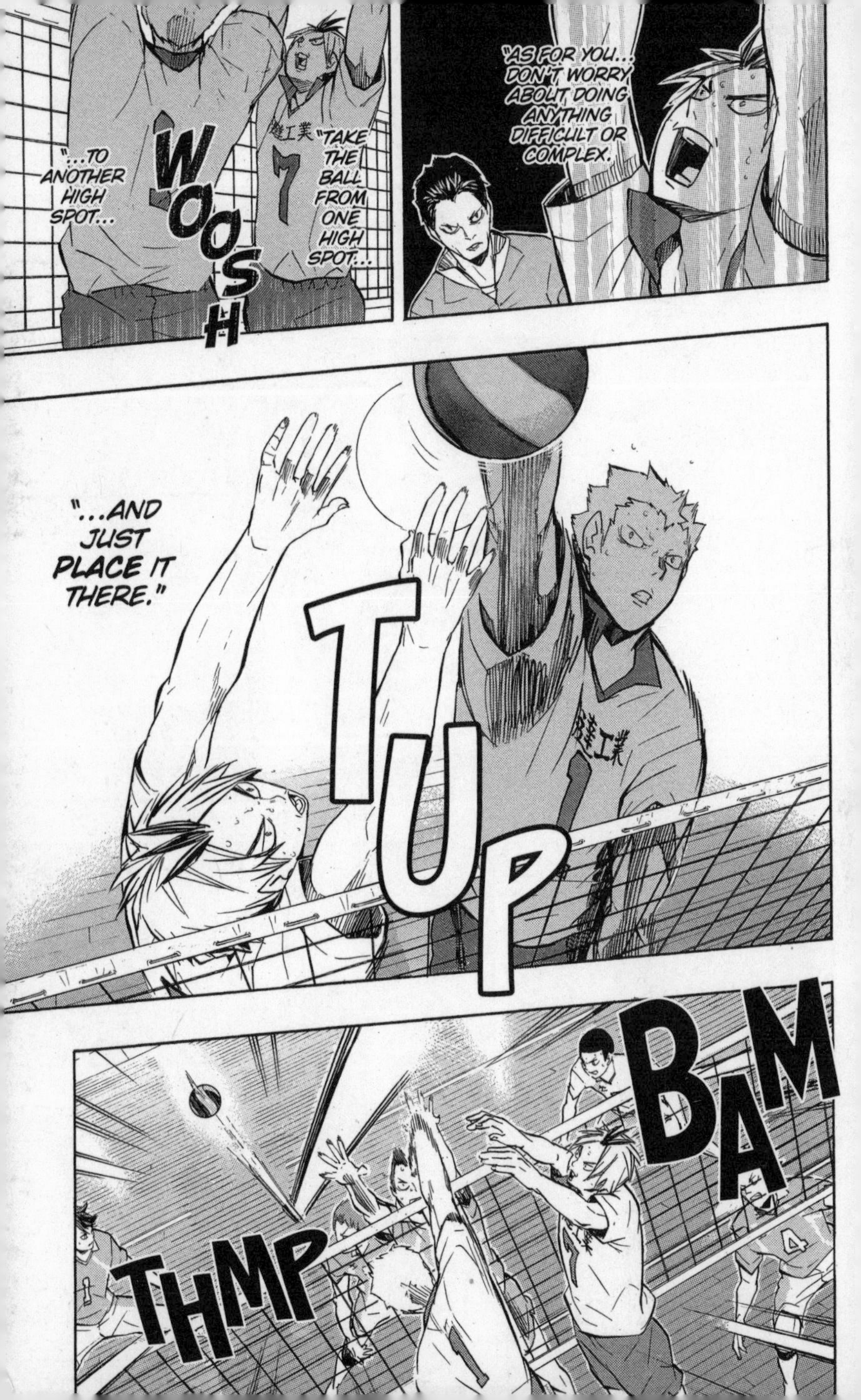
"AS FOR YOU... DON'T WORRY ABOUT DOING ANYTHING DIFFICULT OR COMPLEX.
"TAKE THE BALL FROM ONE HIGH SPOT...
"...TO ANOTHER HIGH SPOT...
WOOSH
"...AND JUST PLACE IT THERE."
TUP
BAM
THMP

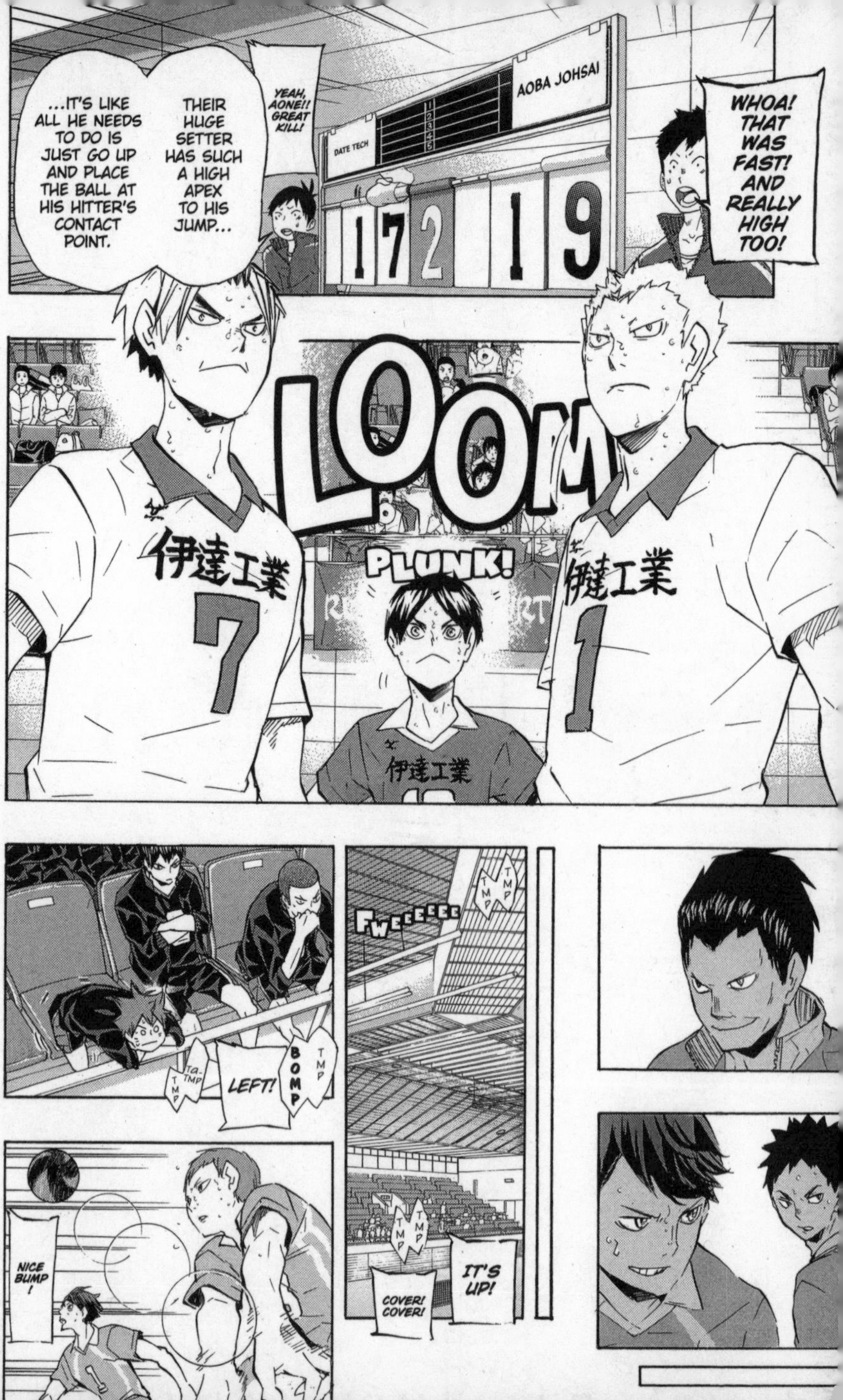
WHOA! THAT WAS FAST! AND REALLY HIGH TOO!
AOBA JOHSAI
DATE TECH
17 2 19
YEAH, AONE!! GREAT KILL!
THEIR HUGE SETTER HAS SUCH A HIGH APEX TO HIS JUMP...
...IT'S LIKE ALL HE NEEDS TO DO IS JUST GO UP AND PLACE THE BALL AT HIS HITTER'S CONTACT POINT.
LOOM
PLUNK!
伊達工業
伊達工業
伊達工業
TMP TMP
FWEEEEEE
TMP TMP
IT'S UP!
COVER! COVER!
TMP
BOMP
LEFT!
Ta-TMP TMP
NICE BUMP!

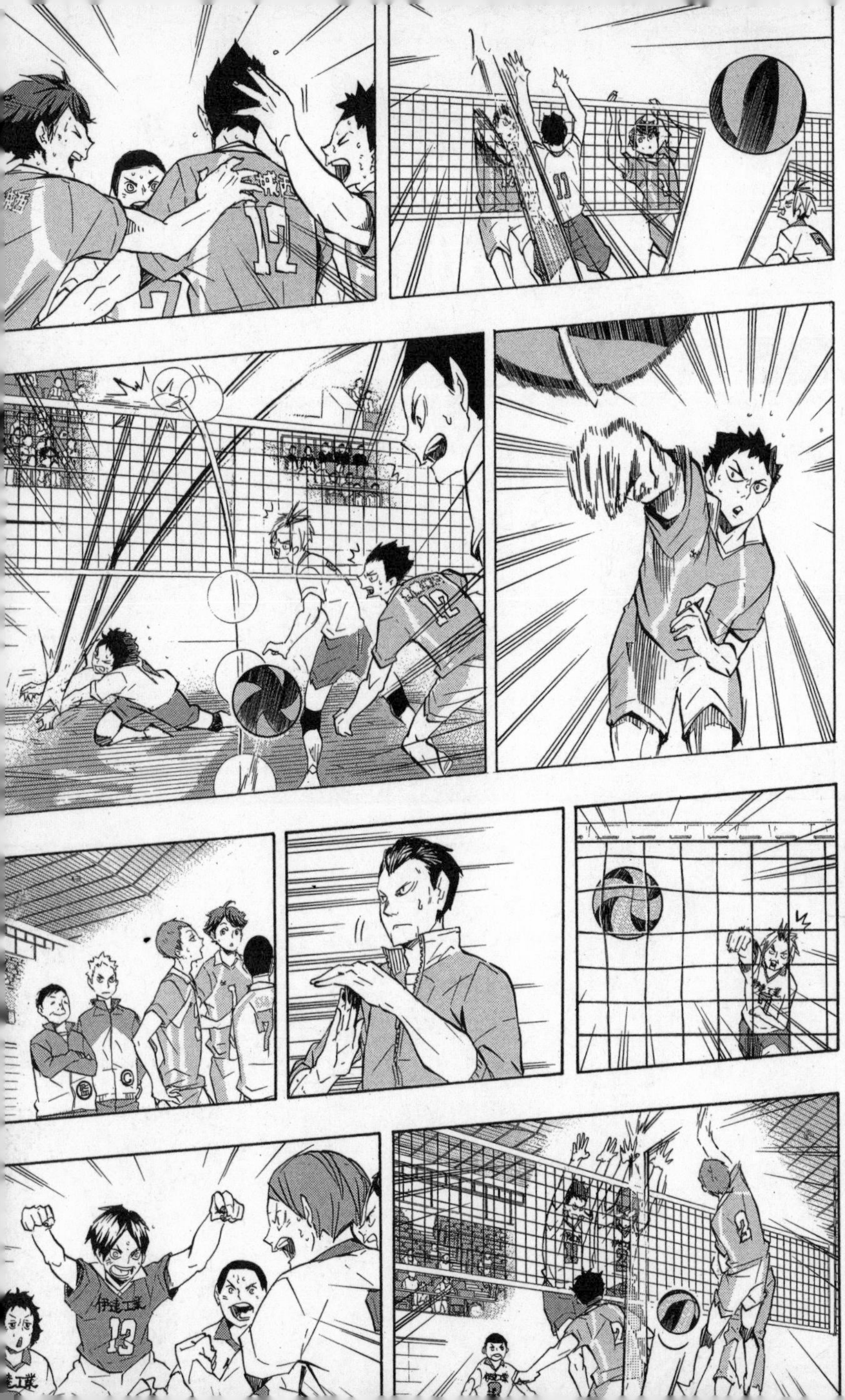

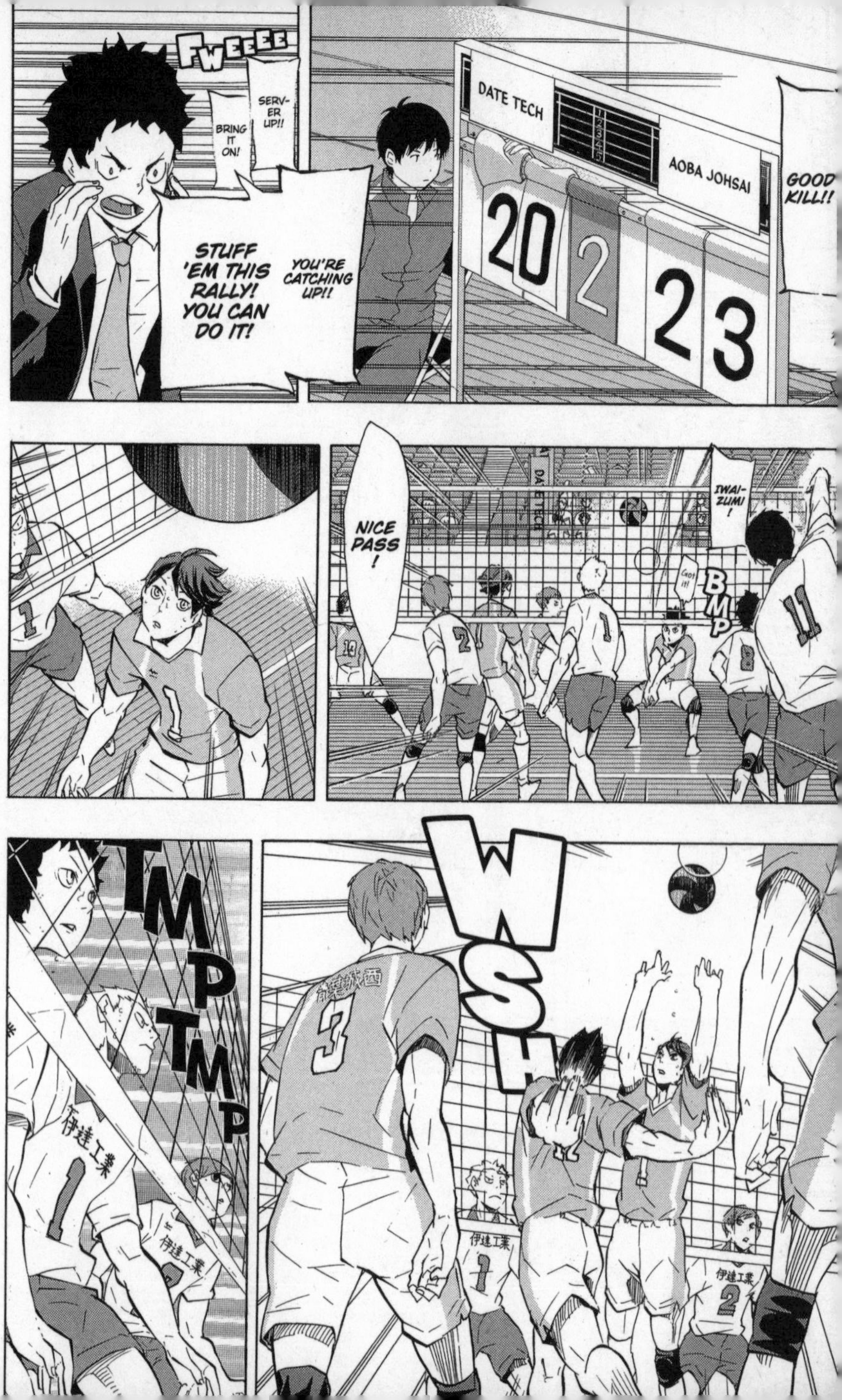
GOOD KILL!!
DATE TECH
AOBA JOHSAI
20
23
FWEEEE
SERVER UP!!
BRING IT ON!
YOU'RE CATCHING UP!!
STUFF 'EM THIS RALLY! YOU CAN DO IT!
IWAIZUMI!
Got it!
BMP
NICE PASS!
WSH
TMP TMP TMP

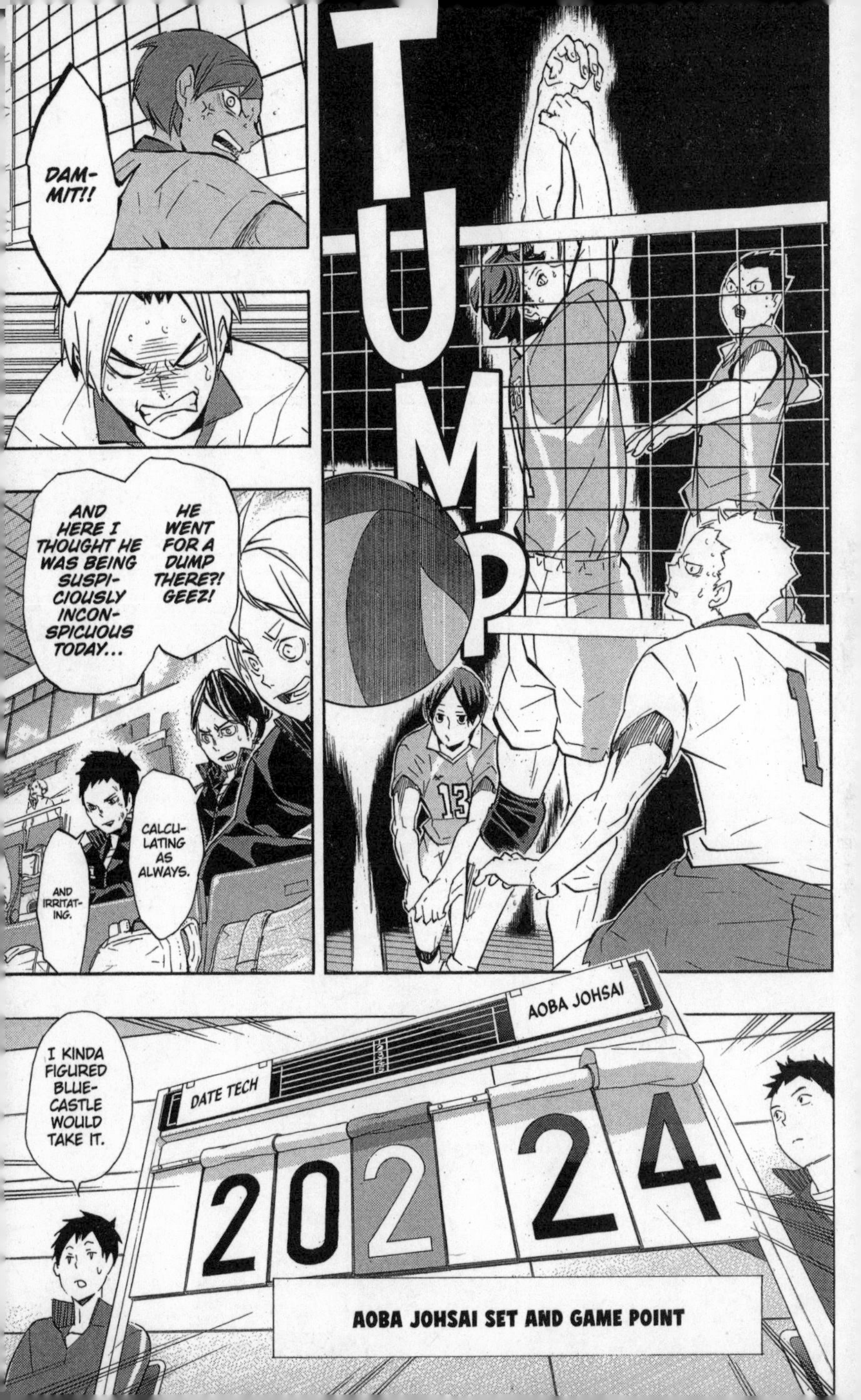
DUMP
DAM-MIT!!
HE WENT FOR A DUMP THERE?! GEEZ!
AND HERE I THOUGHT HE WAS BEING SUSPICIOUSLY INCONSPICUOUS TODAY...
CALCULATING AS ALWAYS.
AND IRRITATING.
AOBA JOHSAI
DATE TECH
20
24
I KINDA FIGURED BLUE-CASTLE WOULD TAKE IT.
AOBA JOHSAI SET AND GAME POINT

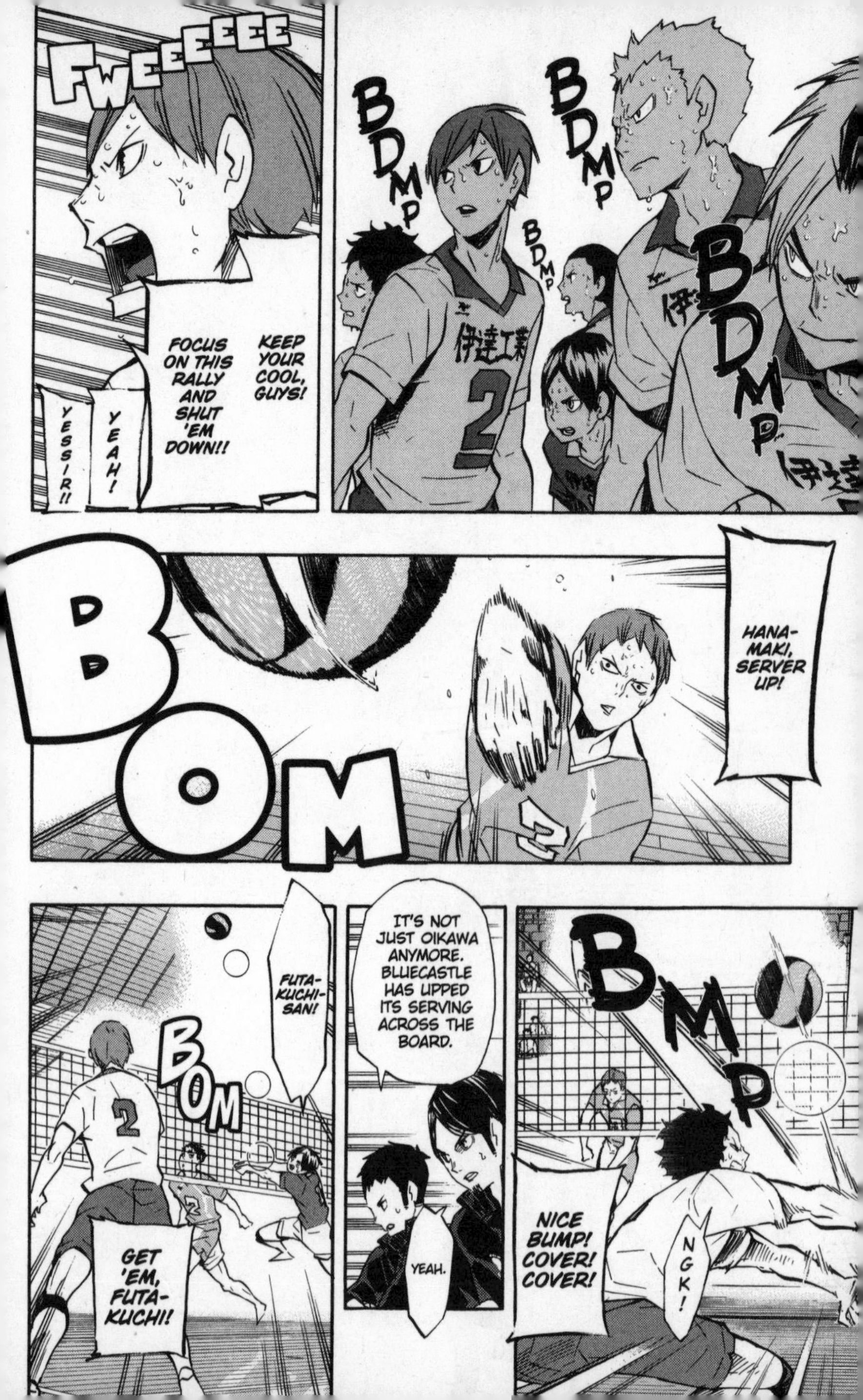
BDMP
BDMP
BDMP
BDMP
FWEEEEEE
KEEP YOUR COOL, GUYS!
FOCUS ON THIS RALLY AND SHUT 'EM DOWN!!
YEAH!
YESSIR!!
HANA-MAKI, SERVER UP!
BOOM
BMP
NGK!
NICE BUMP! COVER! COVER!
IT'S NOT JUST OIKAWA ANYMORE. BLUECASTLE HAS UPPED ITS SERVING ACROSS THE BOARD.
YEAH.
FUTA-KUCHI-SAN!
BOM
GET 'EM, FUTA-KUCHI!

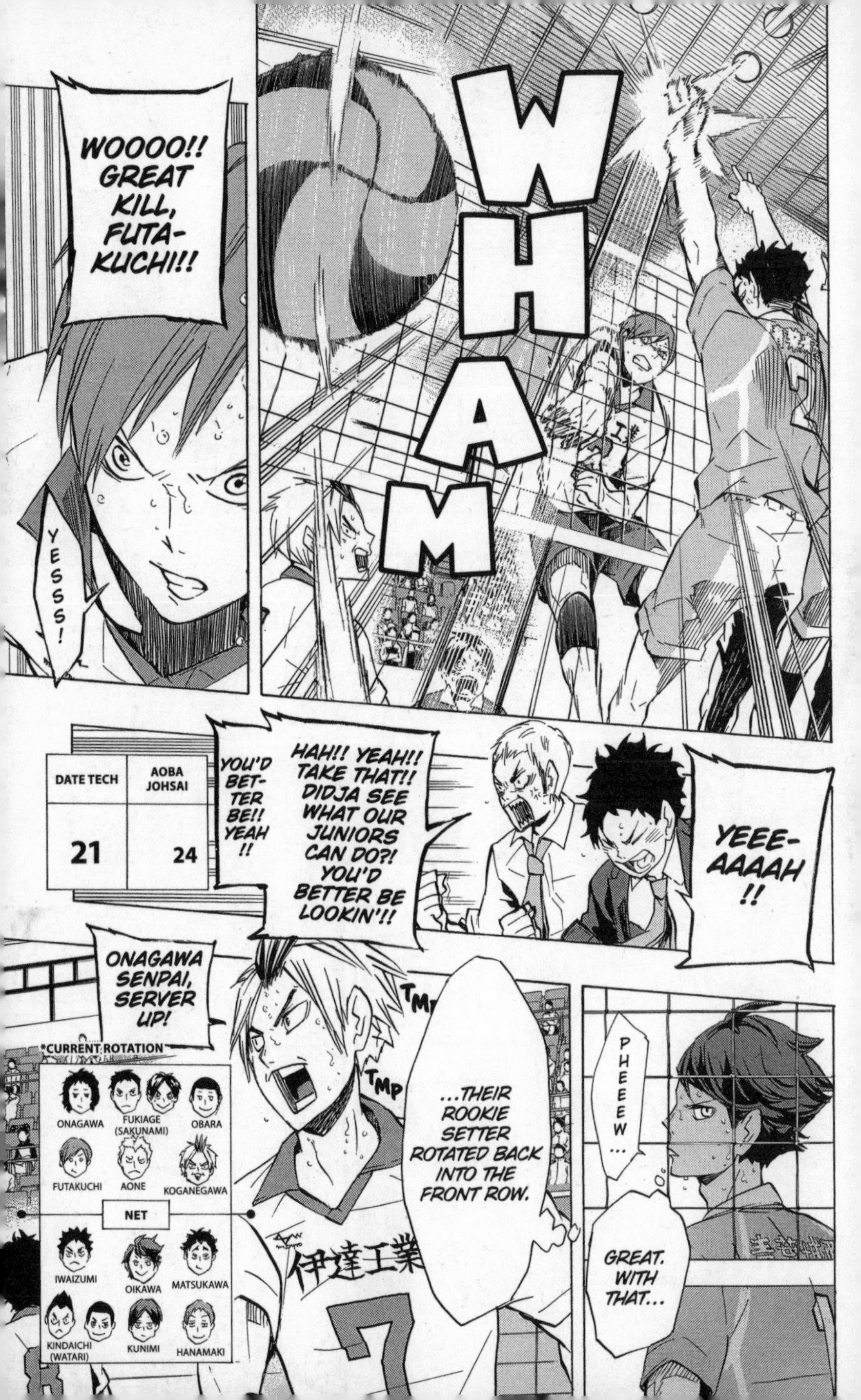
WHAM
WOOOO!! GREAT KILL, FUTA-KUCHI!!
YESSS!
YEEE-AAAAH!!
HAH!! YEAH!! TAKE THAT!! DIDJA SEE WHAT OUR JUNIORS CAN DO?! YOU'D BETTER BE LOOKIN'!!
YOU'D BET-TER BE!! YEAH!!
DATE TECH
21
AOBA JOHSAI
24
PHEEEW...
GREAT. WITH THAT...
...THEIR ROOKIE SETTER ROTATED BACK INTO THE FRONT ROW.
TMP
TMP
伊達工業
ONAGAWA SENPAI, SERVER UP!
*CURRENT ROTATION
ONAGAWA
FUKIAGE (SAKUNAMI)
OBARA
FUTAKUCHI
AONE
KOGANEGAWA
NET
IWAIZUMI
OIKAWA
MATSUKAWA
KINDAICHI (WATARI)
KUNIMI
HANAMAKI

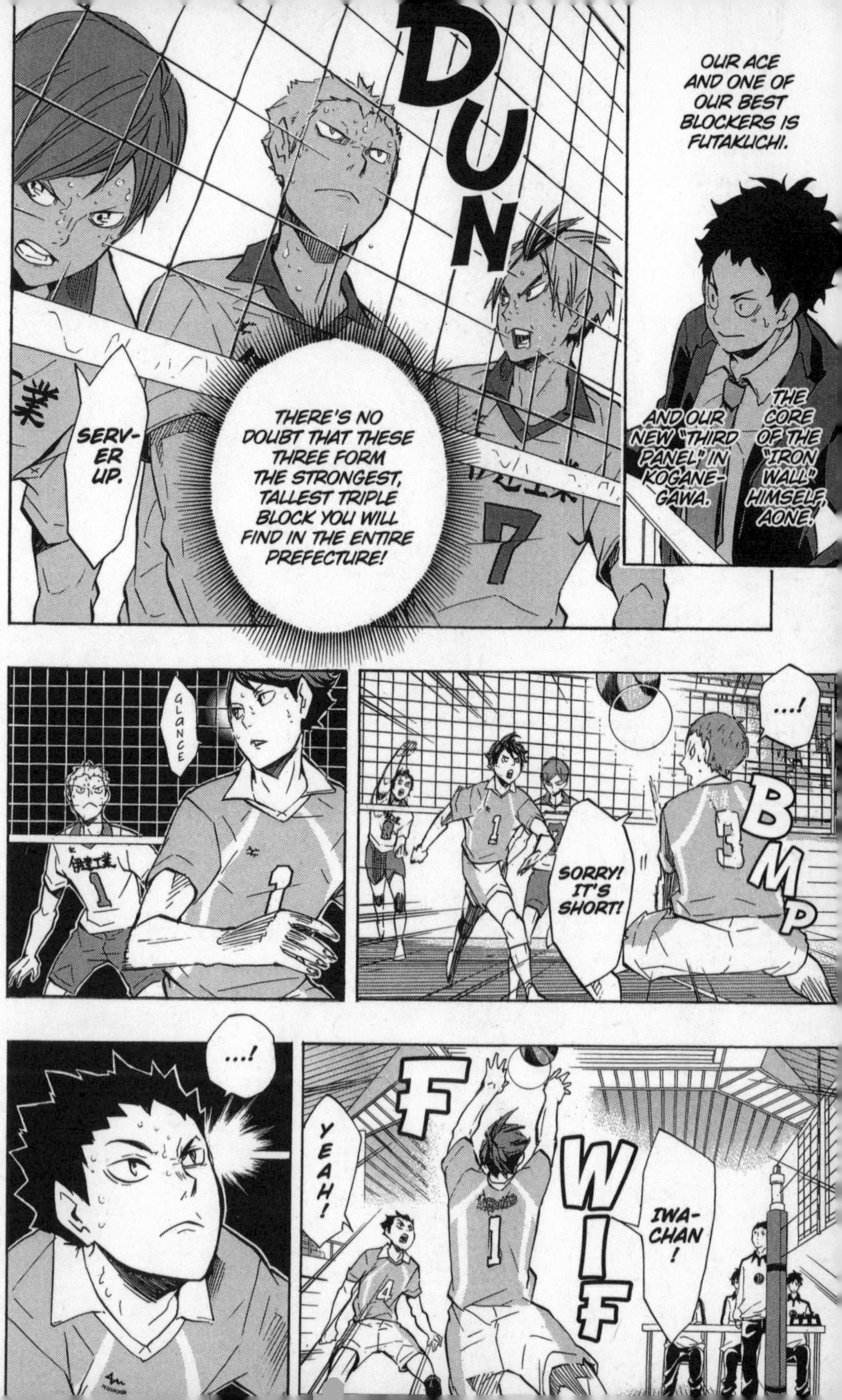
OUR ACE AND ONE OF OUR BEST BLOCKERS IS FUTAKUCHI.
THE CORE OF THE "IRON WALL" HIMSELF, AONE!
AND OUR NEW "THIRD PANEL" IN KOGANEGAWA.
DUN
THERE'S NO DOUBT THAT THESE THREE FORM THE STRONGEST, TALLEST TRIPLE BLOCK YOU WILL FIND IN THE ENTIRE PREFECTURE!
SERVER UP.
...!
BMP
SORRY! IT'S SHORT!
GLANCE
FWIF
IWA-CHAN!
YEAH!
...!

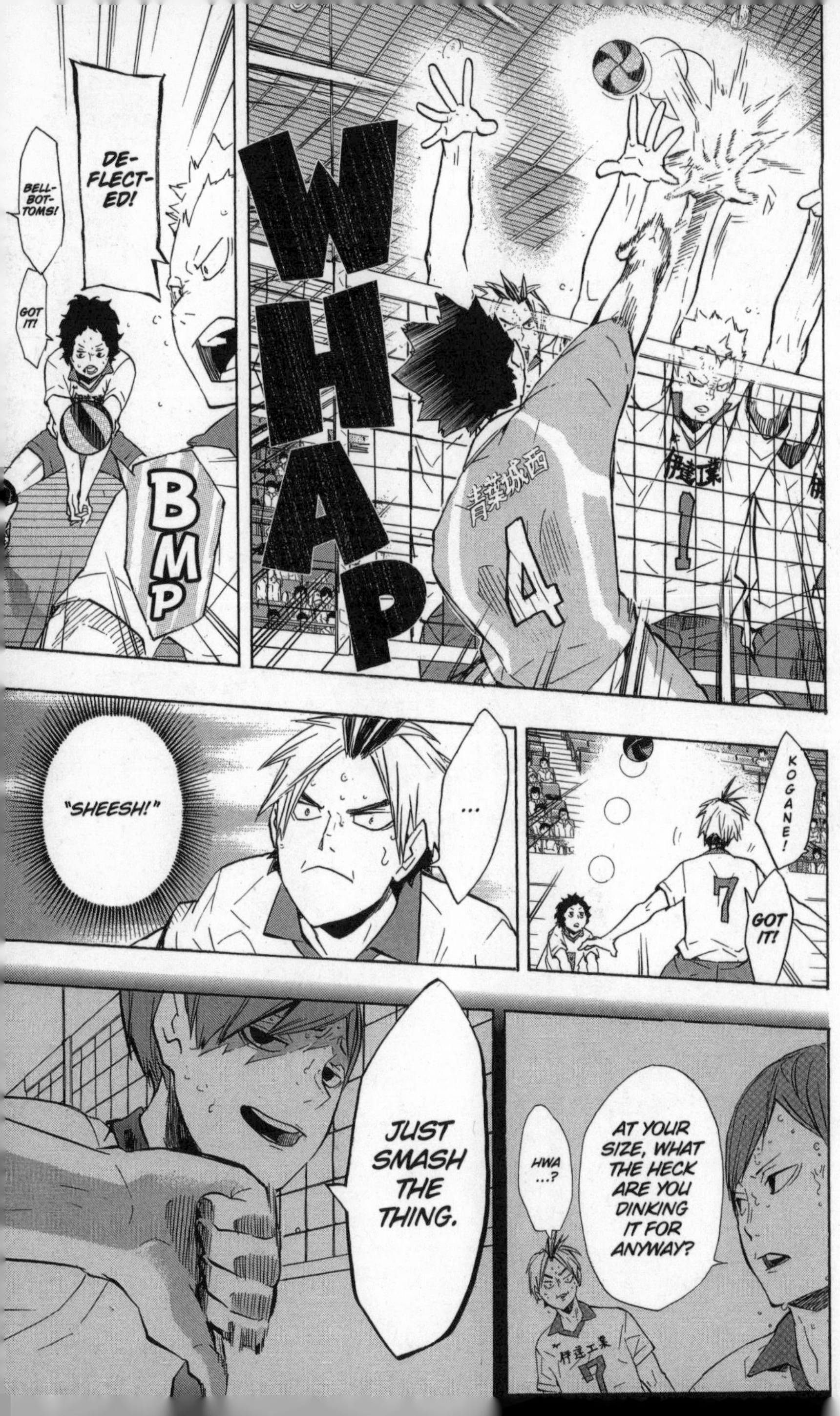
WHAP
DE-FLECTED!
BELL-BOTTOMS!
GOT IT!
BMP
KOGANE!
GOT IT!
...
"SHEESH!"
AT YOUR SIZE, WHAT THE HECK ARE YOU DINKING IT FOR ANYWAY?
HWA...?
JUST SMASH THE THING.

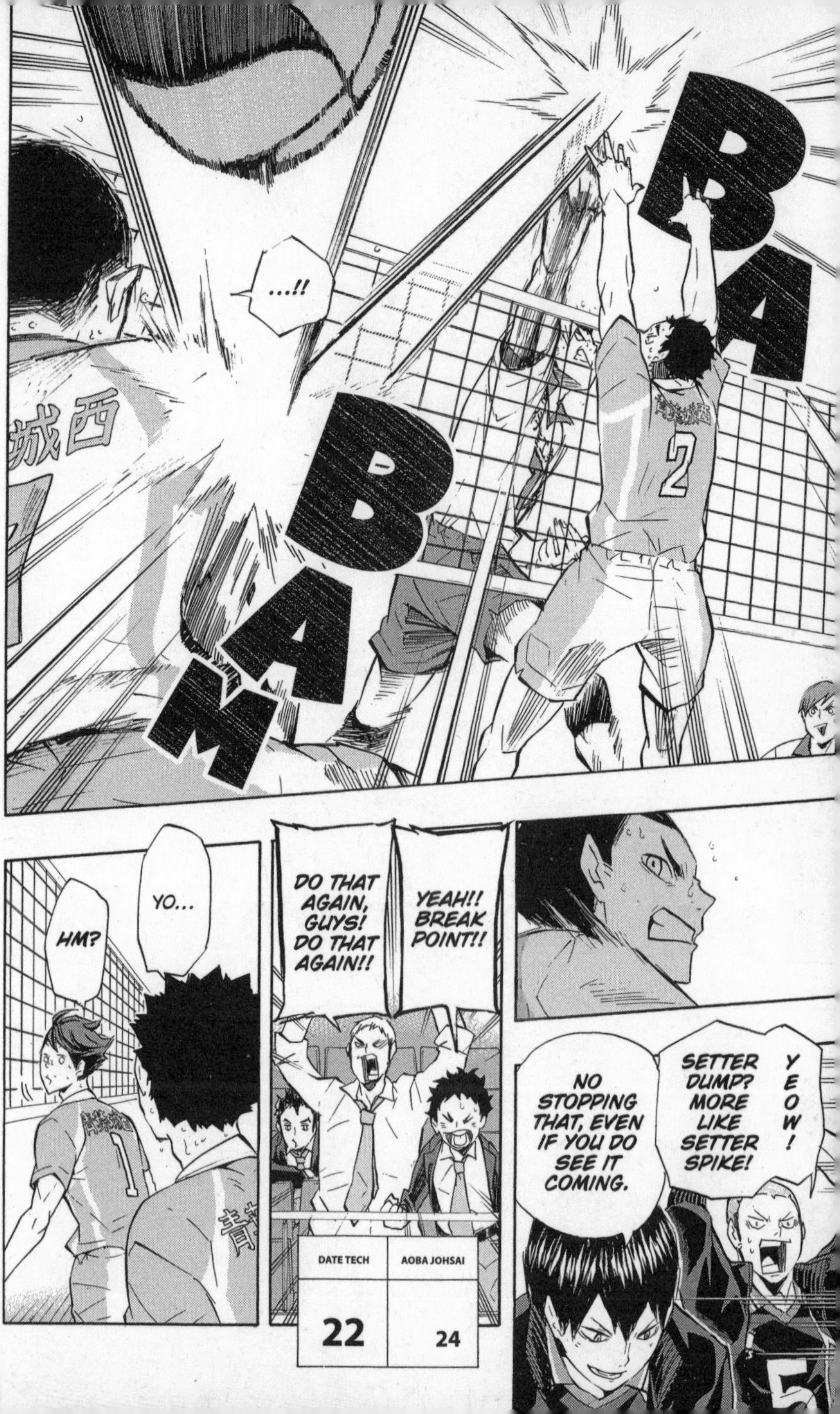
BA
...!!
BAM
YEOW!
SETTER DUMP? MORE LIKE SETTER SPIKE!
NO STOPPING THAT, EVEN IF YOU DO SEE IT COMING.
YEAH!! BREAK POINT!!
DO THAT AGAIN, GUYS! DO THAT AGAIN!!
DATE TECH
AOBA JOHSAI
22
24
YO...
HM?

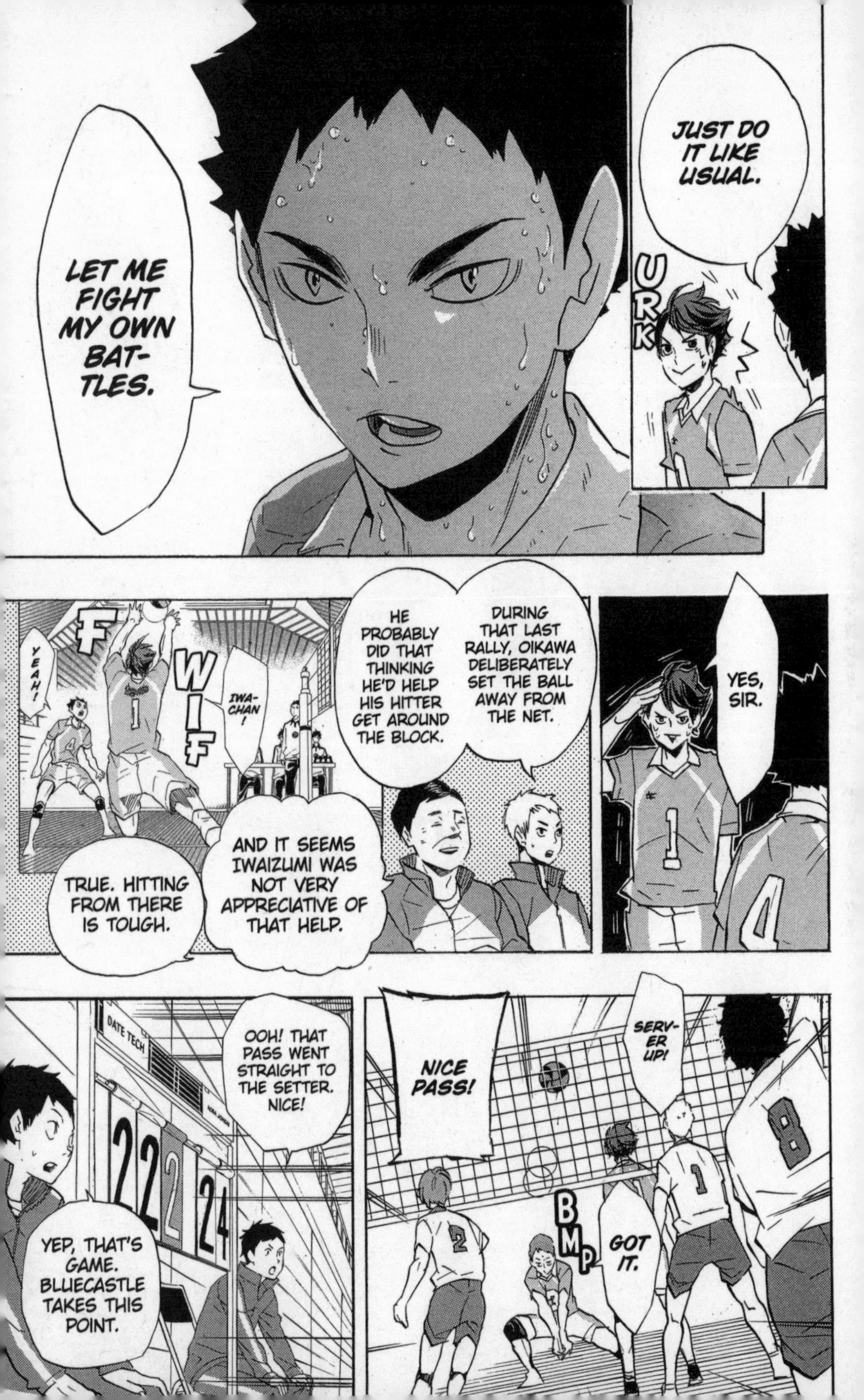
JUST DO IT LIKE USUAL.
URK
LET ME FIGHT MY OWN BAT-TLES.
YES, SIR.
DURING THAT LAST RALLY, OIKAWA DELIBERATELY SET THE BALL AWAY FROM THE NET.
HE PROBABLY DID THAT THINKING HE'D HELP HIS HITTER GET AROUND THE BLOCK.
AND IT SEEMS IWAIZUMI WAS NOT VERY APPRECIATIVE OF THAT HELP.
TRUE. HITTING FROM THERE IS TOUGH.
IWA-CHAN!
WIF
F
YEAH!
SERV-ER UP!
NICE PASS!
GOT IT.
BMP
OOH! THAT PASS WENT STRAIGHT TO THE SETTER. NICE!
DATE TECH
YEP, THAT'S GAME. BLUECASTLE TAKES THIS POINT.

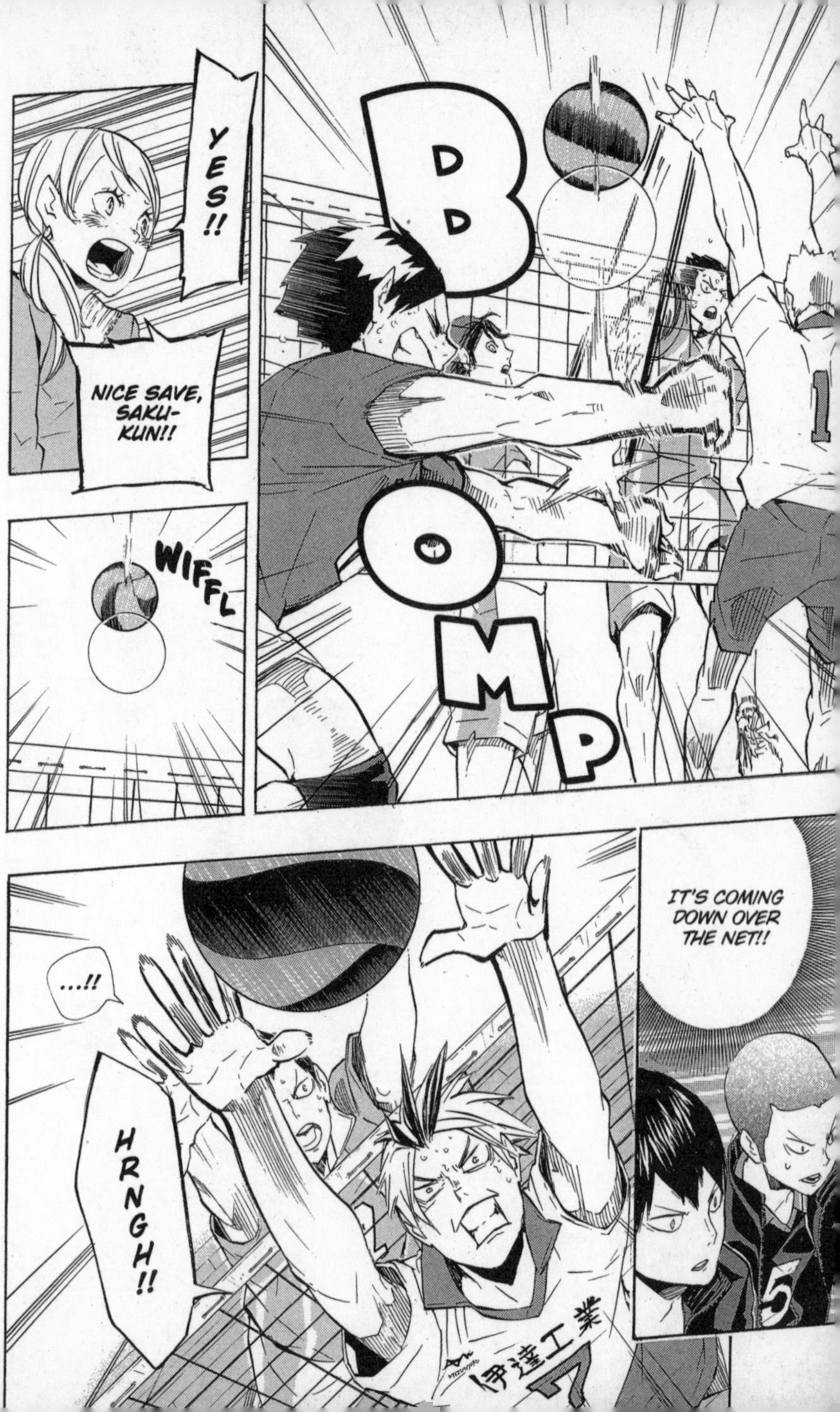
BOMP
YES!!
NICE SAVE, SAKU-KUN!!
WIFFL
IT'S COMING DOWN OVER THE NET!!
...!!
HRNGH!!
伊達工業

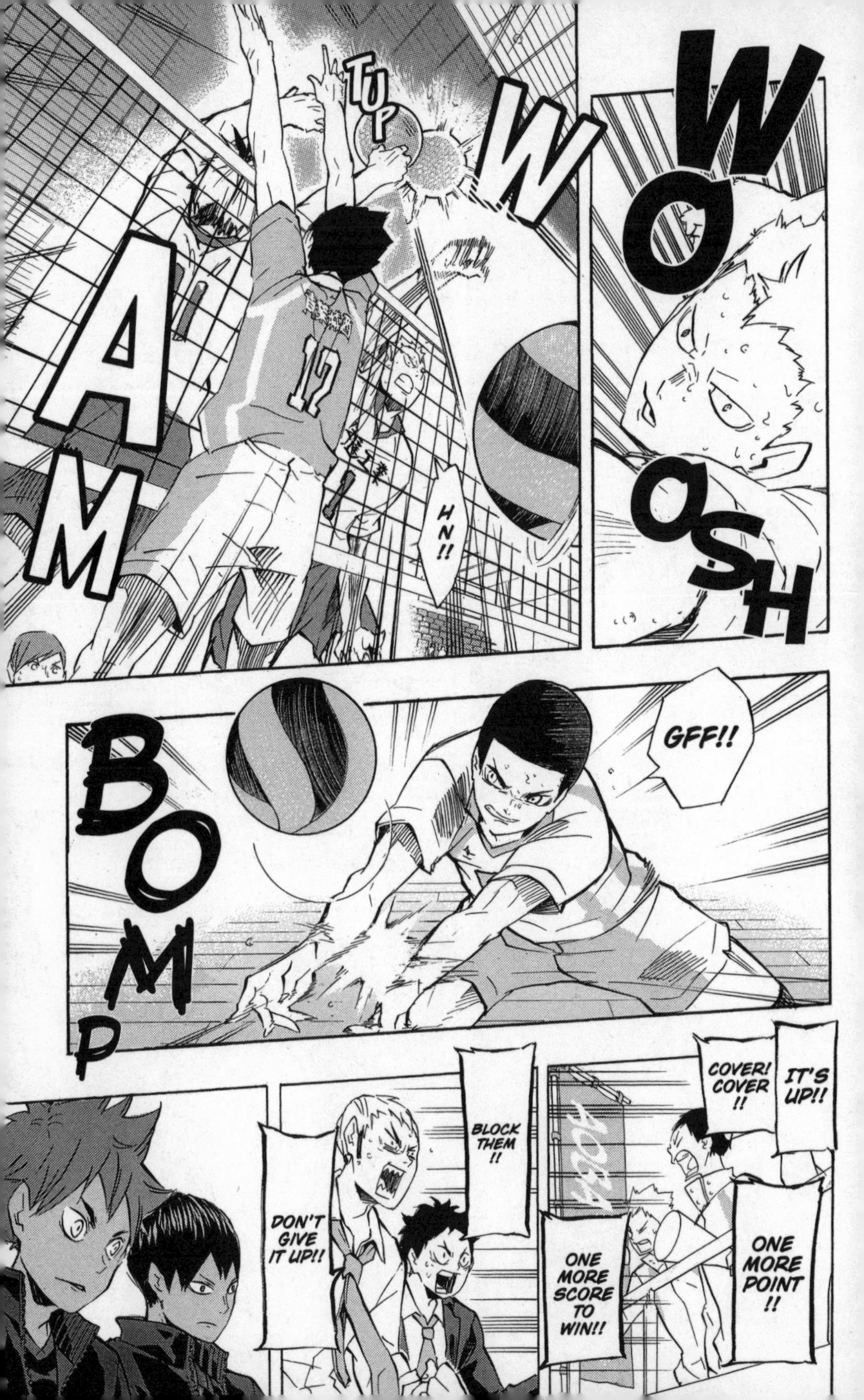

WOOSH
TUP
WAM
HN!!
GFF!!
BOOMP
IT'S UP!!
COVER! COVER!!
ONE MORE POINT!!
ONE MORE SCORE TO WIN!!
BLOCK THEM!!
DON'T GIVE IT UP!!

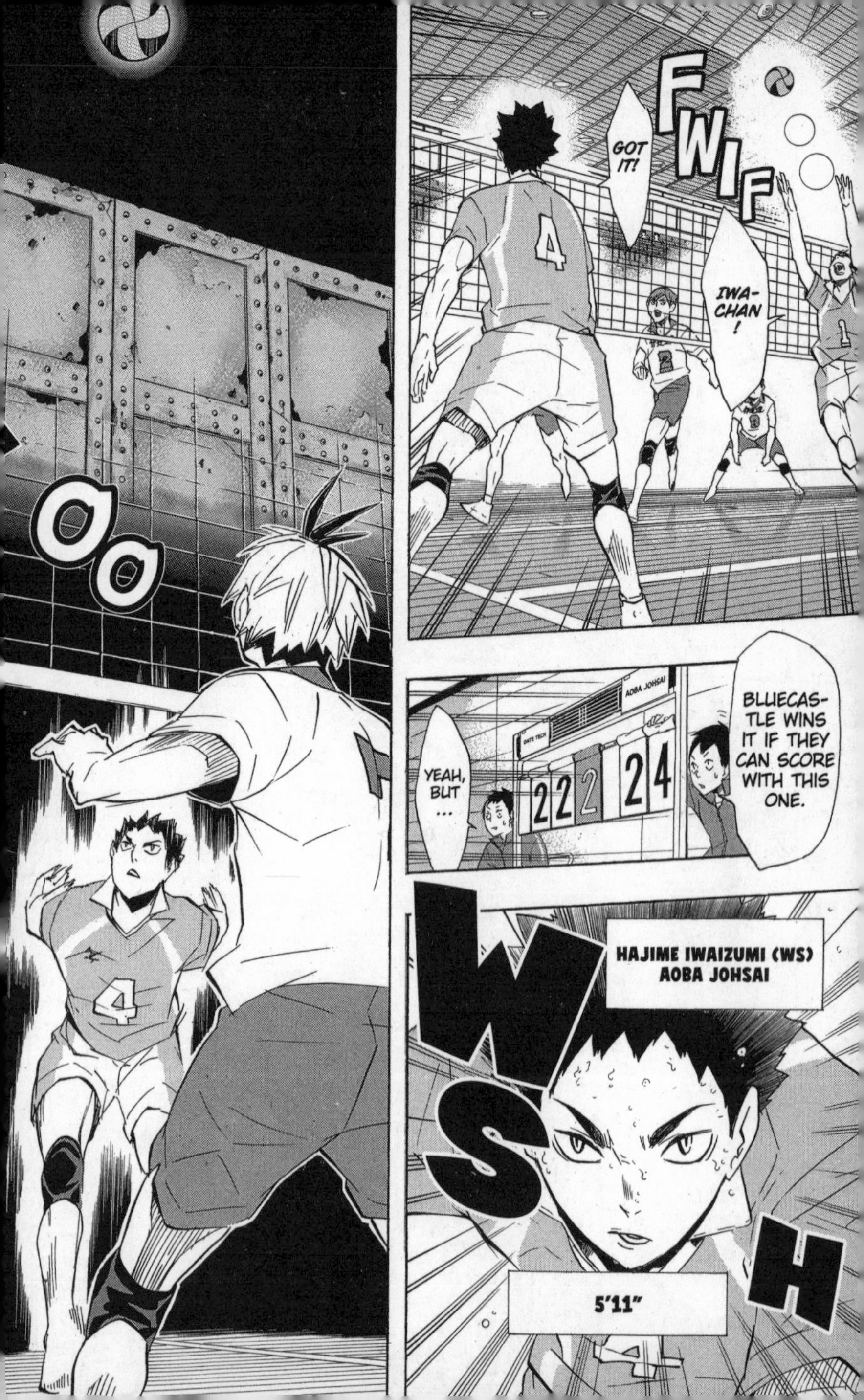
FWIF
GOT IT!
IWA-CHAN!
BLUECASTLE WINS IT IF THEY CAN SCORE WITH THIS ONE.
AOBA JOHSAI
DATE TECH
22
24
YEAH, BUT...
WHSH
HAJIME IWAIZUMI (WS)
AOBA JOHSAI
5'11"
OO

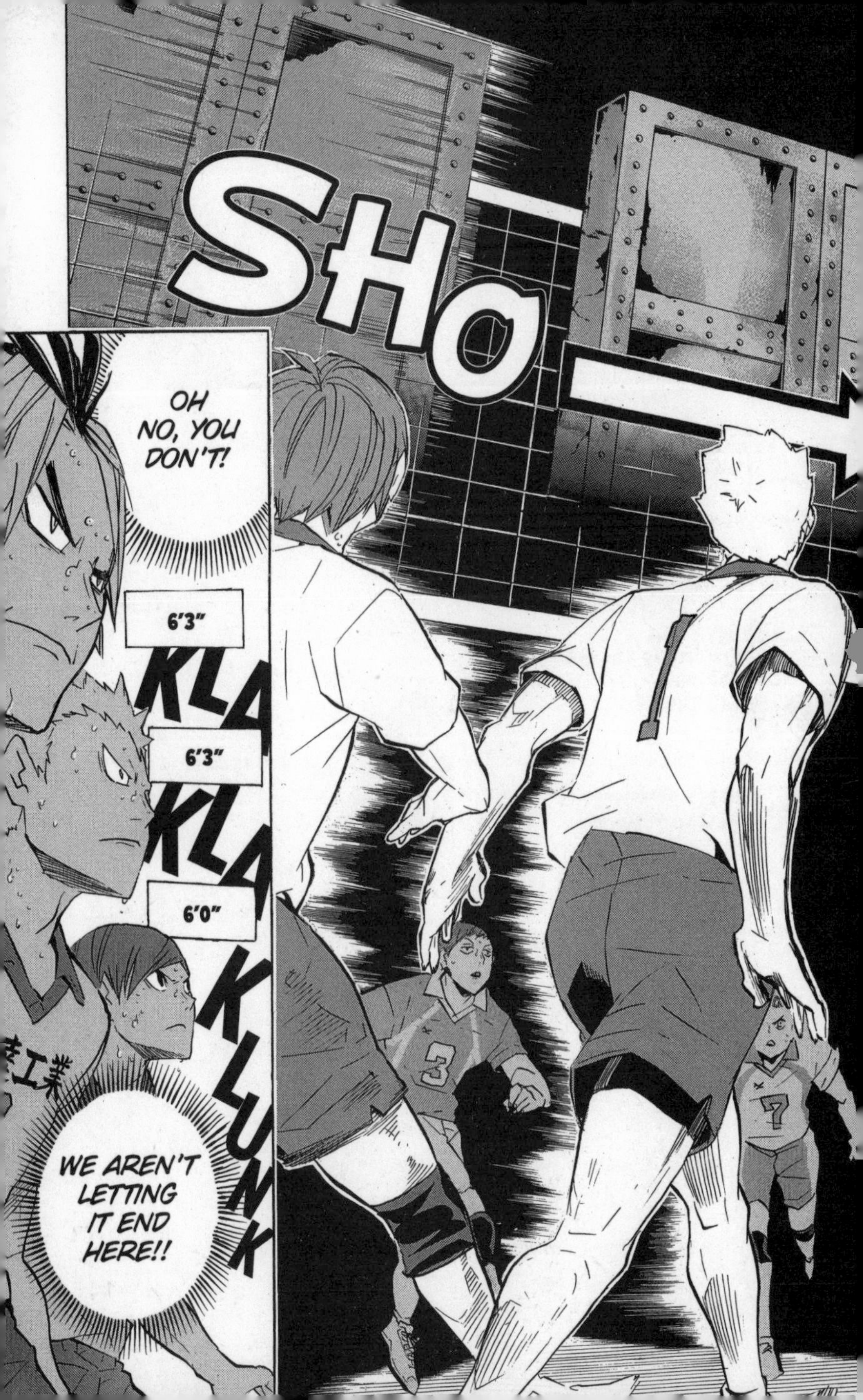
SHO
OH NO, YOU DON'T!
6'3"
KLA
6'3"
KLA
6'0"
KLUNK
WE AREN'T LETTING IT END HERE!!

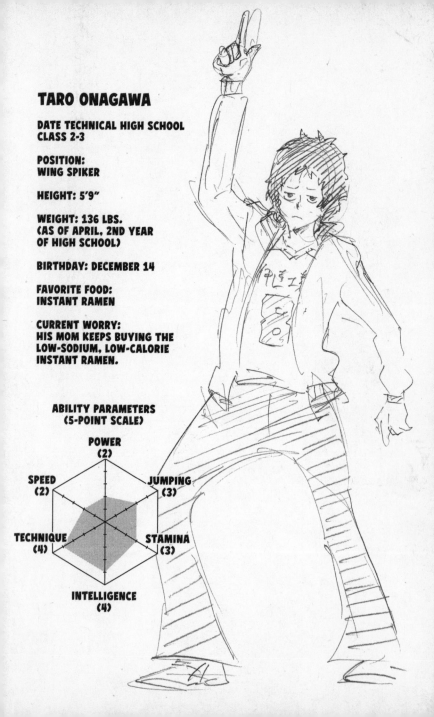

TARO ONAGAWA

DATE TECHNICAL HIGH SCHOOL
CLASS 2-3

POSITION:
WING SPIKER

HEIGHT: 5'9"

WEIGHT: 136 LBS.
(AS OF APRIL, 2ND YEAR OF HIGH SCHOOL)

BIRTHDAY: DECEMBER 14

FAVORITE FOOD:
INSTANT RAMEN

CURRENT WORRY:
HIS MOM KEEPS BUYING THE LOW-SODIUM, LOW-CALORIE INSTANT RAMEN.

ABILITY PARAMETERS
(5-POINT SCALE)

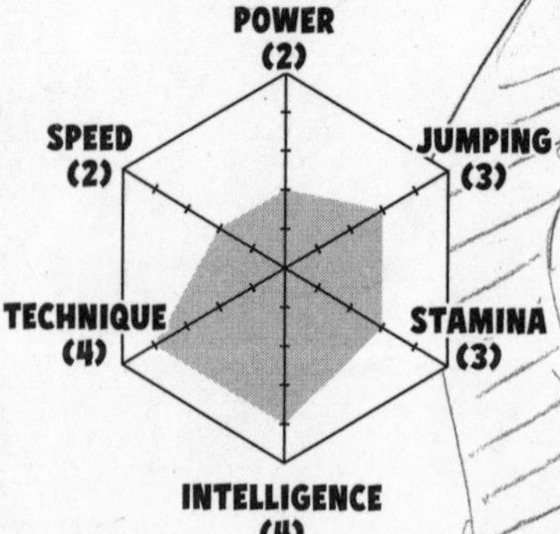
POWER
(2)
JUMPING
(3)
STAMINA
(3)
INTELLIGENCE
(4)
TECHNIQUE
(4)
SPEED
(2)

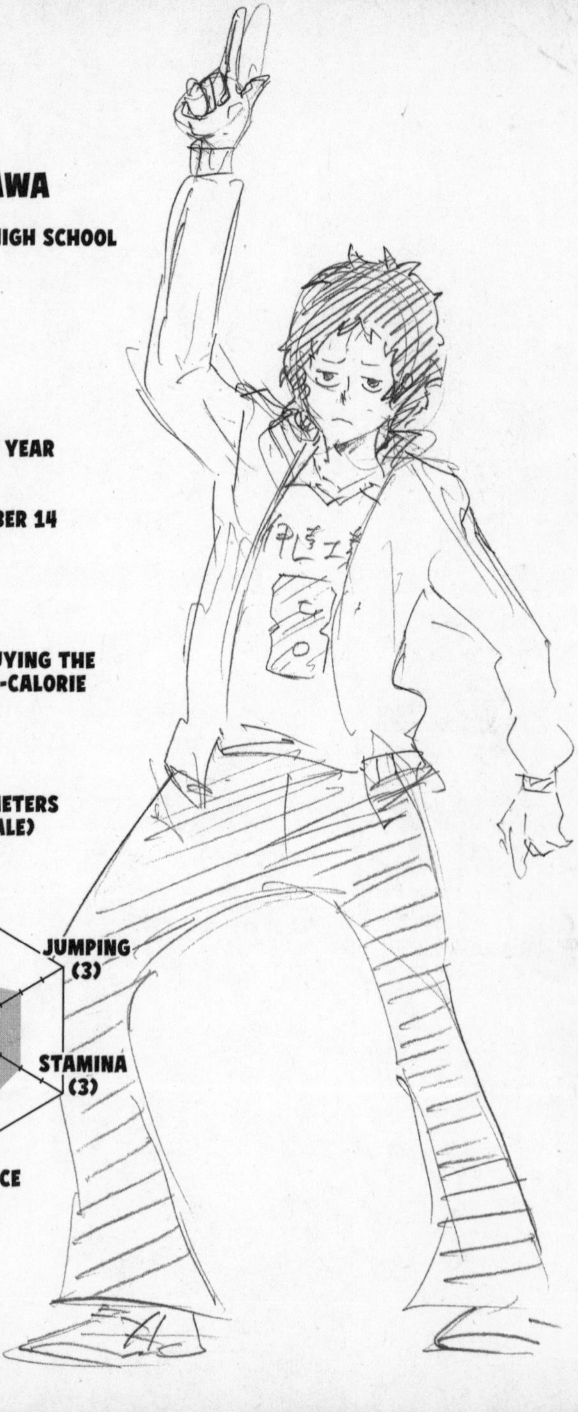

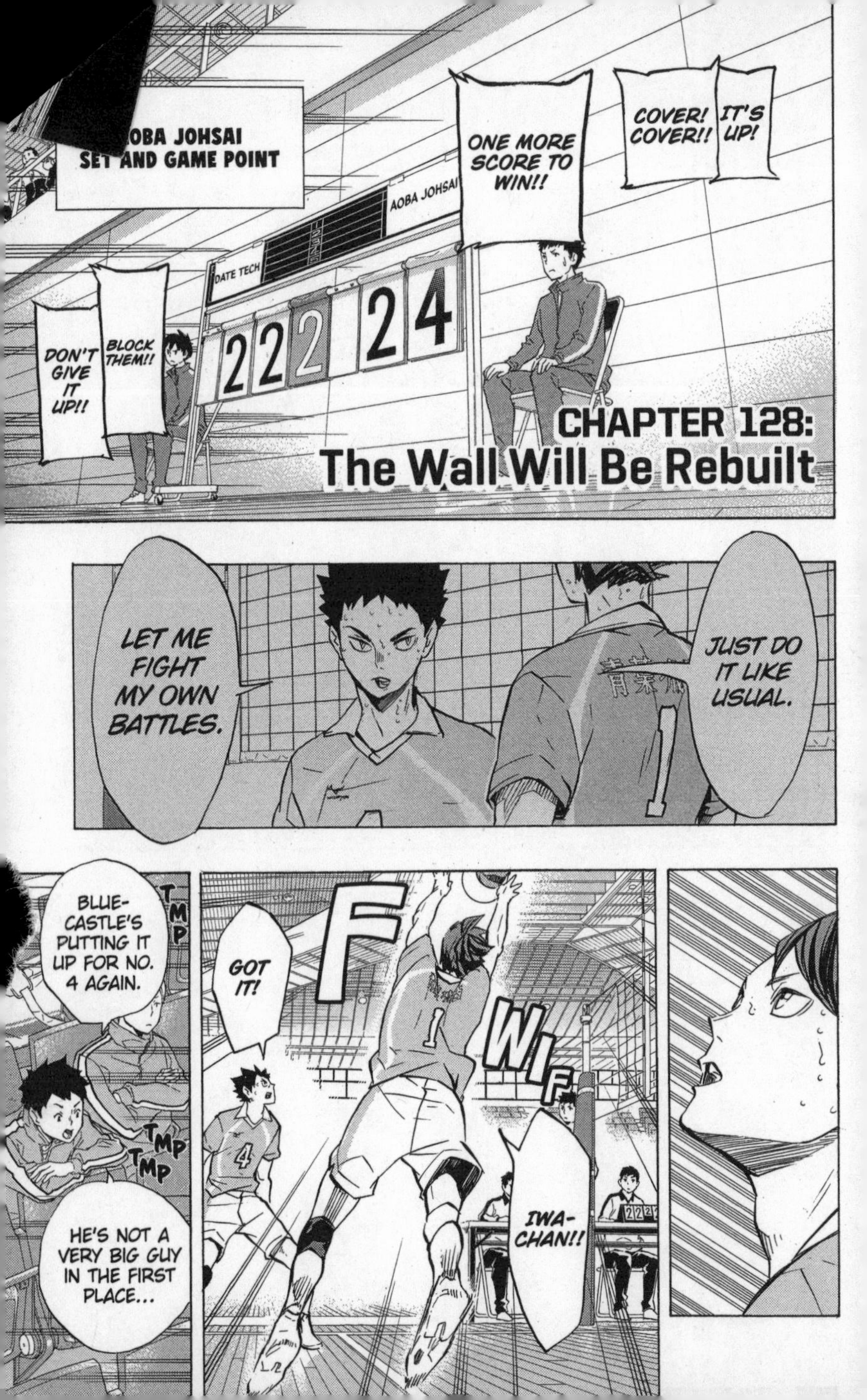
IT'S UP!
COVER! COVER!!
ONE MORE SCORE TO WIN!!
AOBA JOHSAI
AOBA JOHSAI SET AND GAME POINT
DATE TECH
22 24
BLOCK THEM!!
DON'T GIVE IT UP!!
CHAPTER 128:
The Wall Will Be Rebuilt
JUST DO IT LIKE USUAL.
LET ME FIGHT MY OWN BATTLES.
F
WIF
GOT IT!
IWA-CHAN!!
TMP
BLUE-CASTLE'S PUTTING IT UP FOR NO. 4 AGAIN.
TMP TMP
HE'S NOT A VERY BIG GUY IN THE FIRST PLACE...

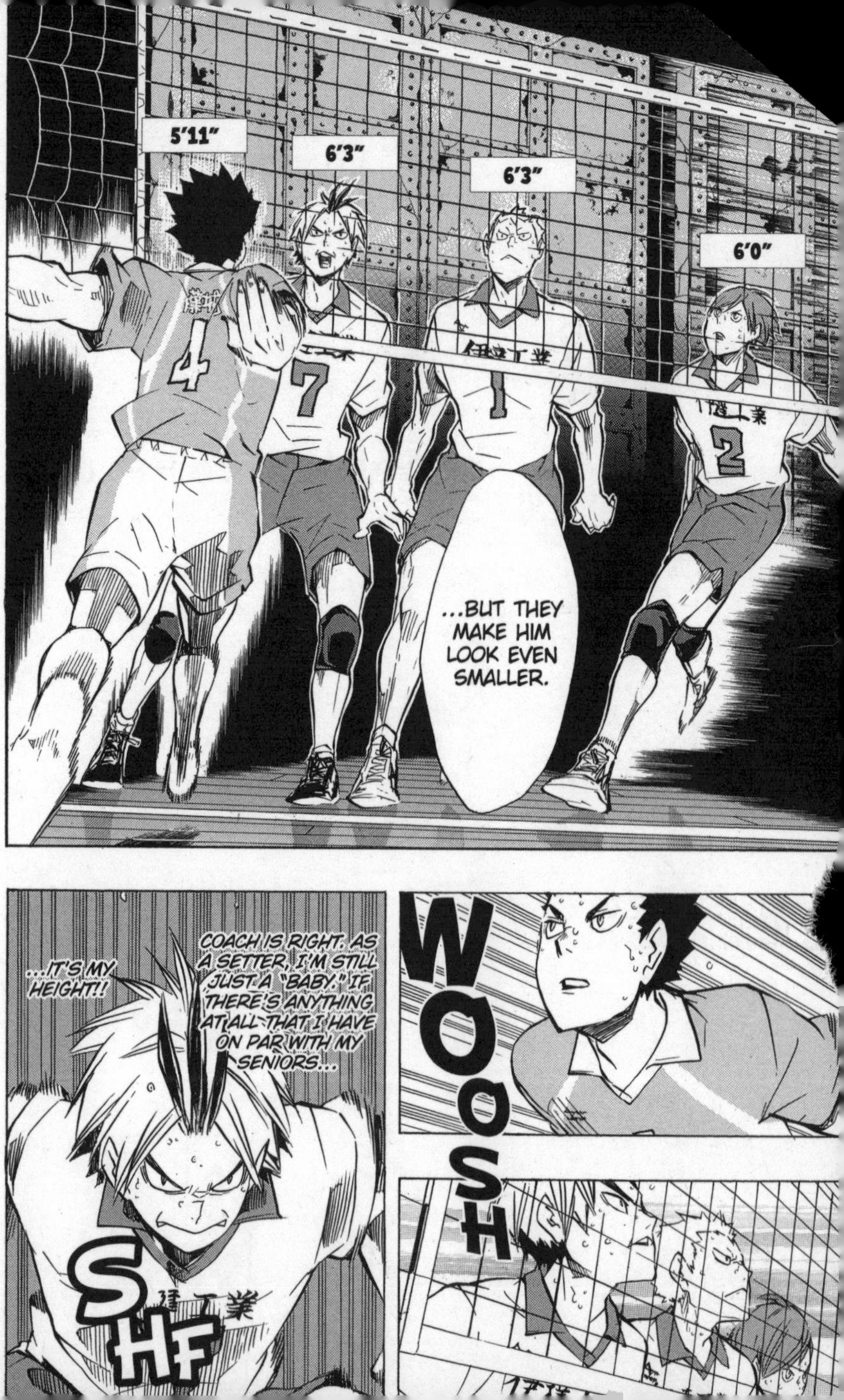
6'0"
6'3"
6'3"
5'11"
...BUT THEY MAKE HIM LOOK EVEN SMALLER.
WOOSH
COACH IS RIGHT. AS A SETTER, I'M STILL JUST A "BABY." IF THERE'S ANYTHING AT ALL THAT I HAVE ON PAR WITH MY SENIORS...
...IT'S MY HEIGHT!!
SHF

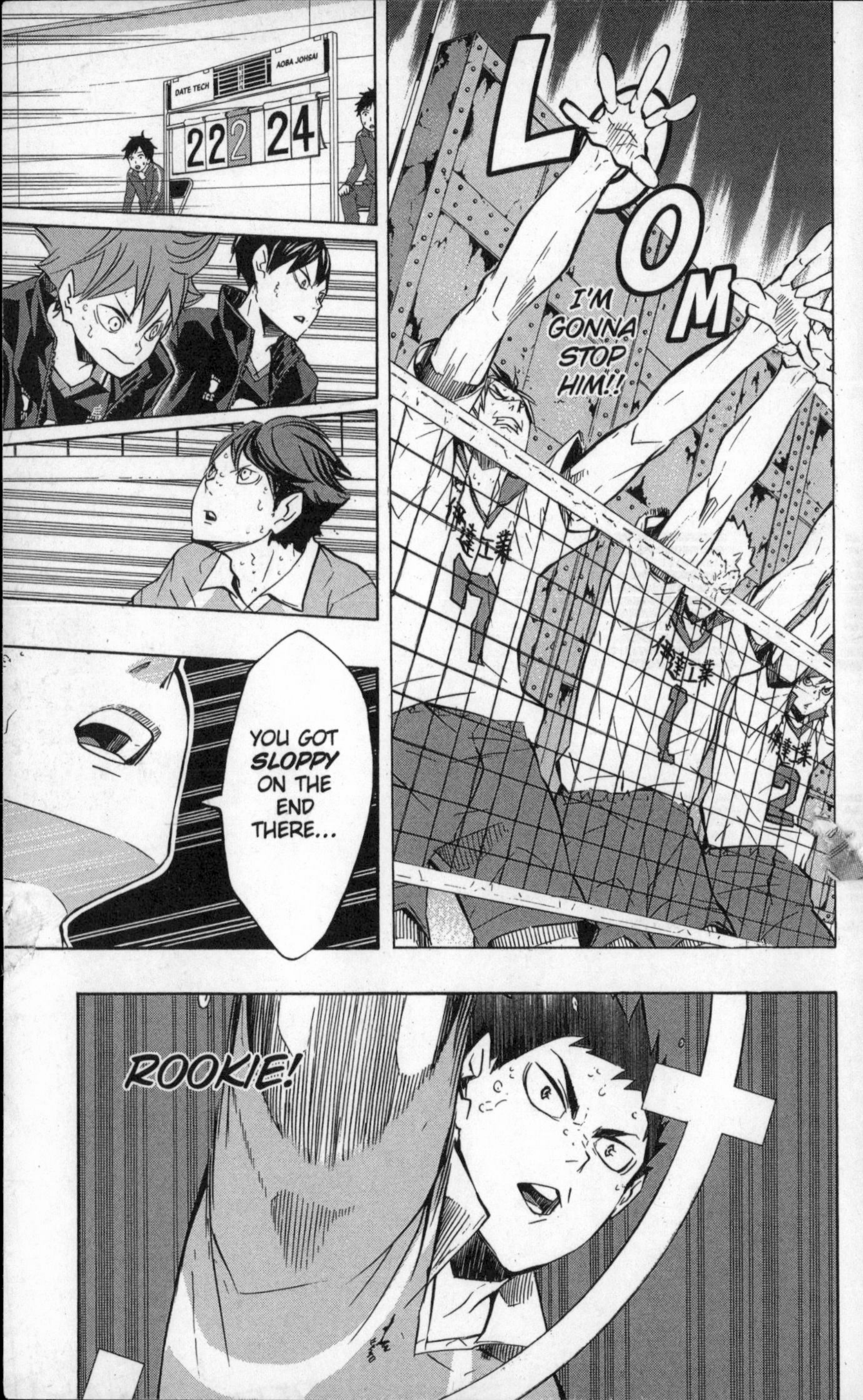
LOOM
I'M GONNA STOP HIM!!
DATE TECH
AOBA JOHSAI
22 2 24
YOU GOT SLOPPY ON THE END THERE...
ROOKIE!

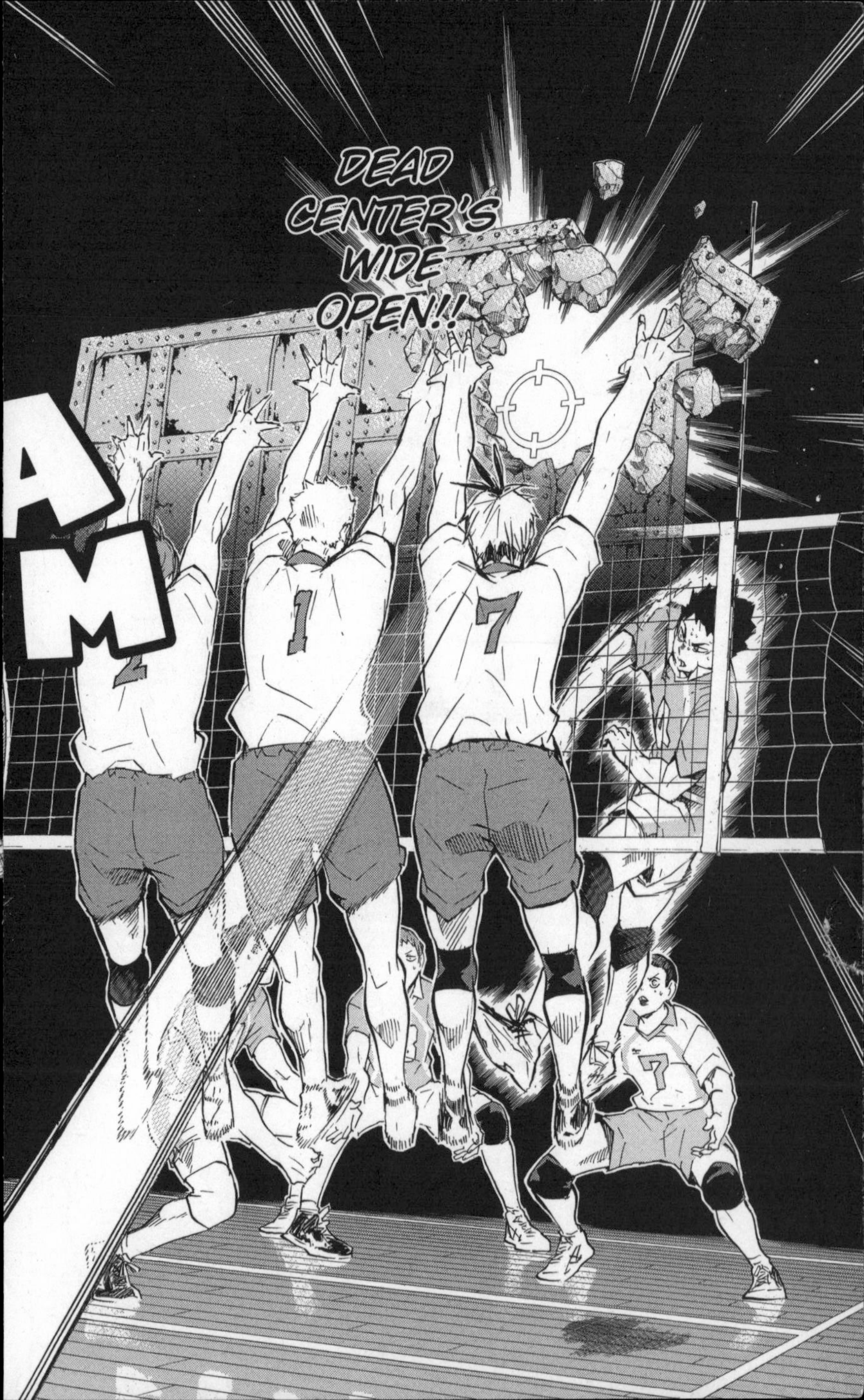
DEAD CENTER'S WIDE OPEN!!

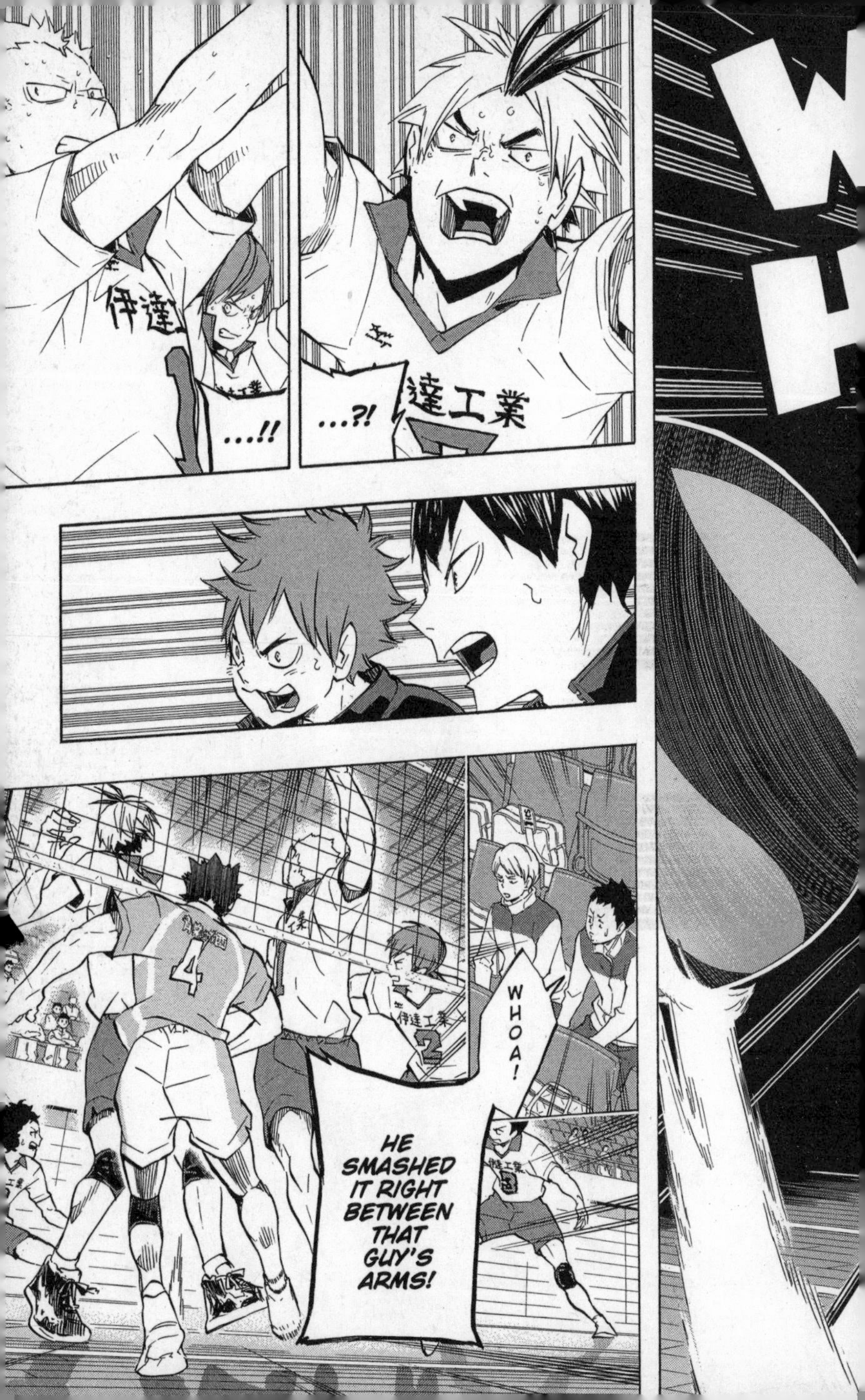
WH
...?!
...!!
WHOA!
HE SMASHED IT RIGHT BETWEEN THAT GUY'S ARMS!

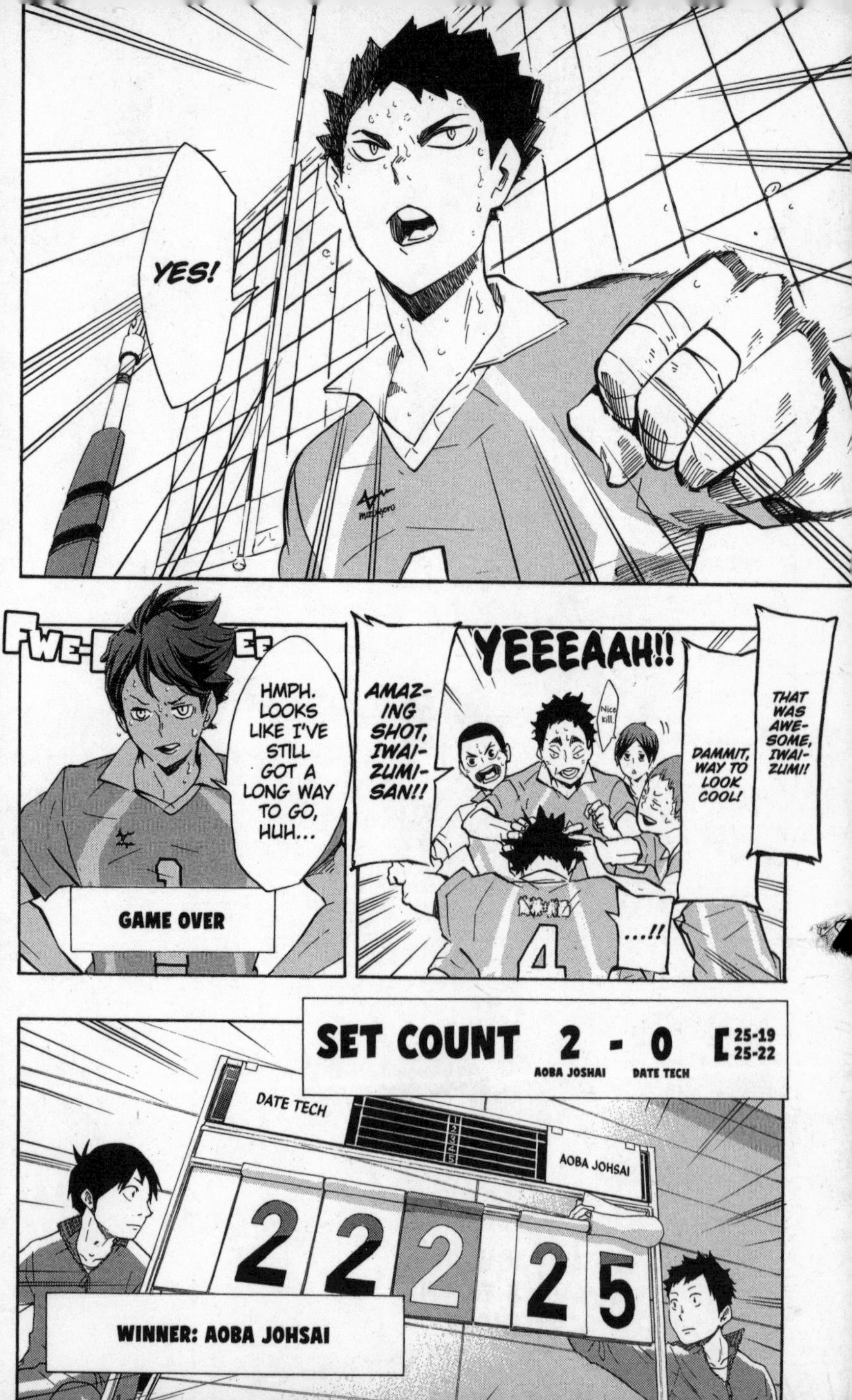
YES!
YEEEAAH!!
THAT WAS AWESOME, IWAIZUMI!
DAMMIT, WAY TO LOOK COOL!
Nice kill.
AMAZING SHOT, IWAIZUMI-SAN!!
...!!
HMPH. LOOKS LIKE I'VE STILL GOT A LONG WAY TO GO, HUH...
GAME OVER
SET COUNT 2 - 0
AOBA JOSHAI
DATE TECH
25-19
25-22
DATE TECH
AOBA JOHSAI
22
25
WINNER: AOBA JOHSAI

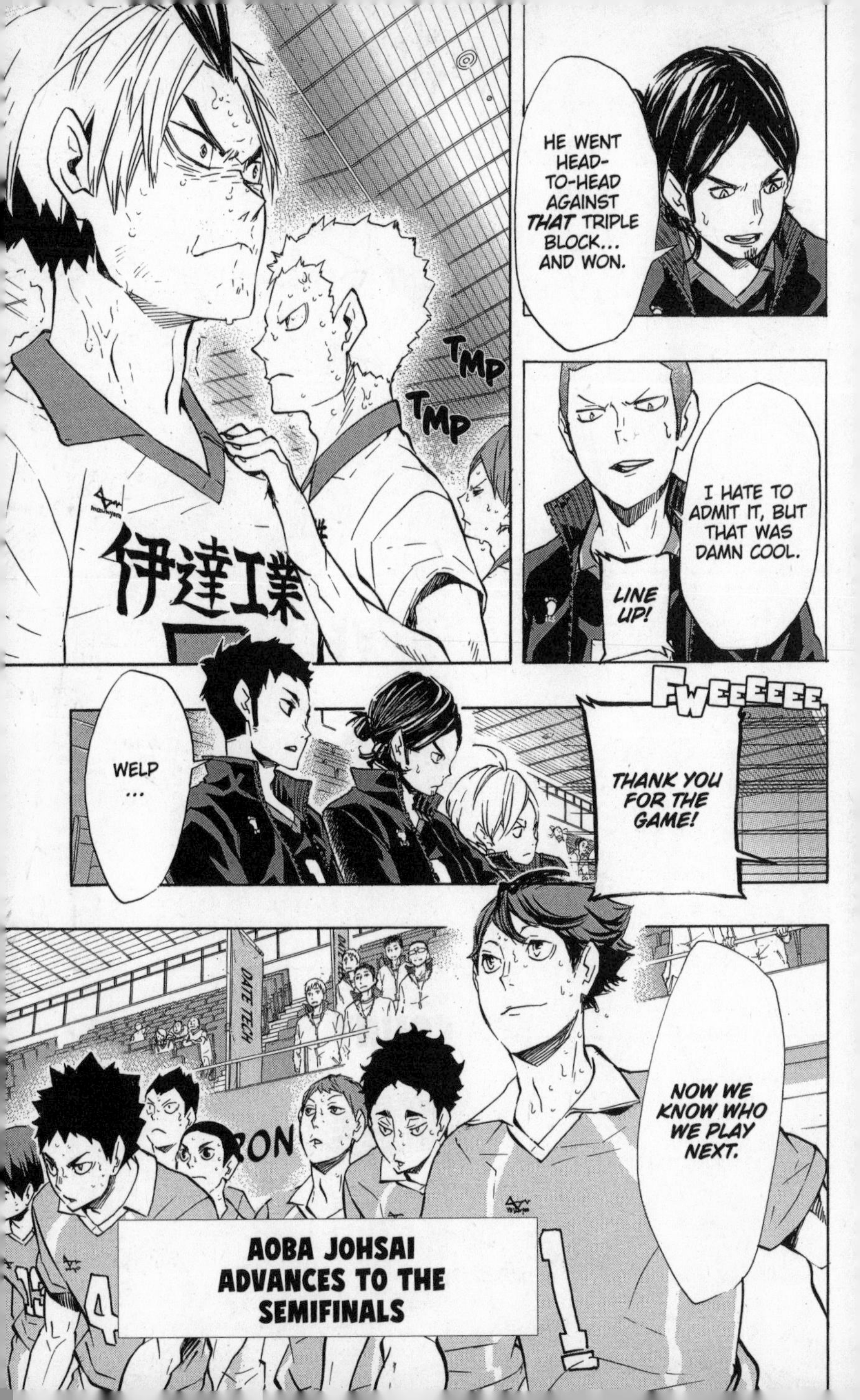
HE WENT HEAD-TO-HEAD AGAINST *THAT* TRIPLE BLOCK... AND WON.
I HATE TO ADMIT IT, BUT THAT WAS DAMN COOL.
LINE UP!
TMP
TMP
伊達工業
FWEEEEEE
THANK YOU FOR THE GAME!
WELP ...
NOW WE KNOW WHO WE PLAY NEXT.
DATE TECH
AOBA JOHSAI ADVANCES TO THE SEMIFINALS

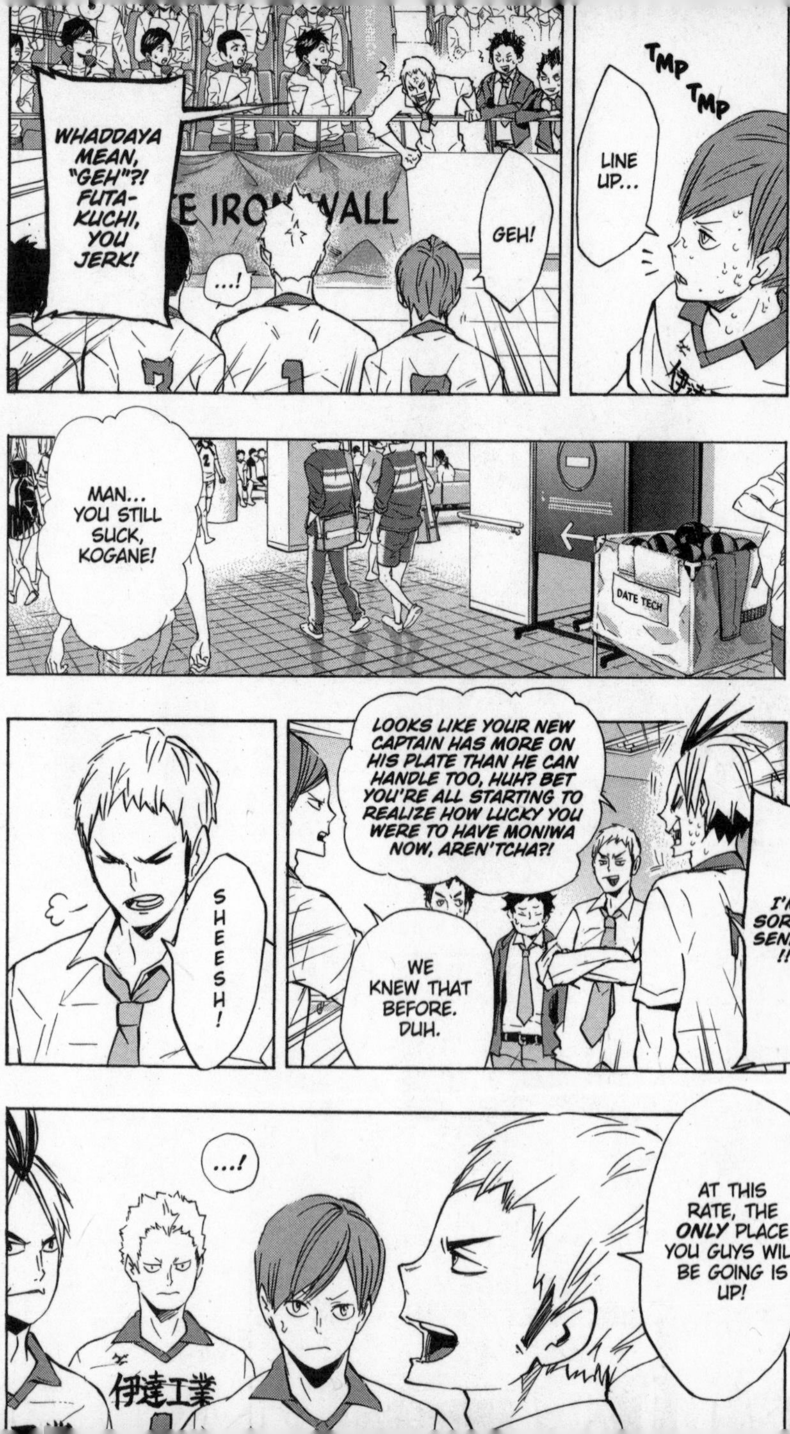
TMP TMP
LINE UP...
GEH!
...!
WHADDAYA MEAN, "GEH"?! FUTA-KUCHI, YOU JERK!
MAN... YOU STILL SUCK, KOGANE!
DATE TECH
I'M SORRY, SENPAI!!
LOOKS LIKE YOUR NEW CAPTAIN HAS MORE ON HIS PLATE THAN HE CAN HANDLE TOO, HUH? BET YOU'RE ALL STARTING TO REALIZE HOW LUCKY YOU WERE TO HAVE MONIWA NOW, AREN'TCHA?!
WE KNEW THAT BEFORE. DUH.
SHEESH!
AT THIS RATE, THE ONLY PLACE YOU GUYS WILL BE GOING IS UP!
...!

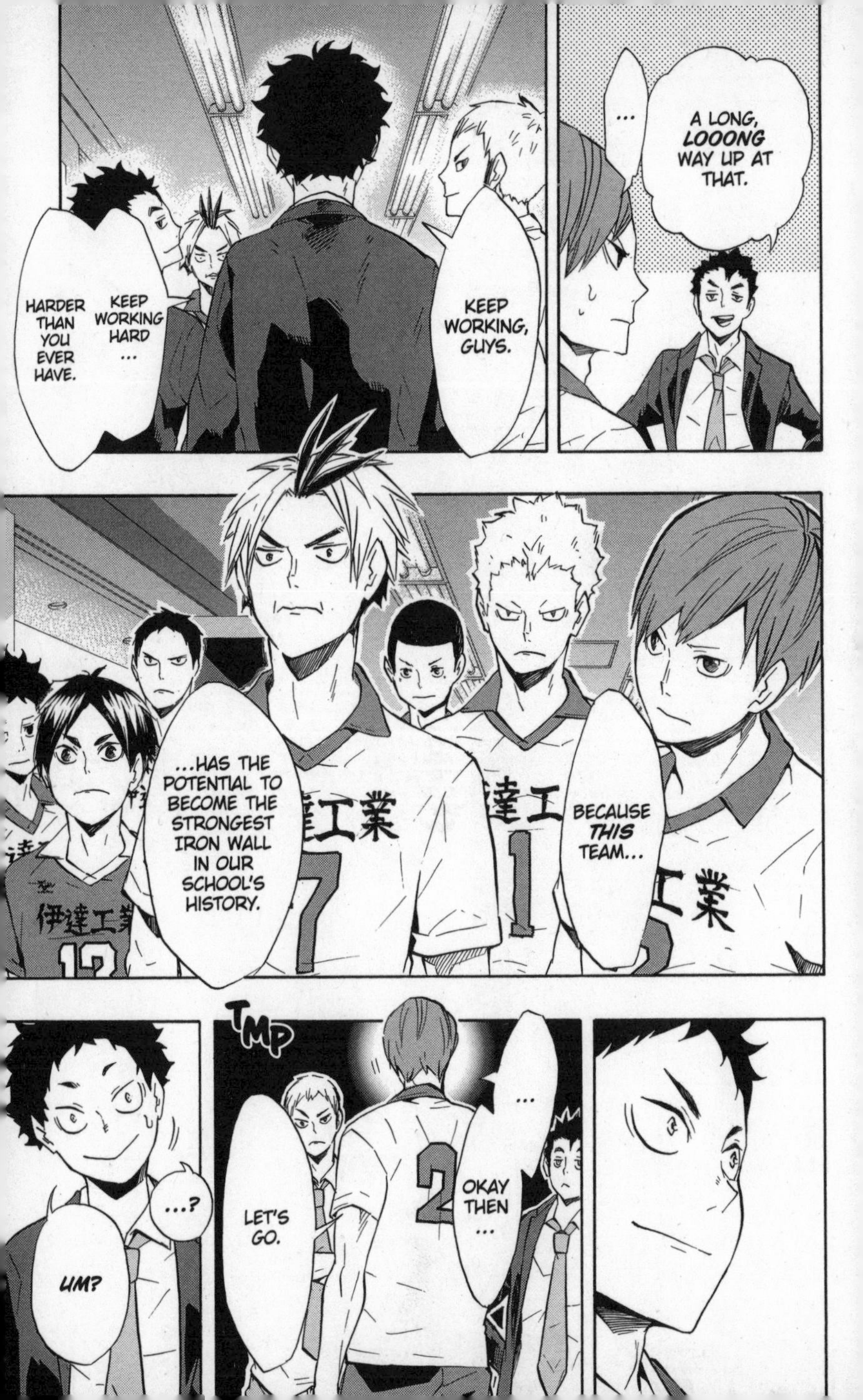
A LONG, LOOONG WAY UP AT THAT.
...
KEEP WORKING, GUYS.
KEEP WORKING HARD ...
HARDER THAN YOU EVER HAVE.
BECAUSE THIS TEAM...
...HAS THE POTENTIAL TO BECOME THE STRONGEST IRON WALL IN OUR SCHOOL'S HISTORY.
...
TMP
OKAY THEN ...
LET'S GO.
...?
UM?

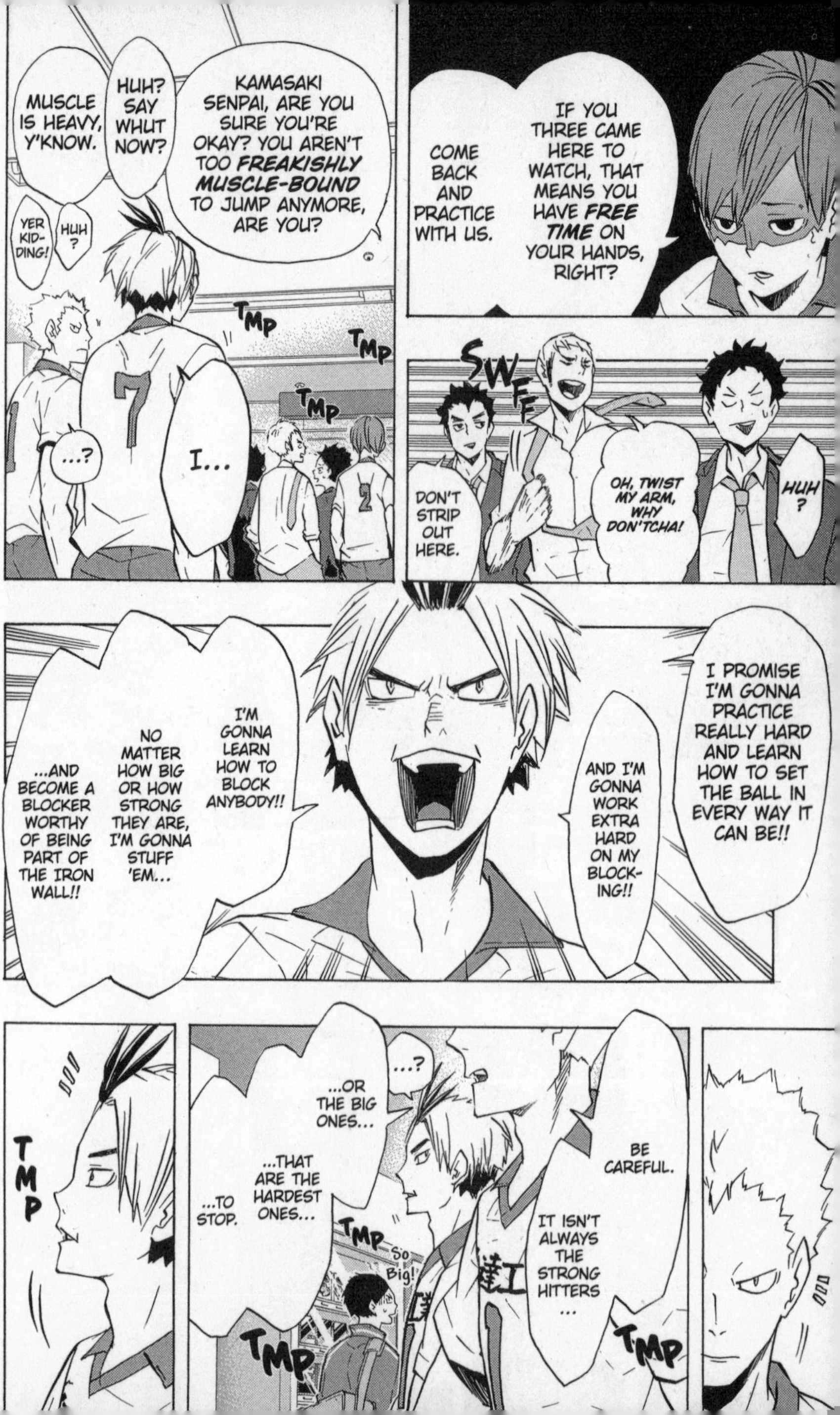
IF YOU THREE CAME HERE TO WATCH, THAT MEANS YOU HAVE FREE TIME ON YOUR HANDS, RIGHT?
COME BACK AND PRACTICE WITH US.
KAMASAKI SENPAI, ARE YOU SURE YOU'RE OKAY? YOU AREN'T TOO FREAKISHLY MUSCLE-BOUND TO JUMP ANYMORE, ARE YOU?
HUH? SAY WHUT NOW?
MUSCLE IS HEAVY, Y'KNOW.
HUH?
YER KID-DING!
HUH?
OH, TWIST MY ARM, WHY DON'TCHA!
SWFF
DON'T STRIP OUT HERE.
TMP
TMP
TMP
I...
...?
I PROMISE I'M GONNA PRACTICE REALLY HARD AND LEARN HOW TO SET THE BALL IN EVERY WAY IT CAN BE!!
AND I'M GONNA WORK EXTRA HARD ON MY BLOCK-ING!!
I'M GONNA LEARN HOW TO BLOCK ANYBODY!!
NO MATTER HOW BIG OR HOW STRONG THEY ARE, I'M GONNA STUFF 'EM...
...AND BECOME A BLOCKER WORTHY OF BEING PART OF THE IRON WALL!!
BE CAREFUL.
IT ISN'T ALWAYS THE STRONG HITTERS...
...?
...OR THE BIG ONES...
...THAT ARE THE HARDEST ONES...
...TO STOP.
TMP
So Big!
TMP
TMP
TMP

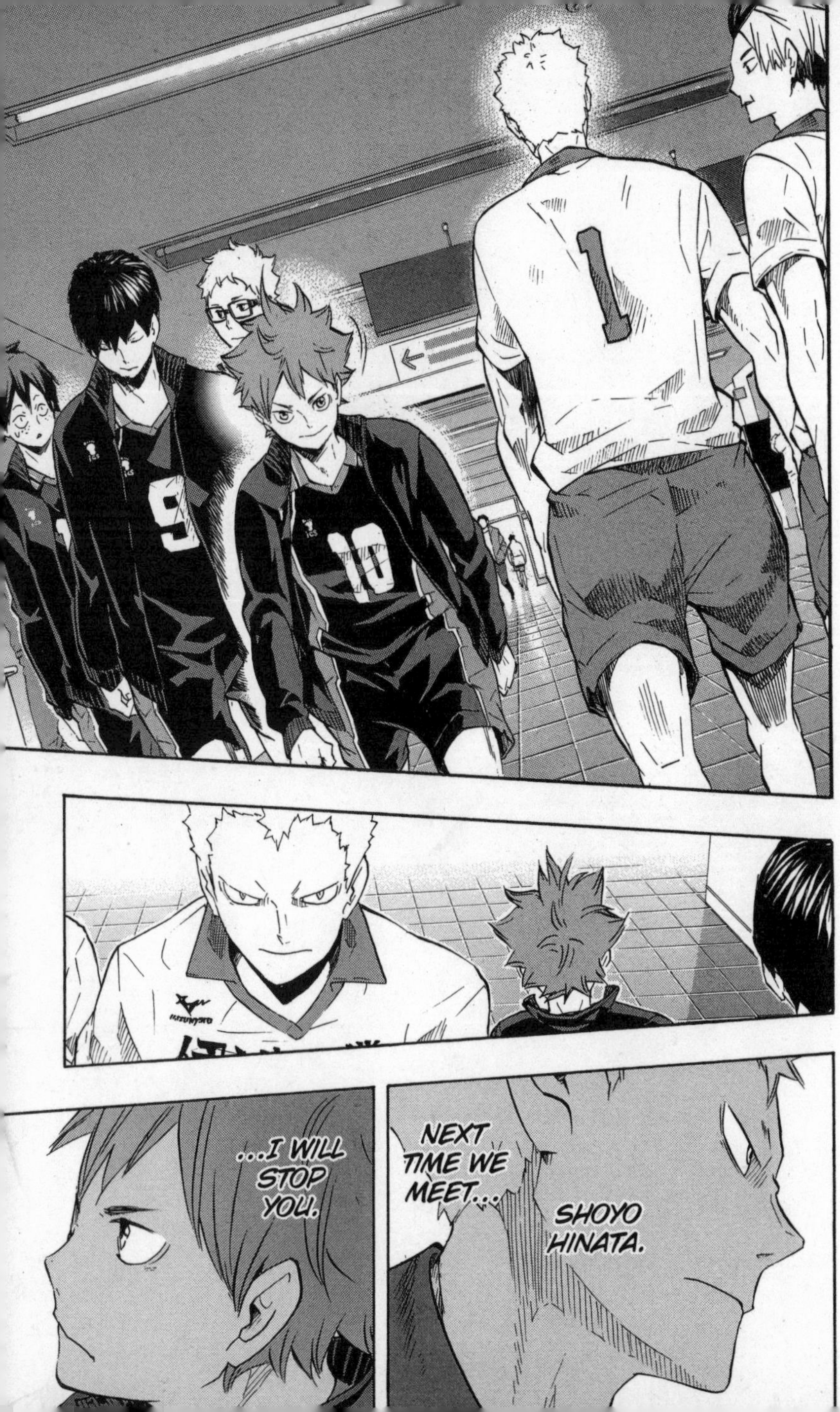
NEXT TIME WE MEET...
SHOYO HINATA.
...I WILL STOP YOU.

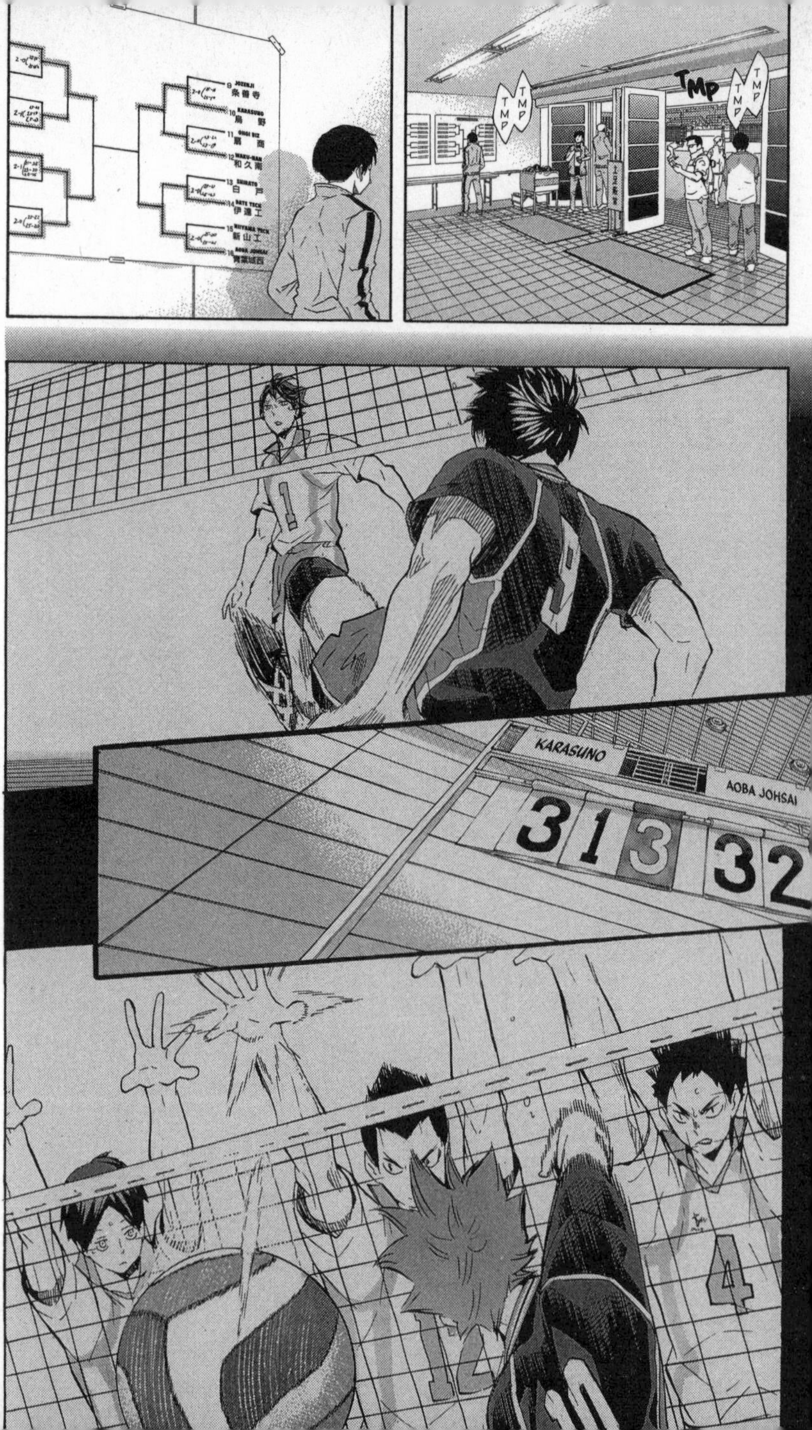
TMP TMP
TMP
TMP TMP
TMP TMP
9 JOZENJI 条善寺
10 KARASUNO 烏野
11 OHGI BIZ 扇商
12 WAKU-NAN 和久南
13 SHIRATO 白戸
14 DATE TECH 伊達工
15 NIIYAMA TECH 新山工
16 AOBA JOHSAI 青葉城西
KARASUNO
AOBA JOHSAI
31 13 32

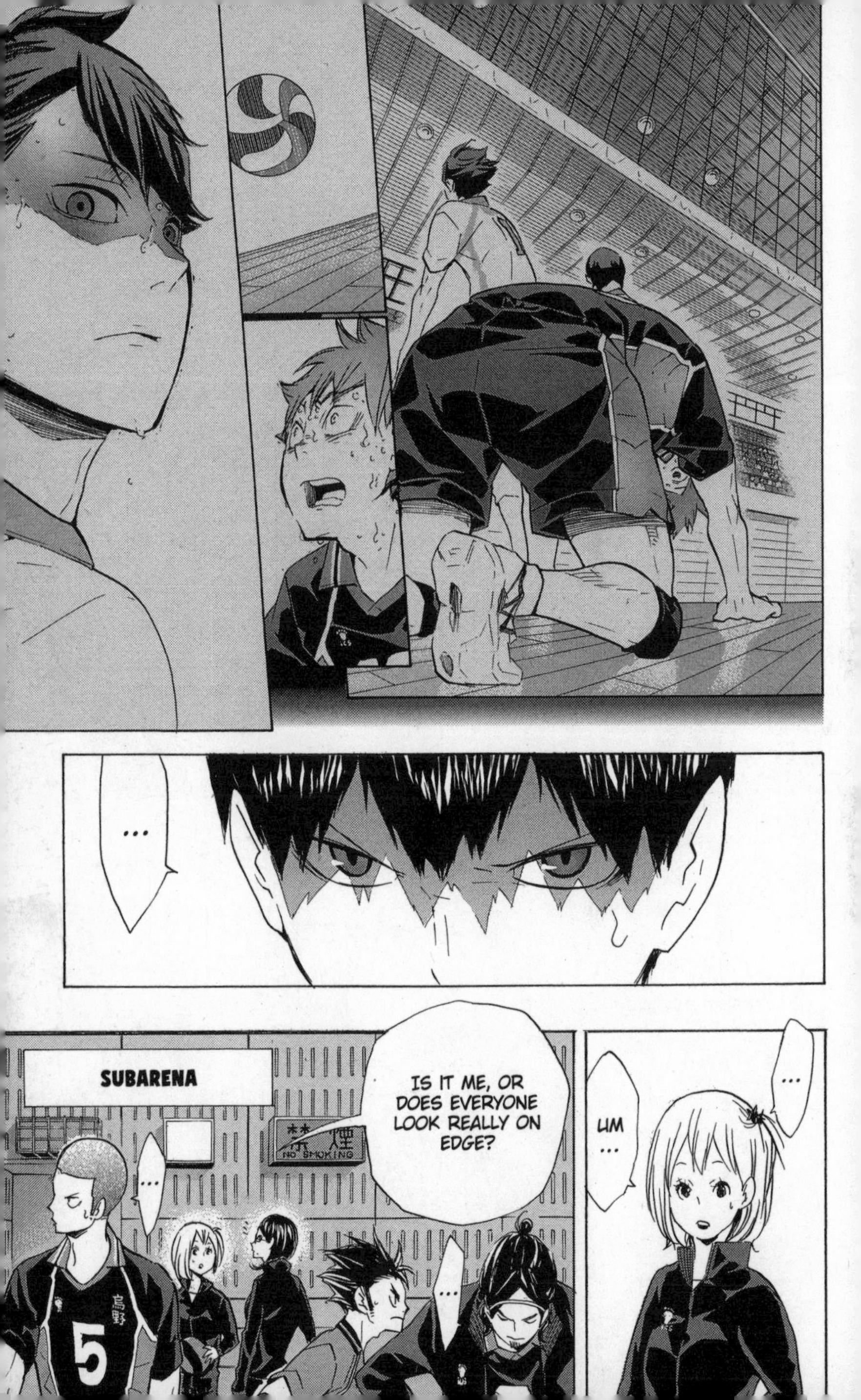
...
...
UM ...
IS IT ME, OR DOES EVERYONE LOOK REALLY ON EDGE?
SUBARENA
禁煙
NO SMOKING
...
...

YES.
IN THE LAST TOURNAMENT, WE GAVE EVERYTHING WE HAD TO BEAT BLUE-CASTLE...
...BUT IT WASN'T ENOUGH. WE LOST.
...
YES?
UM... Y-YACHI-SAN...?
Shimizu...
MP
TMP TMP
BAM
D-DO YOU HAVE ANY ANTACIDS...?
...?!
YAMAGUCHI-KUN!!
ARE YOU OKAY?!
KLCH
SORRY. I JUST GOT REALLY NERVOUS ALL OF A SUDDEN...
WSH
...!
OH!!
BELIEVE IT OR NOT, I HAVE SOME GREAT WAYS FOR DEALING WITH NERVES!
WHRL
WHAT?
YOU DO? LIKE WHAT?
WHEN I GET NERVOUS, I TEND TO GET SUPER WORRIED MY WHOLE LIFE COULD BE IN DANGER, SO I LOOKED UP ALL KINDS OF WAYS TO DEAL WITH NERVES.
You know, before tests and competitions and stuff...
YOU FEAR FOR YOUR LIFE?!
SEE, THE BEST THING TO DO WHEN YOU'RE NERVOUS IS TO SAY SO!
DON'T HOLD STUFF INSIDE. THAT ONLY MAKES IT WORSE. SAYING "OH MY GOSH, I'M SO NERVOUS!" OR "WHAT AM I GOING TO DO?!" OUT LOUD WILL MAKE YOU FEEL BETTER IN THE END.

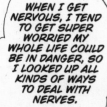

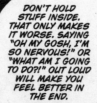

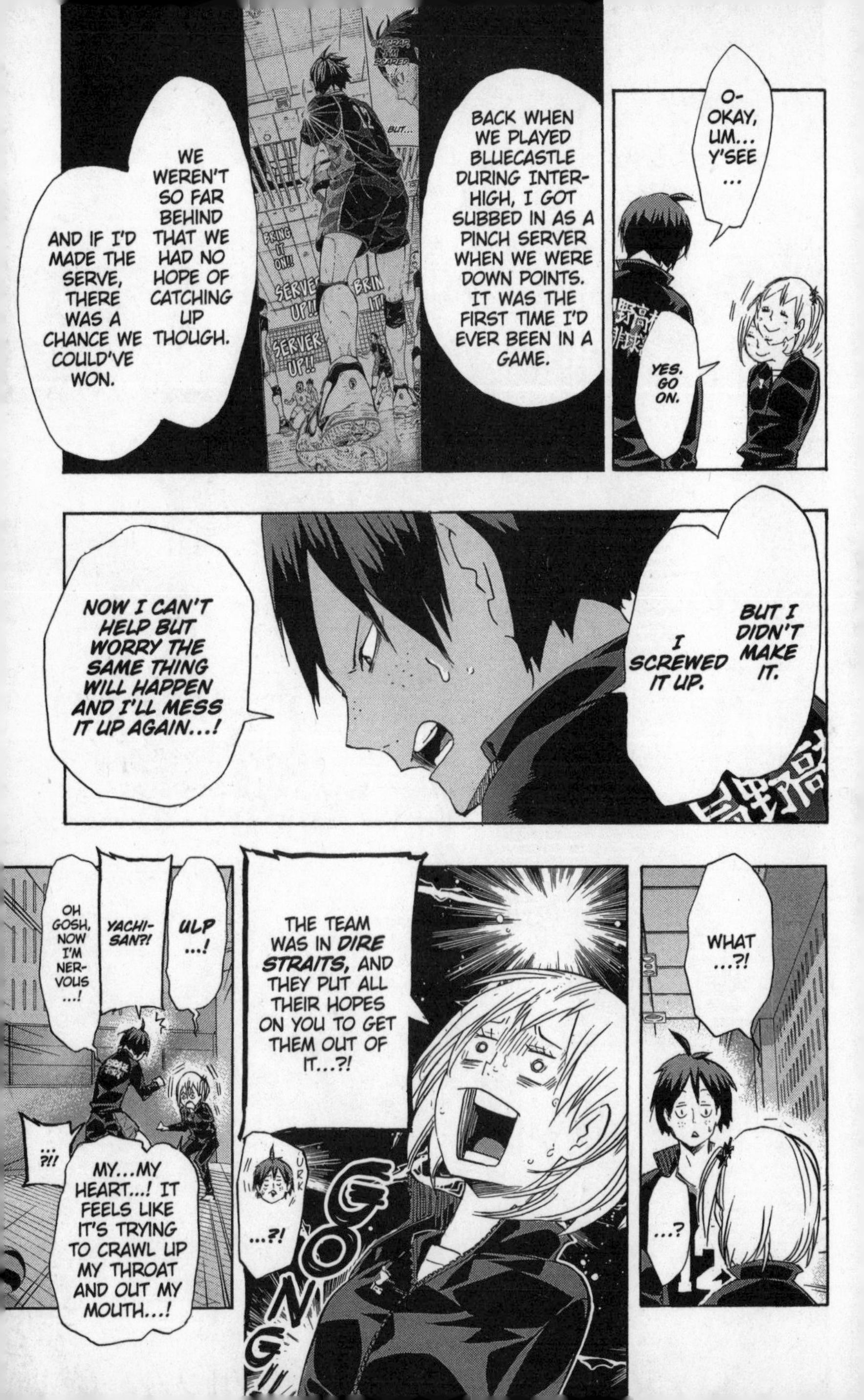
O-OKAY, UM... Y'SEE...
YES. GO ON.
BACK WHEN WE PLAYED BLUECASTLE DURING INTER-HIGH, I GOT SUBBED IN AS A PINCH SERVER WHEN WE WERE DOWN POINTS. IT WAS THE FIRST TIME I'D EVER BEEN IN A GAME.
OH CRAP, I'M SCARED.
BUT...
BRING IT ON!!
SERVER UP!!
BRING IT!!
SERVER UP!!
WE WEREN'T SO FAR BEHIND THAT WE HAD NO HOPE OF CATCHING UP THOUGH.
AND IF I'D MADE THE SERVE, THERE WAS A CHANCE WE COULD'VE WON.
BUT I DIDN'T MAKE IT.
I SCREWED IT UP.
NOW I CAN'T HELP BUT WORRY THE SAME THING WILL HAPPEN AND I'LL MESS IT UP AGAIN...!
WHAT...?!
...?
THE TEAM WAS IN *DIRE STRAITS,* AND THEY PUT ALL THEIR HOPES ON YOU TO GET THEM OUT OF IT...?!
GONG
URK
...?!
ULP...!
YACHI-SAN?!
OH GOSH, NOW I'M NERVOUS...!
...?!!
MY...MY HEART...! IT FEELS LIKE IT'S TRYING TO CRAWL UP MY THROAT AND OUT MY MOUTH...!

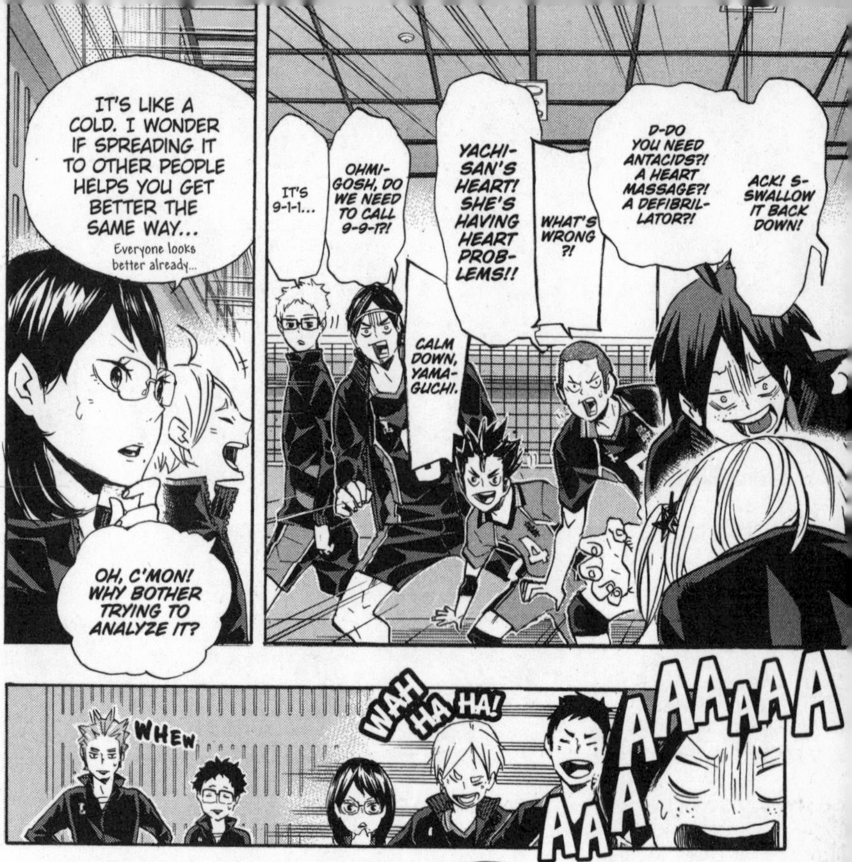
ACK! S-SWALLOW IT BACK DOWN!
D-DO YOU NEED ANTACIDS?! A HEART MASSAGE?! A DEFIBRIL-LATOR?!
WHAT'S WRONG?!
YACHI-SAN'S HEART! SHE'S HAVING HEART PROB-LEMS!!
CALM DOWN, YAMA-GUCHI.
OHMI-GOSH, DO WE NEED TO CALL 9-9-1?!
IT'S 9-1-1...
IT'S LIKE A COLD. I WONDER IF SPREADING IT TO OTHER PEOPLE HELPS YOU GET BETTER THE SAME WAY...
Everyone looks better already...
OH, C'MON! WHY BOTHER TRYING TO ANALYZE IT?
AAAAAAAAAA
WAH HA HA!
WHEW

*JACKET: KARASUNO HIGH SCHOOL VOLLEYBALL CLUB

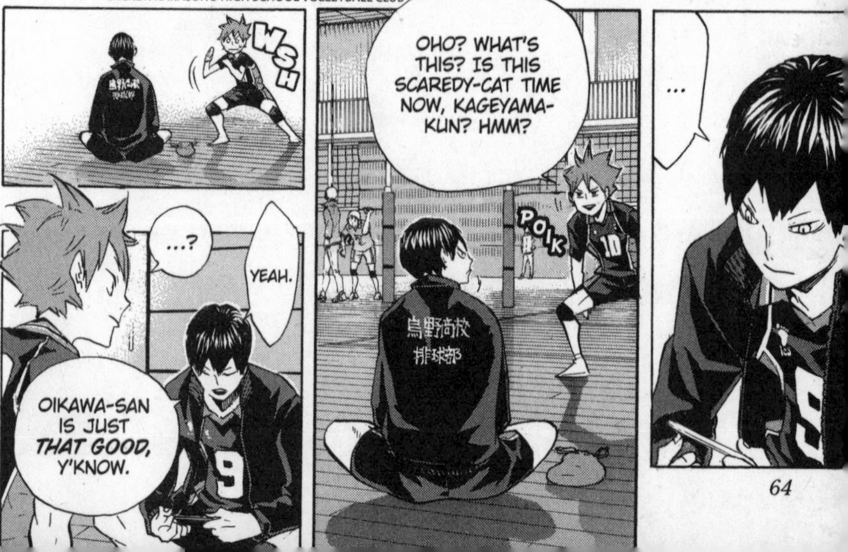
...
OHO? WHAT'S THIS? IS THIS SCAREDY-CAT TIME NOW, KAGEYAMA-KUN? HMM?
POIK
WSH
...?
YEAH.
OIKAWA-SAN IS JUST THAT GOOD, Y'KNOW.

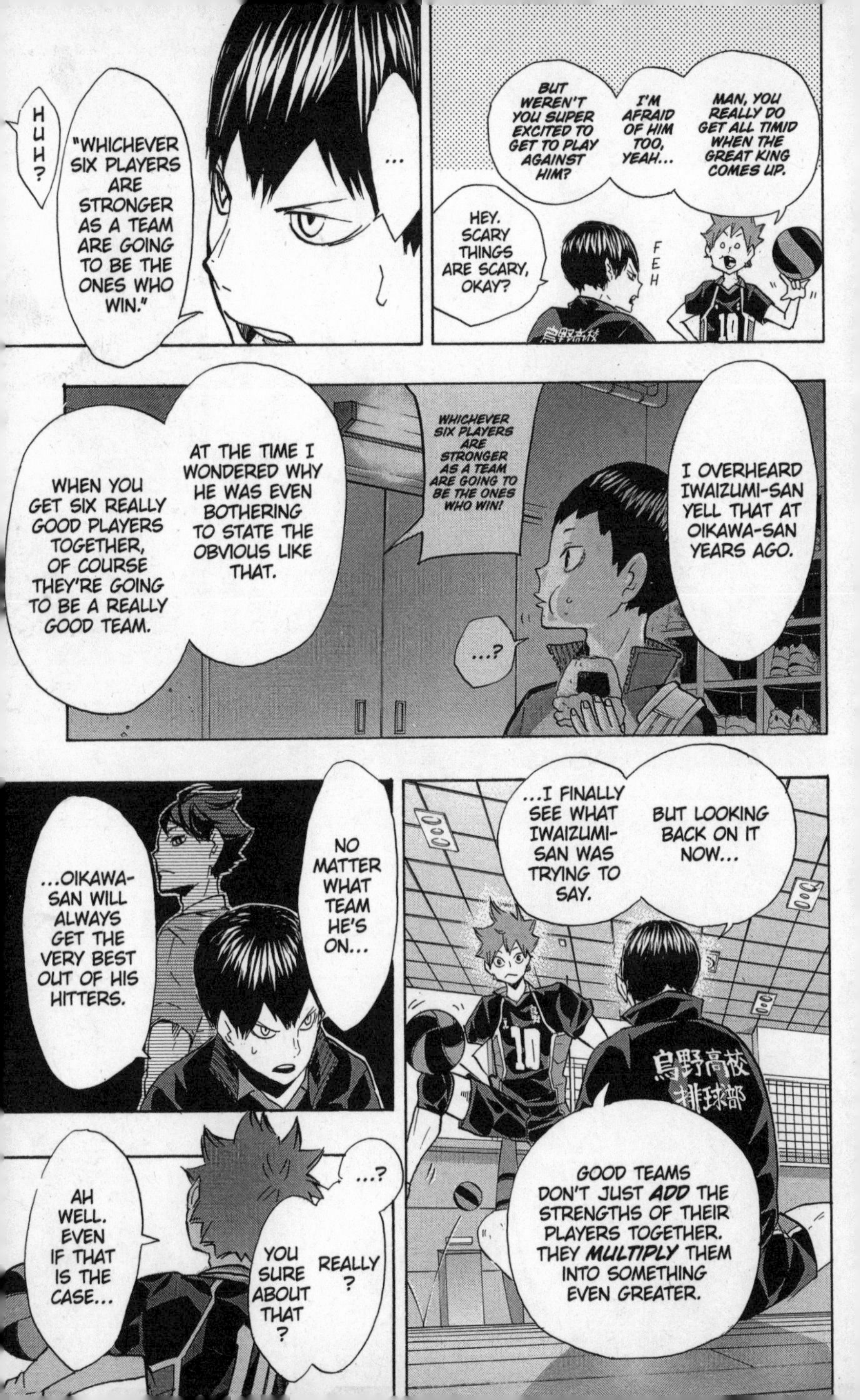
MAN, YOU REALLY DO GET ALL TIMID WHEN THE GREAT KING COMES UP.
I'M AFRAID OF HIM TOO, YEAH...
BUT WEREN'T YOU SUPER EXCITED TO GET TO PLAY AGAINST HIM?
HEY. SCARY THINGS ARE SCARY, OKAY?
FEH
...
HUH?
"WHICHEVER SIX PLAYERS ARE STRONGER AS A TEAM ARE GOING TO BE THE ONES WHO WIN."
I OVERHEARD IWAIZUMI-SAN YELL THAT AT OIKAWA-SAN YEARS AGO.
WHICHEVER SIX PLAYERS ARE STRONGER AS A TEAM ARE GOING TO BE THE ONES WHO WIN!
...?
AT THE TIME I WONDERED WHY HE WAS EVEN BOTHERING TO STATE THE OBVIOUS LIKE THAT.
WHEN YOU GET SIX REALLY GOOD PLAYERS TOGETHER, OF COURSE THEY'RE GOING TO BE A REALLY GOOD TEAM.
BUT LOOKING BACK ON IT NOW...
...I FINALLY SEE WHAT IWAIZUMI-SAN WAS TRYING TO SAY.
GOOD TEAMS DON'T JUST ADD THE STRENGTHS OF THEIR PLAYERS TOGETHER. THEY MULTIPLY THEM INTO SOMETHING EVEN GREATER.
NO MATTER WHAT TEAM HE'S ON...
...OIKAWA-SAN WILL ALWAYS GET THE VERY BEST OUT OF HIS HITTERS.
...?
REALLY?
YOU SURE ABOUT THAT?
AH WELL. EVEN IF THAT IS THE CASE...

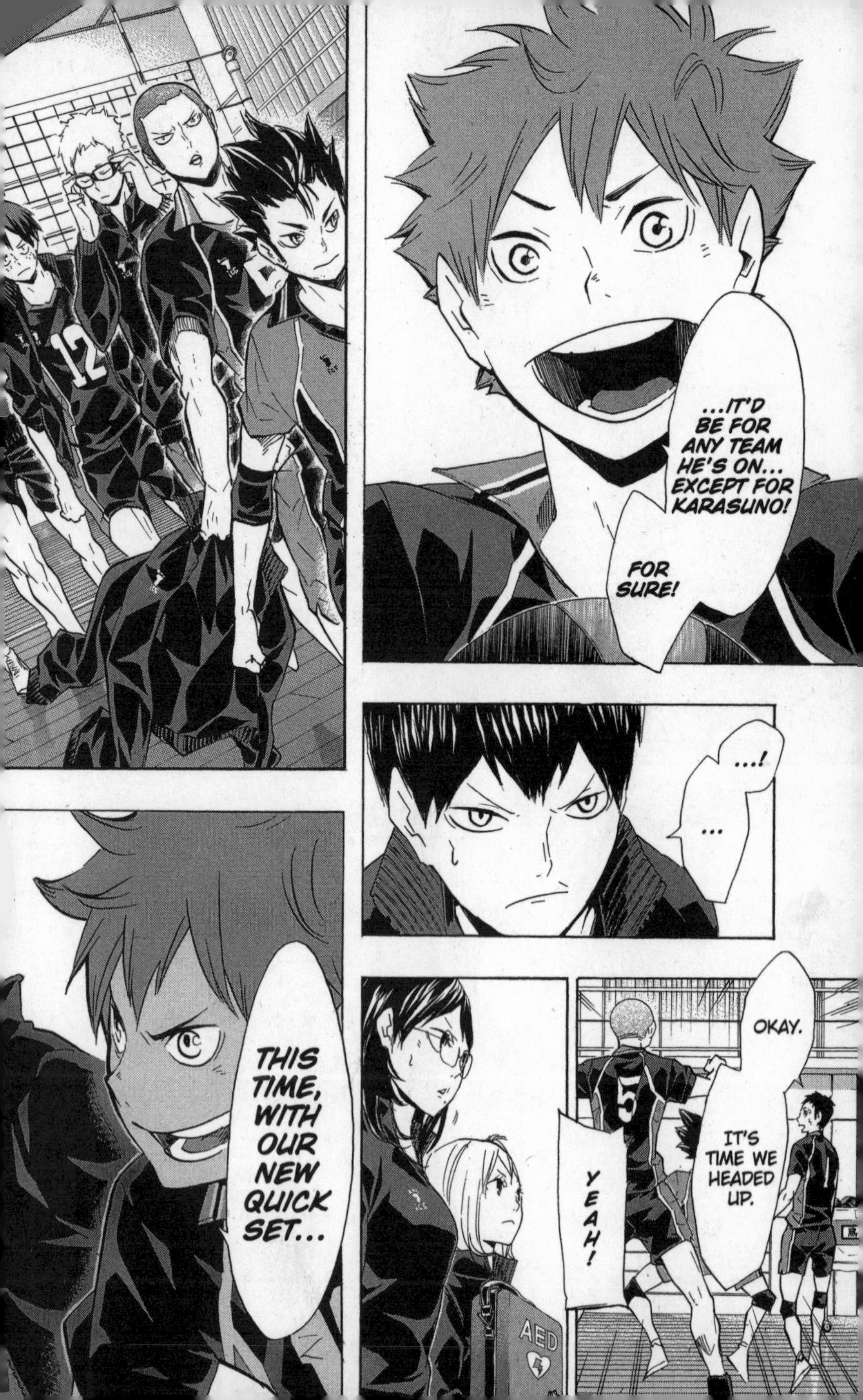

...IT'D BE FOR ANY TEAM HE'S ON... EXCEPT FOR KARASUNO!
FOR SURE!
...!
...
THIS TIME, WITH OUR NEW QUICK SET...
OKAY.
IT'S TIME WE HEADED UP.
YEAH!
AED

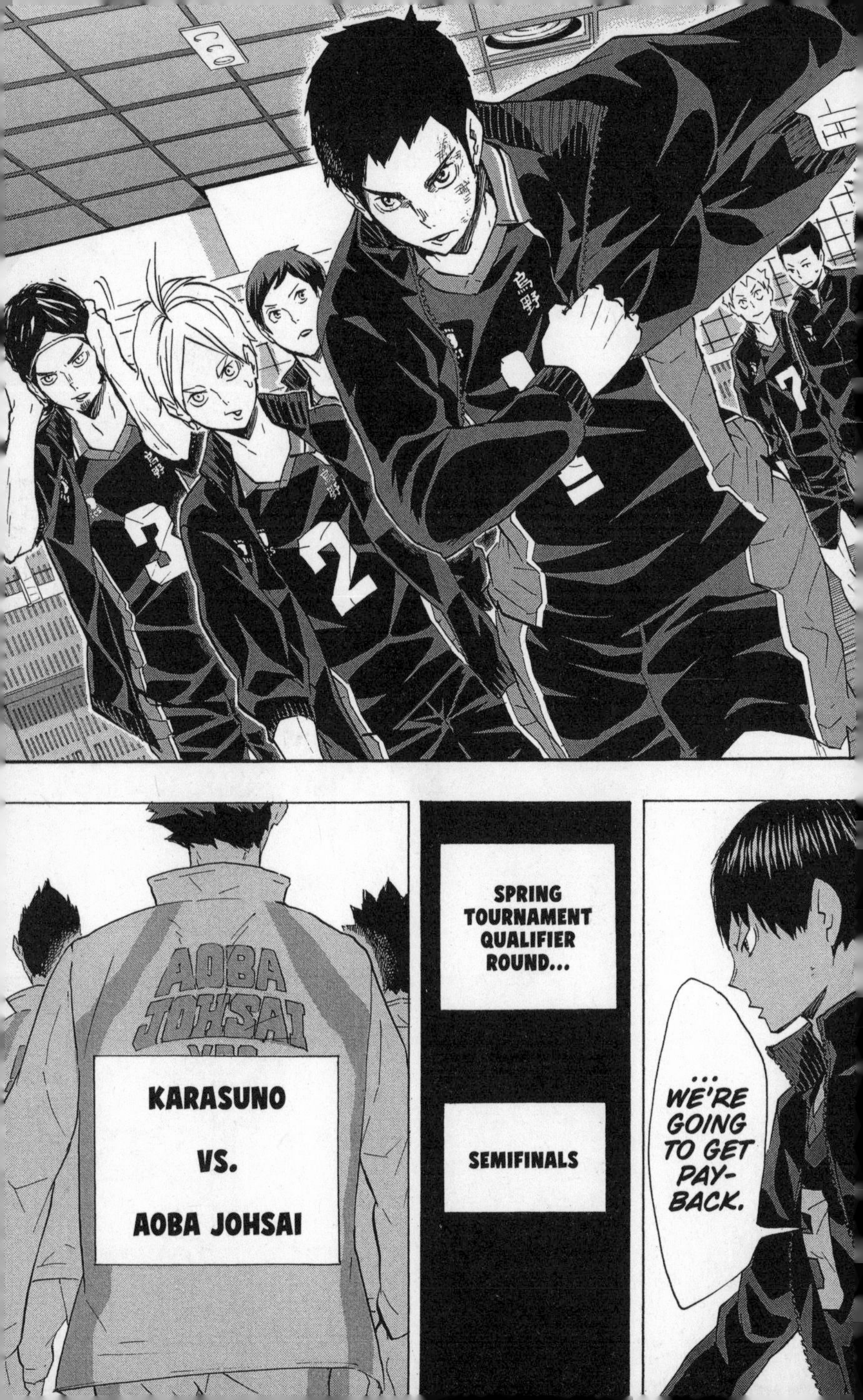
...WE'RE GOING TO GET PAY-BACK.
SPRING TOURNAMENT QUALIFIER ROUND...
SEMIFINALS
AOBA JOHSAI
KARASUNO VS. AOBA JOHSAI

JINGO FUKIAGE

DATE TECHNICAL HIGH SCHOOL
CLASS 1-3

POSITION:
MIDDLE BLOCKER

HEIGHT: 6'1"

WEIGHT: 162 LBS.
(AS OF APRIL, 1ST YEAR
OF HIGH SCHOOL)

ABILITY PARAMETERS
(5-POINT SCALE)

POWER
(3)

SPEED
(2)

JUMPING
(2)

TECHNIQUE
(2)

STAMINA
(3)

INTELLIGENCE
(4)

MAI NAMETSU

DATE TECHNICAL HIGH SCHOOL
CLASS 2-4
VOLLEYBALL CLUB MANAGER

HEIGHT: 5'3"

WEIGHT: 100 LBS.
(AS OF APRIL, 2ND YEAR
OF HIGH SCHOOL)

ABILITY PARAMETERS
(5-POINT SCALE)

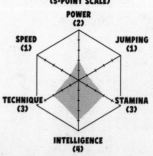

POWER
(2)

SPEED
(1)

JUMPING
(1)

TECHNIQUE
(3)

STAMINA
(3)

INTELLIGENCE
(4)

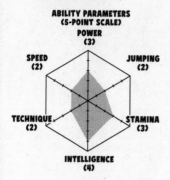

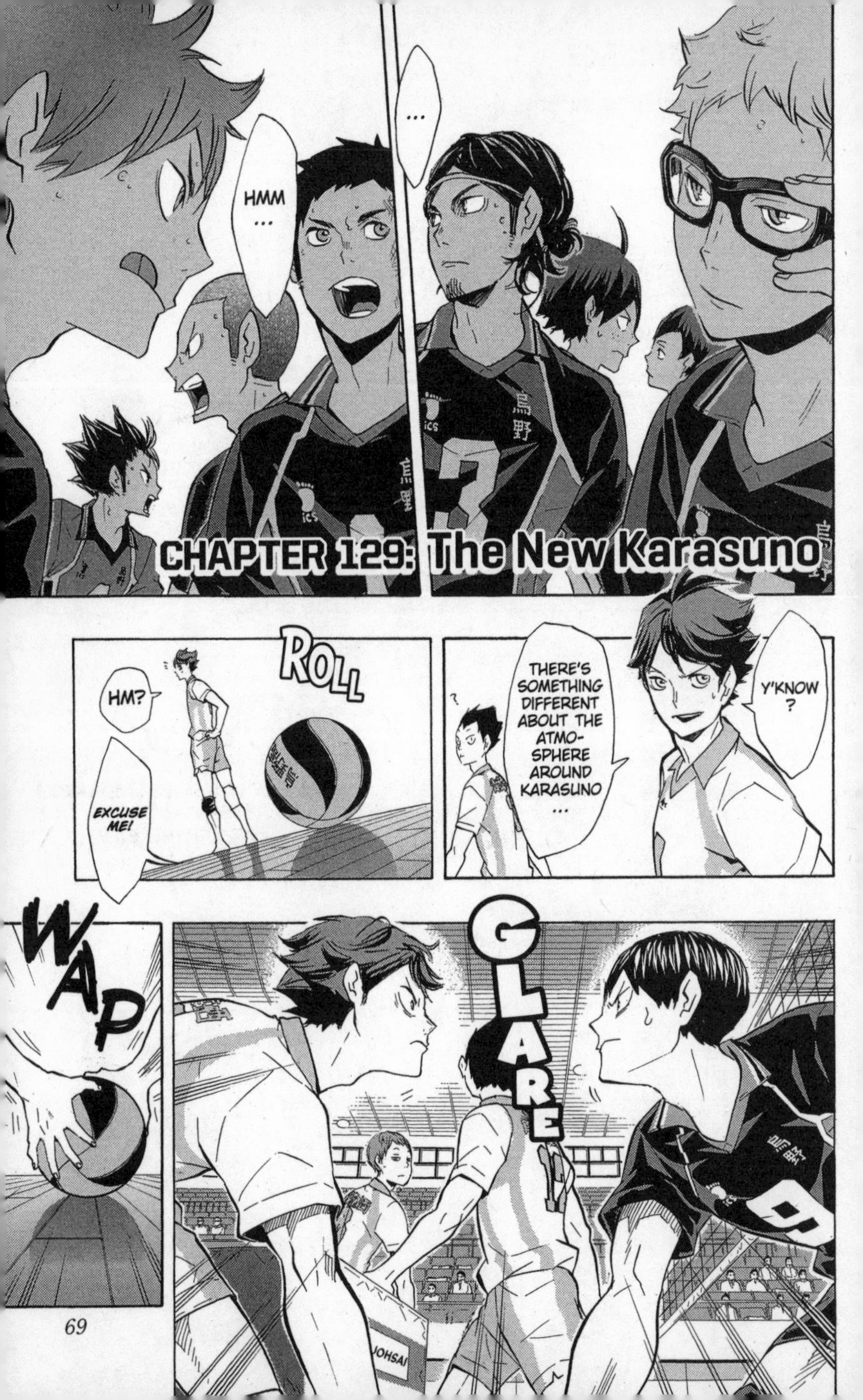
...
HMM ...
CHAPTER 129: The New Karasuno
Y'KNOW ?
THERE'S SOMETHING DIFFERENT ABOUT THE ATMOSPHERE AROUND KARASUNO ...
?
ROLL
HM?
EXCUSE ME!
GLARE
JOHSAI
WAP

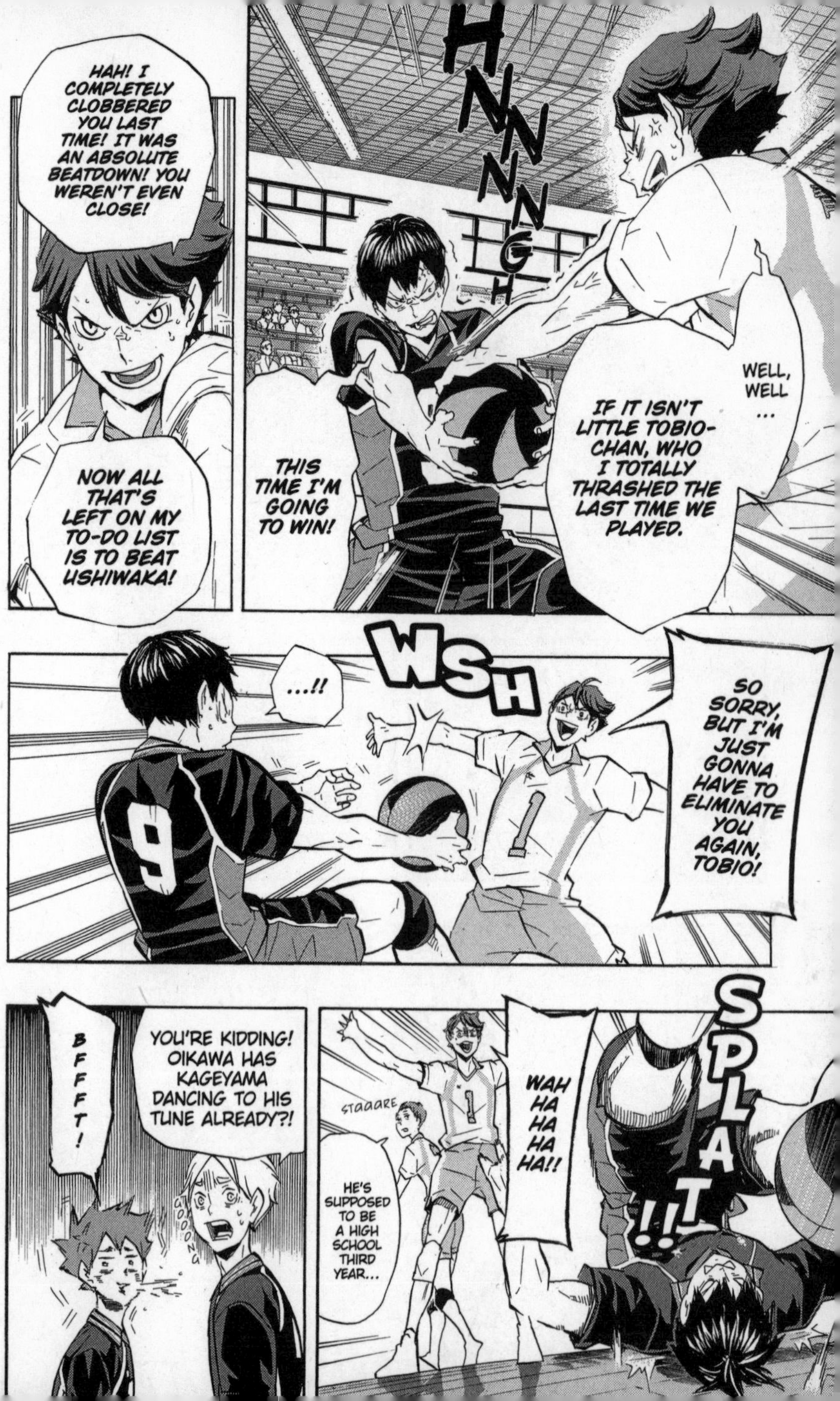

WELL, WELL ...
IF IT ISN'T LITTLE TOBIO-CHAN, WHO I TOTALLY THRASHED THE LAST TIME WE PLAYED.
HNNNNNGH
THIS TIME I'M GOING TO WIN!
HAH! I COMPLETELY CLOBBERED YOU LAST TIME! IT WAS AN ABSOLUTE BEATDOWN! YOU WEREN'T EVEN CLOSE!
NOW ALL THAT'S LEFT ON MY TO-DO LIST IS TO BEAT USHIWAKA!
SO SORRY, BUT I'M JUST GONNA HAVE TO ELIMINATE YOU AGAIN, TOBIO!
WSH
...!!
SPLAT!!
WAH HA HA HA HA HA!!
staaare
HE'S SUPPOSED TO BE A HIGH SCHOOL THIRD YEAR...
YOU'RE KIDDING! OIKAWA HAS KAGEYAMA DANCING TO HIS TUNE ALREADY?!
BFFFT!
GOOOONG

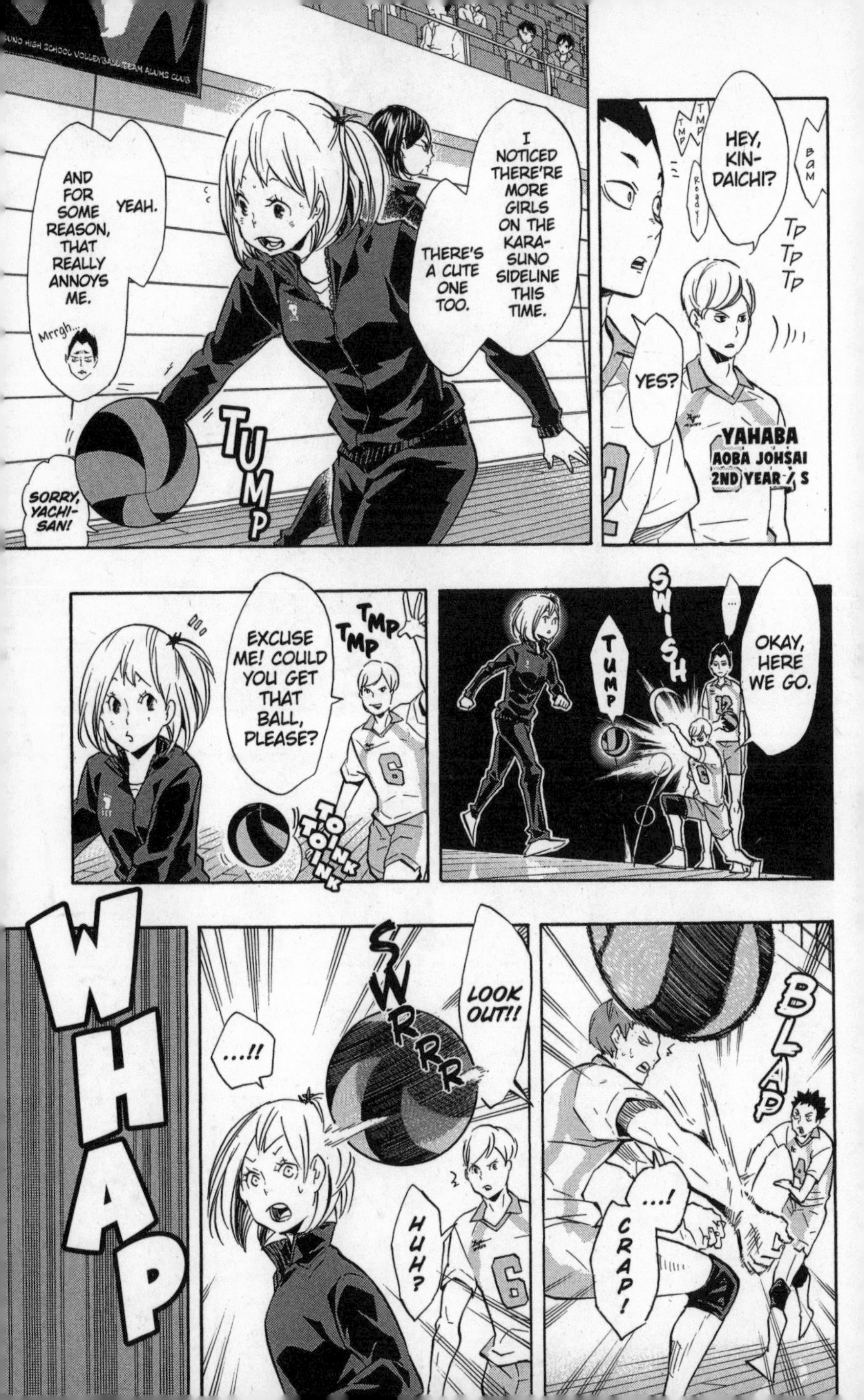
HEY, KIN-DAICHI?
BAM
TMP TMP
Ready
TP TP TP
YES?
YAHABA
AOBA JOHSAI
2ND YEAR / S
UNO HIGH SCHOOL VOLLEYBALL TEAM ALUMS CLUB
I NOTICED THERE'RE MORE GIRLS ON THE KARA-SUNO SIDELINE THIS TIME.
THERE'S A CUTE ONE TOO.
YEAH.
AND FOR SOME REASON, THAT REALLY ANNOYS ME.
Mrrgh...
TUMP
SORRY, YACHI-SAN!
OKAY, HERE WE GO.
...
SWISH
TUMP
EXCUSE ME! COULD YOU GET THAT BALL, PLEASE?
TMP TMP
TOINK TOINK
BLAP
...!
CRAP!
LOOK OUT!!
SWRRR
...!!
HUH?
WHAP

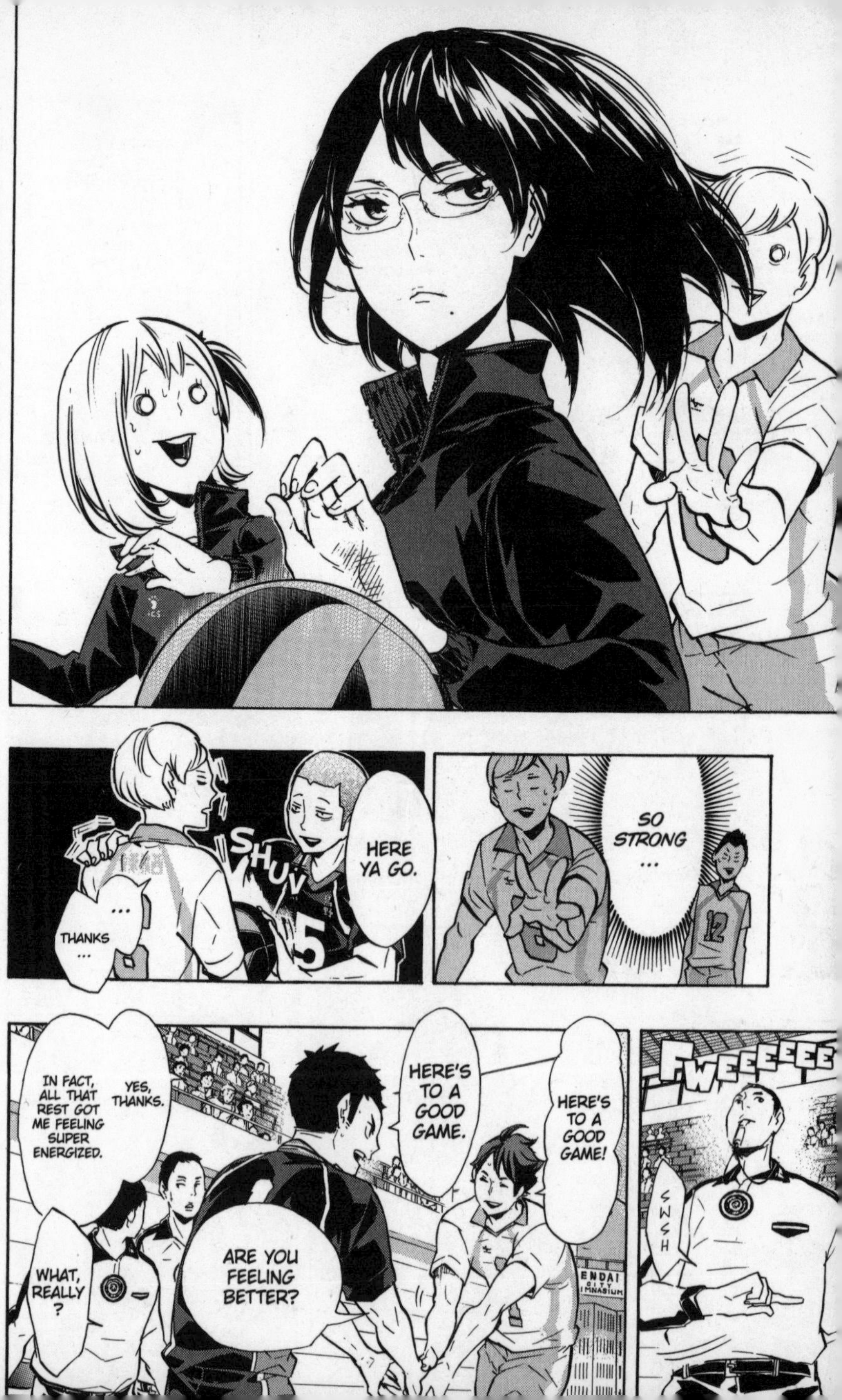
SO STRONG ...
HERE YA GO.
SHUV
...
THANKS ...
FWEEEEEE
SWSH
HERE'S TO A GOOD GAME!
HERE'S TO A GOOD GAME.
ARE YOU FEELING BETTER?
YES, THANKS.
IN FACT, ALL THAT REST GOT ME FEELING SUPER ENERGIZED.
WHAT, REALLY ?

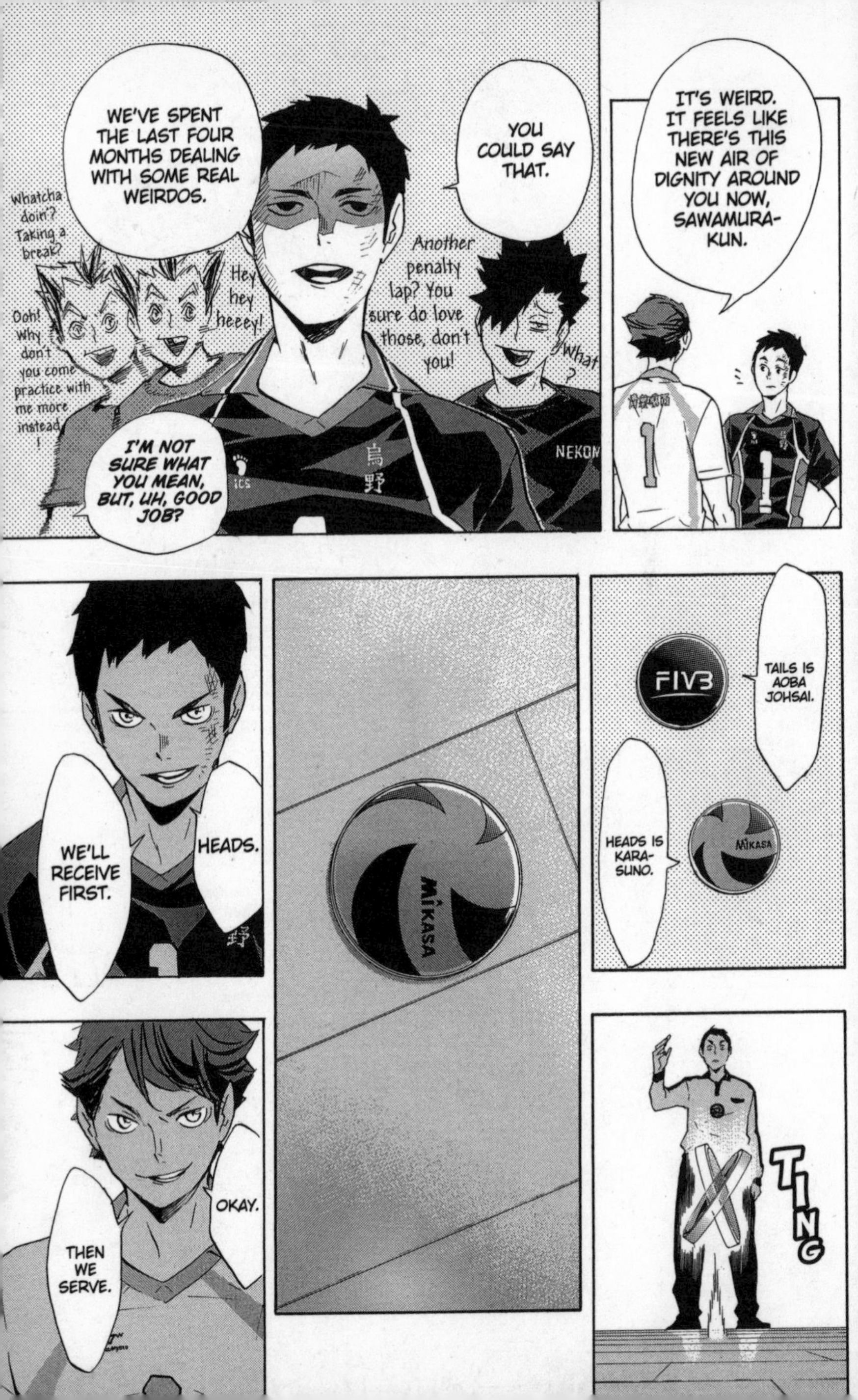
IT'S WEIRD. IT FEELS LIKE THERE'S THIS NEW AIR OF DIGNITY AROUND YOU NOW, SAWAMURA-KUN.
YOU COULD SAY THAT.
WE'VE SPENT THE LAST FOUR MONTHS DEALING WITH SOME REAL WEIRDOS.
Another penalty lap? You sure do love those, don't you!
What?
Hey hey heeey!
Whatcha doin'? Taking a break?
Ooh! Why don't you come practice with me more instead!
I'M NOT SURE WHAT YOU MEAN, BUT, UH, GOOD JOB?
FIVB
TAILS IS AOBA JOHSAI.
HEADS IS KARA-SUNO.
MIKASA
TING
MIKASA
HEADS.
WE'LL RECEIVE FIRST.
OKAY.
THEN WE SERVE.

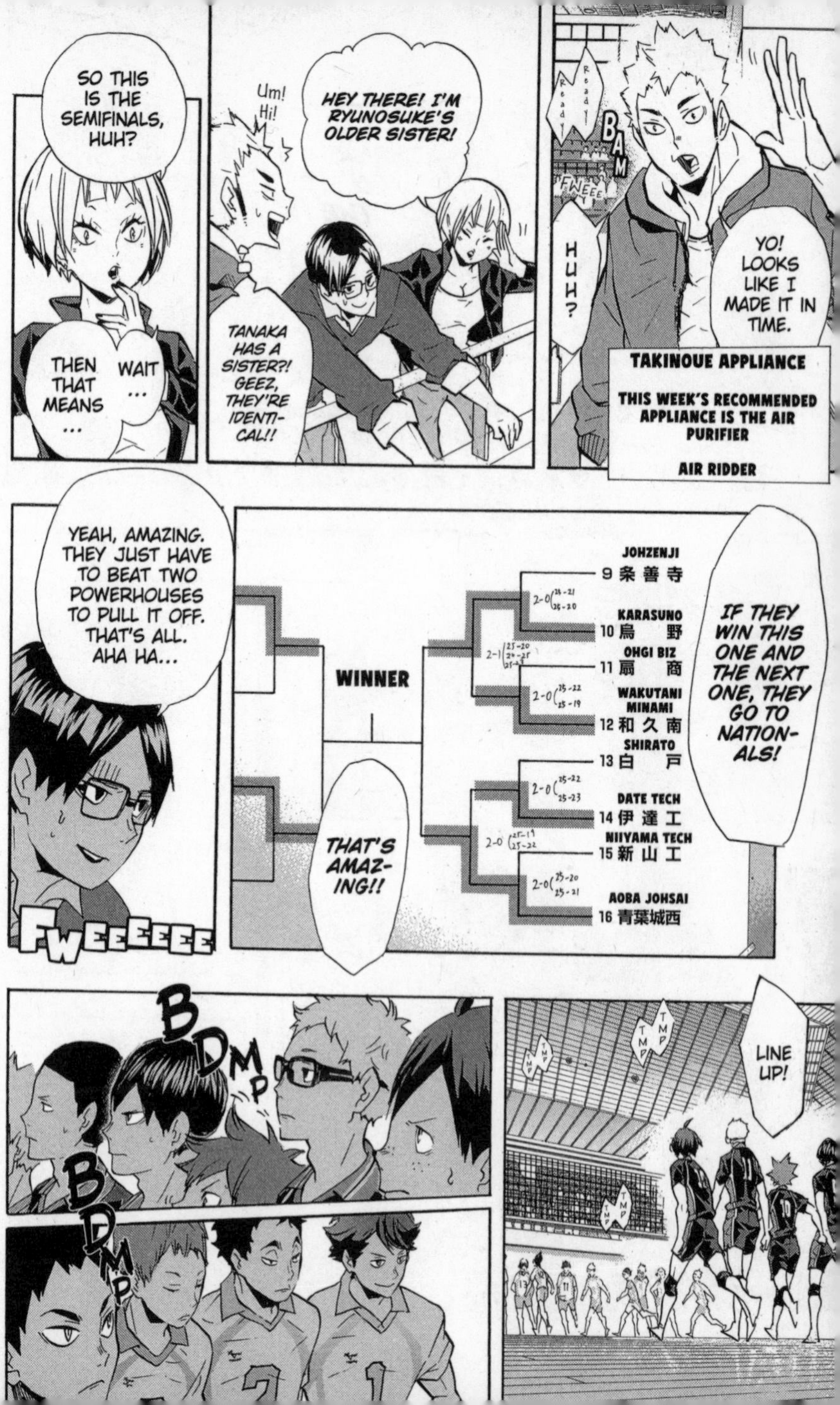
Ready
Ready
BAM
FWEEE
HUH?
YO! LOOKS LIKE I MADE IT IN TIME.
TAKINOUE APPLIANCE
THIS WEEK'S RECOMMENDED APPLIANCE IS THE AIR PURIFIER
AIR RIDDER
HEY THERE! I'M RYUNOSUKE'S OLDER SISTER!
Um! Hi!
TANAKA HAS A SISTER?! GEEZ, THEY'RE IDENTICAL!!
SO THIS IS THE SEMIFINALS, HUH?
WAIT ...
THEN THAT MEANS ...
IF THEY WIN THIS ONE AND THE NEXT ONE, THEY GO TO NATIONALS!
JOHZENJI 9 条善寺
KARASUNO 10 烏野
OHGI BIZ 11 扇商
WAKUTANI MINAMI 12 和久南
SHIRATO 13 白戸
DATE TECH 14 伊達工
NIIYAMA TECH 15 新山工
AOBA JOHSAI 16 青葉城西
2-0 (25-20
2-1 (25-20 24-25
2-0 (25-22 25-19
2-0 (25-22 25-23
2-0 (25-19 25-22
2-0 (25-20 25-21
WINNER
THAT'S AMAZING!!
YEAH, AMAZING. THEY JUST HAVE TO BEAT TWO POWERHOUSES TO PULL IT OFF. THAT'S ALL. AHA HA...
FWEEEEEE
TMP TMP
TMP TMP
TMP TMP
LINE UP!
BDMP
BDMP

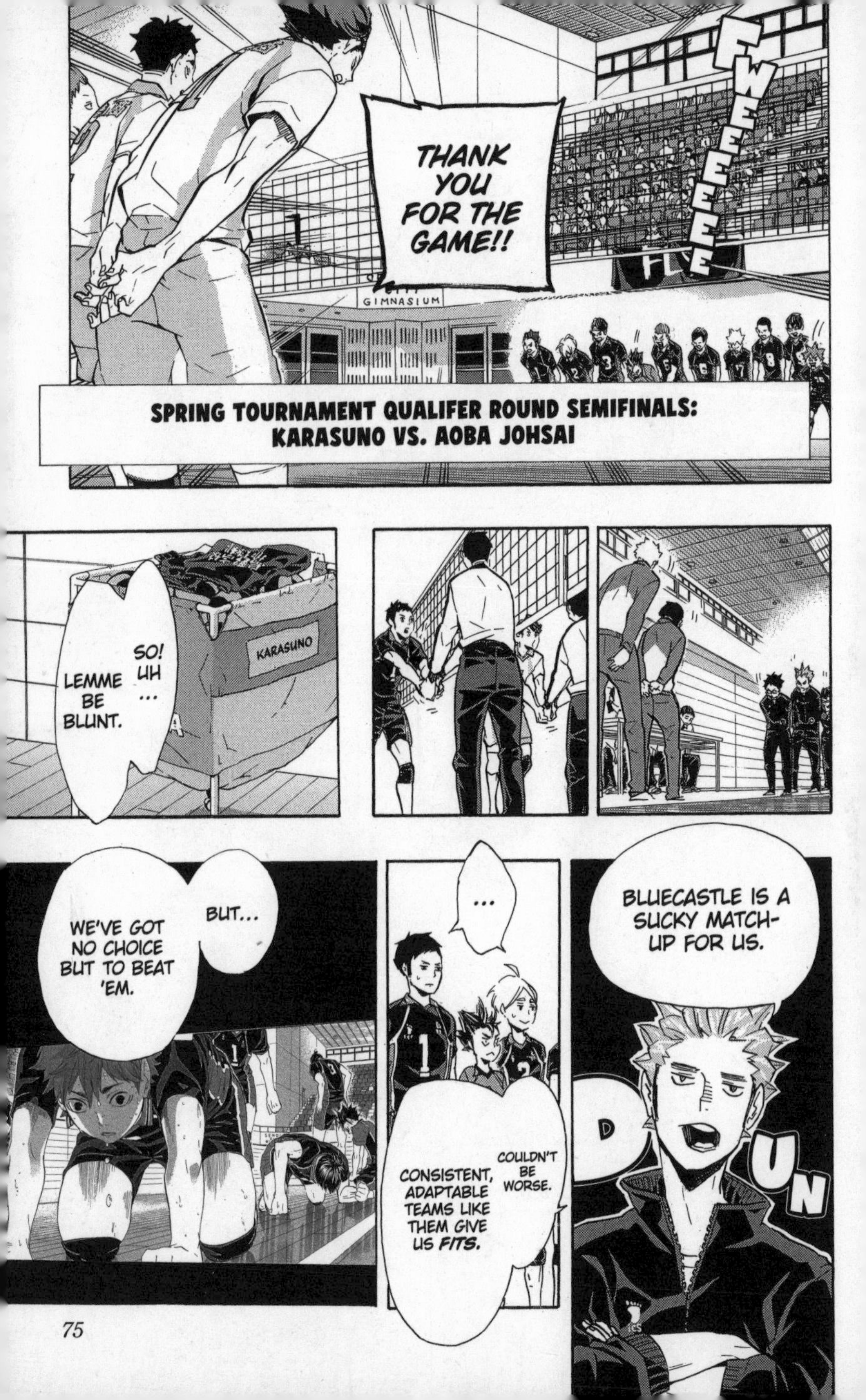
FWEEEEEE
THANK YOU FOR THE GAME!!
GIMNASIUM
SPRING TOURNAMENT QUALIFER ROUND SEMIFINALS: KARASUNO VS. AOBA JOHSAI
KARASUNO
SO! UH ...
LEMME BE BLUNT.
BLUECASTLE IS A SUCKY MATCH-UP FOR US.
DUN
...
COULDN'T BE WORSE.
CONSISTENT, ADAPTABLE TEAMS LIKE THEM GIVE US *FITS*.
BUT...
WE'VE GOT NO CHOICE BUT TO BEAT 'EM.

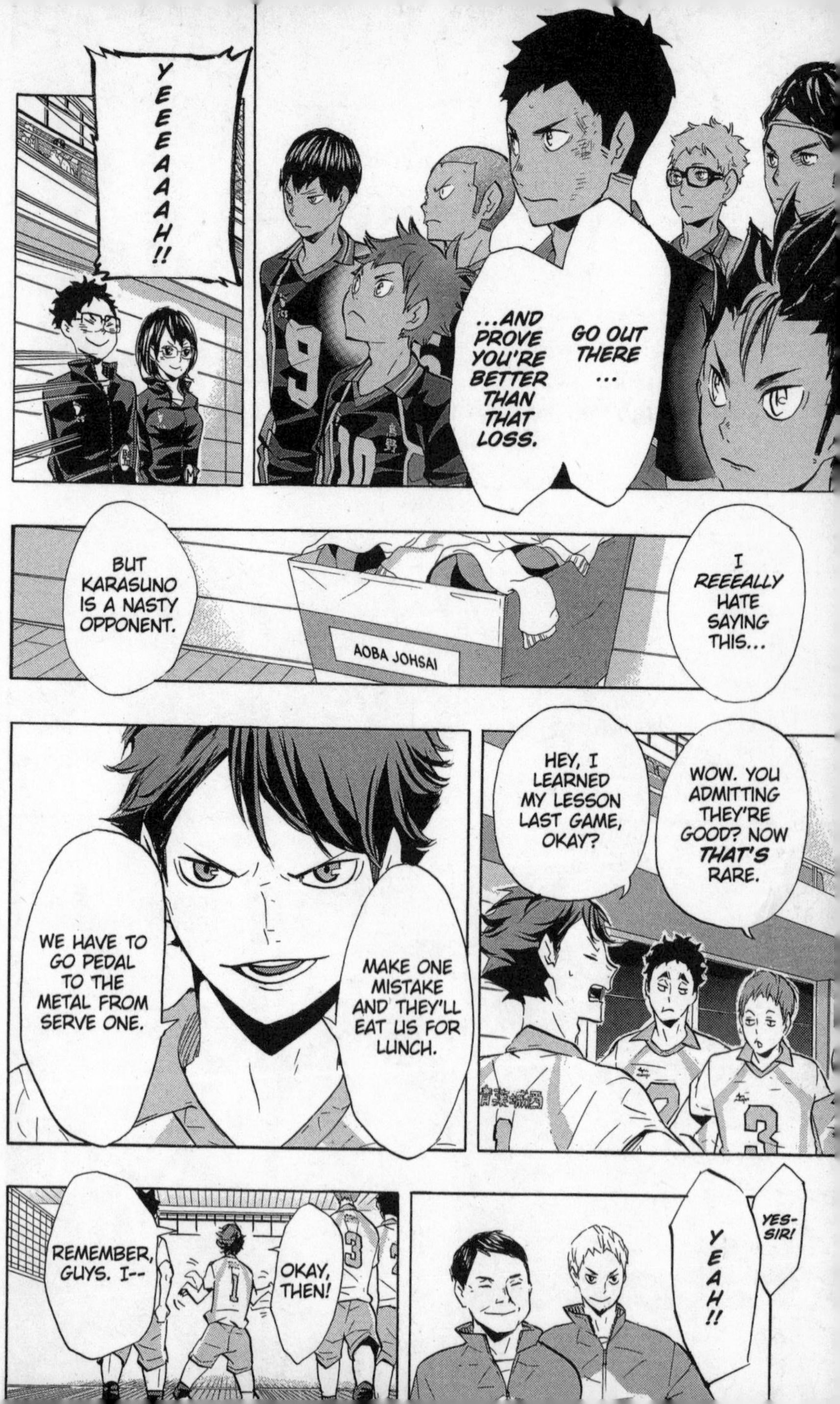
GO OUT THERE ...
...AND PROVE YOU'RE BETTER THAN THAT LOSS.
YEEEAAAAH!!
I REEEALLY HATE SAYING THIS...
BUT KARASUNO IS A NASTY OPPONENT.
AOBA JOHSAI
WOW. YOU ADMITTING THEY'RE GOOD? NOW THAT'S RARE.
HEY, I LEARNED MY LESSON LAST GAME, OKAY?
MAKE ONE MISTAKE AND THEY'LL EAT US FOR LUNCH.
WE HAVE TO GO PEDAL TO THE METAL FROM SERVE ONE.
YES-SIR!
YEAH!!
REMEMBER, GUYS. I--
OKAY, THEN!

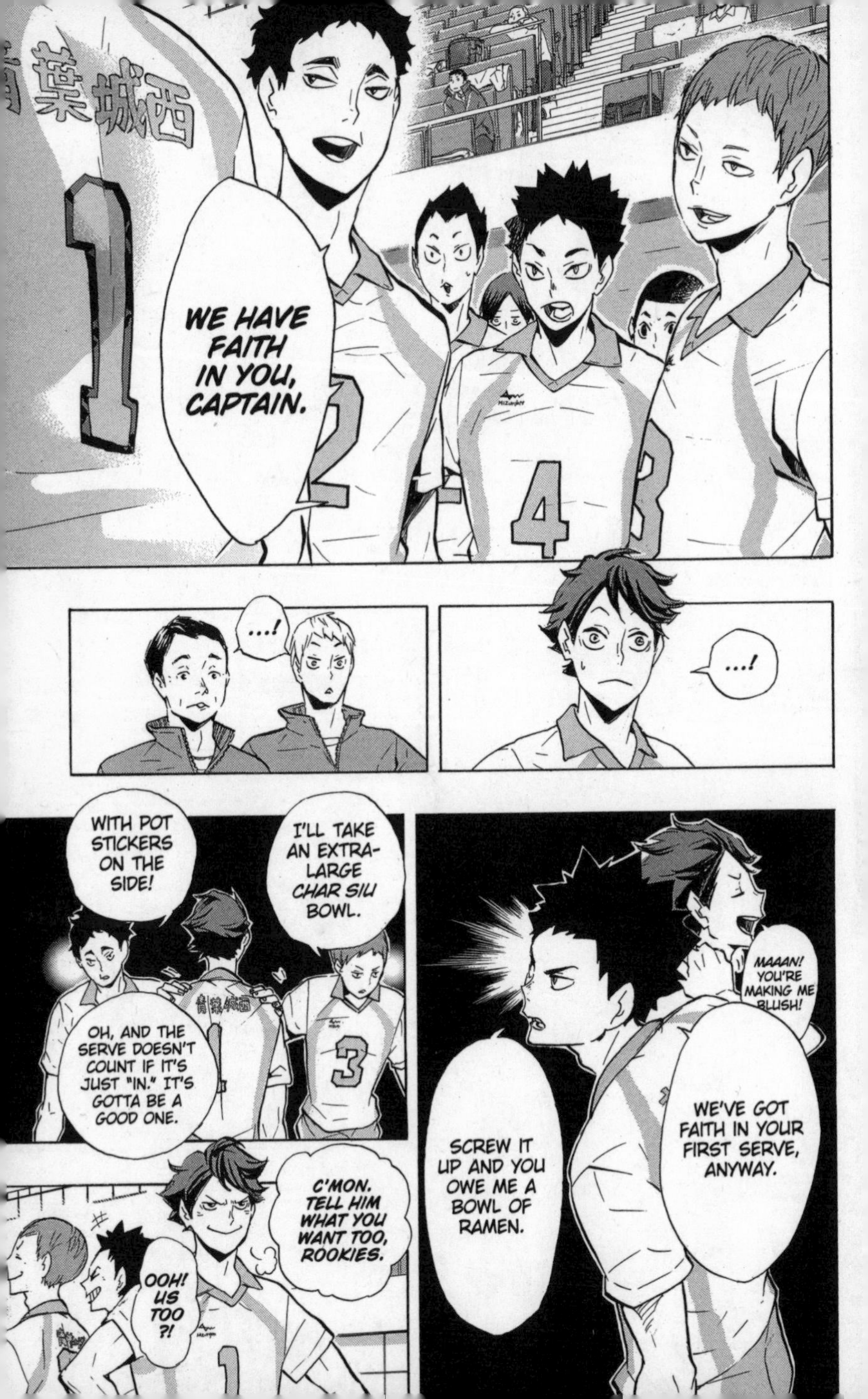
WE HAVE FAITH IN YOU, CAPTAIN.
...!
...!
MAAAN! YOU'RE MAKING ME BLUSH!
WE'VE GOT FAITH IN YOUR FIRST SERVE, ANYWAY.
SCREW IT UP AND YOU OWE ME A BOWL OF RAMEN.
I'LL TAKE AN EXTRA-LARGE CHAR SIU BOWL.
WITH POT STICKERS ON THE SIDE!
OH, AND THE SERVE DOESN'T COUNT IF IT'S JUST "IN." IT'S GOTTA BE A GOOD ONE.
C'MON. TELL HIM WHAT YOU WANT TOO, ROOKIES.
OOH! US TOO?!

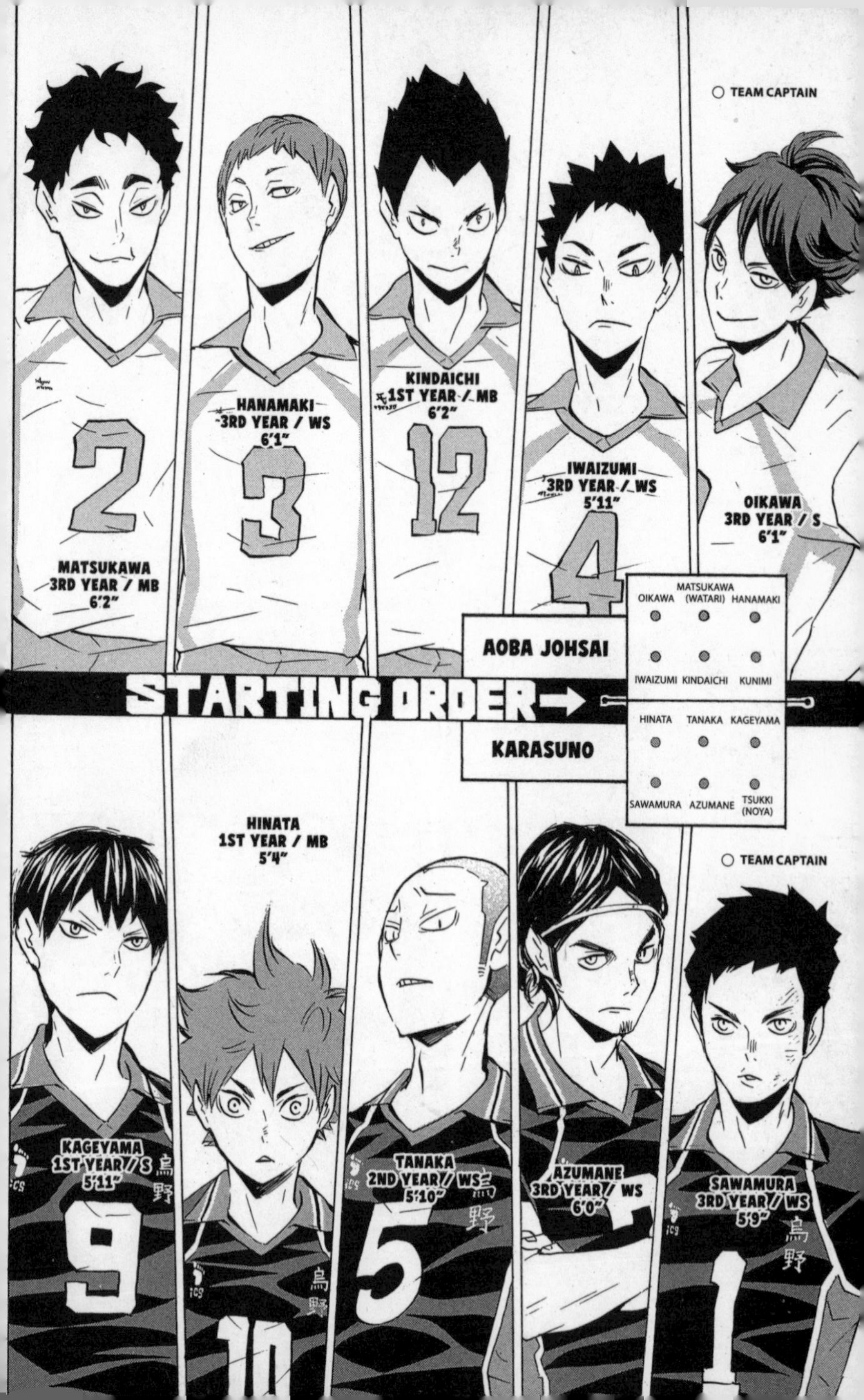
○ TEAM CAPTAIN
OIKAWA
3RD YEAR / S
6'1"
IWAIZUMI
3RD YEAR / WS
5'11"
KINDAICHI
1ST YEAR / MB
6'2"
HANAMAKI
3RD YEAR / WS
6'1"
MATSUKAWA
3RD YEAR / MB
6'2"
STARTING ORDER
AOBA JOHSAI
OIKAWA
MATSUKAWA (WATARI)
HANAMAKI
IWAIZUMI
KINDAICHI
KUNIMI
KARASUNO
HINATA
TANAKA
KAGEYAMA
SAWAMURA
AZUMANE
TSUKKI (NOYA)
○ TEAM CAPTAIN
SAWAMURA
3RD YEAR / WS
5'9"
AZUMANE
3RD YEAR / WS
6'0"
TANAKA
2ND YEAR / WS
5'10"
HINATA
1ST YEAR / MB
5'4"
KAGEYAMA
1ST YEAR / S
5'11"

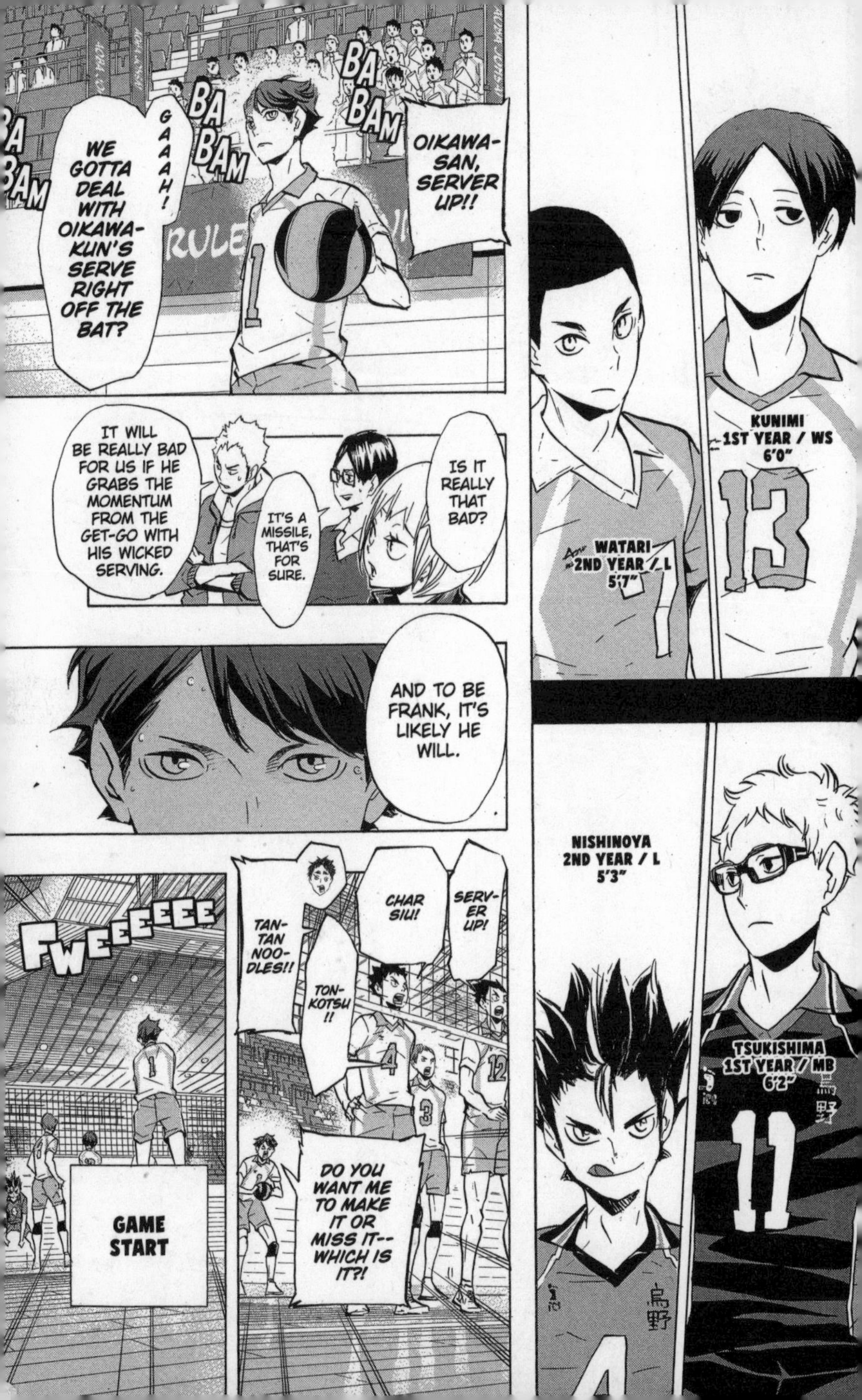
KUNIMI
1ST YEAR / WS
6'0"
WATARI
2ND YEAR / L
5'7"
NISHINOYA
2ND YEAR / L
5'3"
TSUKISHIMA
1ST YEAR / MB
6'2"
BA BAM
OIKAWA-SAN, SERVER UP!!
BA BAM
GAAAAH!
WE GOTTA DEAL WITH OIKAWA-KUN'S SERVE RIGHT OFF THE BAT?
BA BAM
IS IT REALLY THAT BAD?
IT'S A MISSILE, THAT'S FOR SURE.
IT WILL BE REALLY BAD FOR US IF HE GRABS THE MOMENTUM FROM THE GET-GO WITH HIS WICKED SERVING.
AND TO BE FRANK, IT'S LIKELY HE WILL.
SERV-ER UP!
CHAR SIU!
TAN-TAN NOO-DLES!!
TON-KOTSU!!
DO YOU WANT ME TO MAKE IT OR MISS IT-- WHICH IS IT?!
FWEEEEEE
GAME START

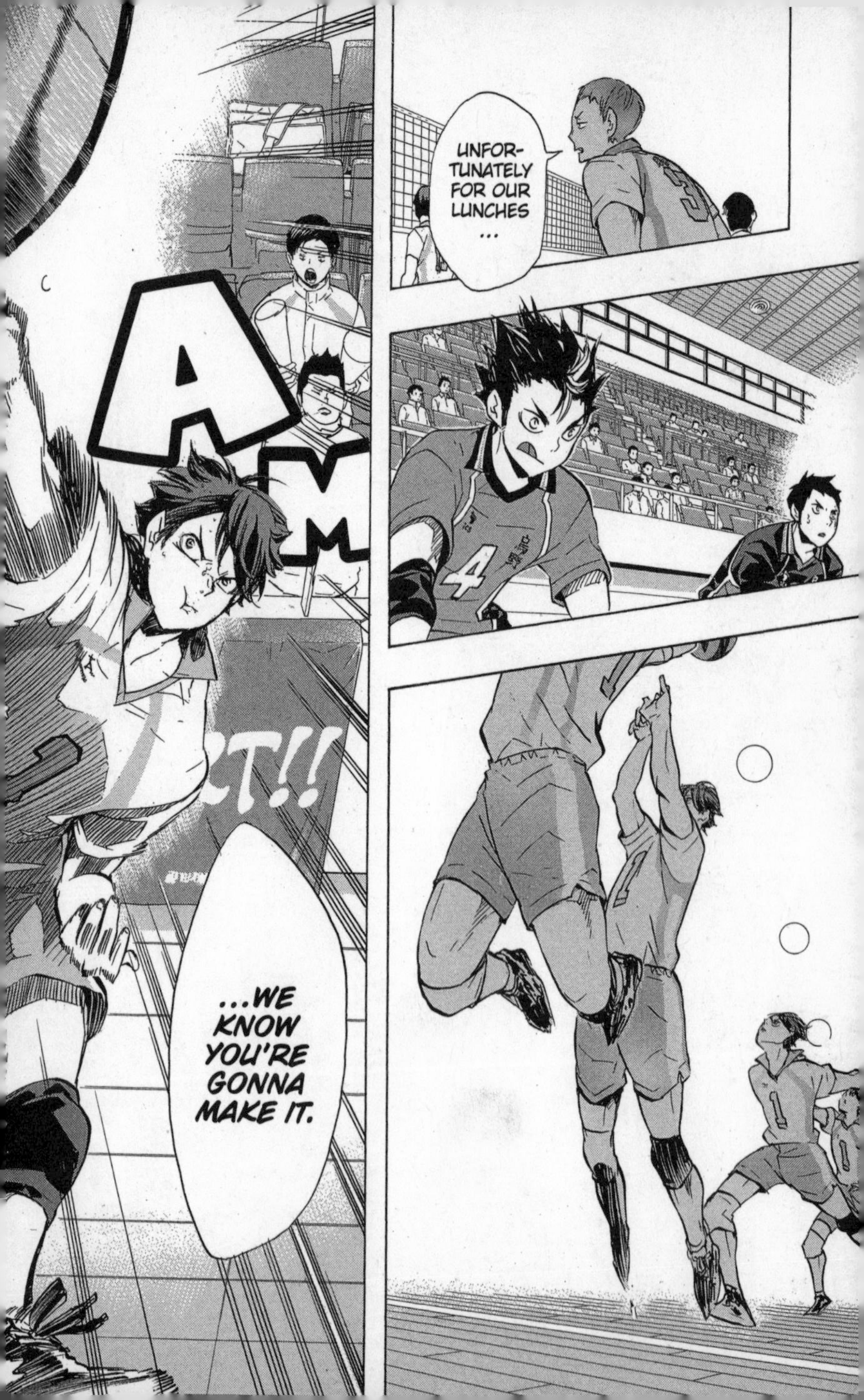
UNFOR-TUNATELY FOR OUR LUNCHES ...
...WE KNOW YOU'RE GONNA MAKE IT.

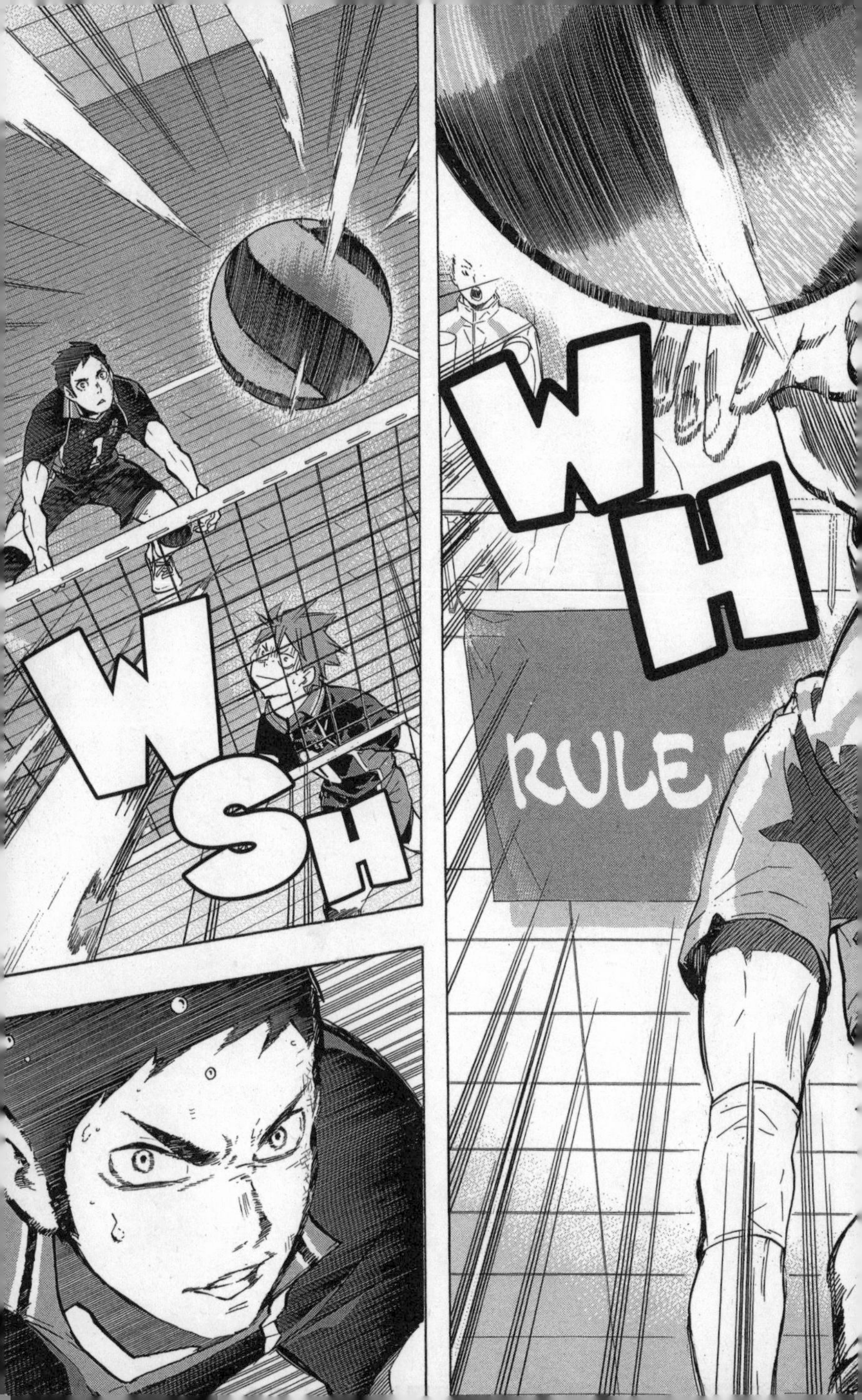
WH
RULE
WSH

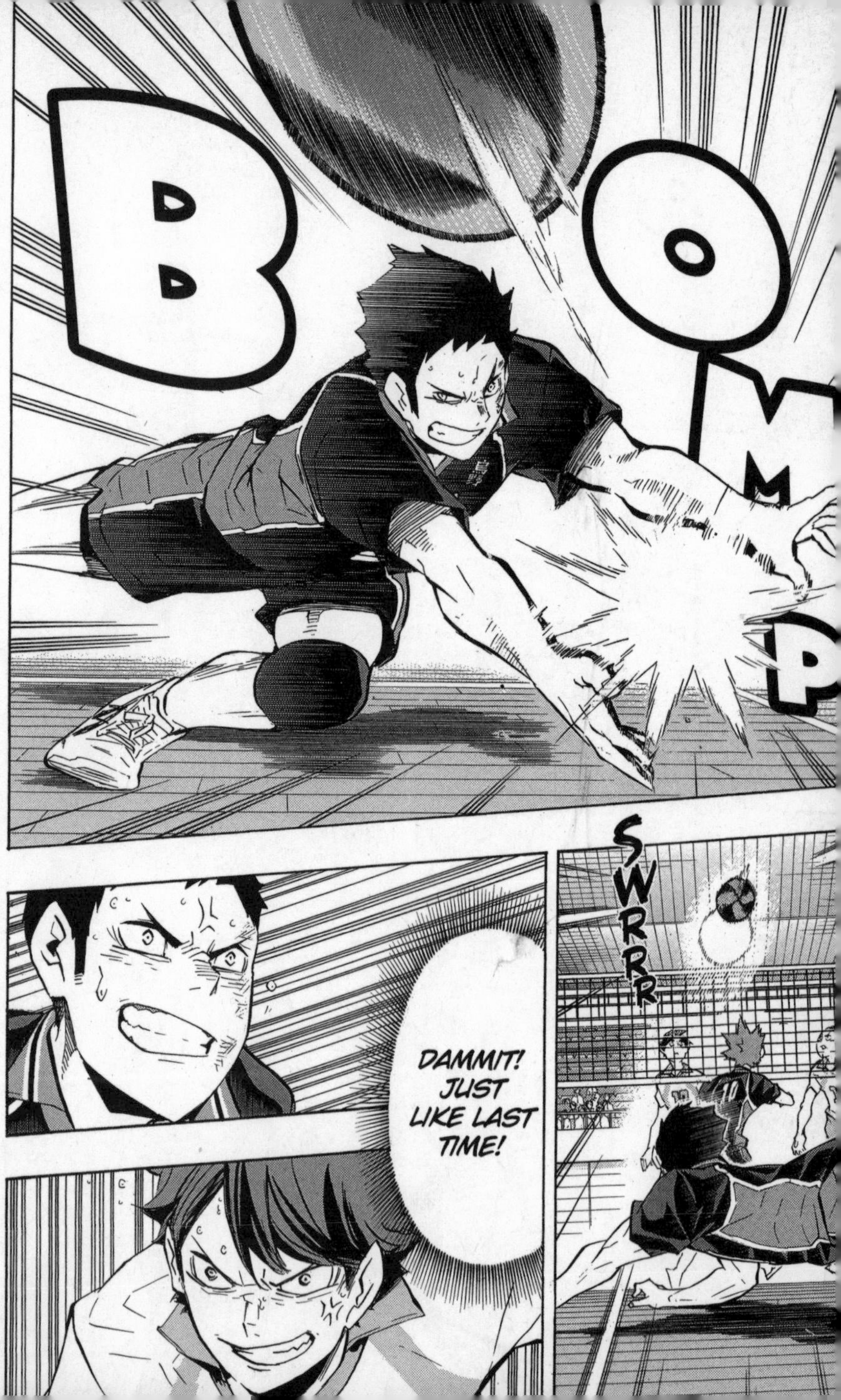
BOOMP
SWRRR
DAMMIT! JUST LIKE LAST TIME!

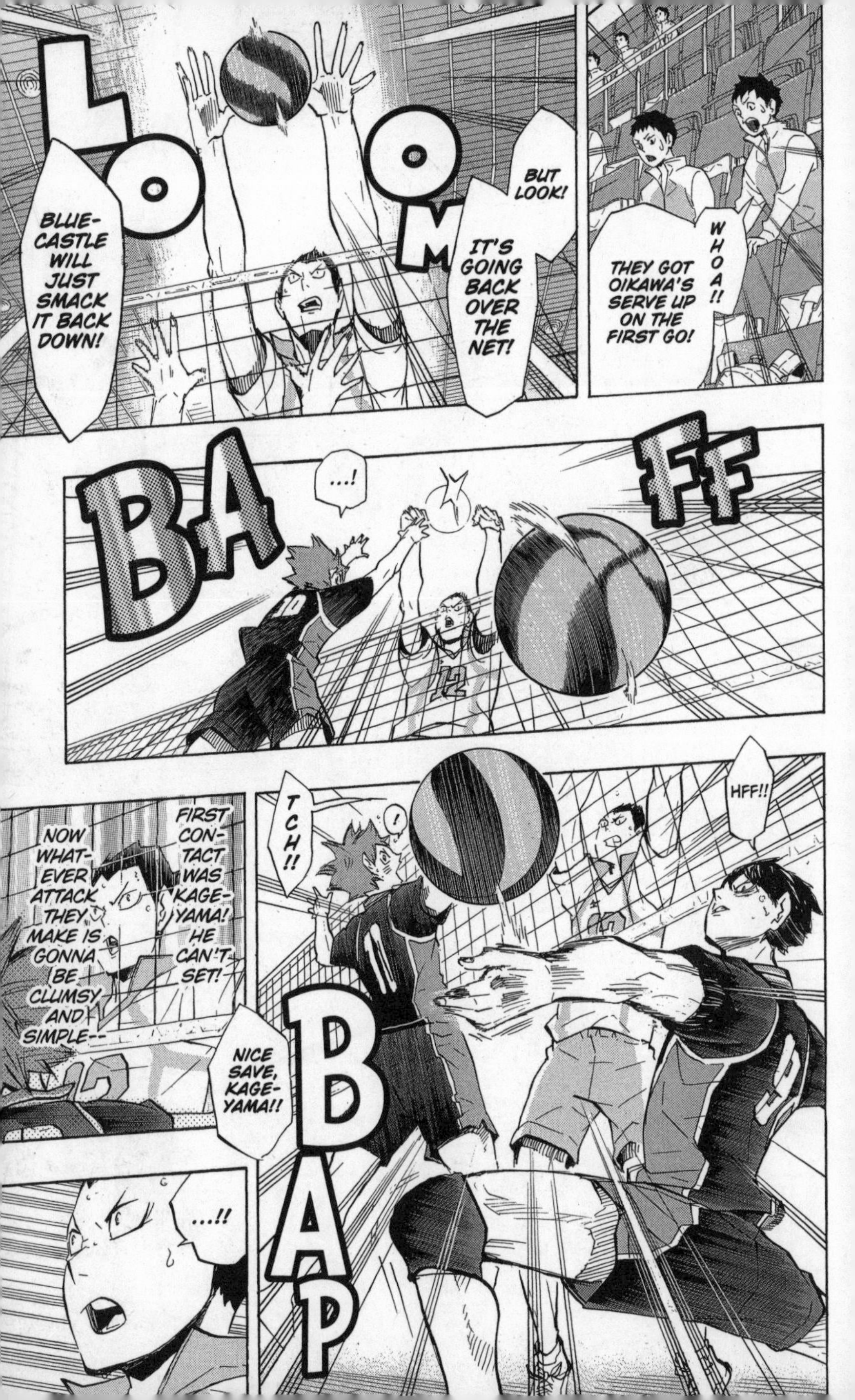
WHOA!!
THEY GOT OIKAWA'S SERVE UP ON THE FIRST GO!
LOOM
BUT LOOK!
IT'S GOING BACK OVER THE NET!
BLUE-CASTLE WILL JUST SMACK IT BACK DOWN!
BAFF
...!
HFF!!
TCH!!
!
NICE SAVE, KAGEYAMA!!
BAP
FIRST CONTACT WAS KAGEYAMA! HE CAN'T SET!
NOW WHATEVER ATTACK THEY MAKE IS GONNA BE CLUMSY AND SIMPLE--
...!!

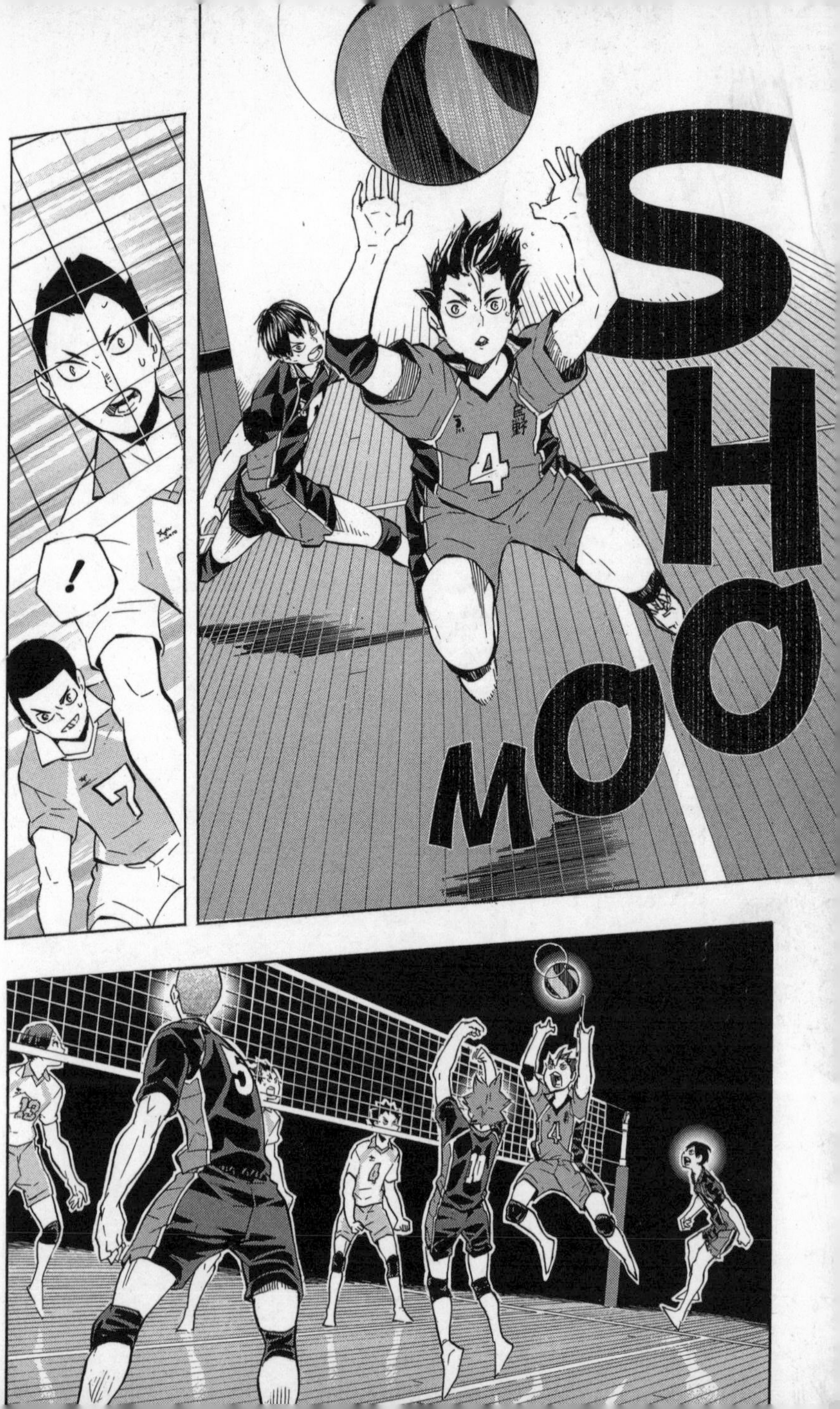
SHOOM
!

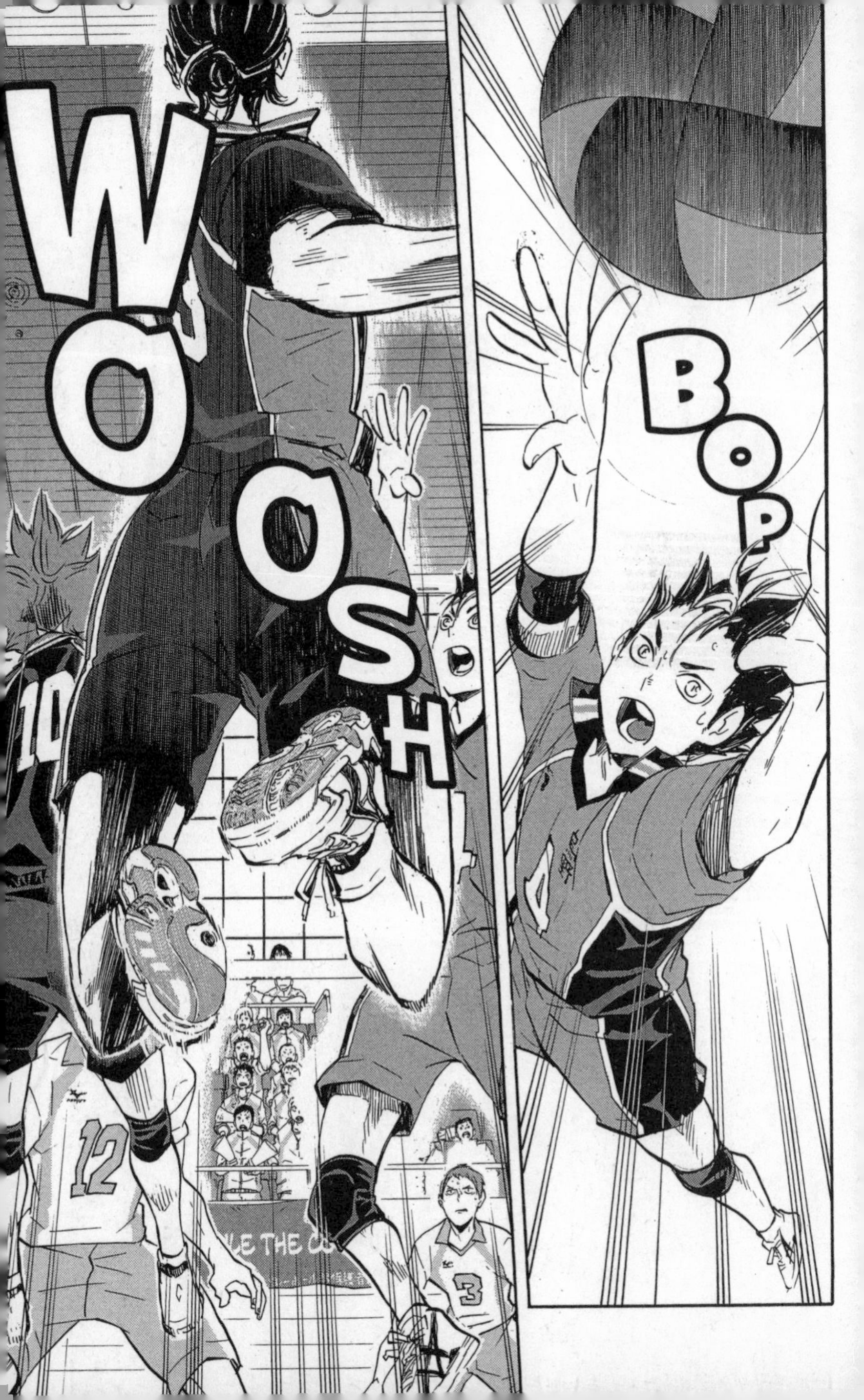
BOP
WOOSH

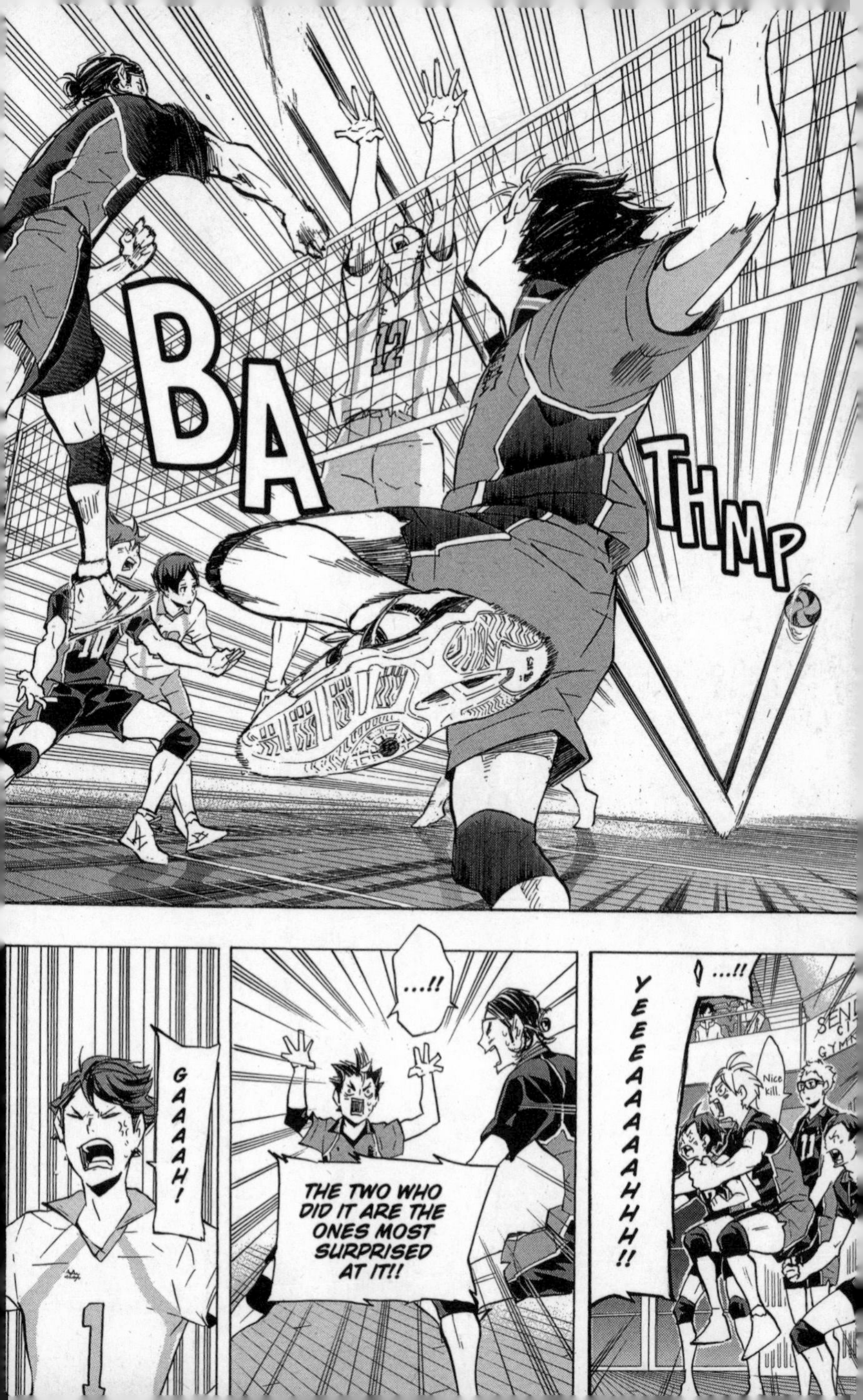
BA
THMP
...!!
YEEEAAAAAAHHH!!
Nice kill.
...!!
THE TWO WHO DID IT ARE THE ONES MOST SURPRISED AT IT!!
GAAAAH!

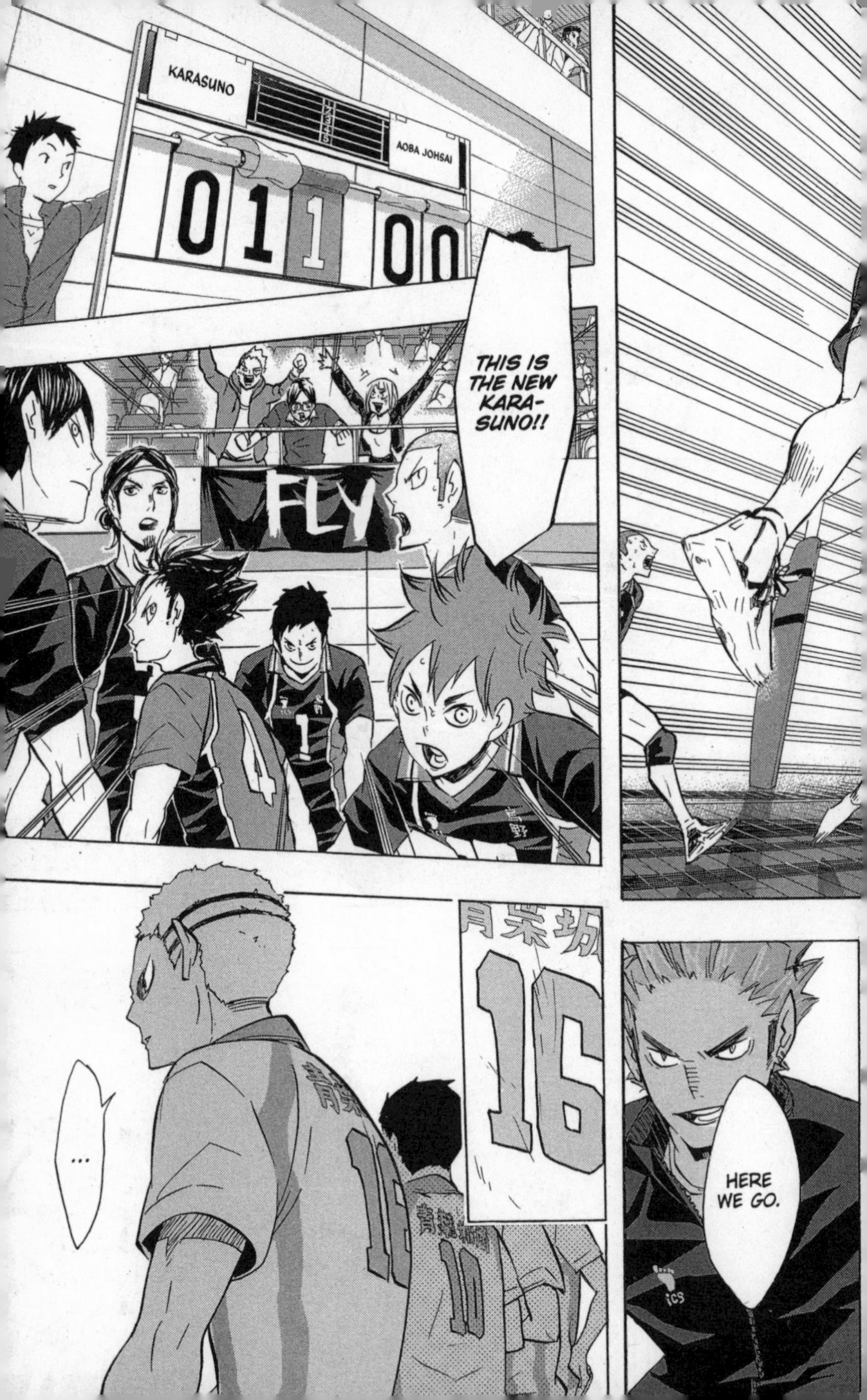
KARASUNO
AOBA JOHSAI
01 1 00
FLY
THIS IS THE NEW KARA-SUNO!!
HERE WE GO.
...

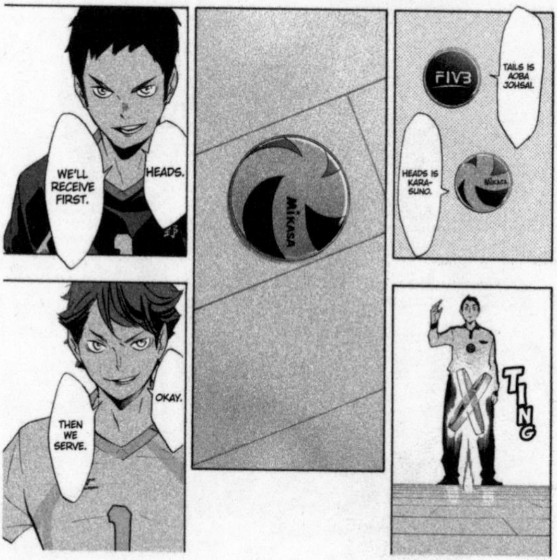
TAILS IS AOBA JOHSAI.
HEADS IS KARA-SUNO.
TING
MIKASA
HEADS.
WE'LL RECEIVE FIRST.
OKAY.
THEN WE SERVE.

↑ THE SCENE ABOVE WAS PUT TOGETHER WITH THE INTENT OF MAKING THE FLOW OF WHAT HAPPENED EASY TO UNDERSTAND AND A LITTLE DRAMATIC (AND TO FIT IT WITHIN THE PAGE COUNT). IN A REAL GAME, THINGS WOULD BE A LITTLE DIFFERENT. SAWAMURA CHOSE THE SERVING ORDER (KARASUNO RECEIVING FIRST), SO OIKAWA WOULD HAVE CHOSEN WHICH SIDE OF THE COURT BLUECASTLE GOT FIRST.

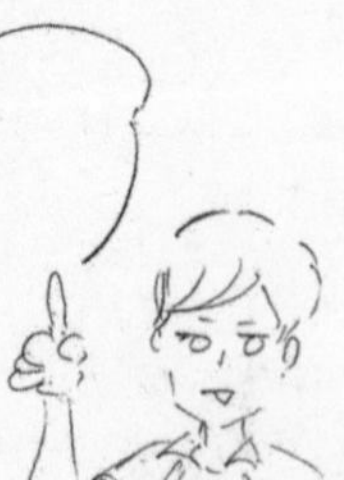

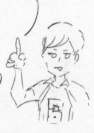

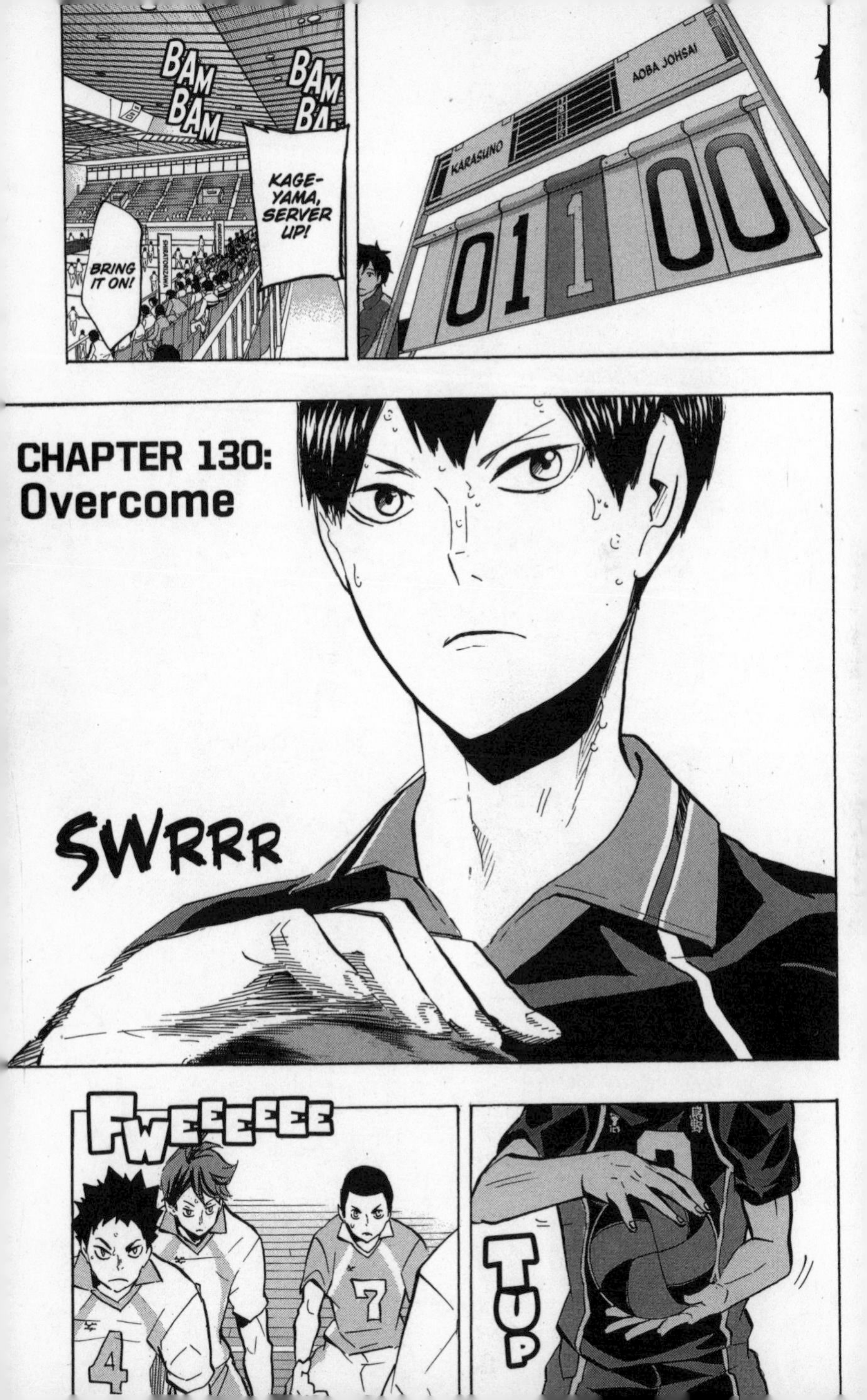
KARASUNO
AOBA JOHSAI
01 1 00
BAM BAM
BAM BA
KAGE-YAMA, SERVER UP!
BRING IT ON!
CHAPTER 130: Overcome
SWRRR
TUP
FWEEEEEE

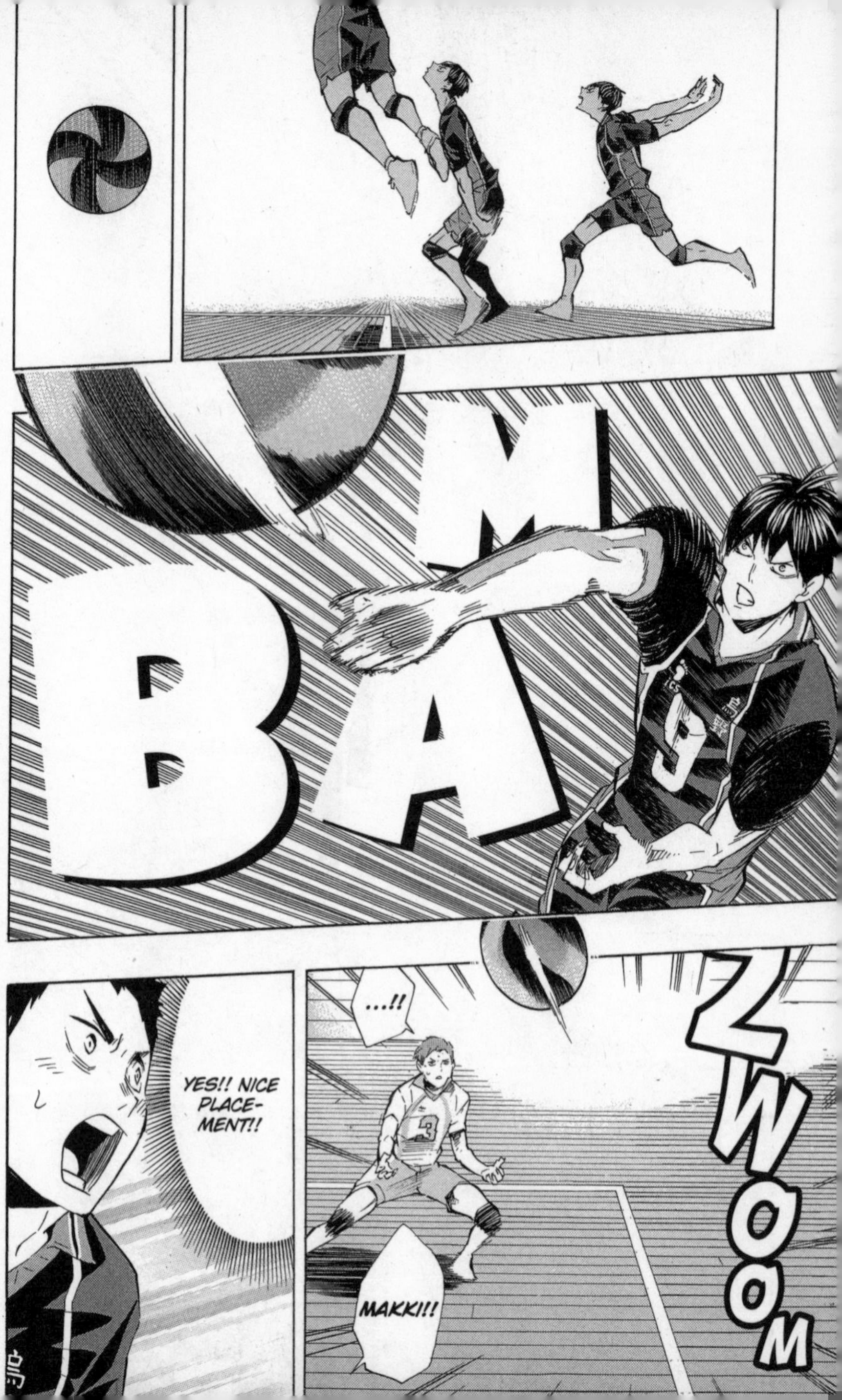
BAM
...!!
ZWOOM
MAKKI!!
YES!! NICE PLACE-MENT!!

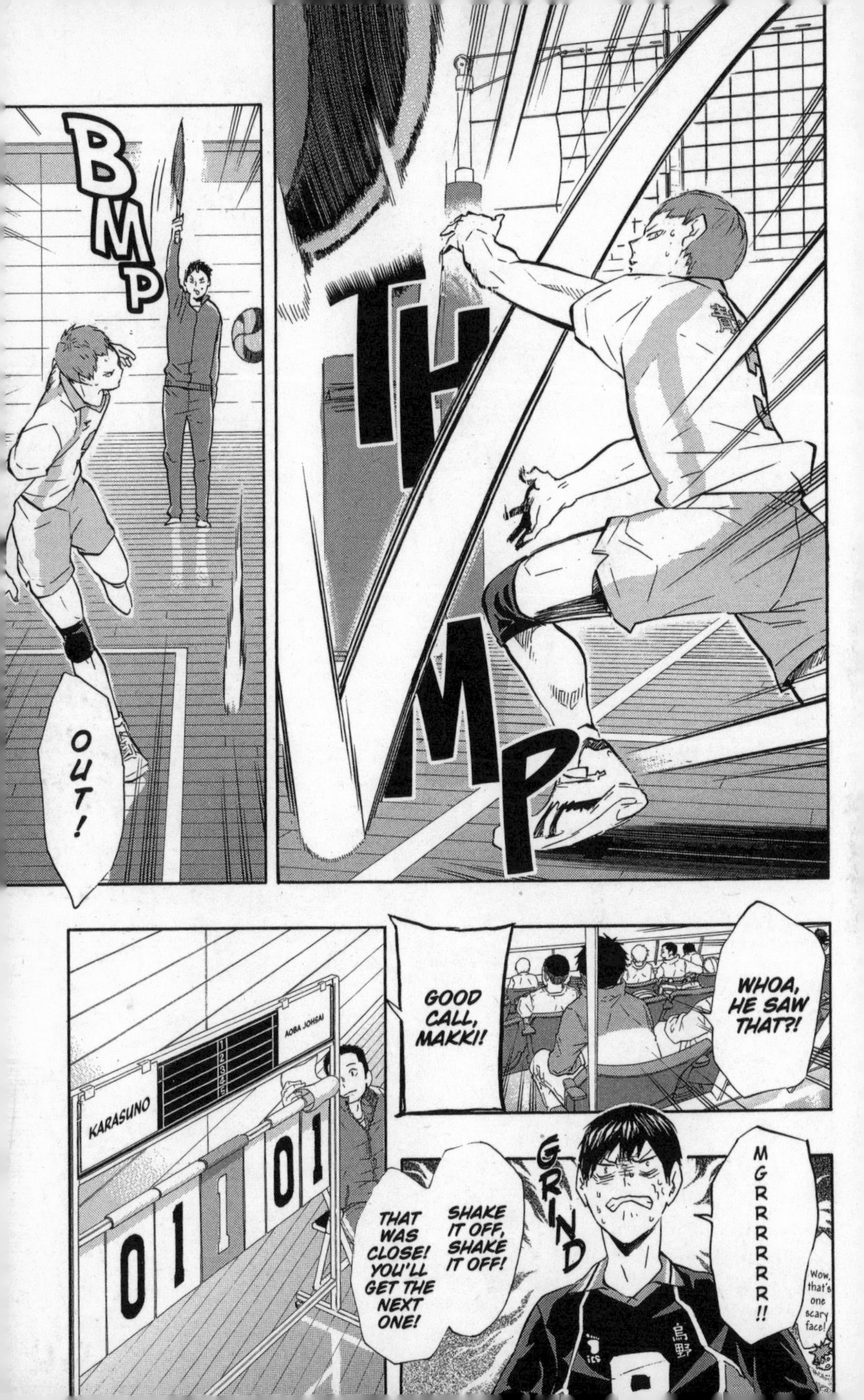
THUMP
BMP
OUT!
WHOA, HE SAW THAT?!
GOOD CALL, MAKKI!
MGRRRRRR!!
GRIND
Wow, that's one scary face!
SHAKE IT OFF, SHAKE IT OFF!
THAT WAS CLOSE! YOU'LL GET THE NEXT ONE!
AOBA JOHSAI
KARASUNO
1 2 3 4 5
01 1 01

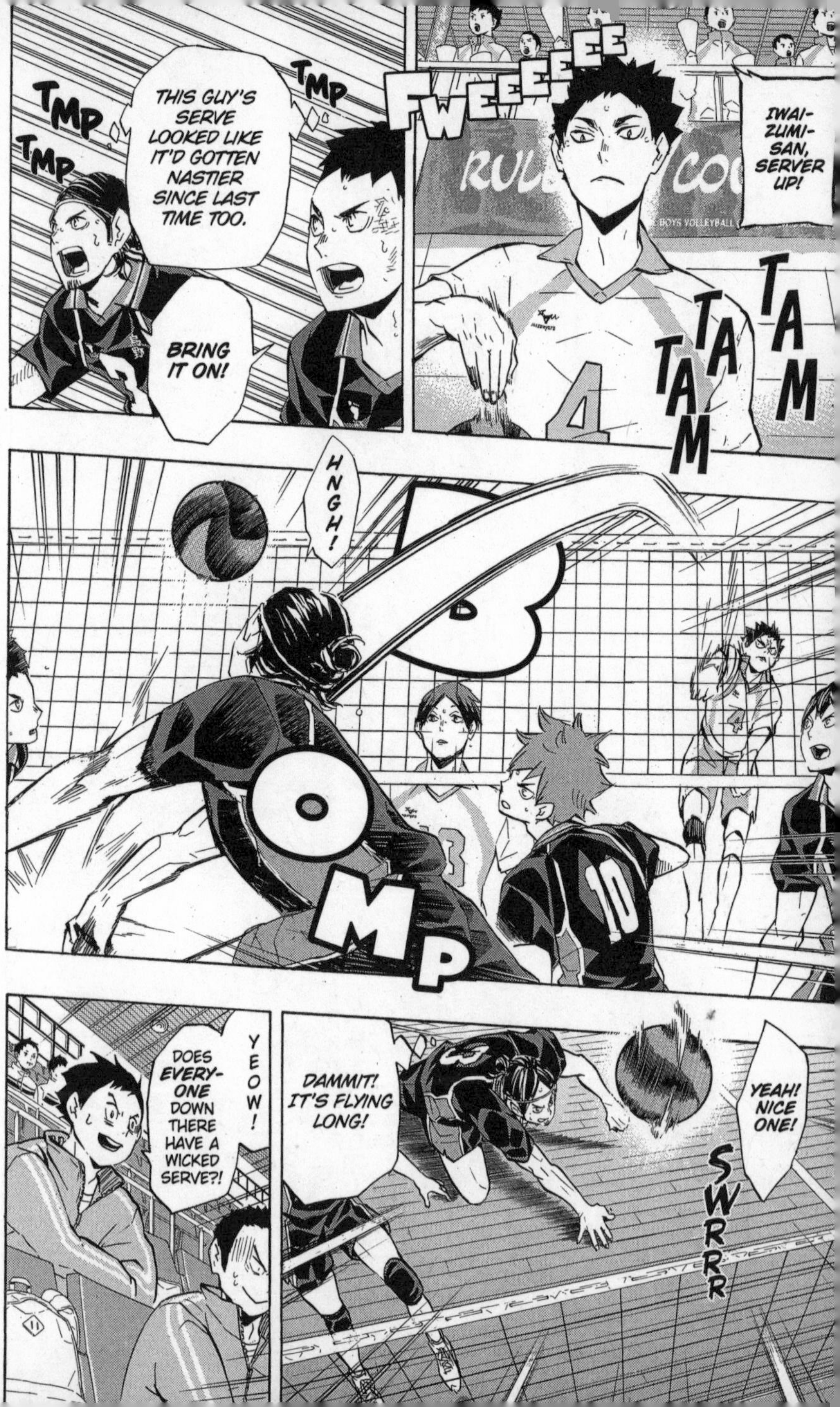
FWEEEEEE
IWAI-ZUMI-SAN, SERVER UP!
TAM TAM TAM
TMP TMP TMP
THIS GUY'S SERVE LOOKED LIKE IT'D GOTTEN NASTIER SINCE LAST TIME TOO.
BRING IT ON!
HNGH!
BOMP
YEAH! NICE ONE!
SWRRR
DAMMIT! IT'S FLYING LONG!
YEOW!
DOES EVERY-ONE DOWN THERE HAVE A WICKED SERVE?!

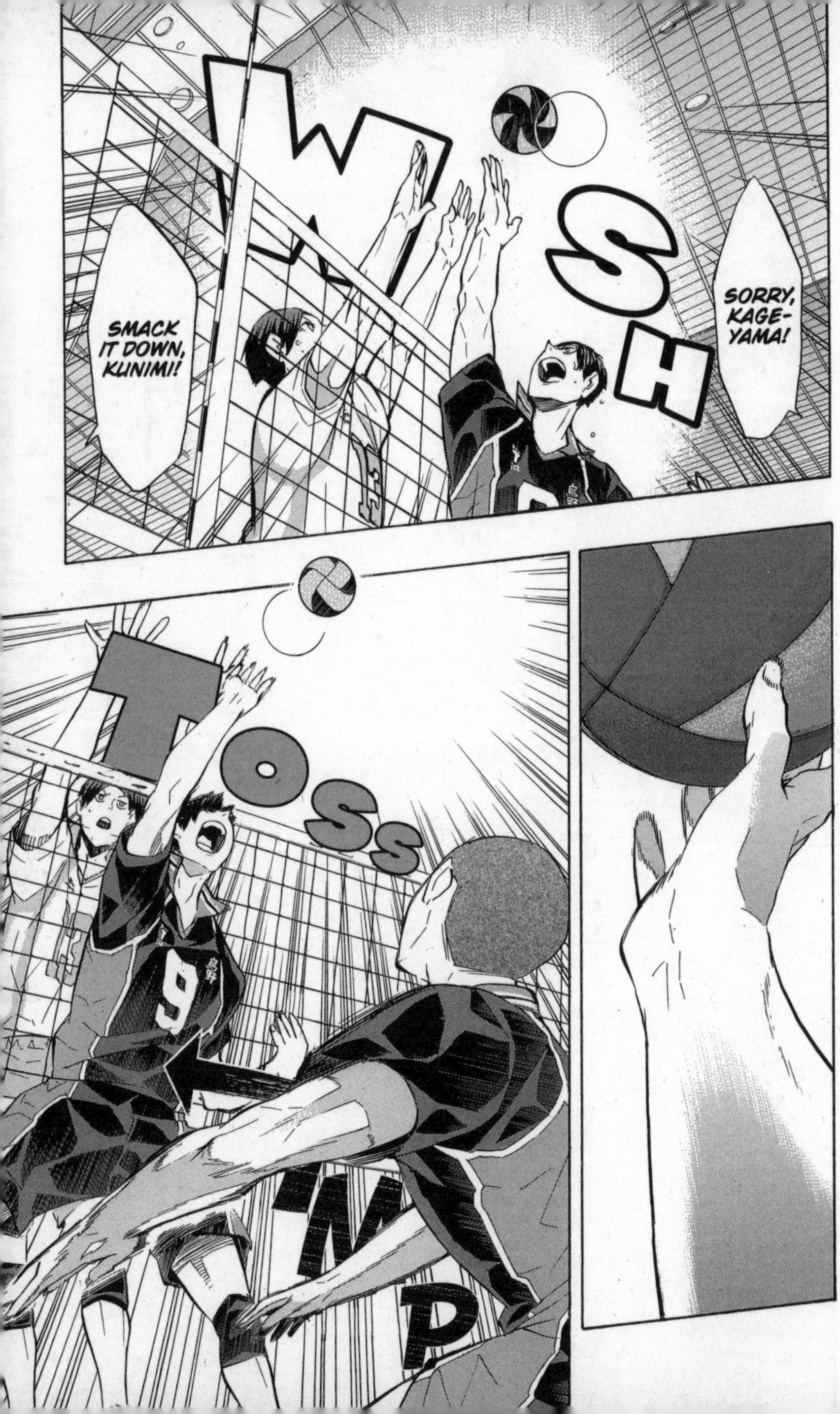

SORRY, KAGE-YAMA!
SMACK IT DOWN, KUNIMI!
TOSS

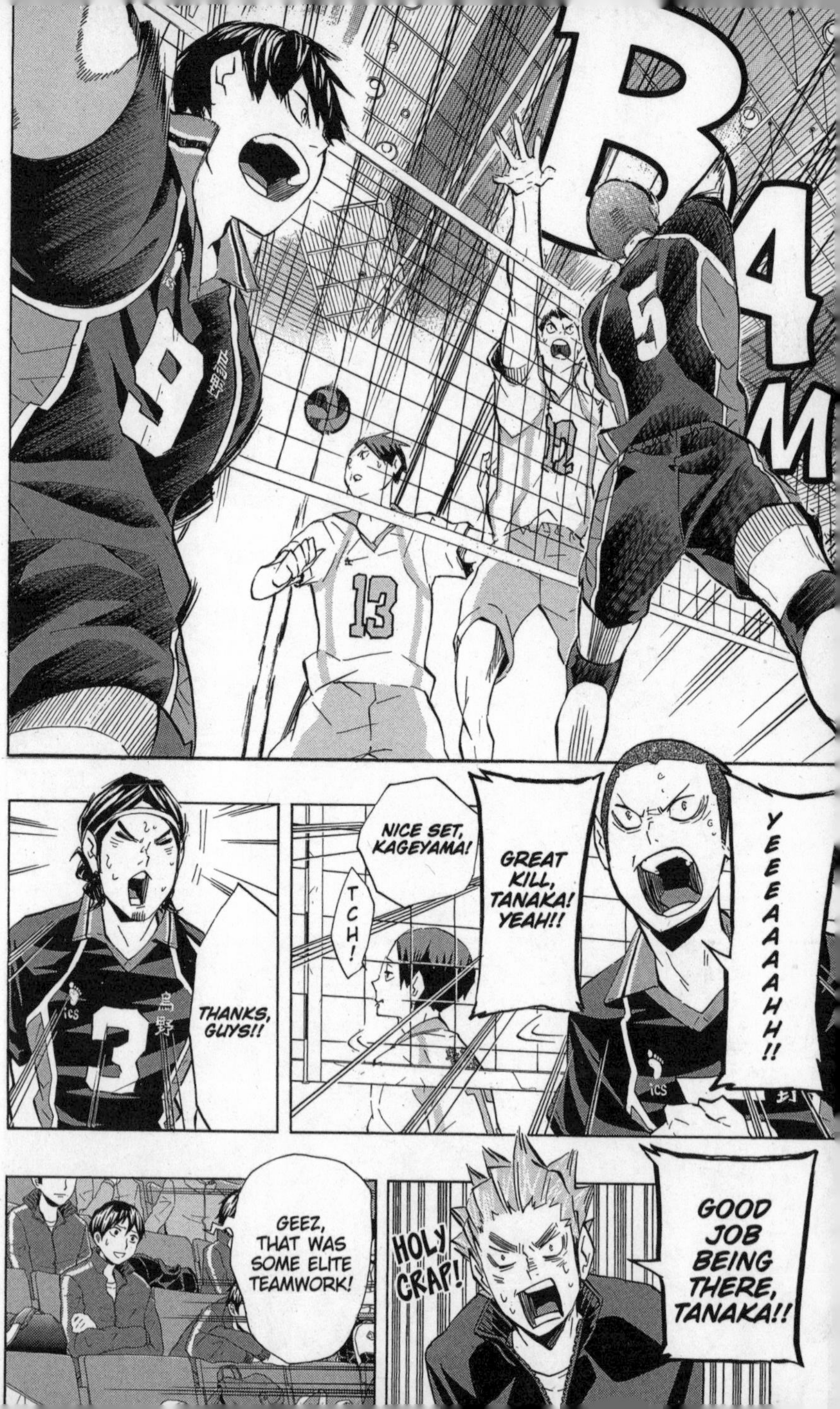

BAM
YEEEEAAAAAHH!!
GREAT KILL, TANAKA! YEAH!!
NICE SET, KAGEYAMA!
TCH!
THANKS, GUYS!!
GOOD JOB BEING THERE, TANAKA!!
HOLY CRAP!
GEEZ, THAT WAS SOME ELITE TEAMWORK!

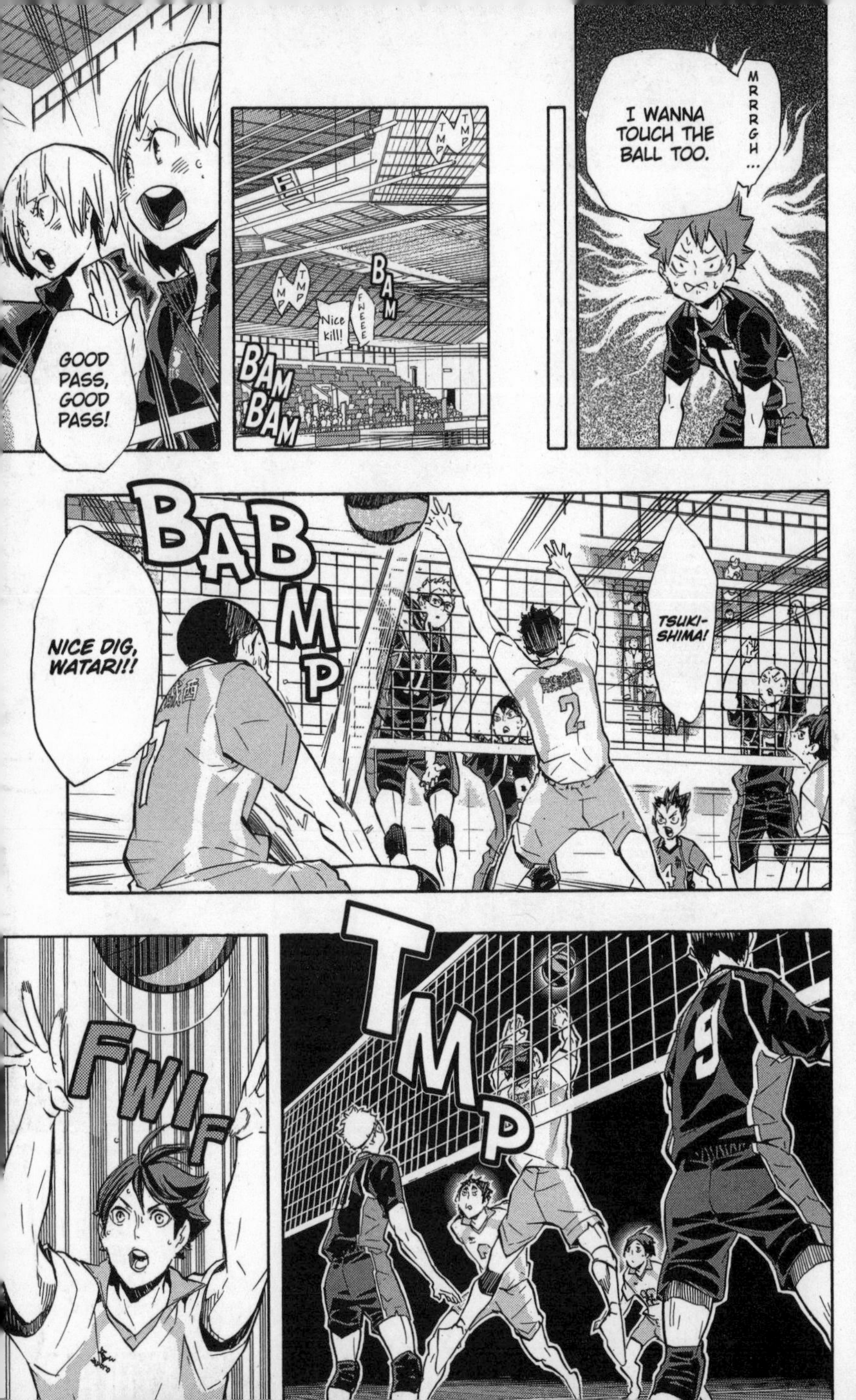
MRRRGH...
I WANNA TOUCH THE BALL TOO.
TMP TMP
BAM
TMP TMP
FWEEE
Nice kill!
BAM BAM BAM BAM
GOOD PASS, GOOD PASS!
TSUKISHIMA!
BABMMP
NICE DIG, WATARI!!
TMP
FWIF

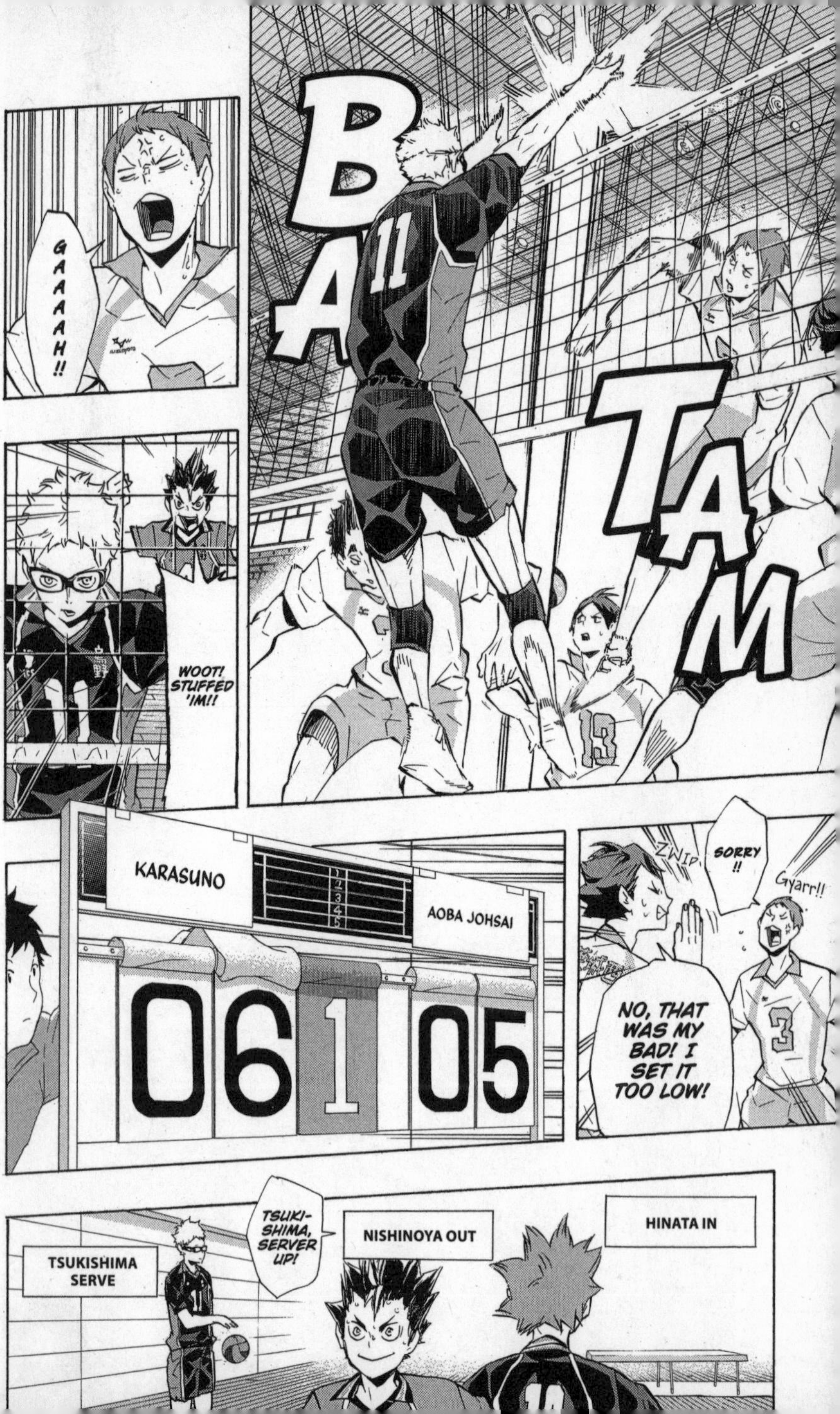
BATAM
GAAAAAH!!
WOOT! STUFFED 'IM!!
ZWIP
SORRY!!
Gyarr!!
NO, THAT WAS MY BAD! I SET IT TOO LOW!
KARASUNO
AOBA JOHSAI
06 1 05
HINATA IN
NISHINOYA OUT
TSUKISHIMA, SERVER UP!
TSUKISHIMA SERVE

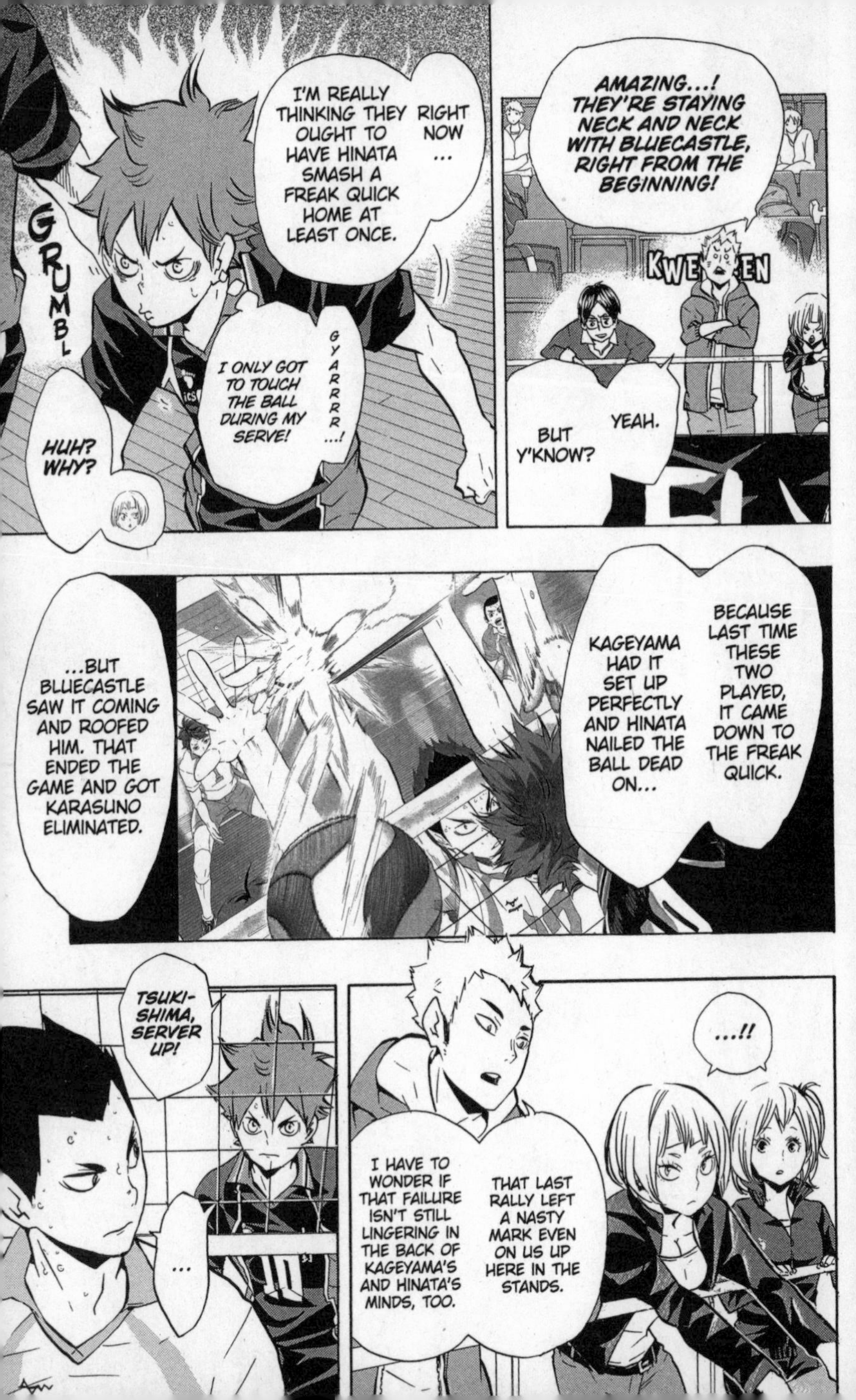
AMAZING...! THEY'RE STAYING NECK AND NECK WITH BLUECASTLE, RIGHT FROM THE BEGINNING!
KWEEEN
YEAH.
BUT Y'KNOW?
RIGHT NOW ... I'M REALLY THINKING THEY OUGHT TO HAVE HINATA SMASH A FREAK QUICK HOME AT LEAST ONCE.
GYARRRR ...!
I ONLY GOT TO TOUCH THE BALL DURING MY SERVE!
GRUMBL
HUH? WHY?
BECAUSE LAST TIME THESE TWO PLAYED, IT CAME DOWN TO THE FREAK QUICK.
KAGEYAMA HAD IT SET UP PERFECTLY AND HINATA NAILED THE BALL DEAD ON...
...BUT BLUECASTLE SAW IT COMING AND ROOFED HIM. THAT ENDED THE GAME AND GOT KARASUNO ELIMINATED.
...!!
THAT LAST RALLY LEFT A NASTY MARK EVEN ON US UP HERE IN THE STANDS.
I HAVE TO WONDER IF THAT FAILURE ISN'T STILL LINGERING IN THE BACK OF KAGEYAMA'S AND HINATA'S MINDS, TOO.
TSUKISHIMA, SERVER UP!
...

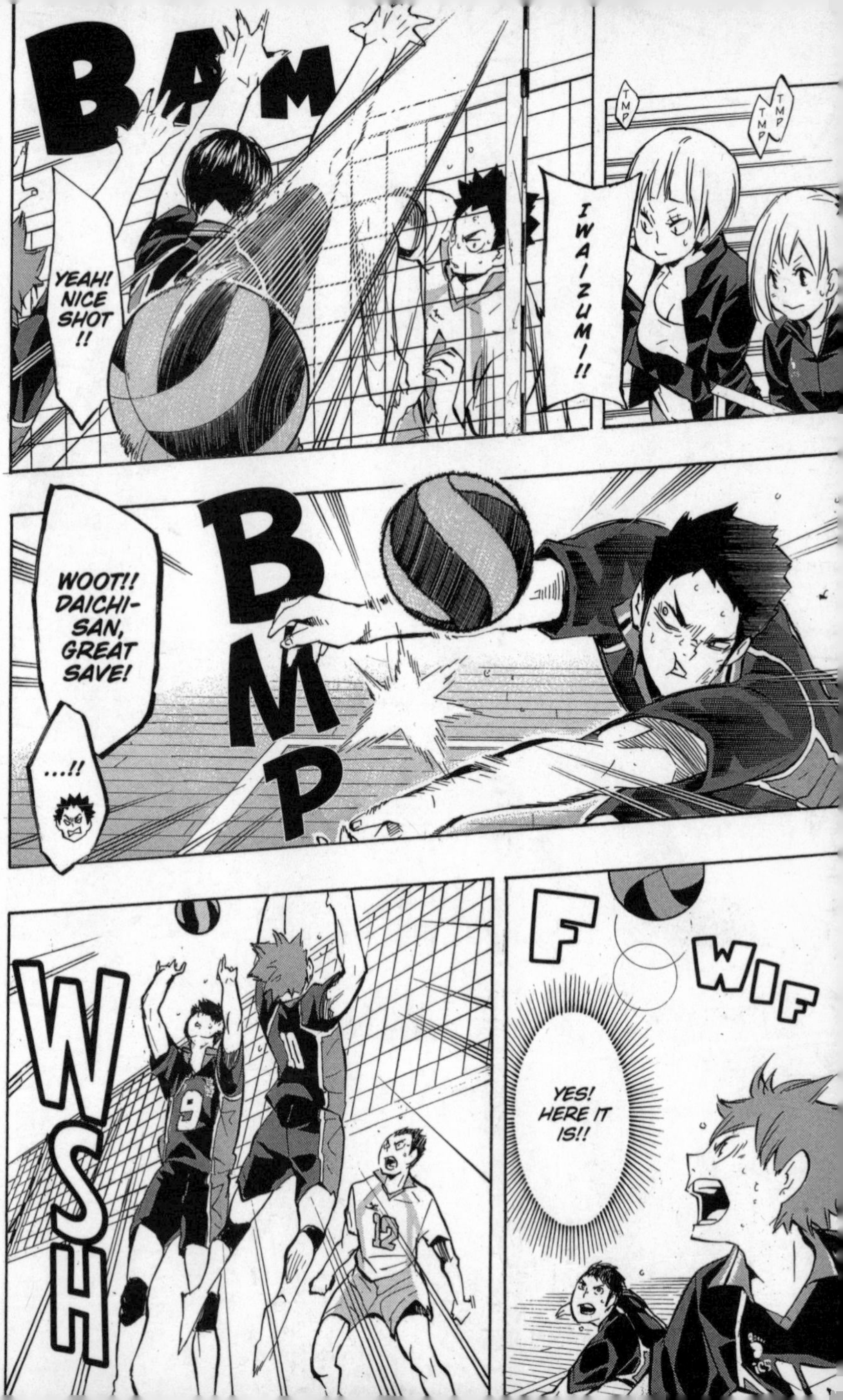

TMP TMP
TMP
IWAIZUMI!!
BAM
YEAH! NICE SHOT!!
BMP
WOOT!! DAICHI-SAN, GREAT SAVE!
...!!
FWIF
YES! HERE IT IS!!
WSH

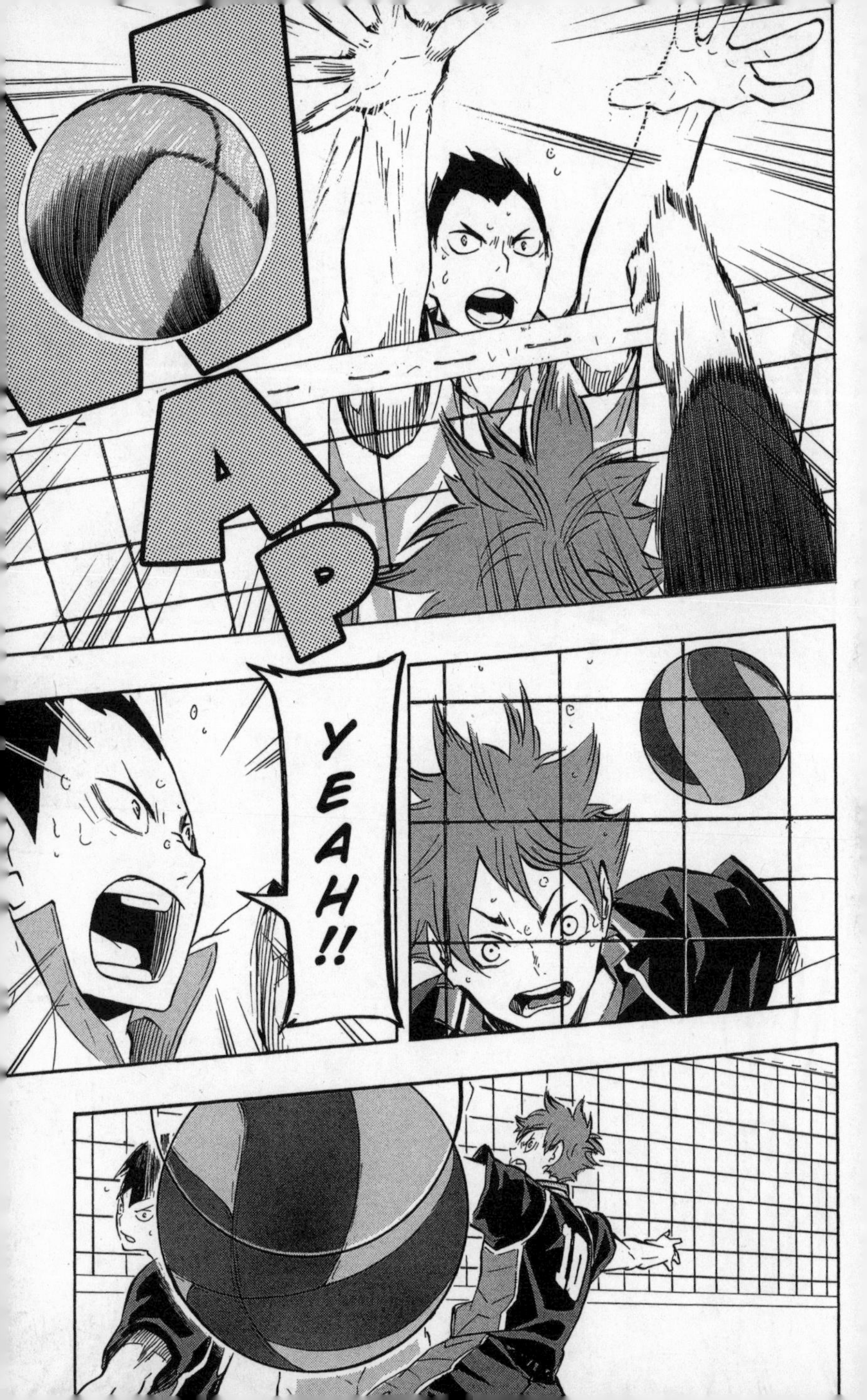
TAP
YEAH!!

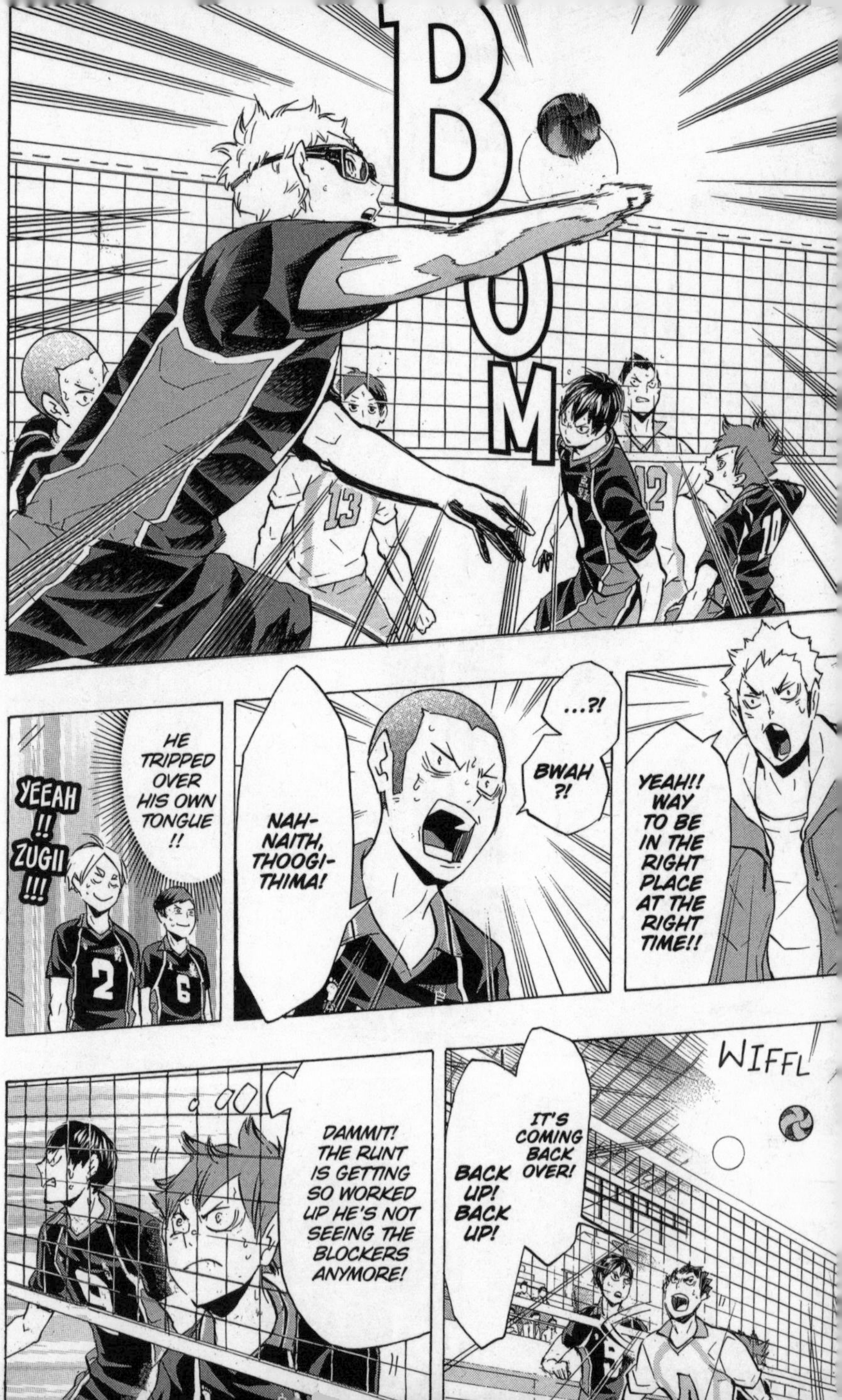
BOOM
YEAH!! WAY TO BE IN THE RIGHT PLACE AT THE RIGHT TIME!!
...?!
BWAH?!
NAH-NAITH, THOOGI-THIMA!
HE TRIPPED OVER HIS OWN TONGUE!!
YEEAH!! ZUGII!!!
WIFFL
IT'S COMING BACK OVER!
BACK UP! BACK UP!
DAMMIT! THE RUNT IS GETTING SO WORKED UP HE'S NOT SEEING THE BLOCKERS ANYMORE!

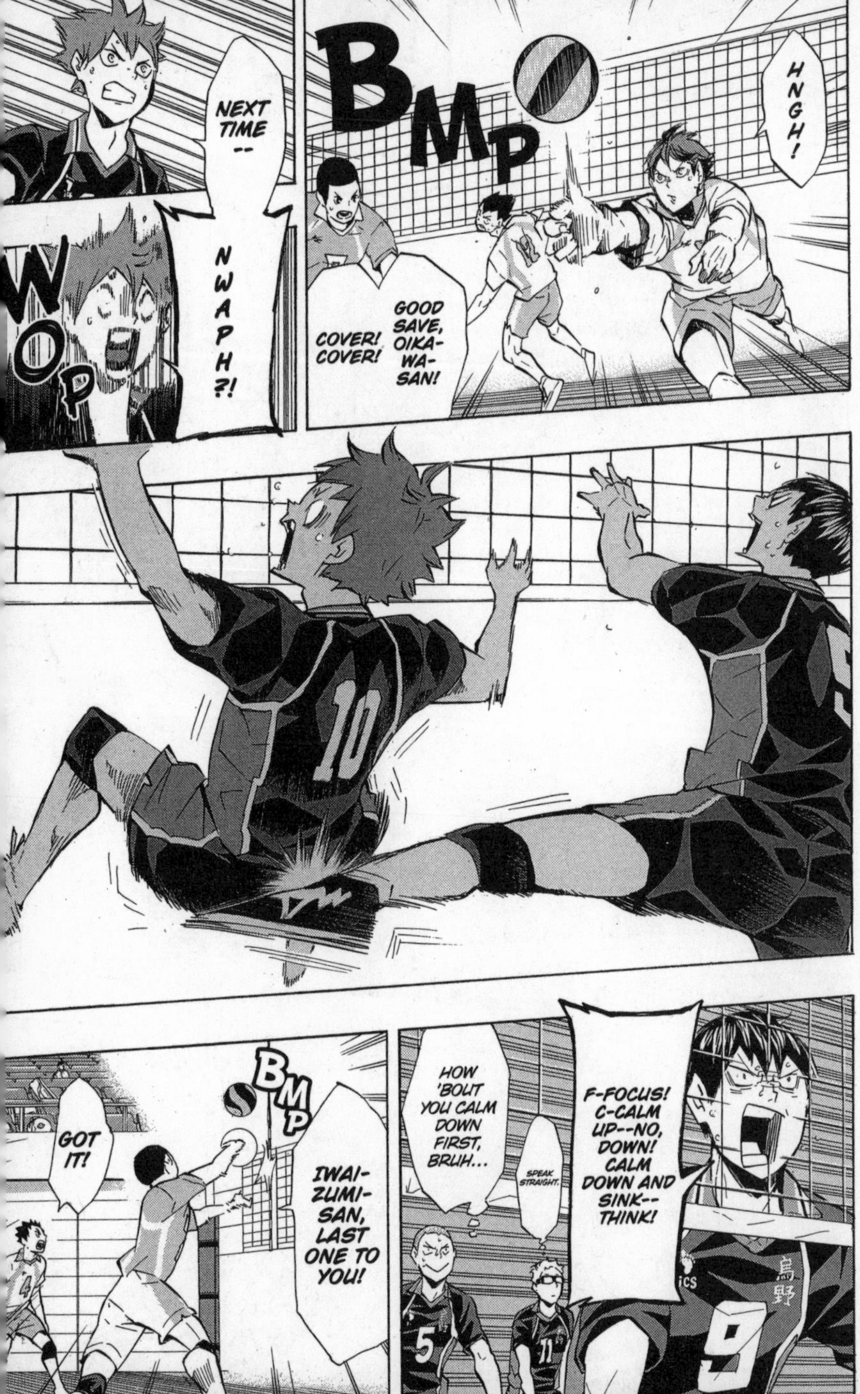
HNGH!
BMP
GOOD SAVE, OIKAWA-SAN!
COVER! COVER!
NEXT TIME --
WOP
NWAPH?!
F-FOCUS! C-CALM UP--NO, DOWN! CALM DOWN AND SINK--THINK!
SPEAK STRAIGHT.
HOW 'BOUT YOU CALM DOWN FIRST, BRUH...
BMP
IWAIZUMI-SAN, LAST ONE TO YOU!
GOT IT!

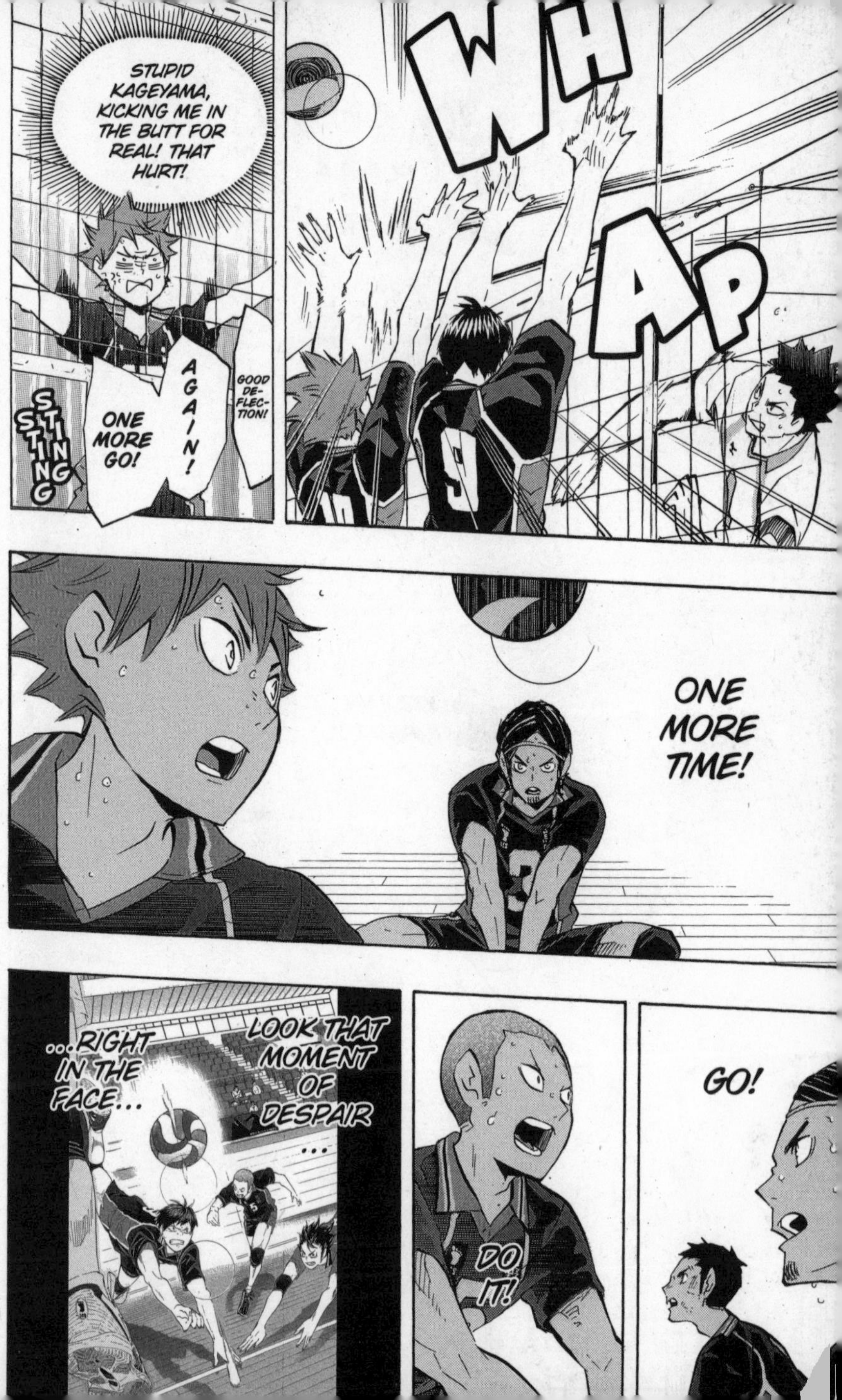
WH
AP
STUPID KAGEYAMA, KICKING ME IN THE BUTT FOR REAL! THAT HURT!
GOOD DEFLECTION!
AGAIN!
ONE MORE GO!
STING STING
ONE MORE TIME!
GO!
DO IT!
LOOK THAT MOMENT OF DESPAIR
...
...RIGHT IN THE FACE...

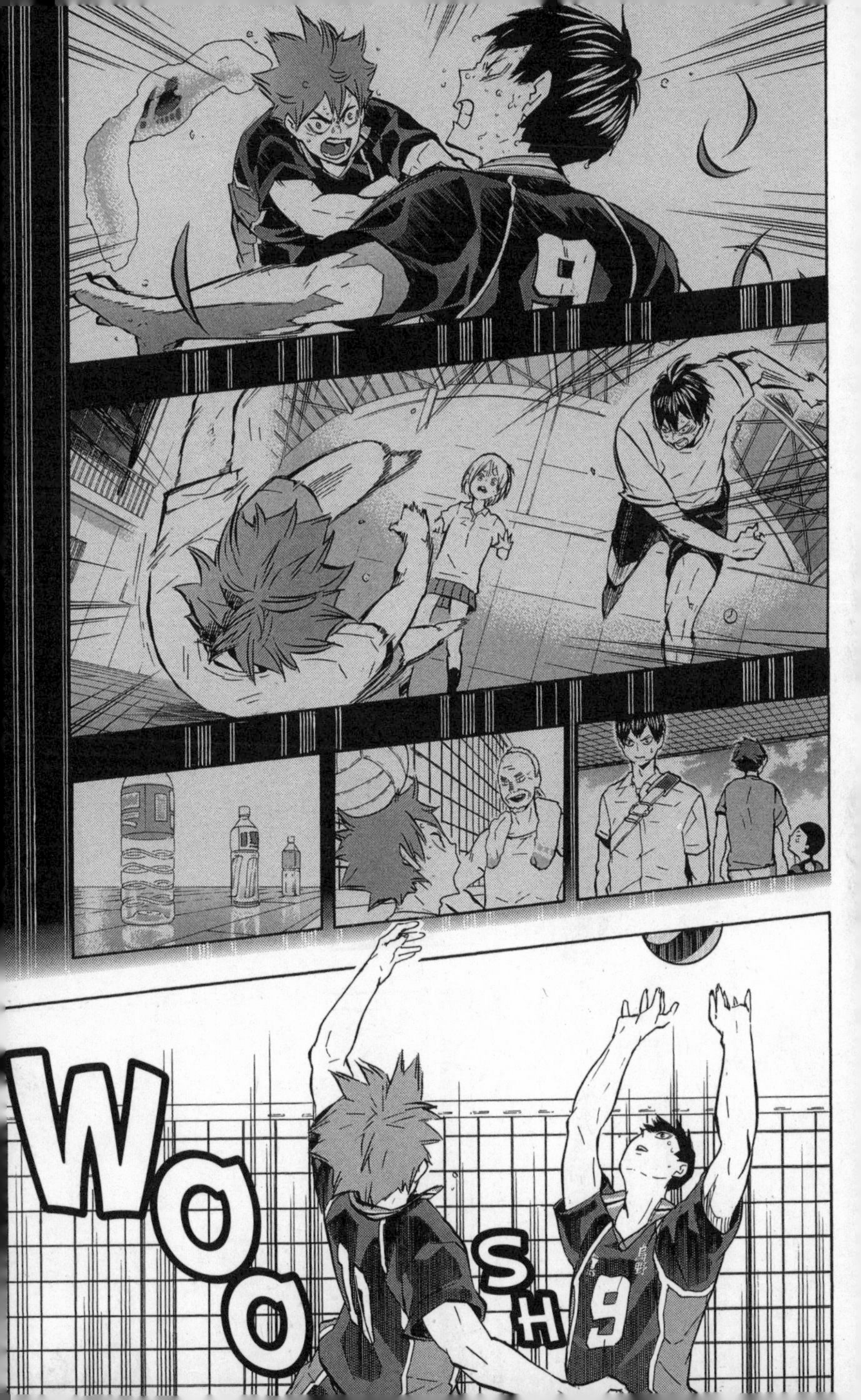
WOOOSH

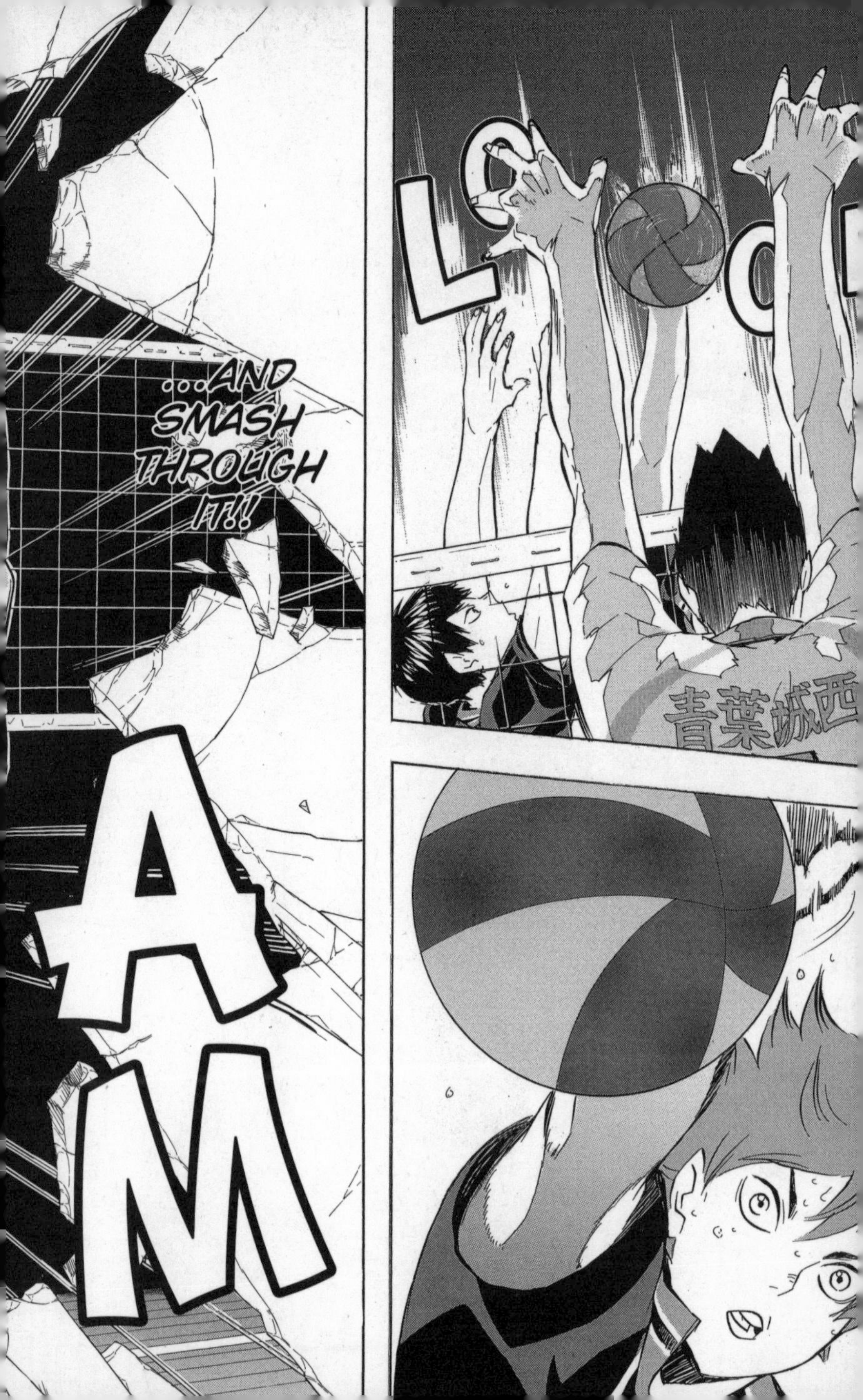
LOO
青葉城西
...AND SMASH THROUGH IT!!
AM

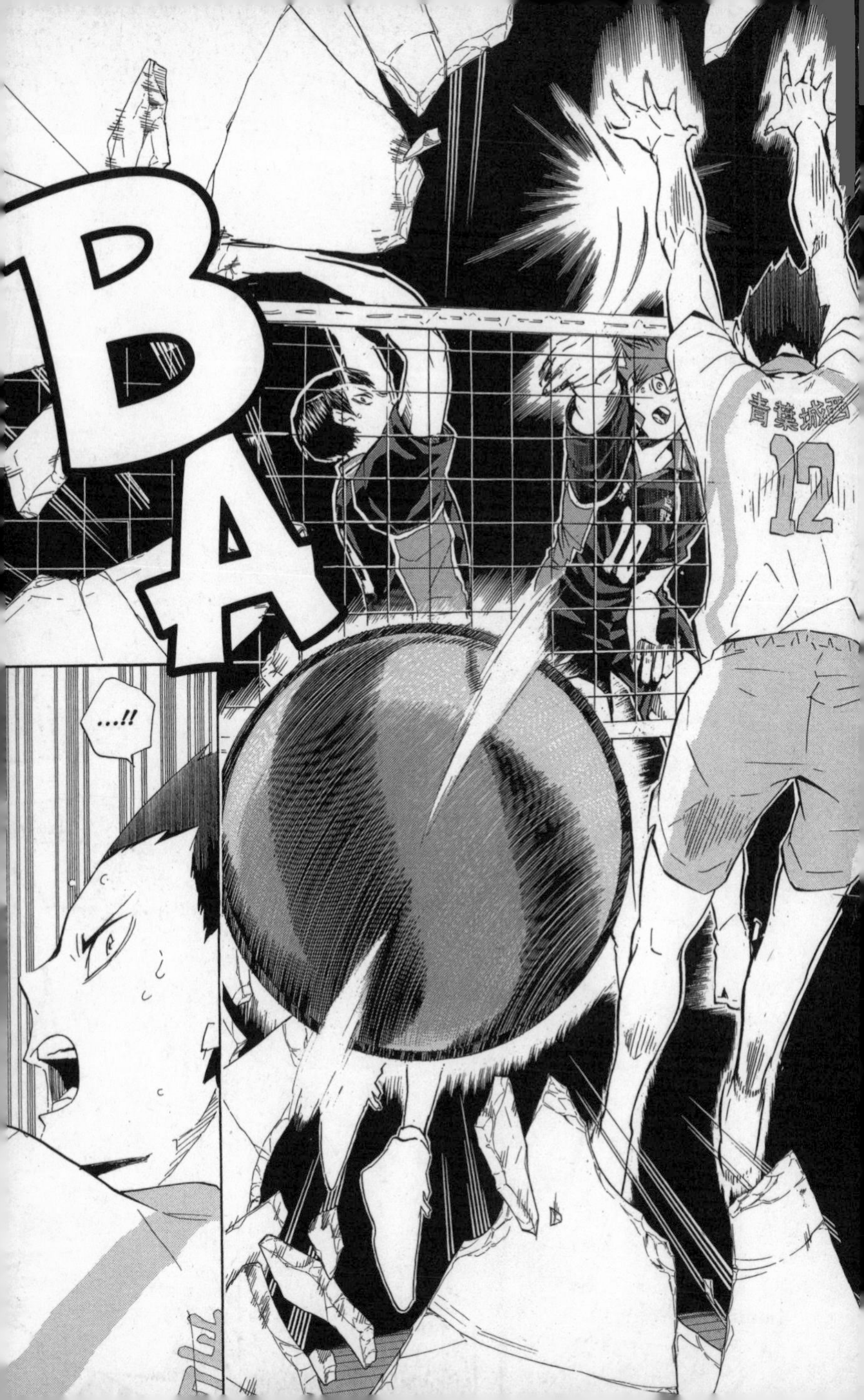

BA
青葉城西
12
...!!

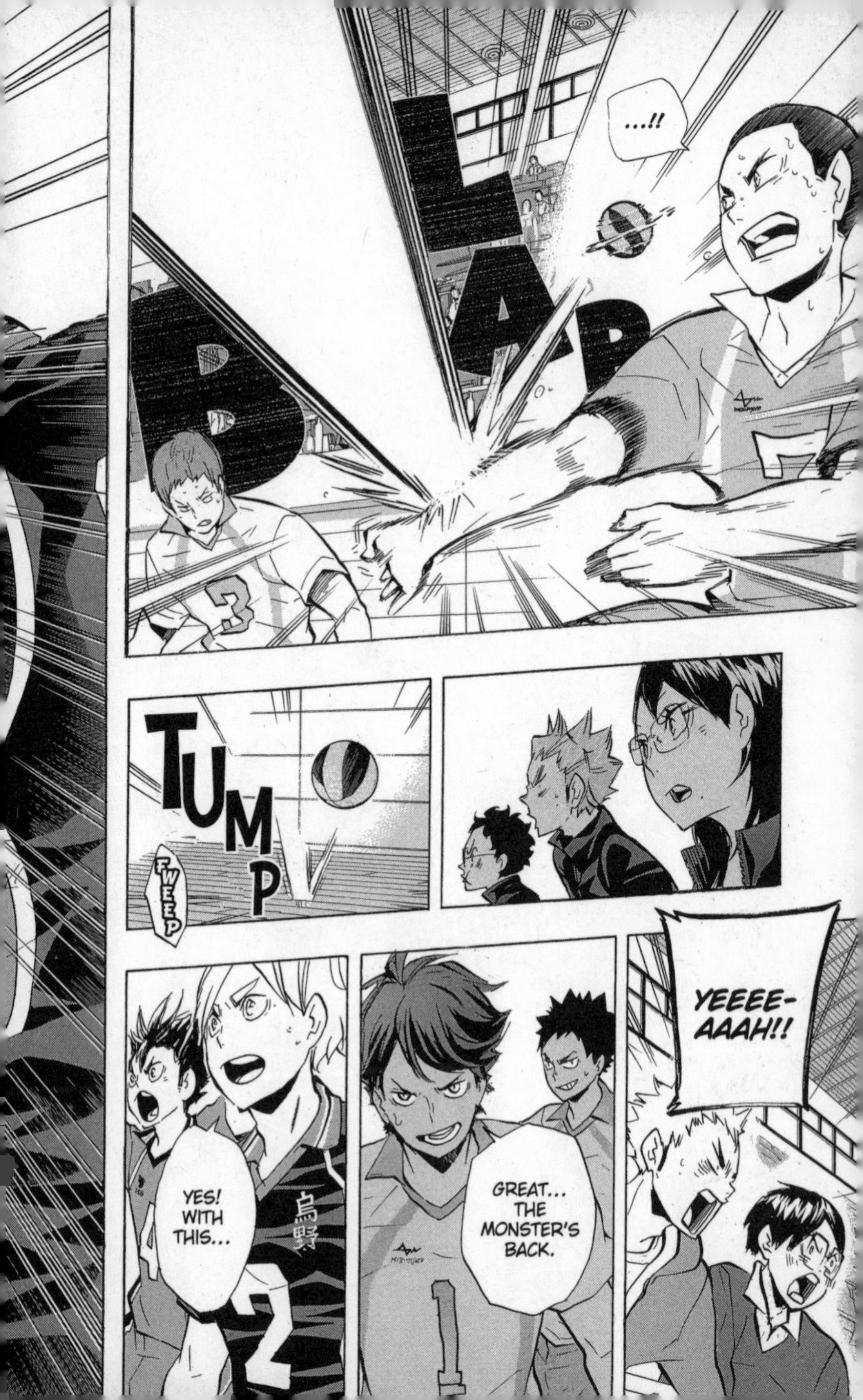
...!!
BLAP
TUMP
FWEEP
YEEEE-AAAH!!
GREAT... THE MONSTER'S BACK.
YES! WITH THIS...

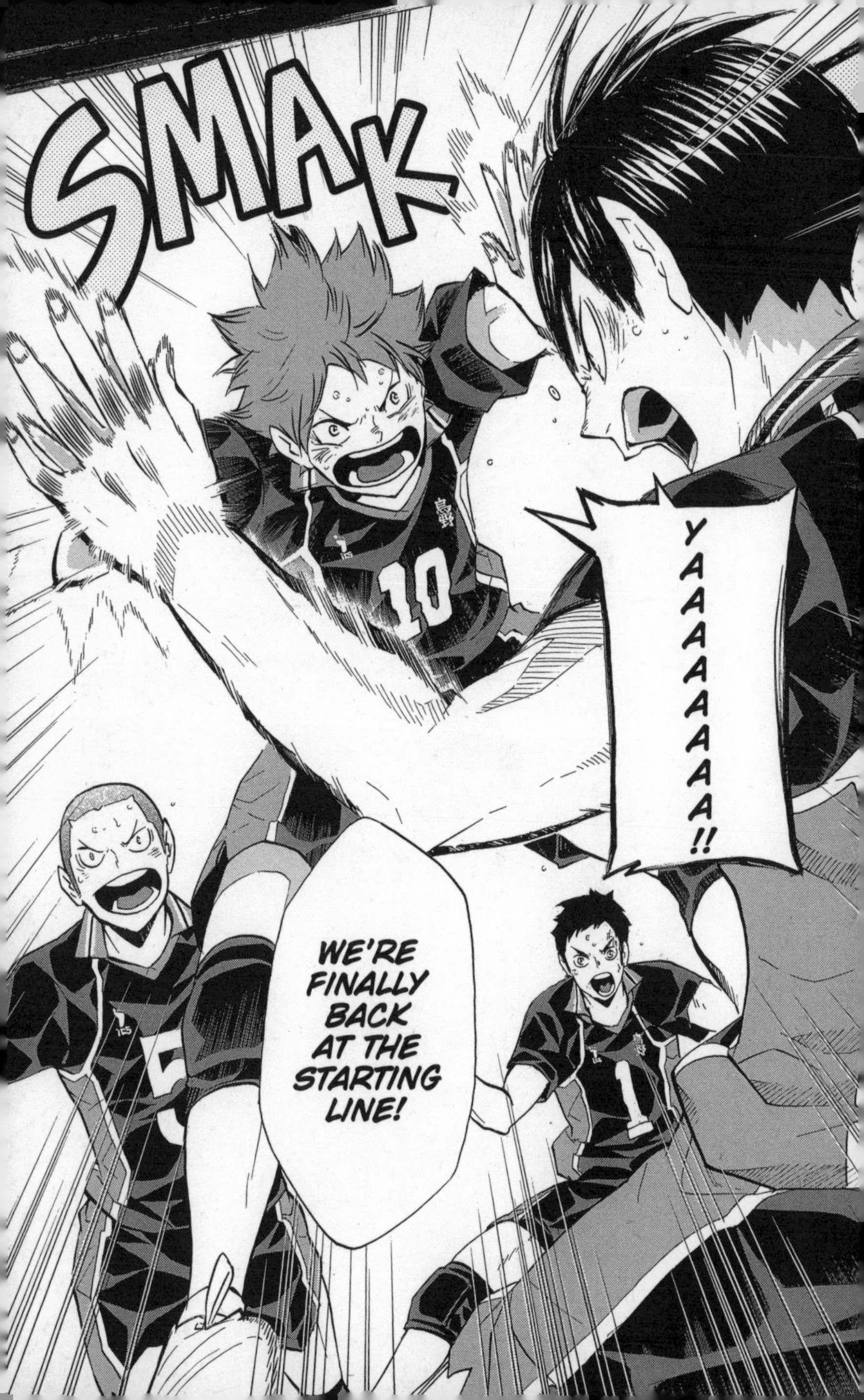
SMAK
YAAAAAAAAAA!!
WE'RE FINALLY BACK AT THE STARTING LINE!

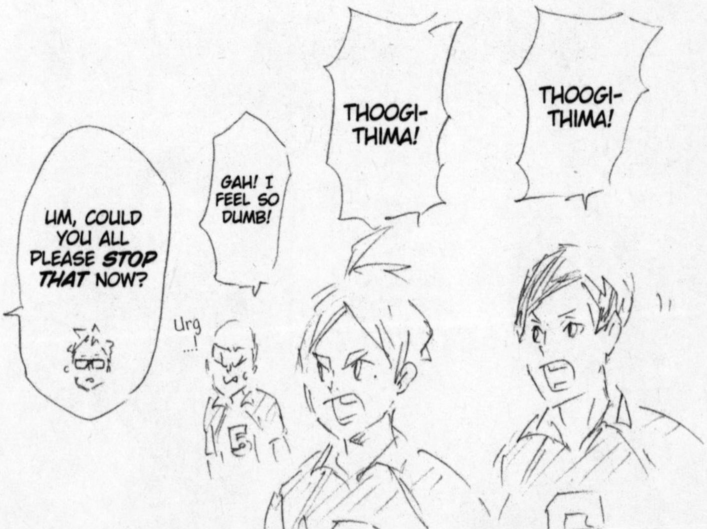
THOOGI-THIMA!
THOOGI-THIMA!
GAH! I FEEL SO DUMB!
UM, COULD YOU ALL PLEASE *STOP THAT* NOW?
Urg...!

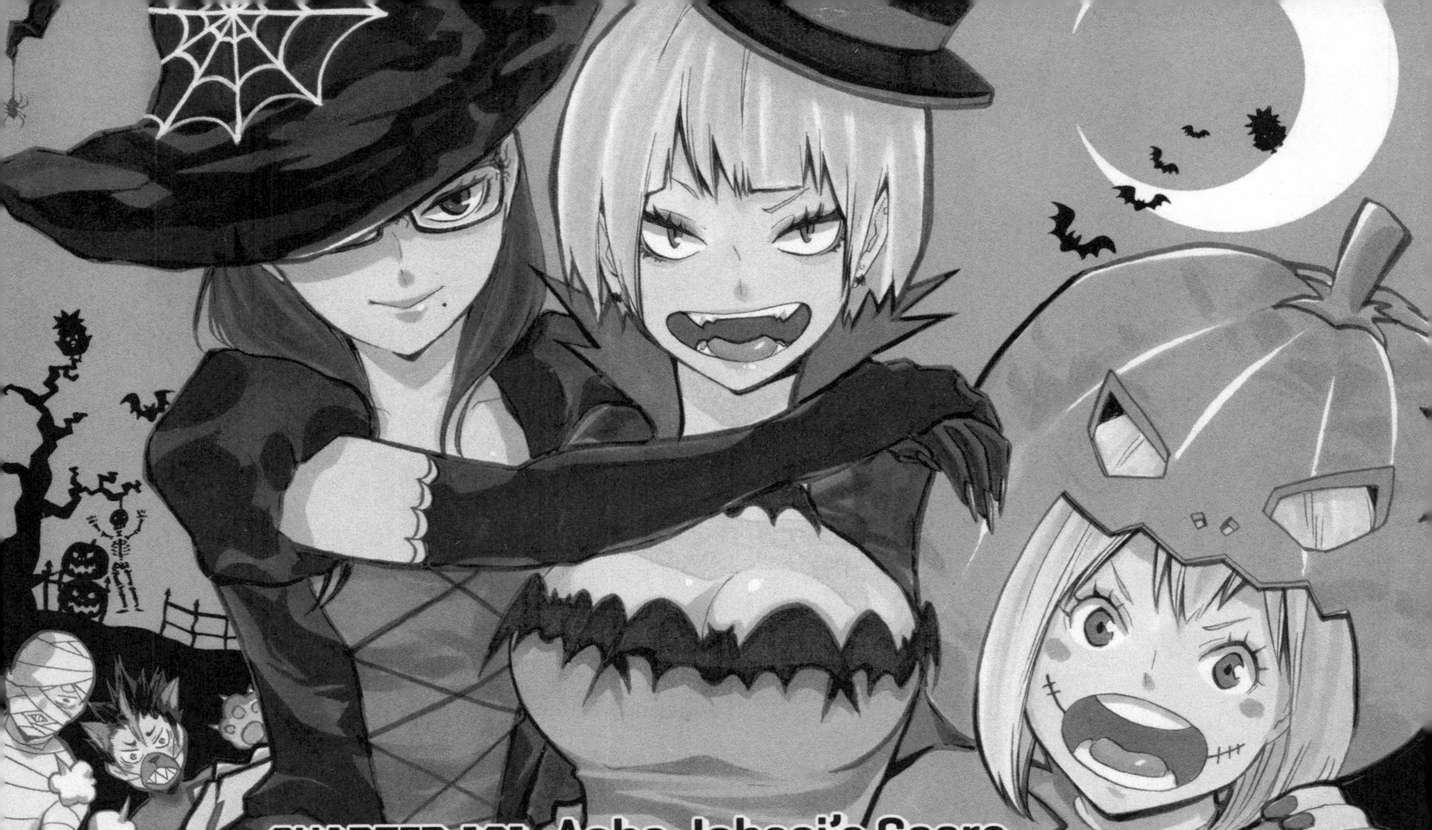

CHAPTER 131: Aoba Johsai's Gears

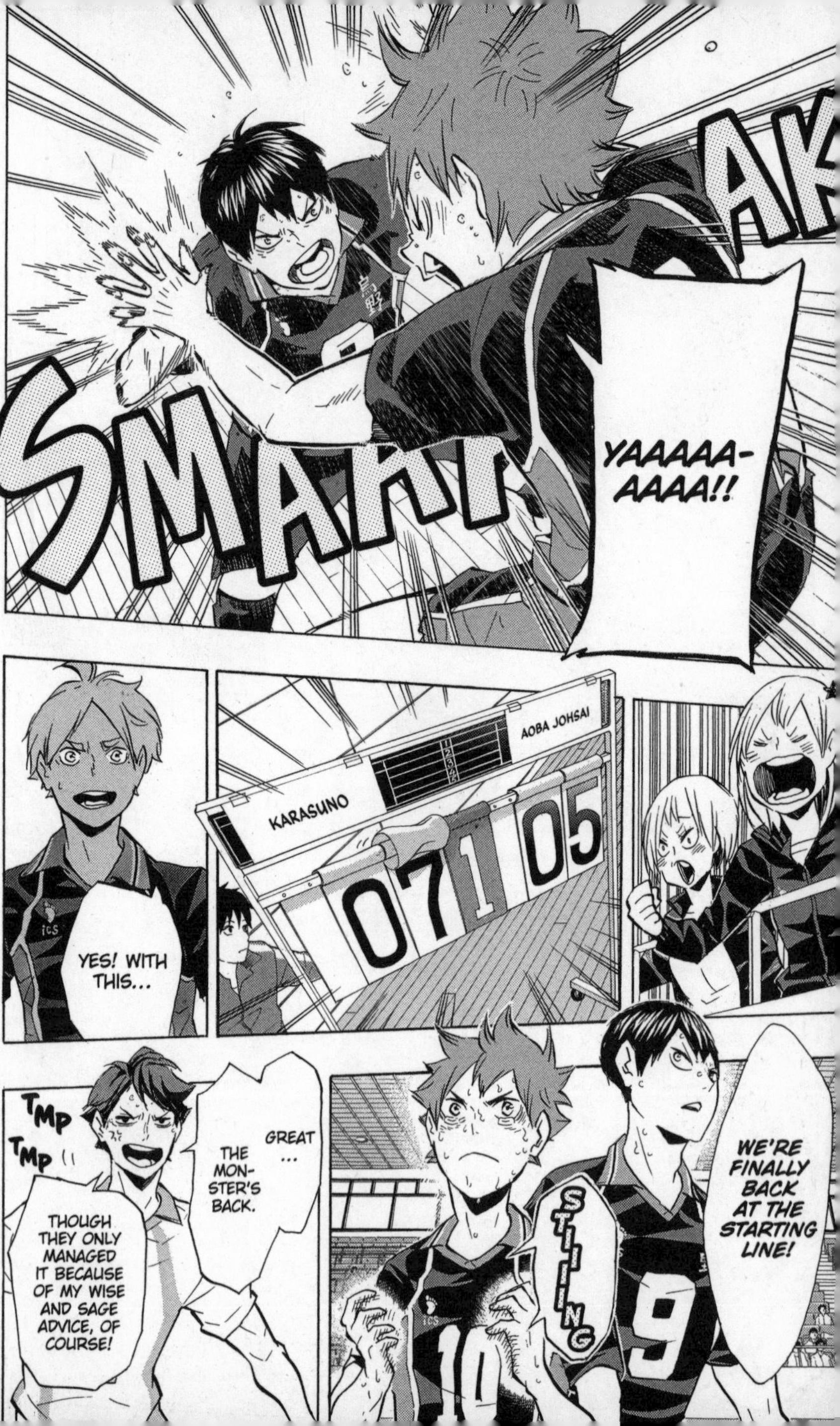
AK
YAAAAA-AAAA!!
SMA
AOBA JOHSAI
KARASUNO
07 1 05
YES! WITH THIS...
WE'RE FINALLY BACK AT THE STARTING LINE!
STING
GREAT ...
THE MONSTER'S BACK.
TMP
TMP
THOUGH THEY ONLY MANAGED IT BECAUSE OF MY WISE AND SAGE ADVICE, OF COURSE!

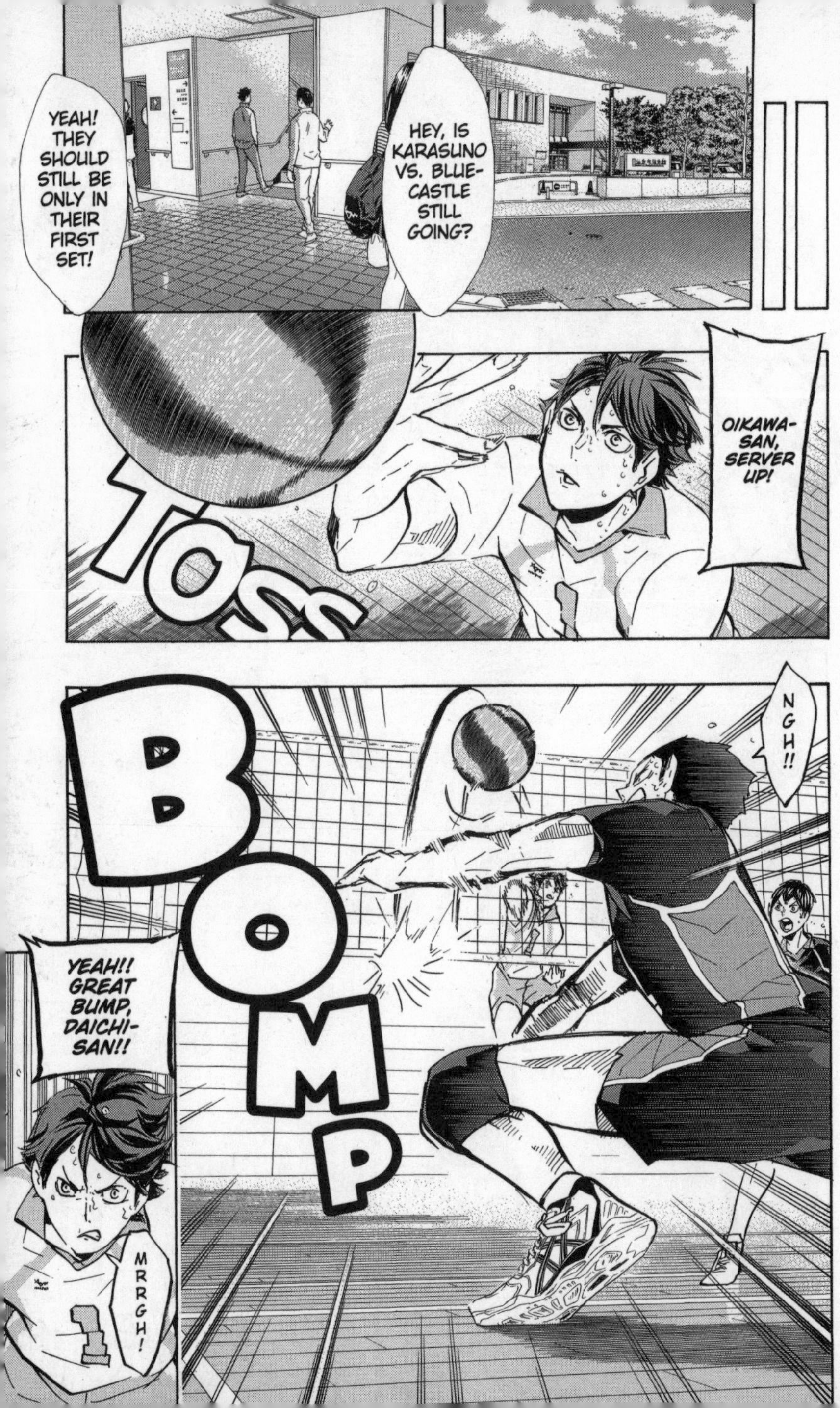
HEY, IS KARASUNO VS. BLUE-CASTLE STILL GOING?
YEAH! THEY SHOULD STILL BE ONLY IN THEIR FIRST SET!
OIKAWA-SAN, SERVER UP!
TOSS
NGH!!
BOMP
YEAH!! GREAT BUMP, DAICHI-SAN!!
MRRGH!

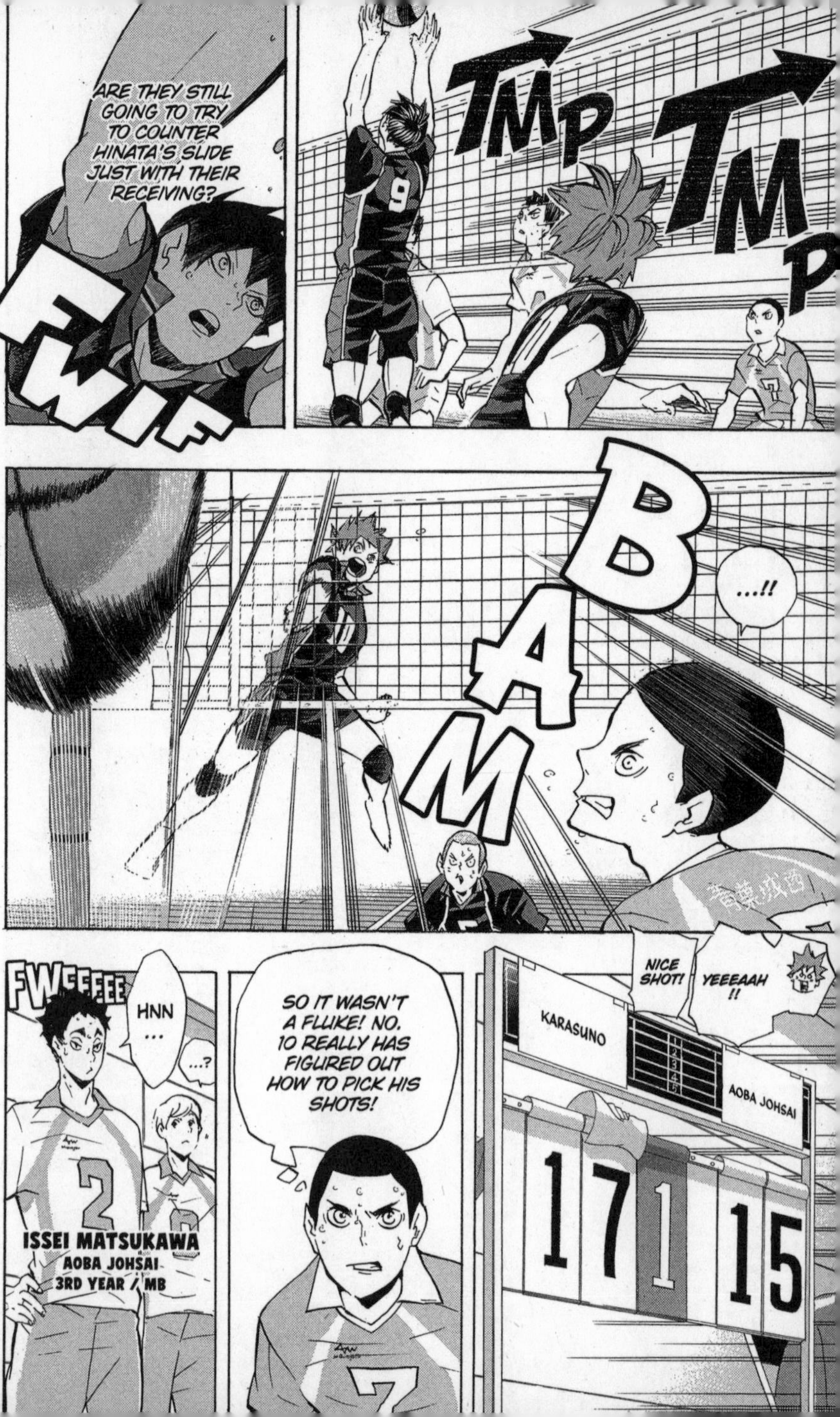
TMP TMP
ARE THEY STILL GOING TO TRY TO COUNTER HINATA'S SLIDE JUST WITH THEIR RECEIVING?
FWIF
BAM
...!!
YEEEAAH !!
NICE SHOT!
KARASUNO
AOBA JOHSAI
17
1
15
SO IT WASN'T A FLUKE! NO. 10 REALLY HAS FIGURED OUT HOW TO PICK HIS SHOTS!
FWEEEEE
HNN ...
...?
ISSEI MATSUKAWA
AOBA JOHSAI
3RD YEAR / MB

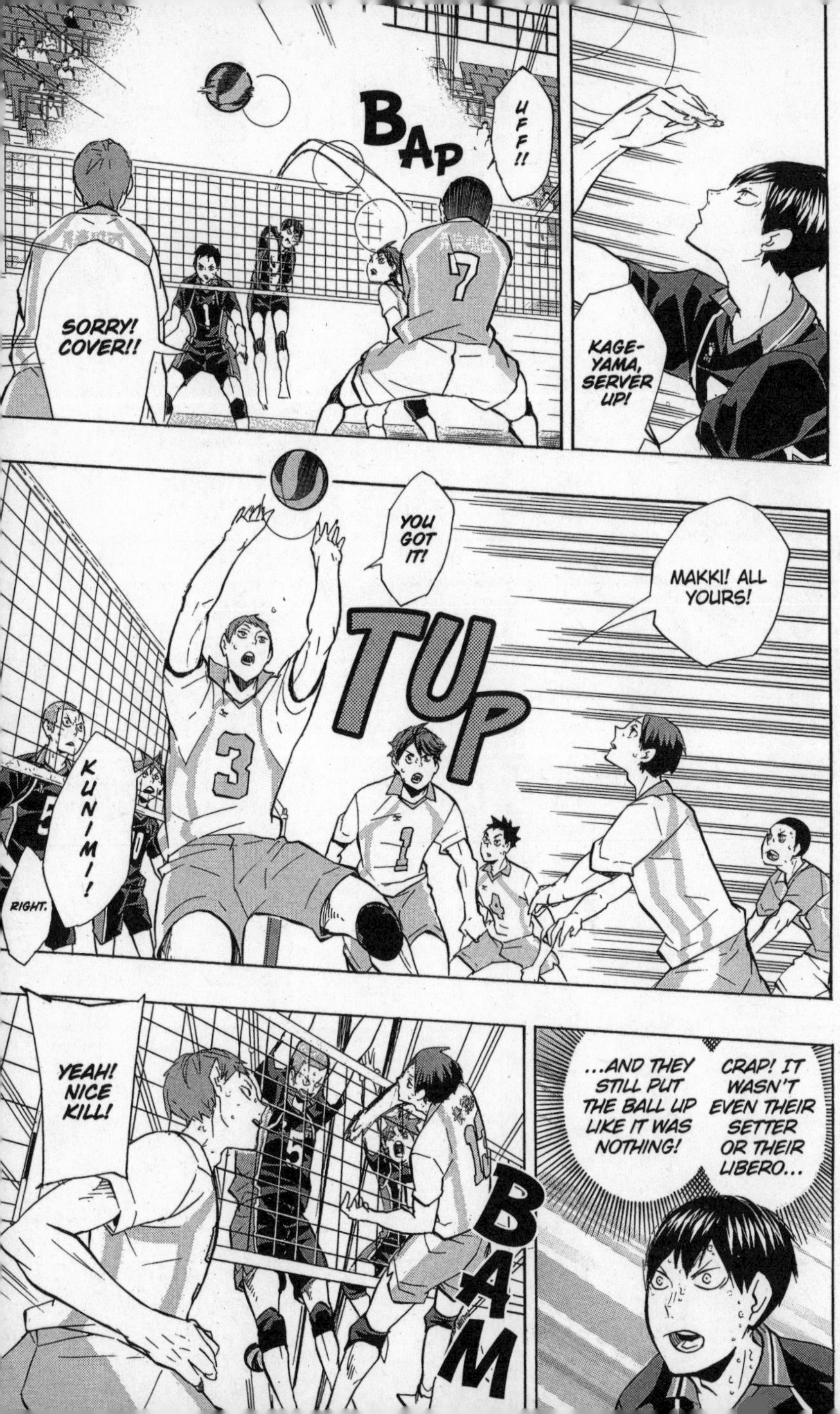
KAGE-YAMA, SERVER UP!
UFF!!
BAP
SORRY! COVER!!
MAKKI! ALL YOURS!
YOU GOT IT!
TUP
KUNIMI!
RIGHT.
CRAP! IT WASN'T EVEN THEIR SETTER OR THEIR LIBERO...
...AND THEY STILL PUT THE BALL UP LIKE IT WAS NOTHING!
BAM
YEAH! NICE KILL!

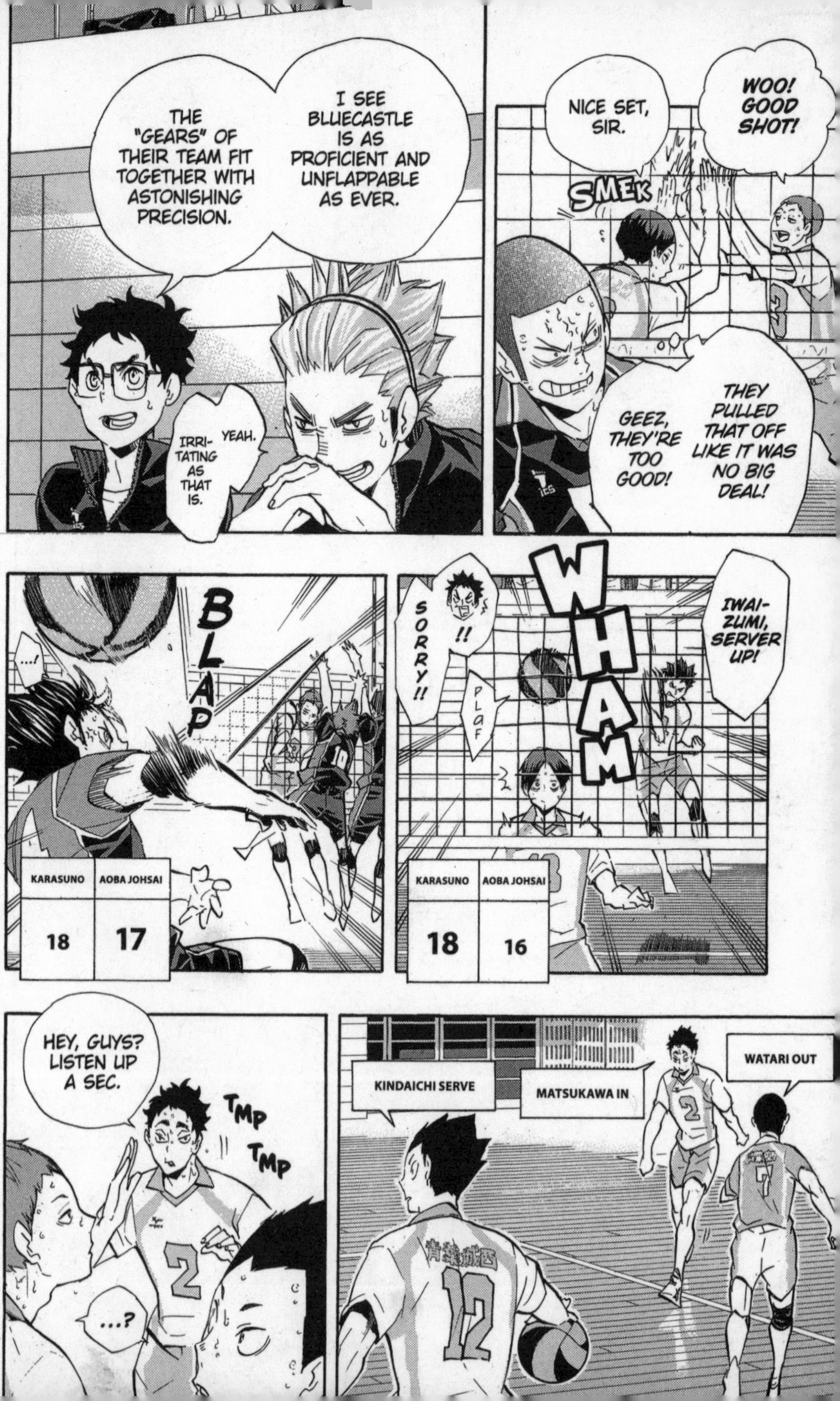
WOO! GOOD SHOT!
NICE SET, SIR.
SMEK
THEY PULLED THAT OFF LIKE IT WAS NO BIG DEAL!
GEEZ, THEY'RE TOO GOOD!
I SEE BLUECASTLE IS AS PROFICIENT AND UNFLAPPABLE AS EVER.
THE "GEARS" OF THEIR TEAM FIT TOGETHER WITH ASTONISHING PRECISION.
YEAH.
IRRITATING AS THAT IS.
IWAIZUMI, SERVER UP!
WHAM
!!
SORRY!!
PLAF
KARASUNO 18
AOBA JOHSAI 16
BLAP
...!
KARASUNO 18
AOBA JOHSAI 17
WATARI OUT
MATSUKAWA IN
KINDAICHI SERVE
HEY, GUYS? LISTEN UP A SEC.
TMP
TMP
...?

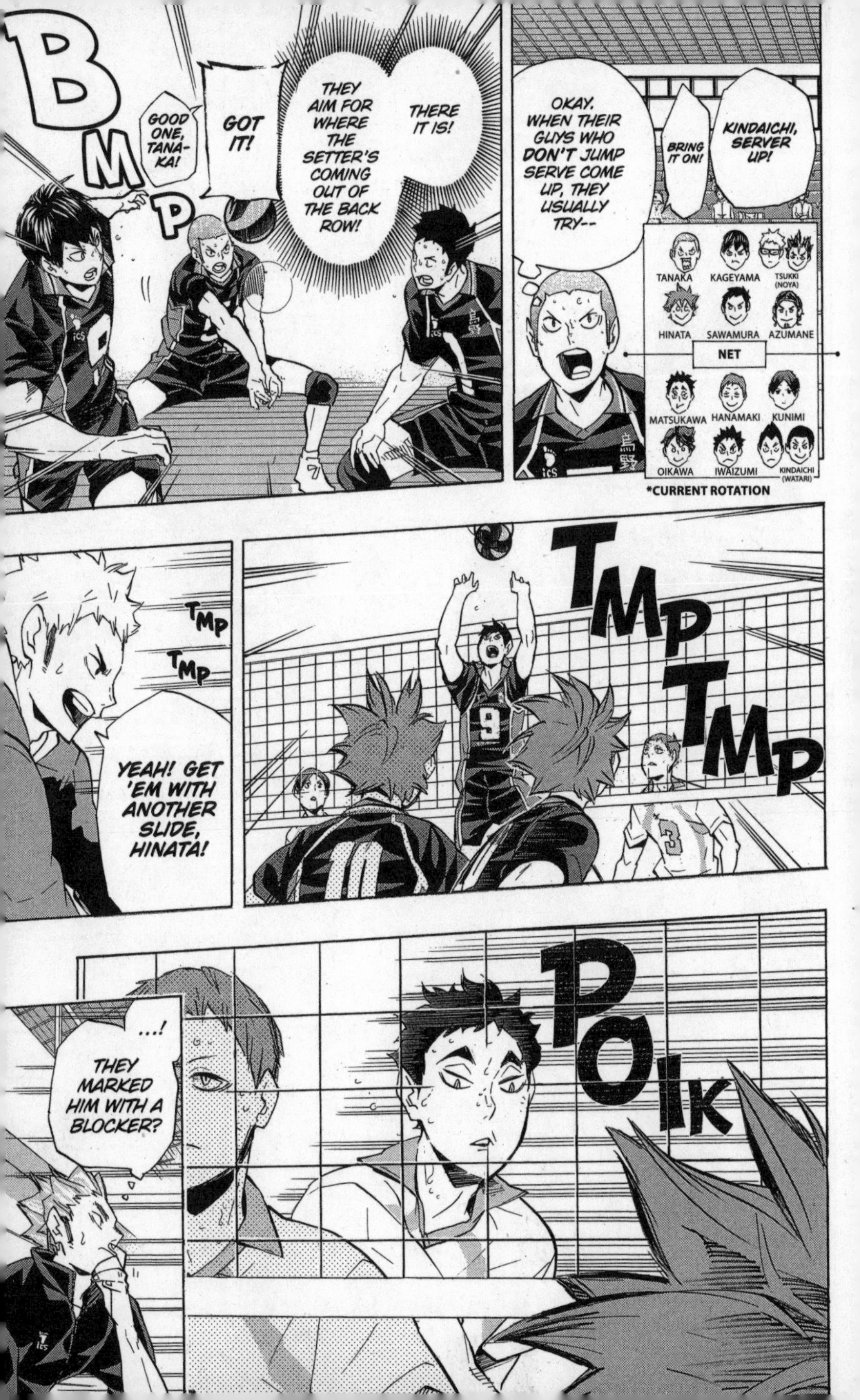

KINDAICHI, SERVER UP!
BRING IT ON!
OKAY. WHEN THEIR GUYS WHO DON'T JUMP SERVE COME UP, THEY USUALLY TRY--
TANAKA
KAGEYAMA
TSUKKI (NOYA)
HINATA
SAWAMURA
AZUMANE
NET
MATSUKAWA
HANAMAKI
KUNIMI
OIKAWA
IWAIZUMI
KINDAICHI (WATARI)
*CURRENT ROTATION
THERE IT IS!
THEY AIM FOR WHERE THE SETTER'S COMING OUT OF THE BACK ROW!
GOT IT!
GOOD ONE, TANAKA!
BMP
TMP TMP
TMP
TMP
YEAH! GET 'EM WITH ANOTHER SLIDE, HINATA!
POIK
...!
THEY MARKED HIM WITH A BLOCKER?

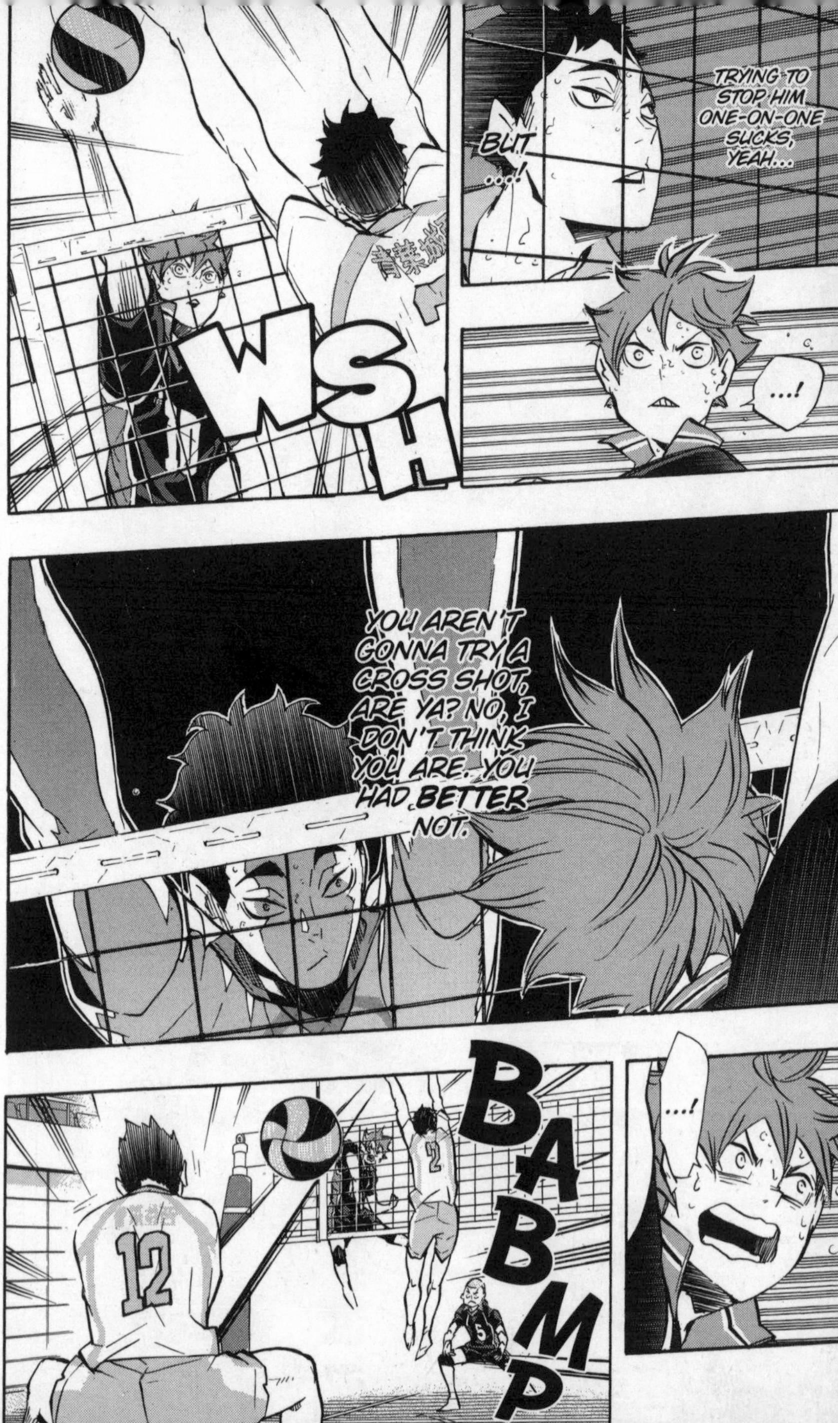
TRYING TO STOP HIM ONE-ON-ONE SUCKS, YEAH...
BUT ...!
...!
WSH
YOU AREN'T GONNA TRY A CROSS SHOT, ARE YA? NO, I DON'T THINK YOU ARE. YOU HAD BETTER NOT.
...!
BABMP

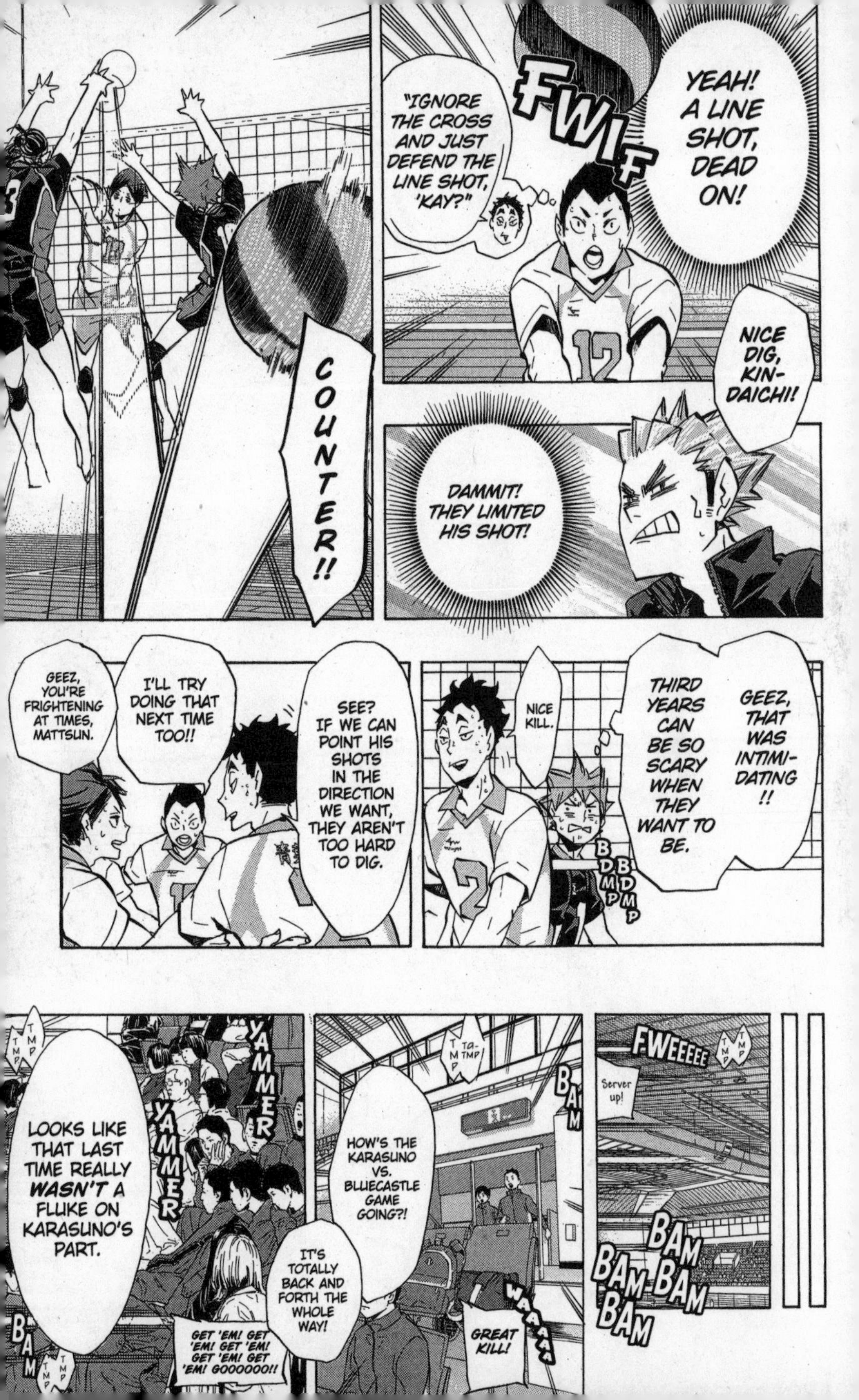
YEAH! A LINE SHOT, DEAD ON!
FWIF
"IGNORE THE CROSS AND JUST DEFEND THE LINE SHOT, 'KAY?"
NICE DIG, KINDAICHI!
DAMMIT! THEY LIMITED HIS SHOT!
COUNTER!!
GEEZ, THAT WAS INTIMIDATING!!
THIRD YEARS CAN BE SO SCARY WHEN THEY WANT TO BE.
NICE KILL.
BDMP BDMP
SEE? IF WE CAN POINT HIS SHOTS IN THE DIRECTION WE WANT, THEY AREN'T TOO HARD TO DIG.
I'LL TRY DOING THAT NEXT TIME TOO!!
GEEZ, YOU'RE FRIGHTENING AT TIMES, MATTSUN.
FWEEEEE
TMP TMP
Server up!
BAM BAM BAM BAM BAM
TMP Ta-TMP
BAM
HOW'S THE KARASUNO VS. BLUECASTLE GAME GOING?!
IT'S TOTALLY BACK AND FORTH THE WHOLE WAY!
WAAAAA
GREAT KILL!
GET 'EM! GET 'EM! GET 'EM! GET 'EM! GET 'EM! GOOOOOO!!
TMP TMP
YAMMER
YAMMER
LOOKS LIKE THAT LAST TIME REALLY *WASN'T* A FLUKE ON KARASUNO'S PART.
BAM
TMP TMP

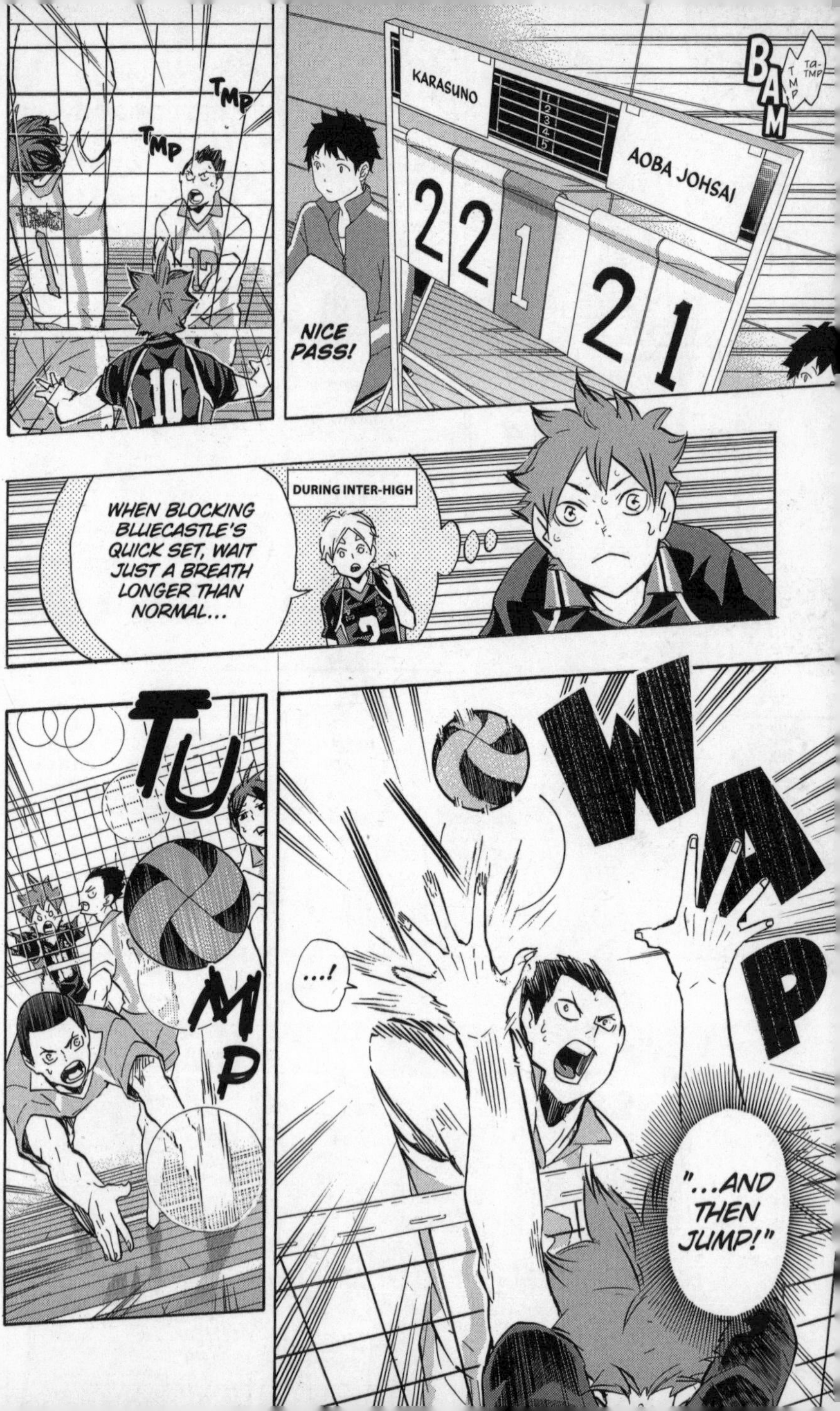
BAM
TA-TMP TMP
KARASUNO
AOBA JOHSAI
22
1
21
NICE PASS!
TMP
TMP
DURING INTER-HIGH
WHEN BLOCKING BLUECASTLE'S QUICK SET, WAIT JUST A BREATH LONGER THAN NORMAL...
WAP
...!
"...AND THEN JUMP!"
TUMP

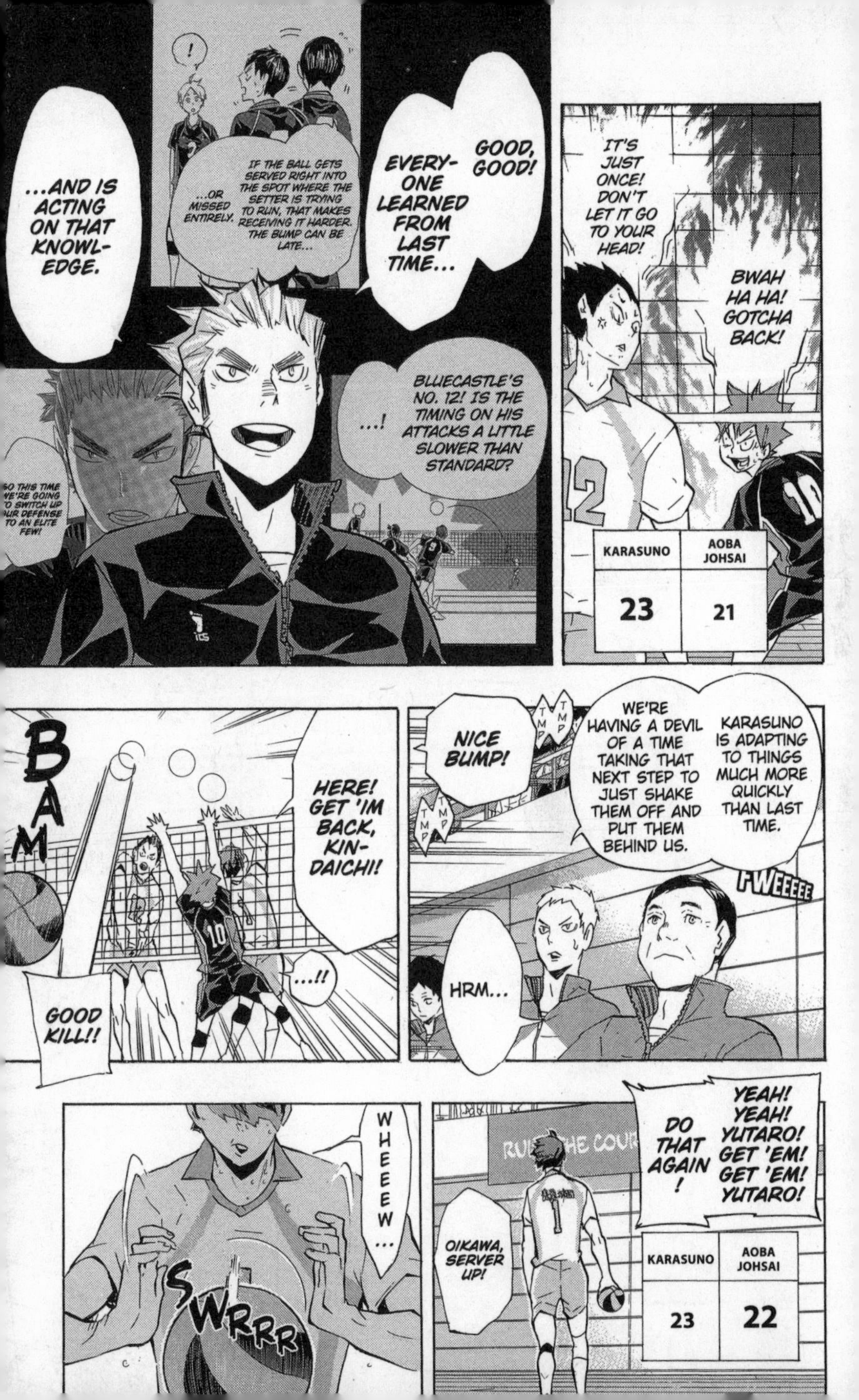
IT'S JUST ONCE! DON'T LET IT GO TO YOUR HEAD!
BWAH HA HA! GOTCHA BACK!
KARASUNO
AOBA JOHSAI
23
21
GOOD, GOOD!
EVERY-ONE LEARNED FROM LAST TIME...
...AND IS ACTING ON THAT KNOWL-EDGE.
!
IF THE BALL GETS SERVED RIGHT INTO THE SPOT WHERE THE SETTER IS TRYING TO RUN, THAT MAKES RECEIVING IT HARDER. THE BUMP CAN BE LATE...
...OR MISSED ENTIRELY.
BLUECASTLE'S NO. 12! IS THE TIMING ON HIS ATTACKS A LITTLE SLOWER THAN STANDARD?
...!
SO THIS TIME WE'RE GOING TO SWITCH UP UR DEFENSE TO AN ELITE FEW!
KARASUNO IS ADAPTING TO THINGS MUCH MORE QUICKLY THAN LAST TIME.
WE'RE HAVING A DEVIL OF A TIME TAKING THAT NEXT STEP TO JUST SHAKE THEM OFF AND PUT THEM BEHIND US.
TMP TMP
NICE BUMP!
TMP TMP
FWEEEEE
HRM...
HERE! GET 'IM BACK, KIN-DAICHI!
BAM
...!!
GOOD KILL!!
YEAH! YEAH! YUTARO! GET 'EM! GET 'EM! YUTARO!
DO THAT AGAIN!
OIKAWA, SERVER UP!
KARASUNO
AOBA JOHSAI
23
22
WHEEEEW...
SWRRR

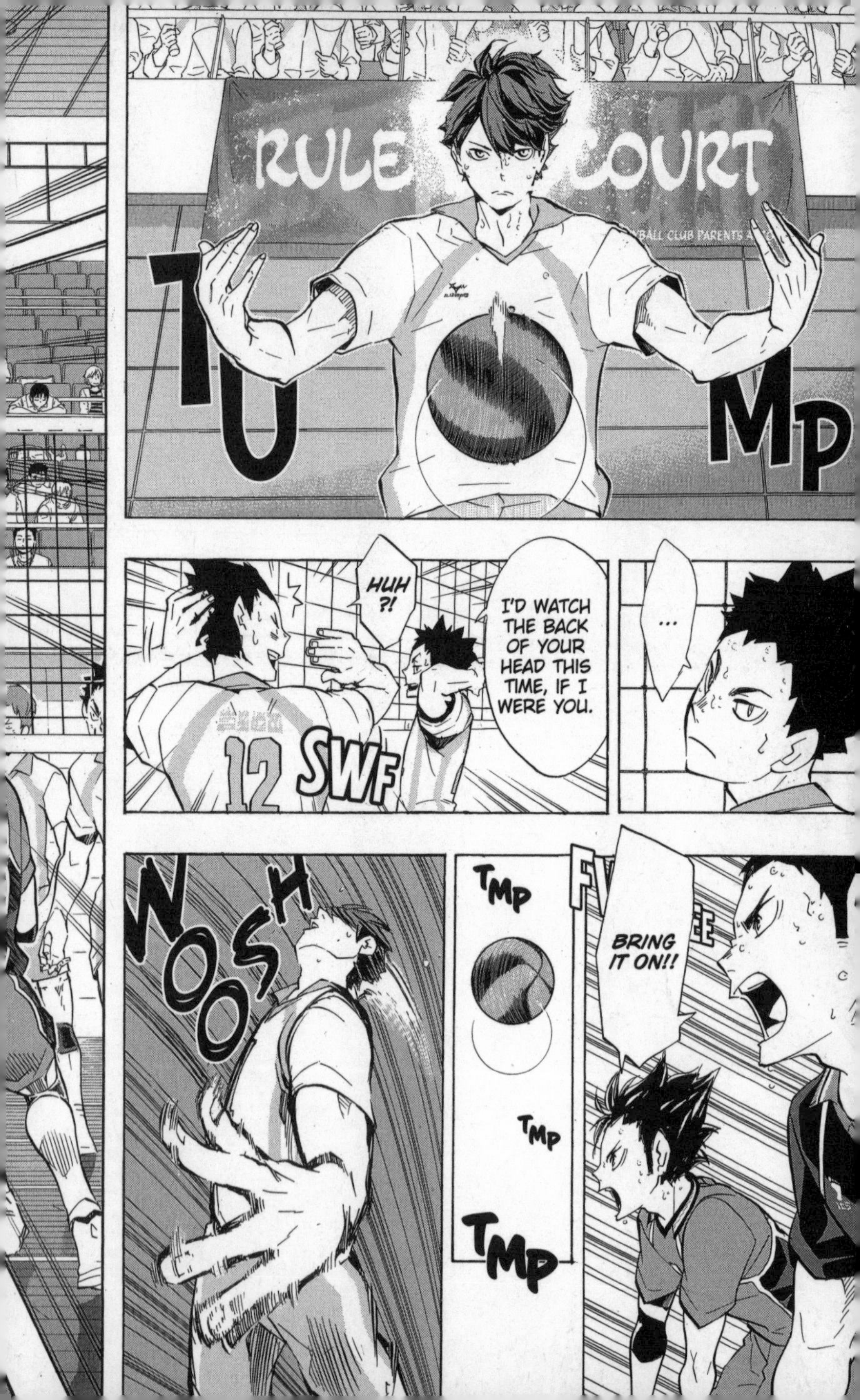
RULE COURT
TUMP
...
I'D WATCH THE BACK OF YOUR HEAD THIS TIME, IF I WERE YOU.
HUH?!
SWF
BRING IT ON!!
TMP
TMP
TMP
WOOSH

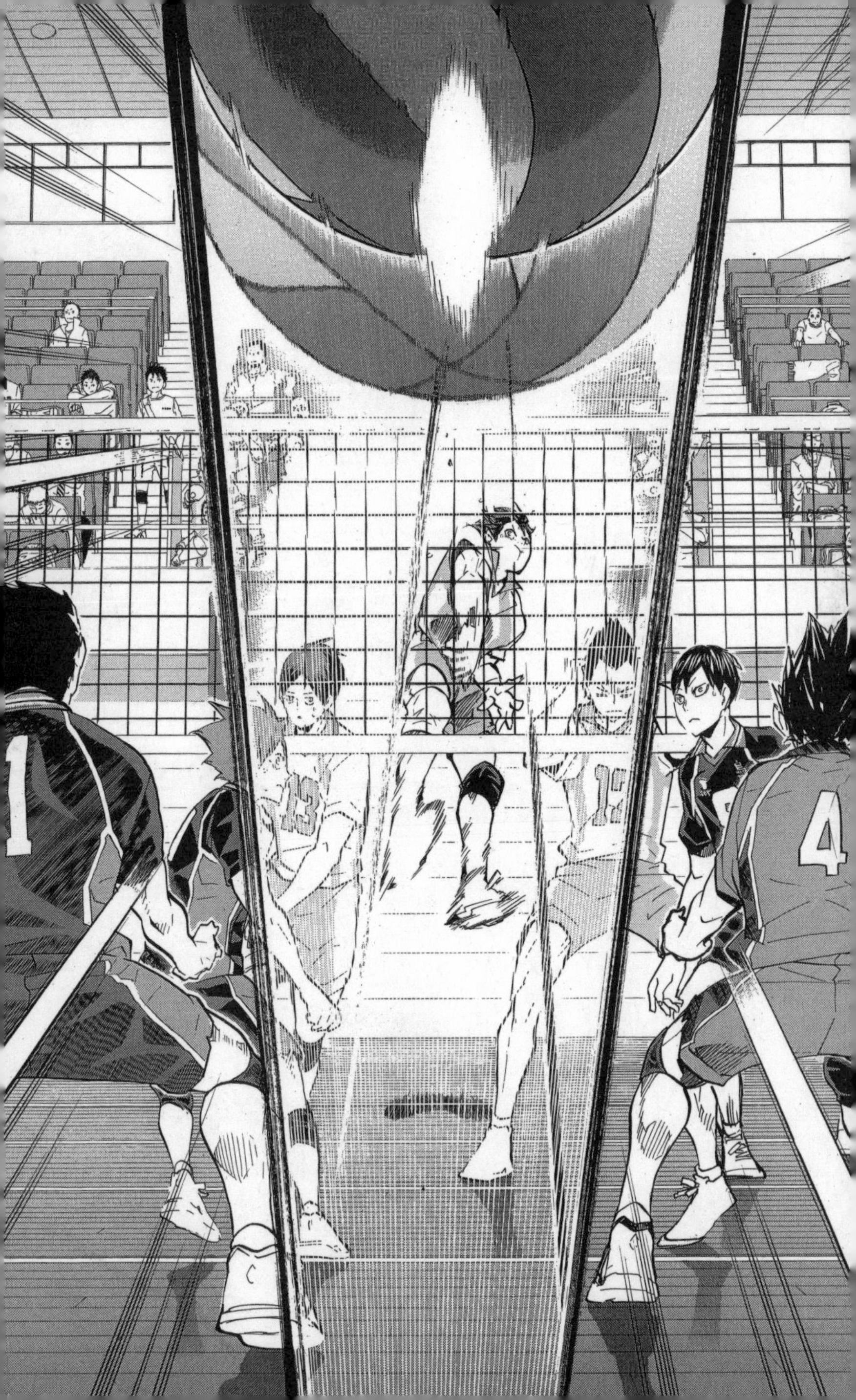

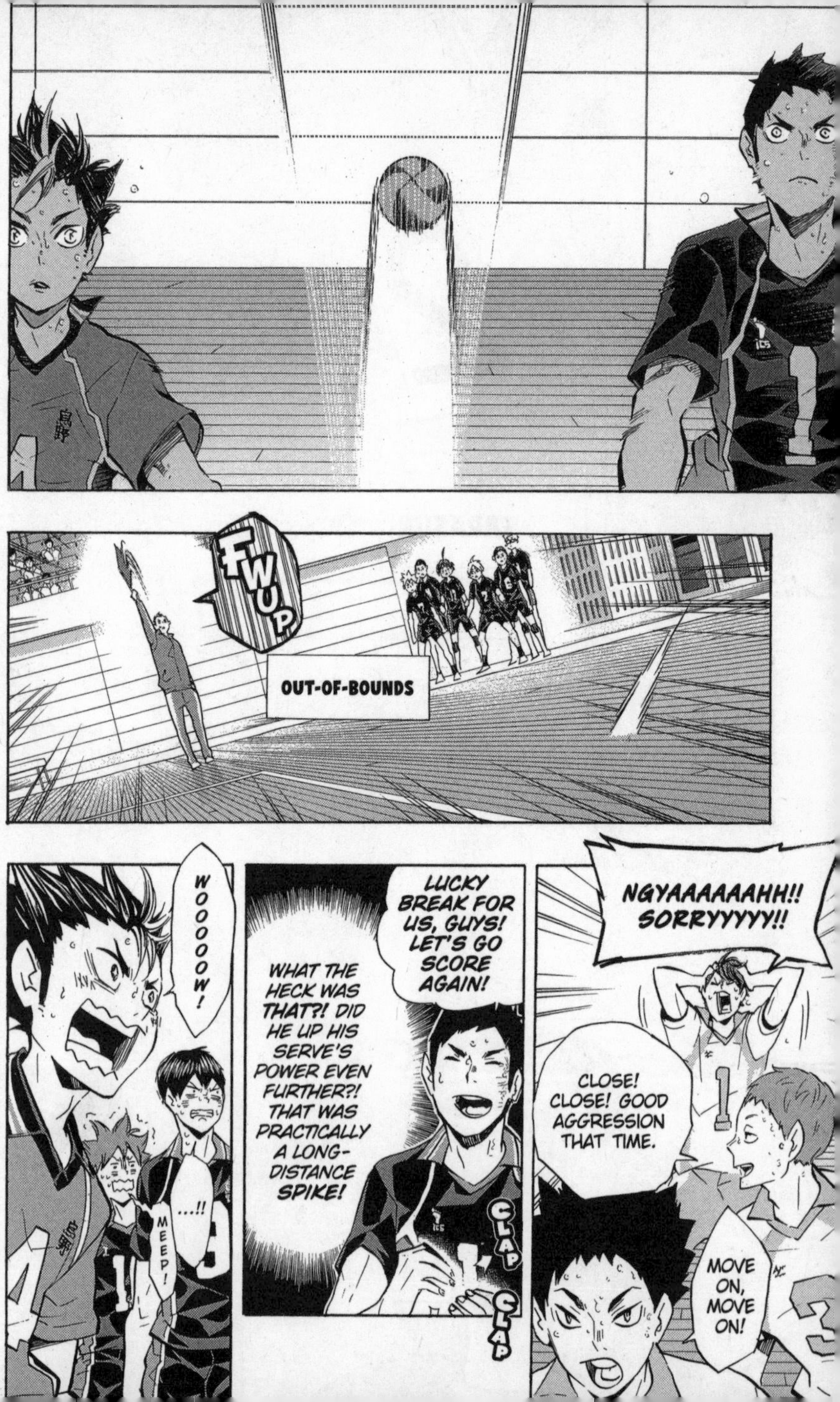
FWUP
OUT-OF-BOUNDS
NGYAAAAAAHH!! SORRYYYYY!!
CLOSE! CLOSE! GOOD AGGRESSION THAT TIME.
MOVE ON, MOVE ON!
LUCKY BREAK FOR US, GUYS! LET'S GO SCORE AGAIN!
WHAT THE HECK WAS THAT?! DID HE UP HIS SERVE'S POWER EVEN FURTHER?! THAT WAS PRACTICALLY A LONG-DISTANCE SPIKE!
CLAP
CLAP
WOOOOOOW!
...!!
MEEP!

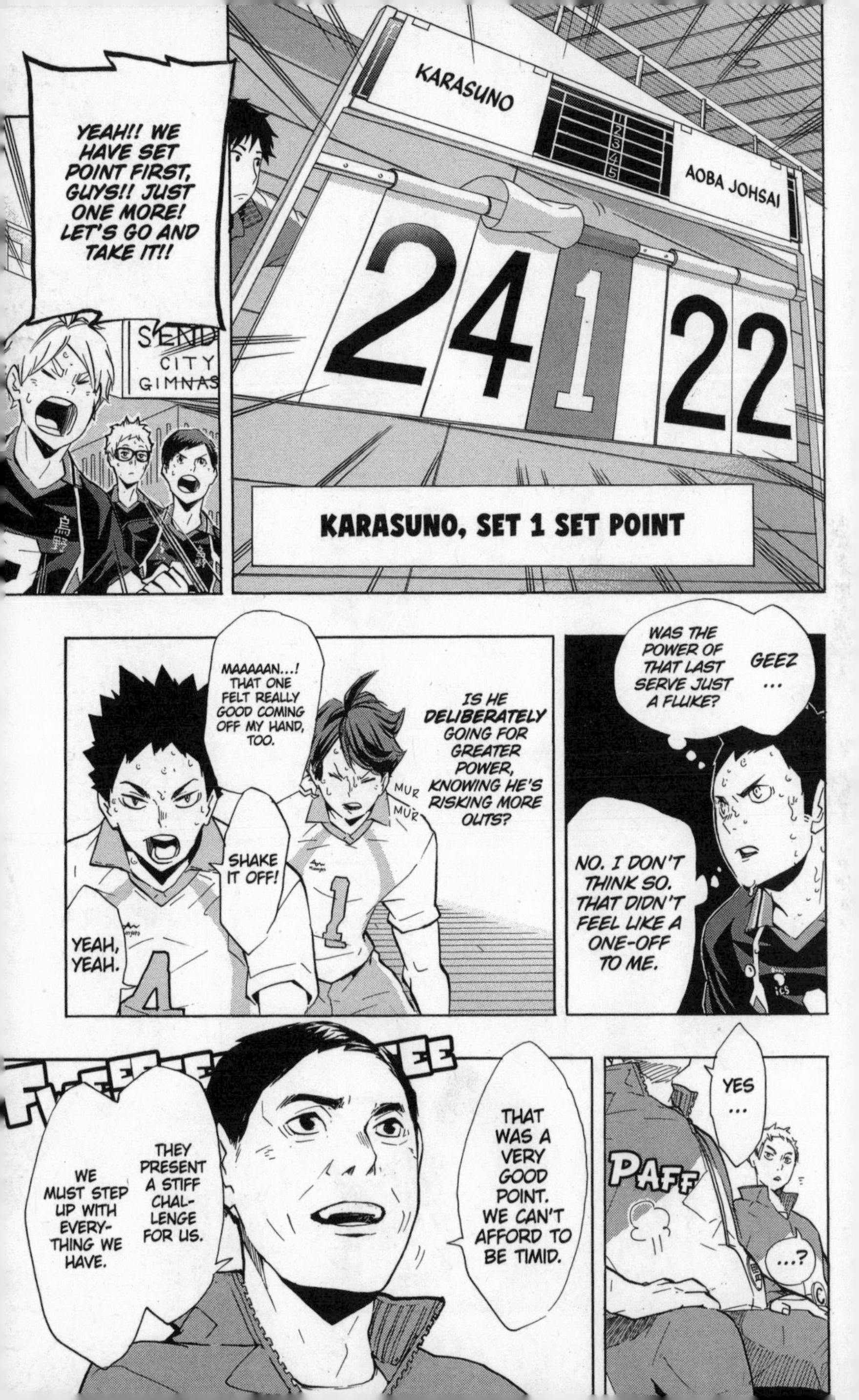
KARASUNO
AOBA JOHSAI
24 1 22
KARASUNO, SET 1 SET POINT
YEAH!! WE HAVE SET POINT FIRST, GUYS!! JUST ONE MORE! LET'S GO AND TAKE IT!!
GEEZ ...
WAS THE POWER OF THAT LAST SERVE JUST A FLUKE?
NO. I DON'T THINK SO. THAT DIDN'T FEEL LIKE A ONE-OFF TO ME.
MAAAAAN...! THAT ONE FELT REALLY GOOD COMING OFF MY HAND, TOO.
IS HE DELIBERATELY GOING FOR GREATER POWER, KNOWING HE'S RISKING MORE OUTS?
MUR MUR
SHAKE IT OFF!
YEAH, YEAH.
YES ...
PAFF
...?
THAT WAS A VERY GOOD POINT. WE CAN'T AFFORD TO BE TIMID.
THEY PRESENT A STIFF CHAL-LENGE FOR US.
WE MUST STEP UP WITH EVERY-THING WE HAVE.

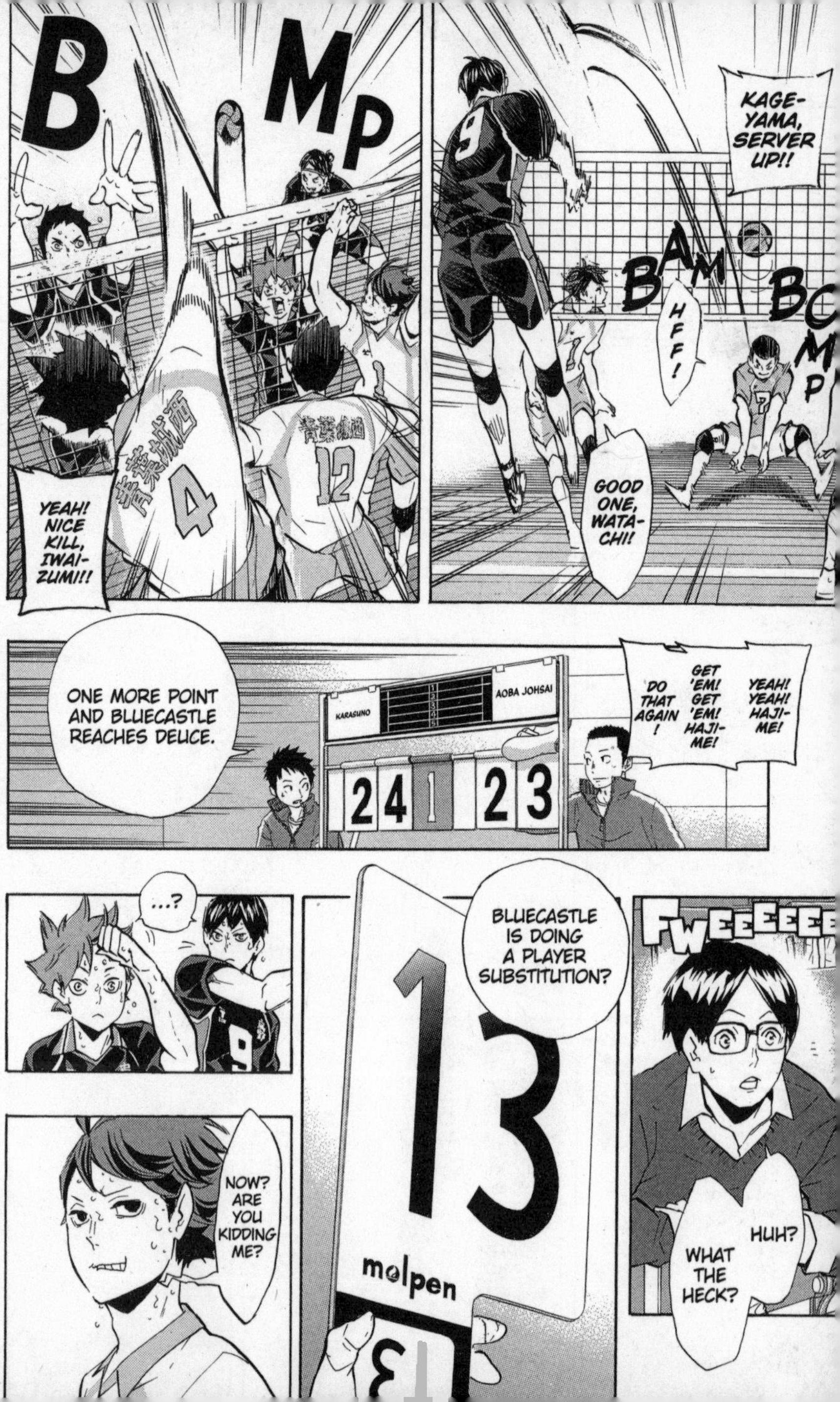
KAGE-YAMA, SERVER UP!!
BAM
HFF!
BOMP
GOOD ONE, WATA-CHI!
BMP
YEAH! NICE KILL, IWAI-ZUMI!!
YEAH! YEAH! HAJI-ME!
GET 'EM! GET 'EM! HAJI-ME!
DO THAT AGAIN!
AOBA JOHSAI
KARASUNO
24 1 23
ONE MORE POINT AND BLUECASTLE REACHES DEUCE.
FWEEEEEE
BLUECASTLE IS DOING A PLAYER SUBSTITUTION?
13
molpen
...?
HUH?
WHAT THE HECK?
NOW? ARE YOU KIDDING ME?

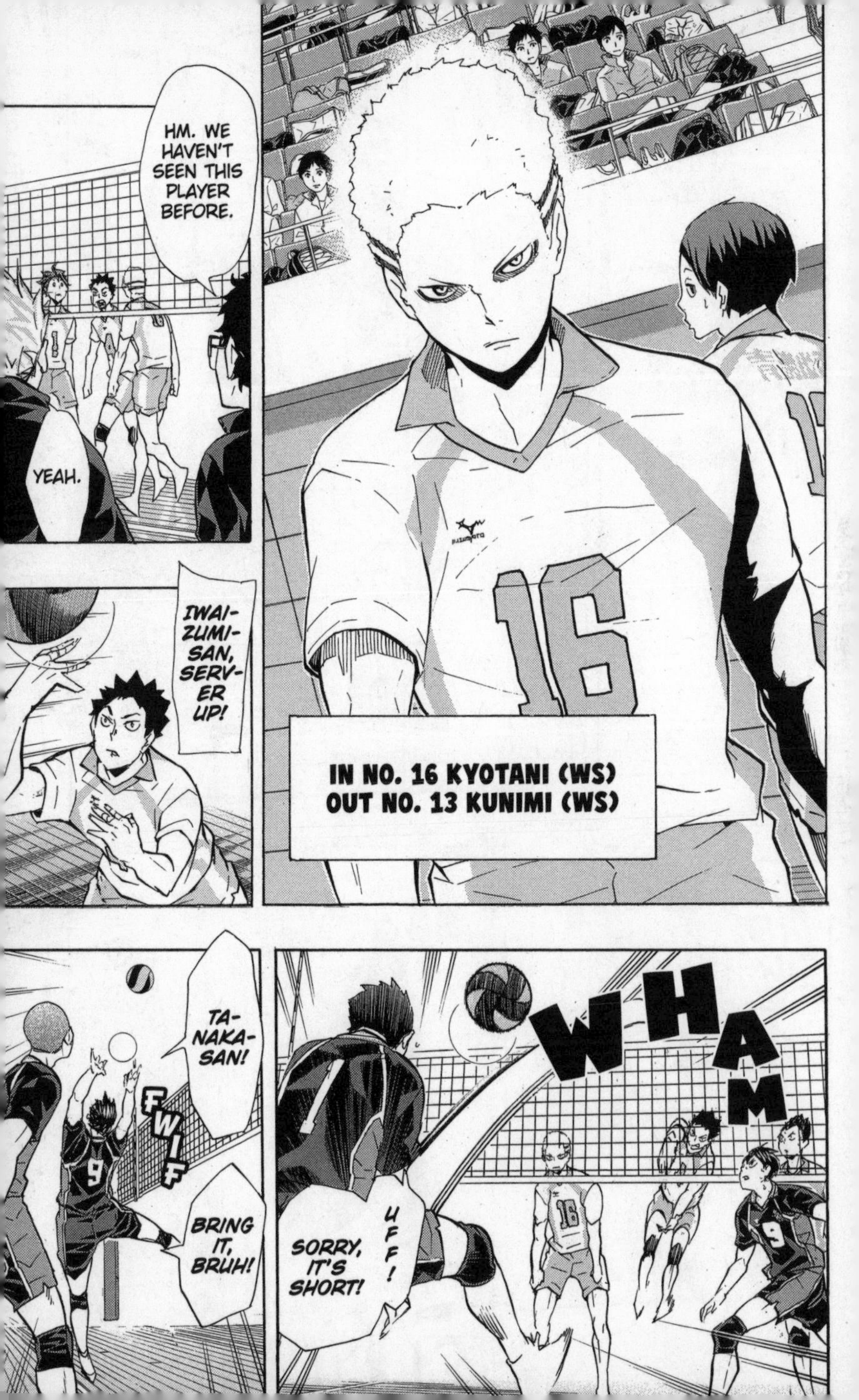

IN NO. 16 KYOTANI (WS)
OUT NO. 13 KUNIMI (WS)
HM. WE HAVEN'T SEEN THIS PLAYER BEFORE.
YEAH.
IWAIZUMI-SAN, SERVER UP!
WHAM
SORRY, IT'S SHORT!
UFF!
TANAKA-SAN!
FWIF
BRING IT, BRUH!

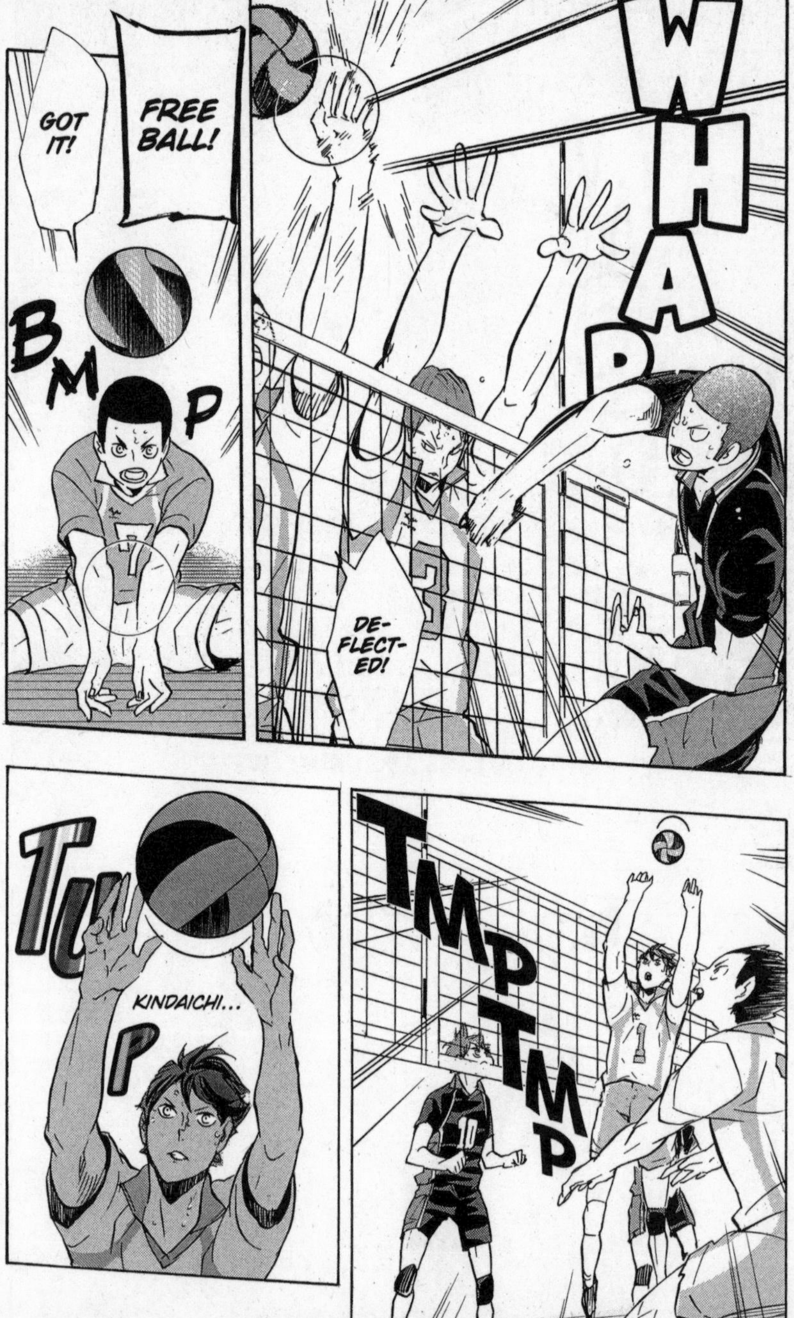
WHAP
DE-FLECT-ED!
FREE BALL!
GOT IT!
BMP
TMP TMP
TUP
KINDAICHI...

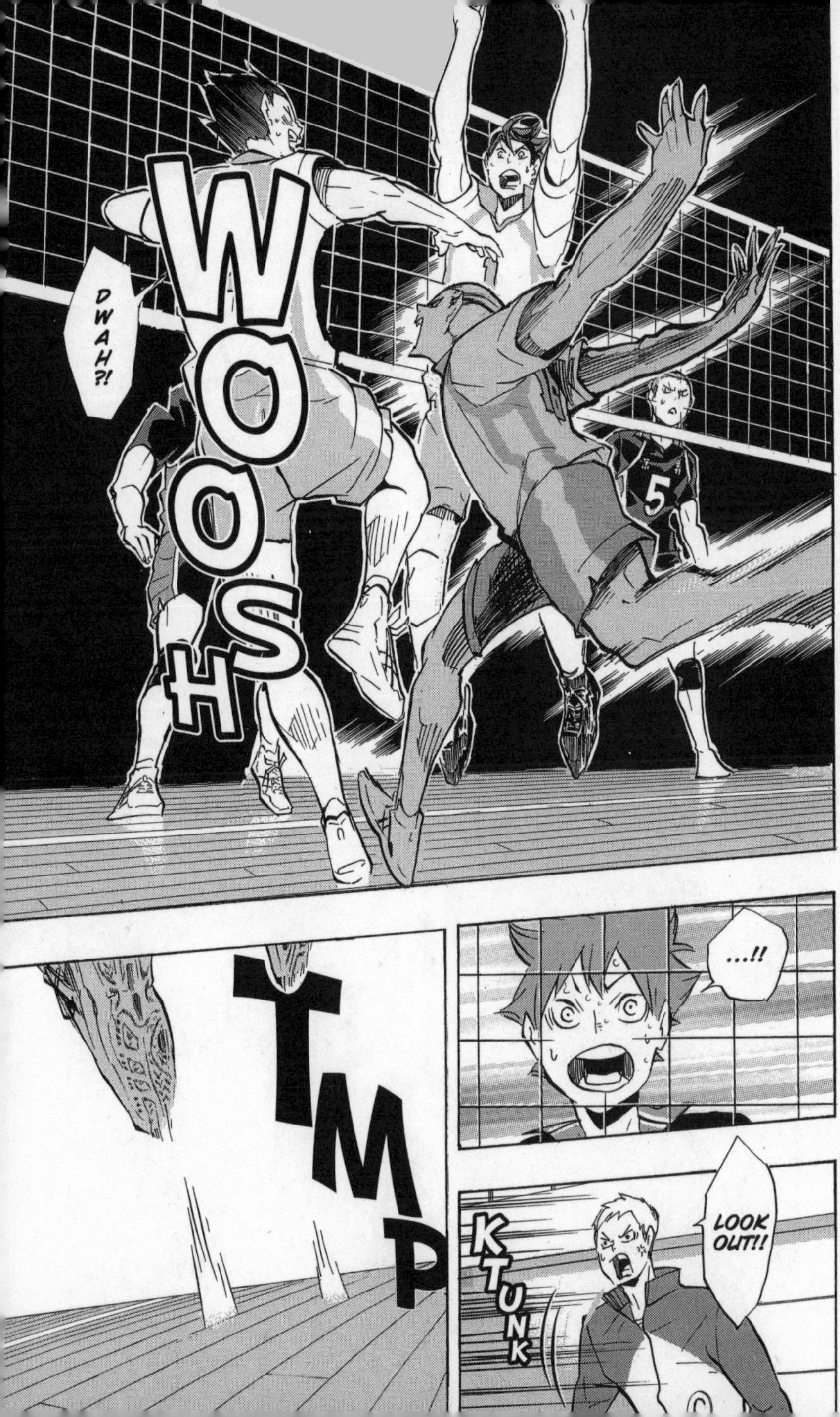
WOOOSH
DWAH?!
...!!
LOOK OUT!!
KTUNK
TMP

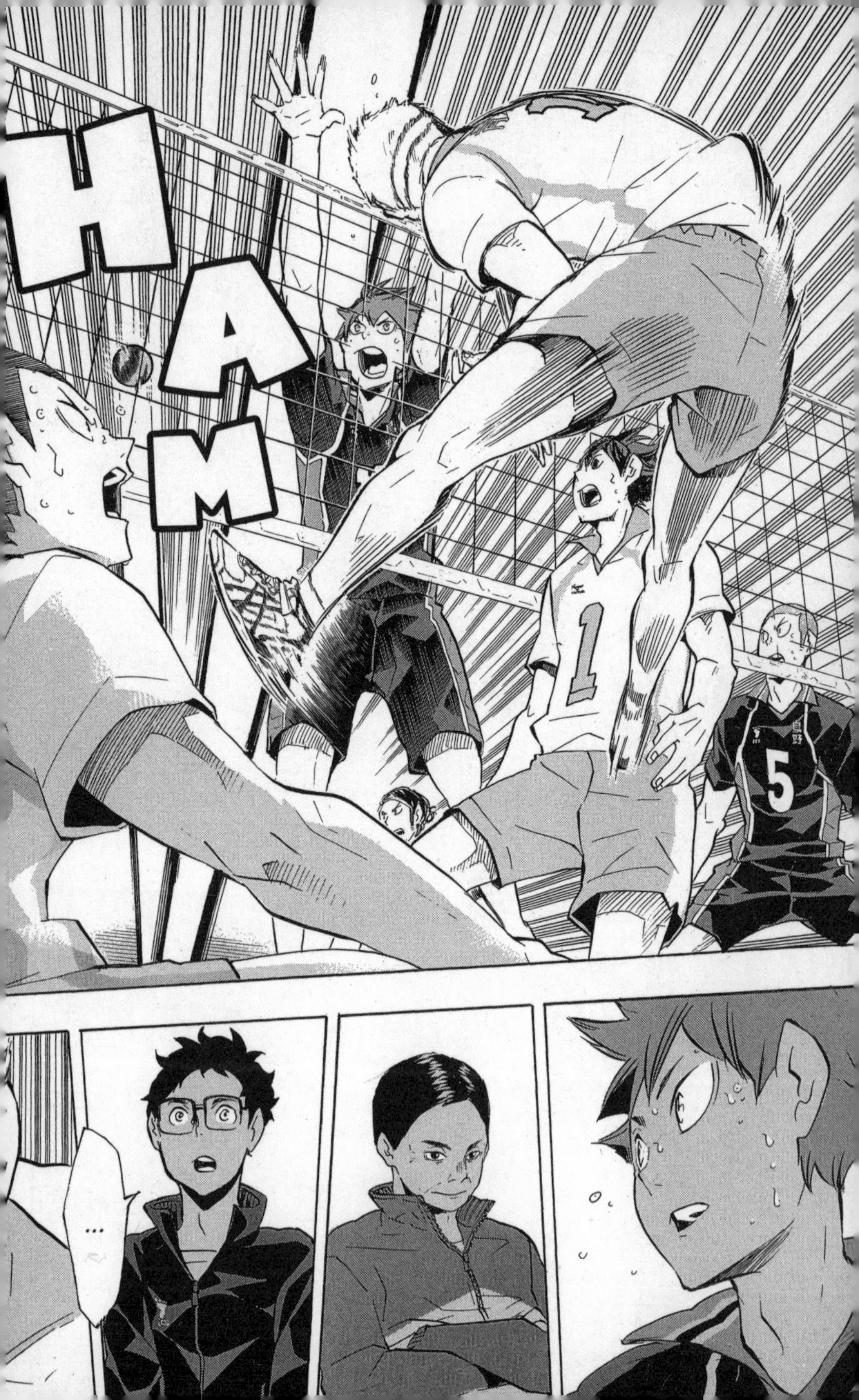

WHAM
...

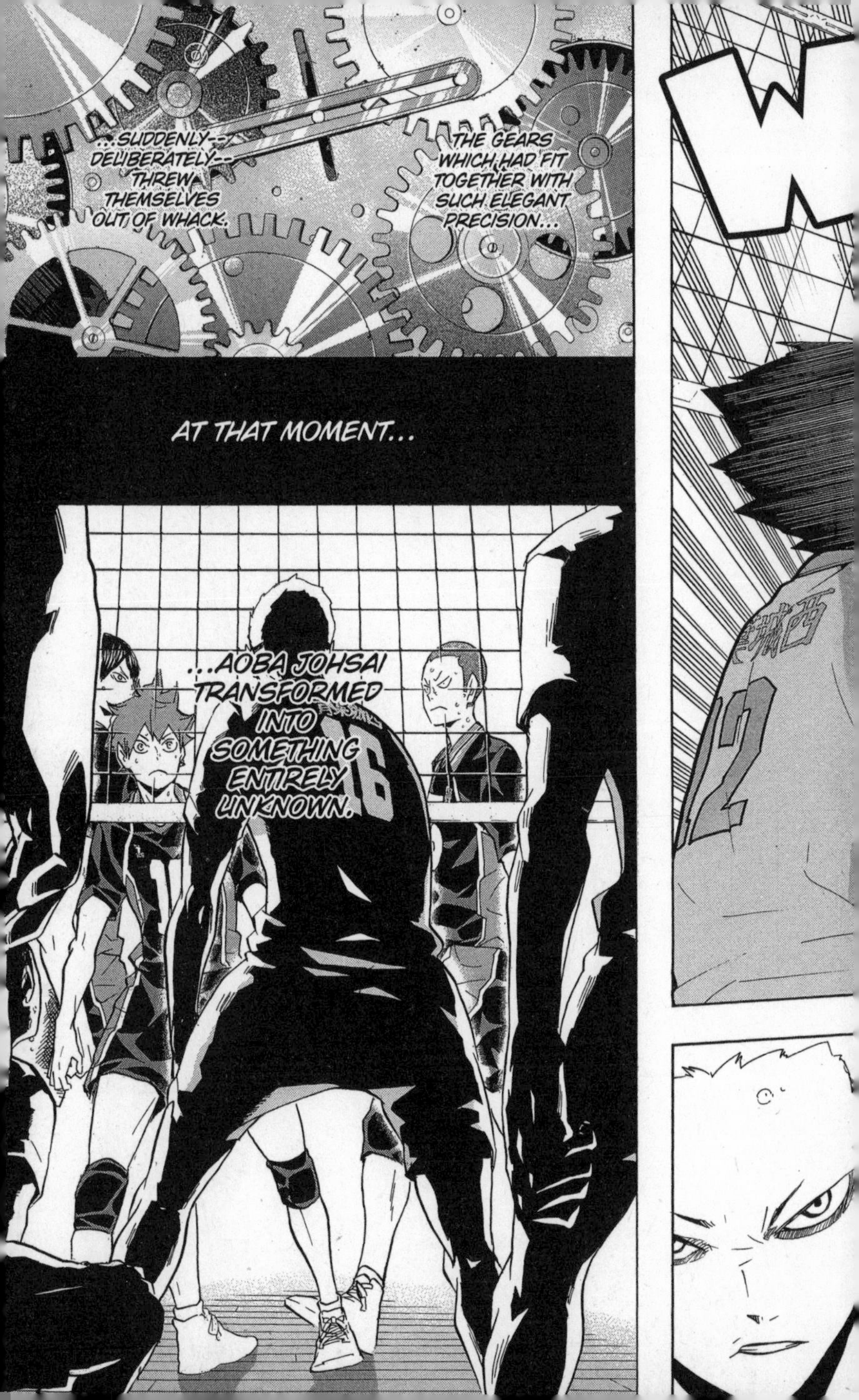
W
THE GEARS WHICH HAD FIT TOGETHER WITH SUCH ELEGANT PRECISION...
...SUDDENLY-- DELIBERATELY-- THREW THEMSELVES OUT OF WHACK.
AT THAT MOMENT...
...AOBA JOHSAI TRANSFORMED INTO SOMETHING ENTIRELY UNKNOWN.

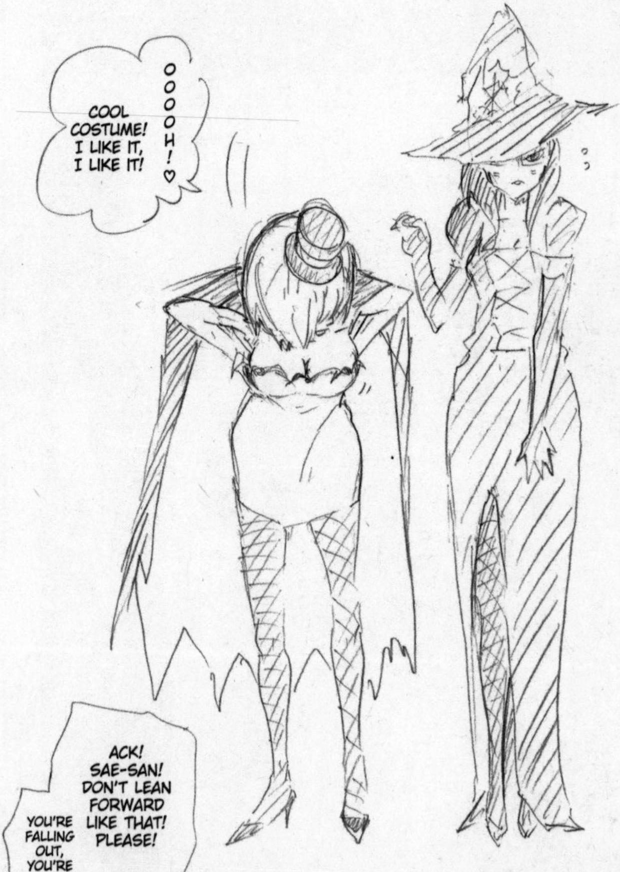
OOOOH!♡
COOL COSTUME! I LIKE IT, I LIKE IT!
ACK! SAE-SAN! DON'T LEAN FORWARD LIKE THAT! PLEASE!
YOU'RE FALLING OUT, YOU'RE FALLING OUT!

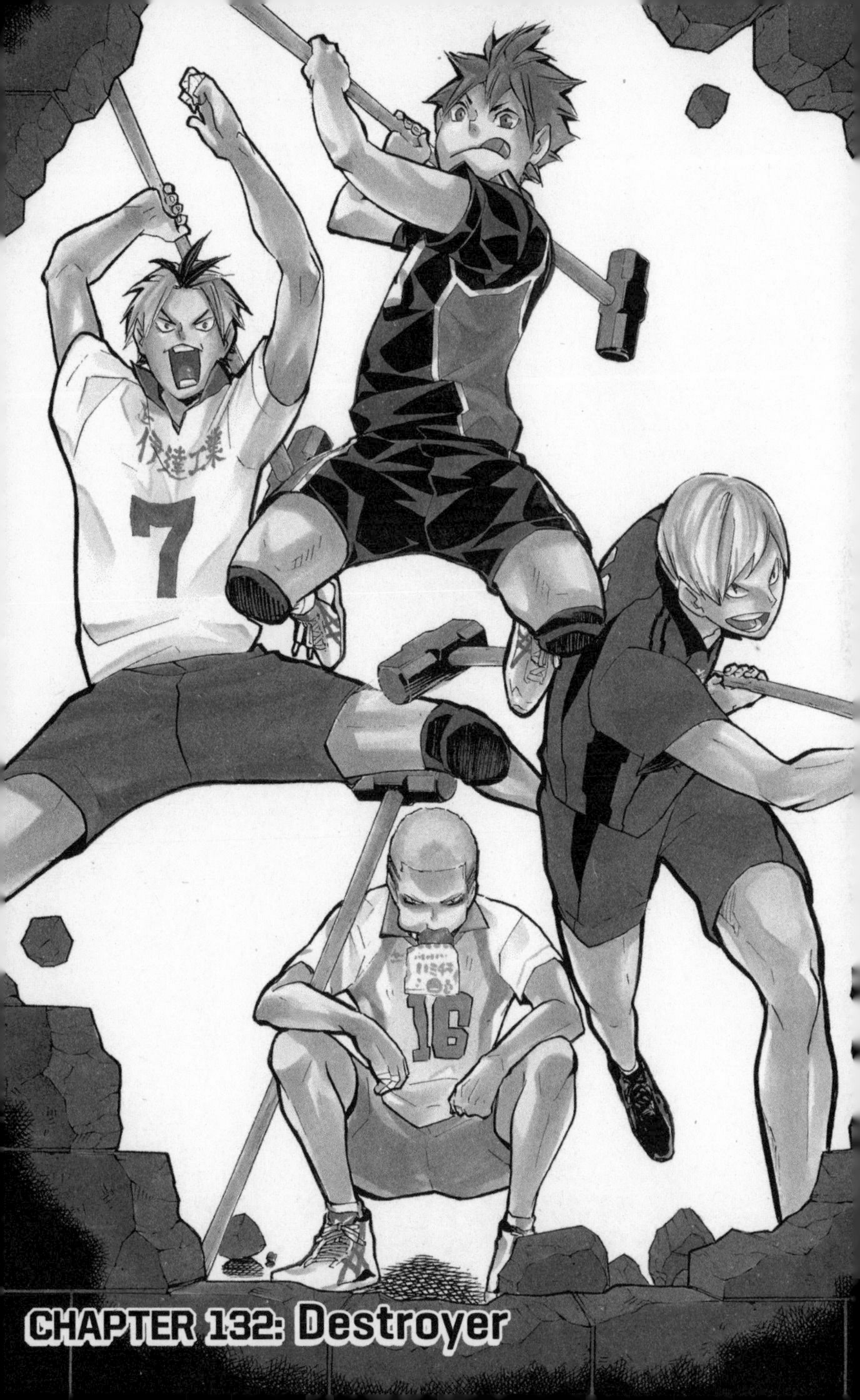
伊達工業
7
16

CHAPTER 132: Destroyer

HAIKYU!!

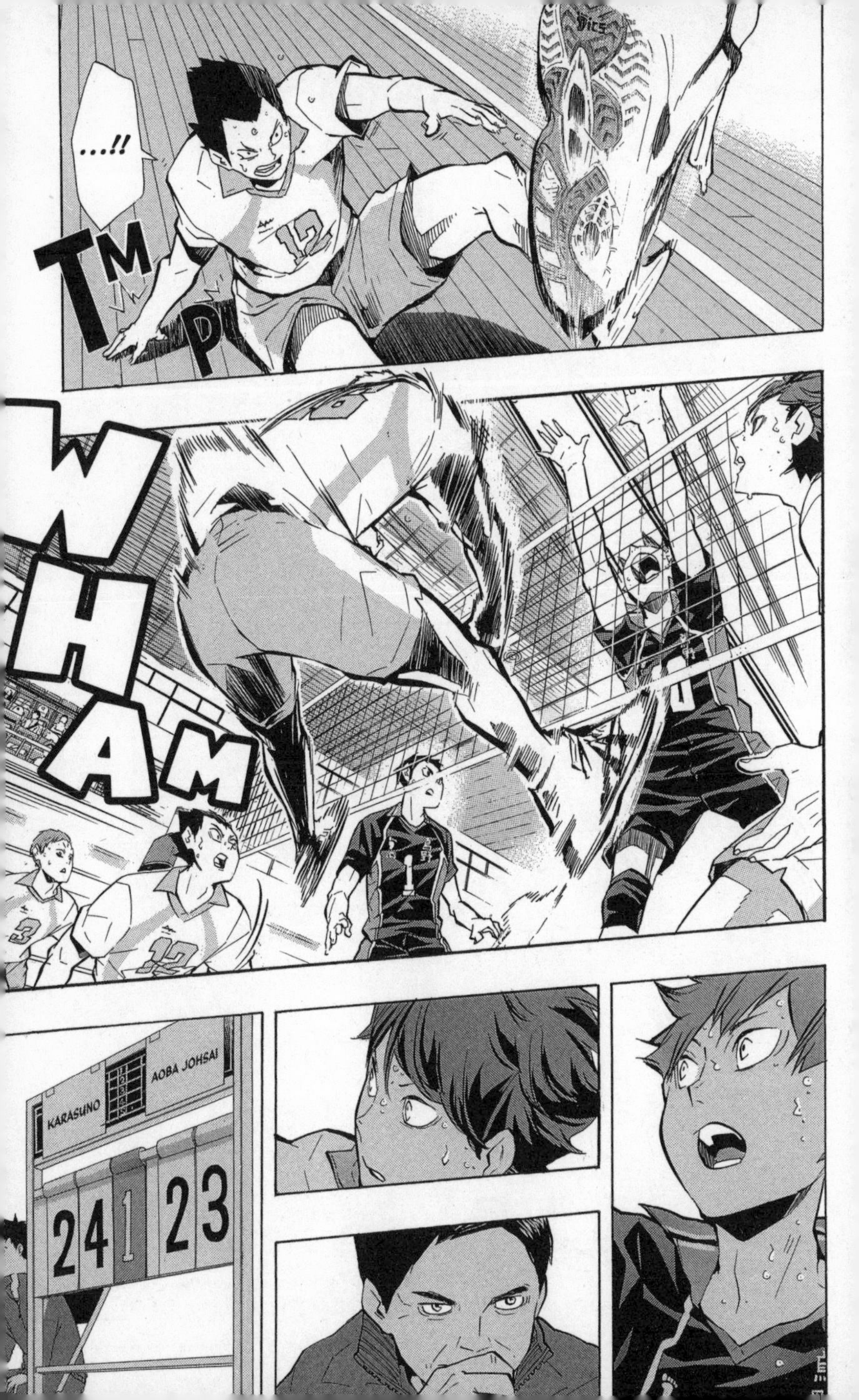
...!!
TMP
WHAM
AOBA JOHSAI
KARASUNO
24
1
23

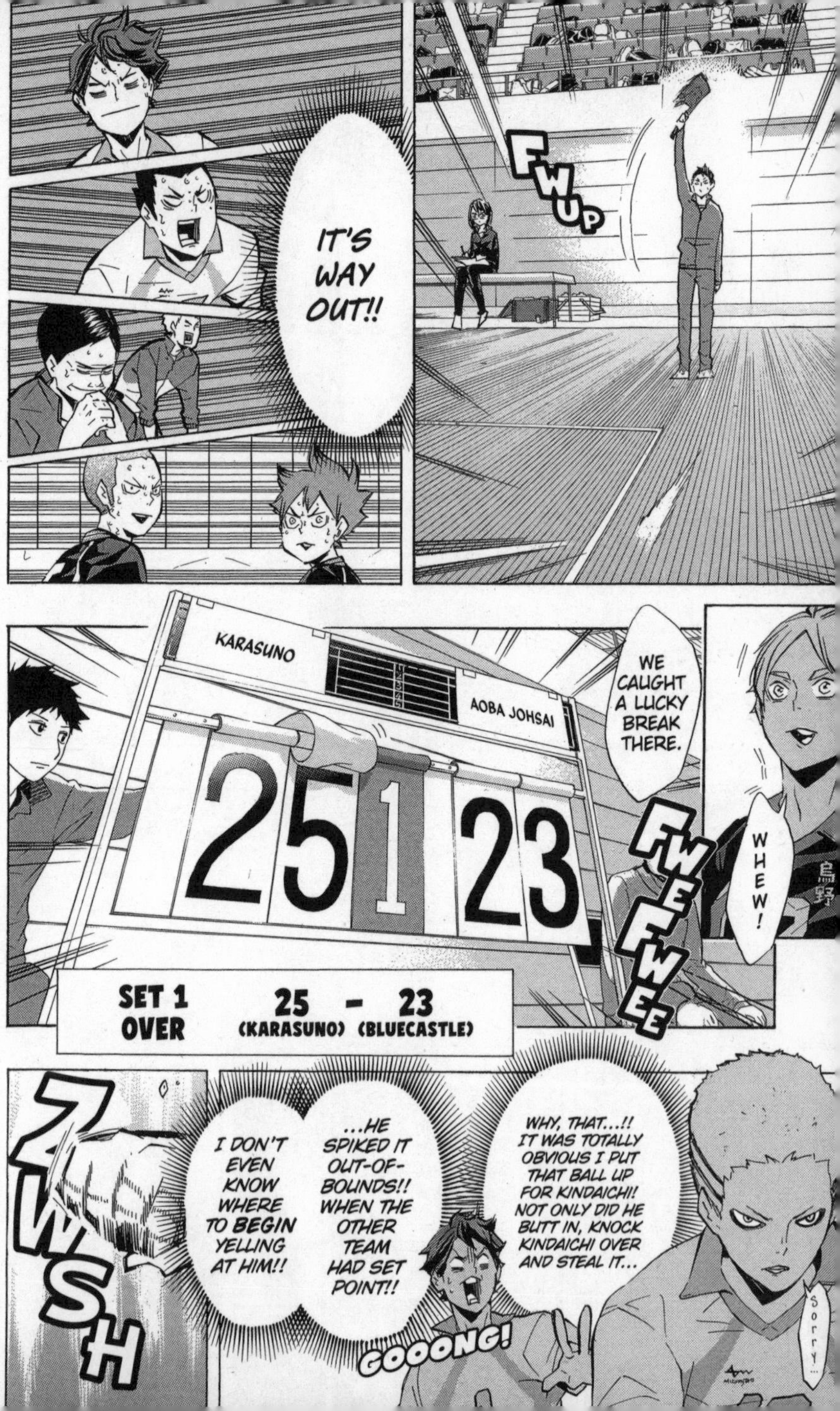
FWUP
IT'S WAY OUT!!
WE CAUGHT A LUCKY BREAK THERE.
WHEW!
KARASUNO
AOBA JOHSAI
25 1 23
FWEEFWEE
SET 1 OVER 25 - 23 (KARASUNO) (BLUECASTLE)
WHY, THAT...!! IT WAS TOTALLY OBVIOUS I PUT THAT BALL UP FOR KINDAICHI! NOT ONLY DID HE BUTT IN, KNOCK KINDAICHI OVER AND STEAL IT...
Sorry...
...HE SPIKED IT OUT-OF-BOUNDS!! WHEN THE OTHER TEAM HAD SET POINT!!
I DON'T EVEN KNOW WHERE TO BEGIN YELLING AT HIM!!
GOOONG!
ZWSH

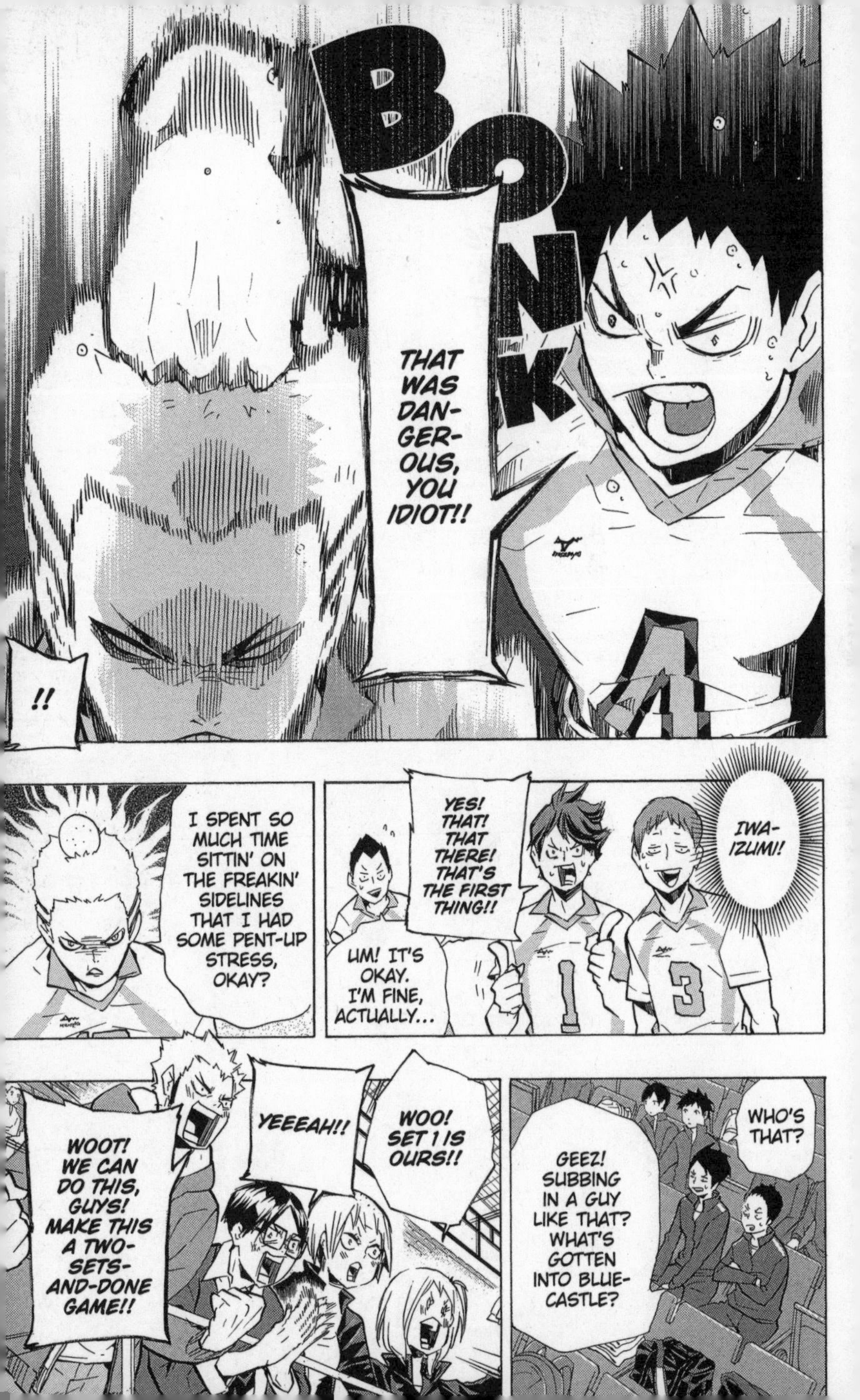
BONK
THAT WAS DANGEROUS, YOU IDIOT!!
!!
IWAIZUMI!
YES! THAT! THAT THERE! THAT'S THE FIRST THING!!
UM! IT'S OKAY. I'M FINE, ACTUALLY...
I SPENT SO MUCH TIME SITTIN' ON THE FREAKIN' SIDELINES THAT I HAD SOME PENT-UP STRESS, OKAY?
WHO'S THAT?
GEEZ! SUBBING IN A GUY LIKE THAT? WHAT'S GOTTEN INTO BLUE-CASTLE?
WOO! SET 1 IS OURS!!
YEEEAH!!
WOOT! WE CAN DO THIS, GUYS! MAKE THIS A TWO-SETS-AND-DONE GAME!!

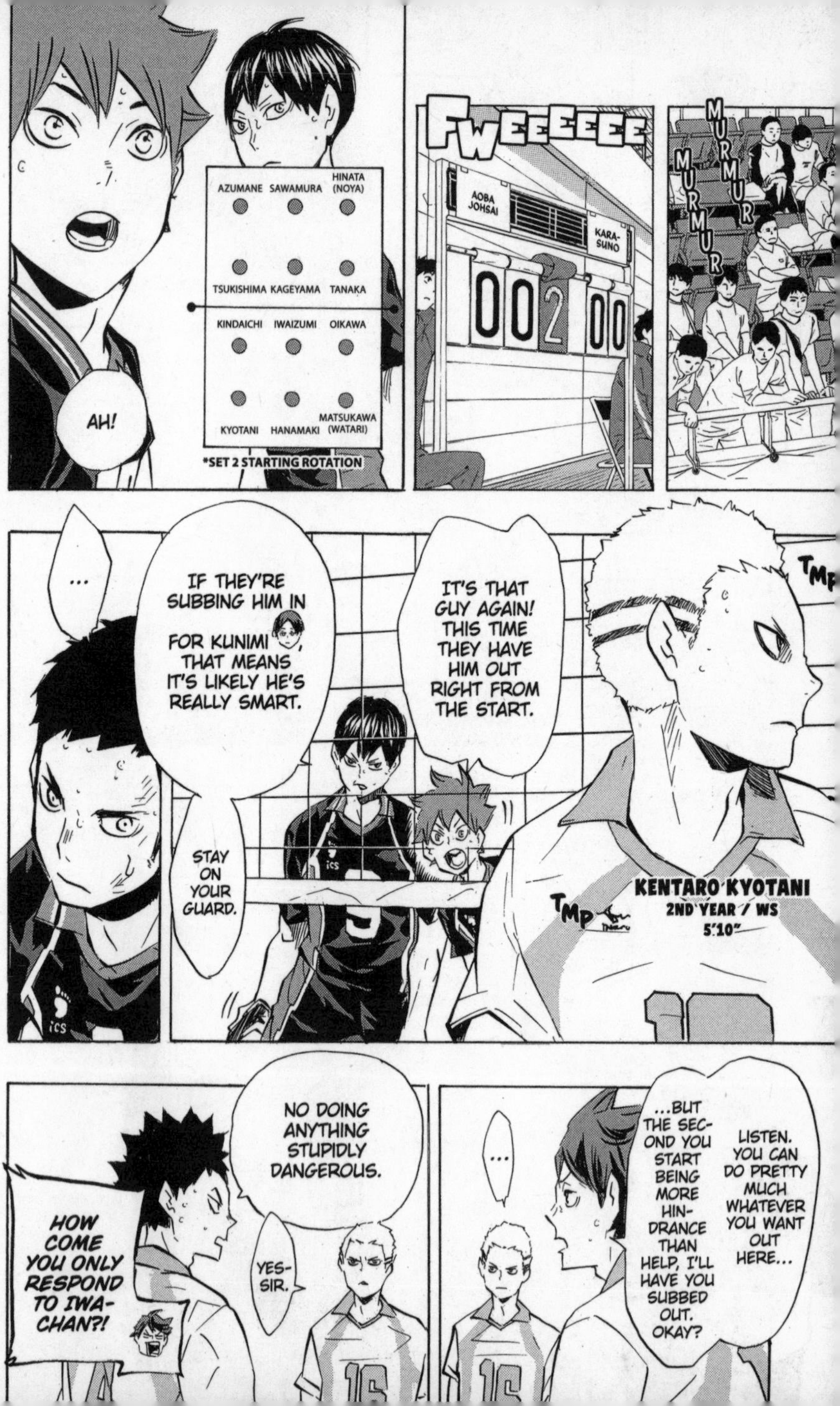
MURMUR
MURMUR
MURMUR
FWEEEEEE
AOBA JOHSAI
KARA-SUNO
00 2 00
HINATA (NOYA)
SAWAMURA
AZUMANE
TANAKA
KAGEYAMA
TSUKISHIMA
OIKAWA
IWAIZUMI
KINDAICHI
MATSUKAWA (WATARI)
HANAMAKI
KYOTANI
*SET 2 STARTING ROTATION
AH!
TMP
KENTARO KYOTANI
2ND YEAR / WS
5'10"
TMP
IT'S THAT GUY AGAIN! THIS TIME THEY HAVE HIM OUT RIGHT FROM THE START.
IF THEY'RE SUBBING HIM IN FOR KUNIMI, THAT MEANS IT'S LIKELY HE'S REALLY SMART.
STAY ON YOUR GUARD.
...
LISTEN. YOU CAN DO PRETTY MUCH WHATEVER YOU WANT OUT HERE...
...BUT THE SECOND YOU START BEING MORE HINDRANCE THAN HELP, I'LL HAVE YOU SUBBED OUT. OKAY?
...
NO DOING ANYTHING STUPIDLY DANGEROUS.
YES-SIR.
HOW COME YOU ONLY RESPOND TO IWA-CHAN?!

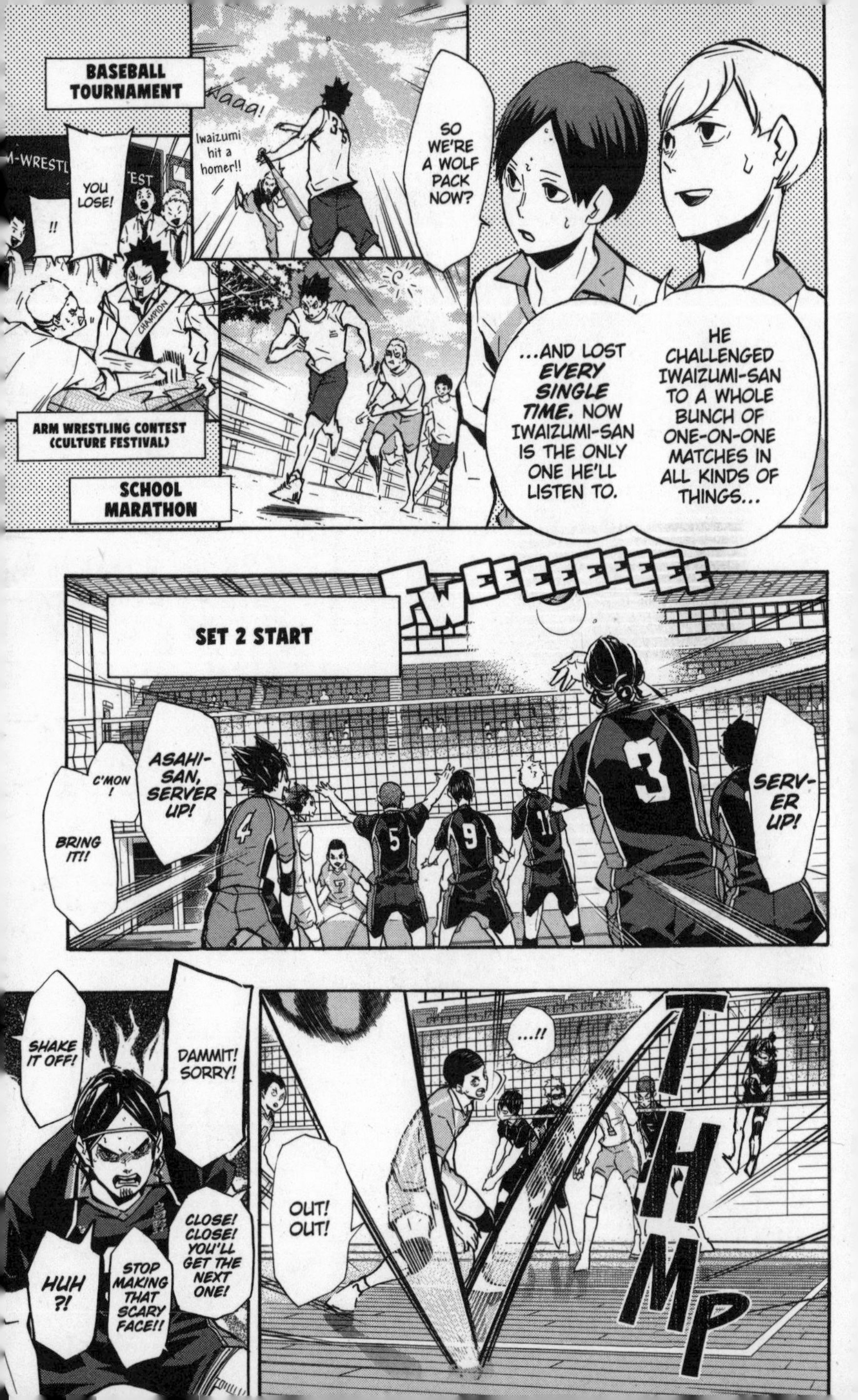
SO WE'RE A WOLF PACK NOW?
HE CHALLENGED IWAIZUMI-SAN TO A WHOLE BUNCH OF ONE-ON-ONE MATCHES IN ALL KINDS OF THINGS...
...AND LOST EVERY SINGLE TIME. NOW IWAIZUMI-SAN IS THE ONLY ONE HE'LL LISTEN TO.
BASEBALL TOURNAMENT
Kaaaa!
Iwaizumi hit a homer!!
YOU LOSE!
!!
ARM WRESTLING CONTEST (CULTURE FESTIVAL)
SCHOOL MARATHON
TWEEEEEEEEE
SET 2 START
SERV-ER UP!
ASAHI-SAN, SERVER UP!
C'MON!
BRING IT!!
...!!
THMP
OUT! OUT!
DAMMIT! SORRY!
SHAKE IT OFF!
CLOSE! CLOSE! YOU'LL GET THE NEXT ONE!
STOP MAKING THAT SCARY FACE!!
HUH?!

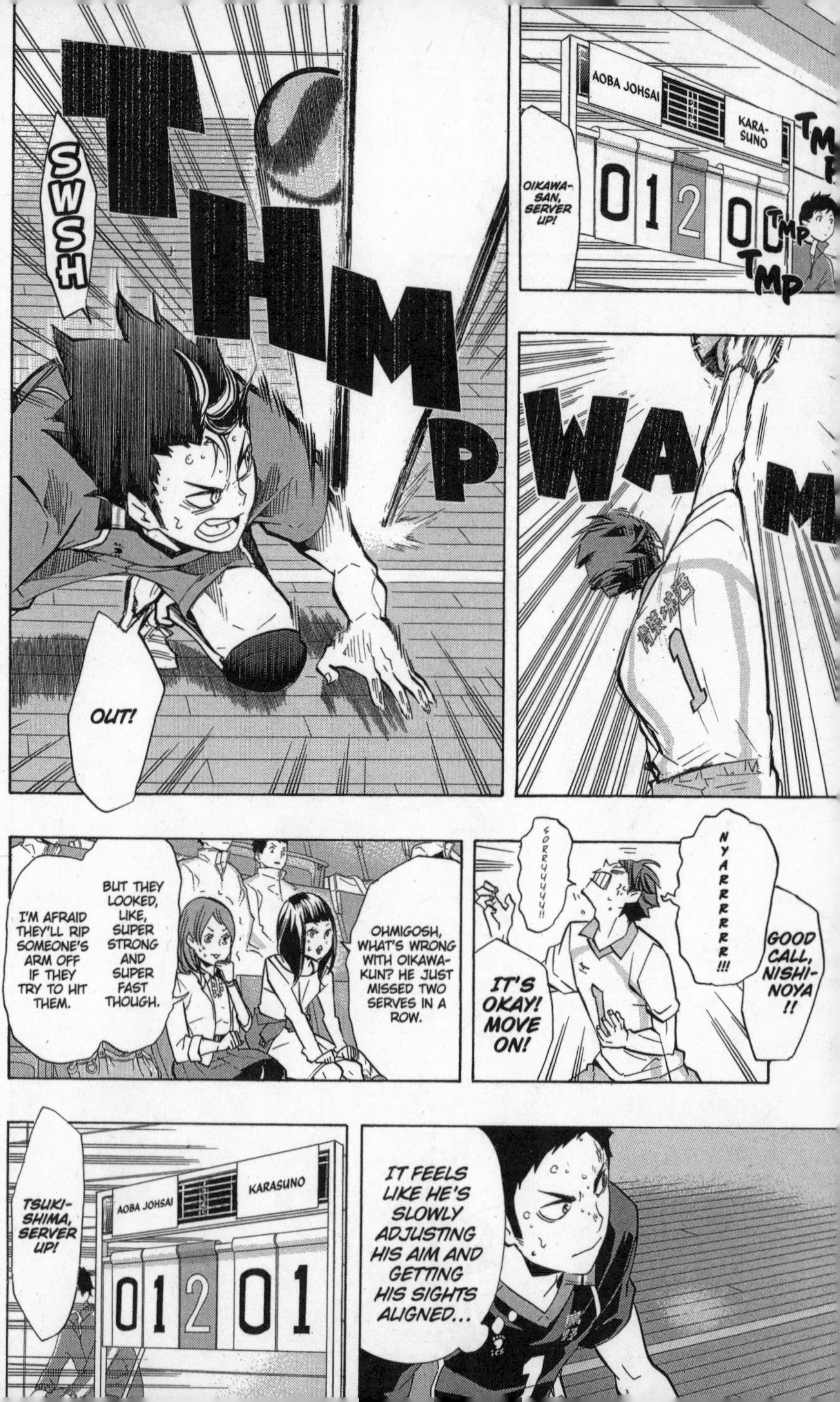

AOBA JOHSAI
KARA-SUNO
01 2 00
OIKAWA-SAN, SERVER UP!
TMP
TMP
TMP
WHAM
THMP
SWSH
OUT!
GOOD CALL, NISHINOYA!!
NYARRRRRR!!!
SORRYYYYY!!
IT'S OKAY! MOVE ON!
OHMIGOSH, WHAT'S WRONG WITH OIKAWA-KUN? HE JUST MISSED TWO SERVES IN A ROW.
BUT THEY LOOKED, LIKE, SUPER STRONG AND SUPER FAST THOUGH.
I'M AFRAID THEY'LL RIP SOMEONE'S ARM OFF IF THEY TRY TO HIT THEM.
IT FEELS LIKE HE'S SLOWLY ADJUSTING HIS AIM AND GETTING HIS SIGHTS ALIGNED...
TSUKISHIMA, SERVER UP!
AOBA JOHSAI
KARASUNO
01 2 01

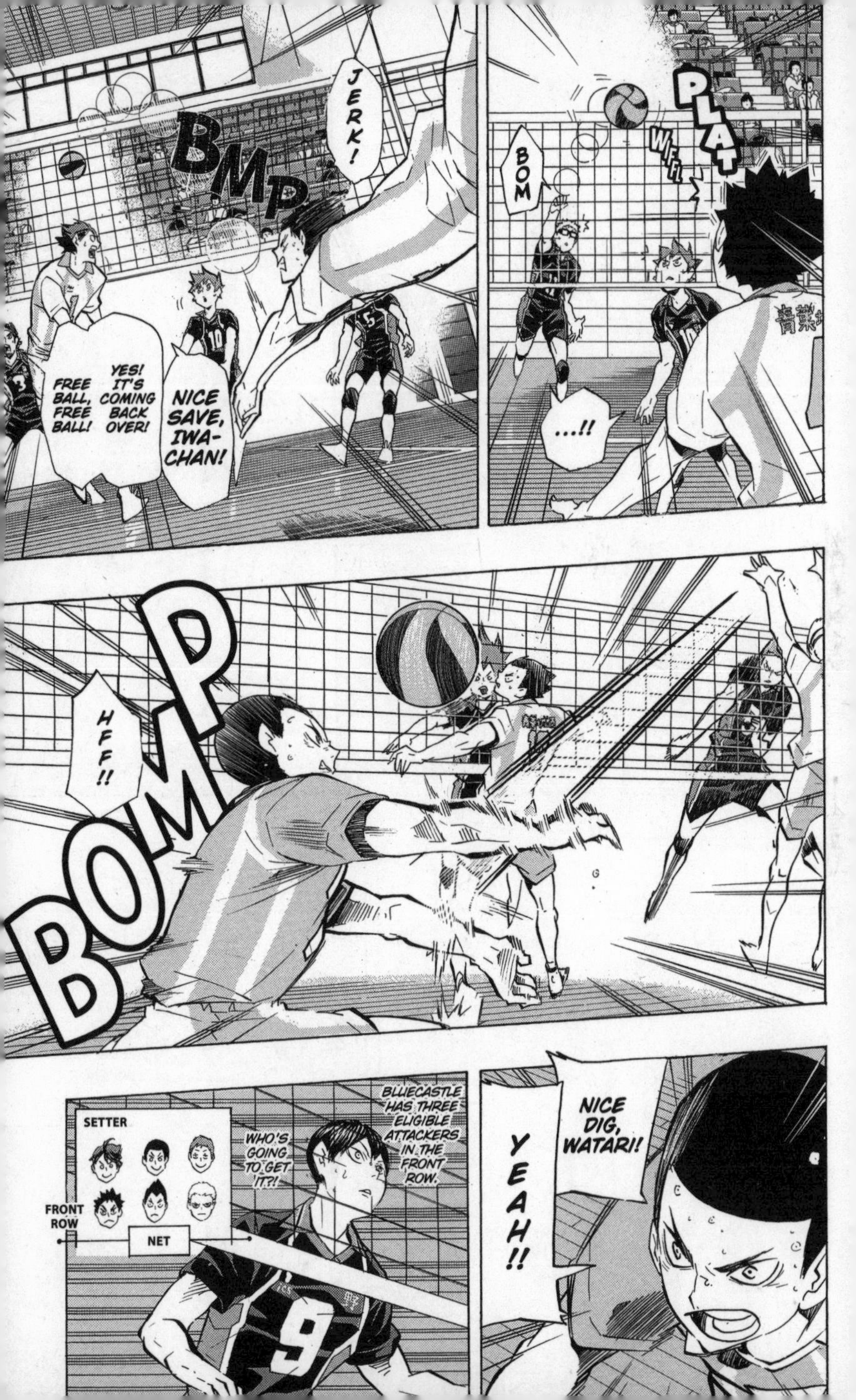
PLAT
WIFFL
BOM
...!!
JERK!
BMP
NICE SAVE, IWA-CHAN!
YES! IT'S COMING BACK OVER!
FREE BALL, FREE BALL!
HFF!!
BOMP
NICE DIG, WATARI!
YEAH!!
BLUECASTLE HAS THREE ELIGIBLE ATTACKERS IN THE FRONT ROW.
WHO'S GOING TO GET IT?!
SETTER
FRONT ROW
NET

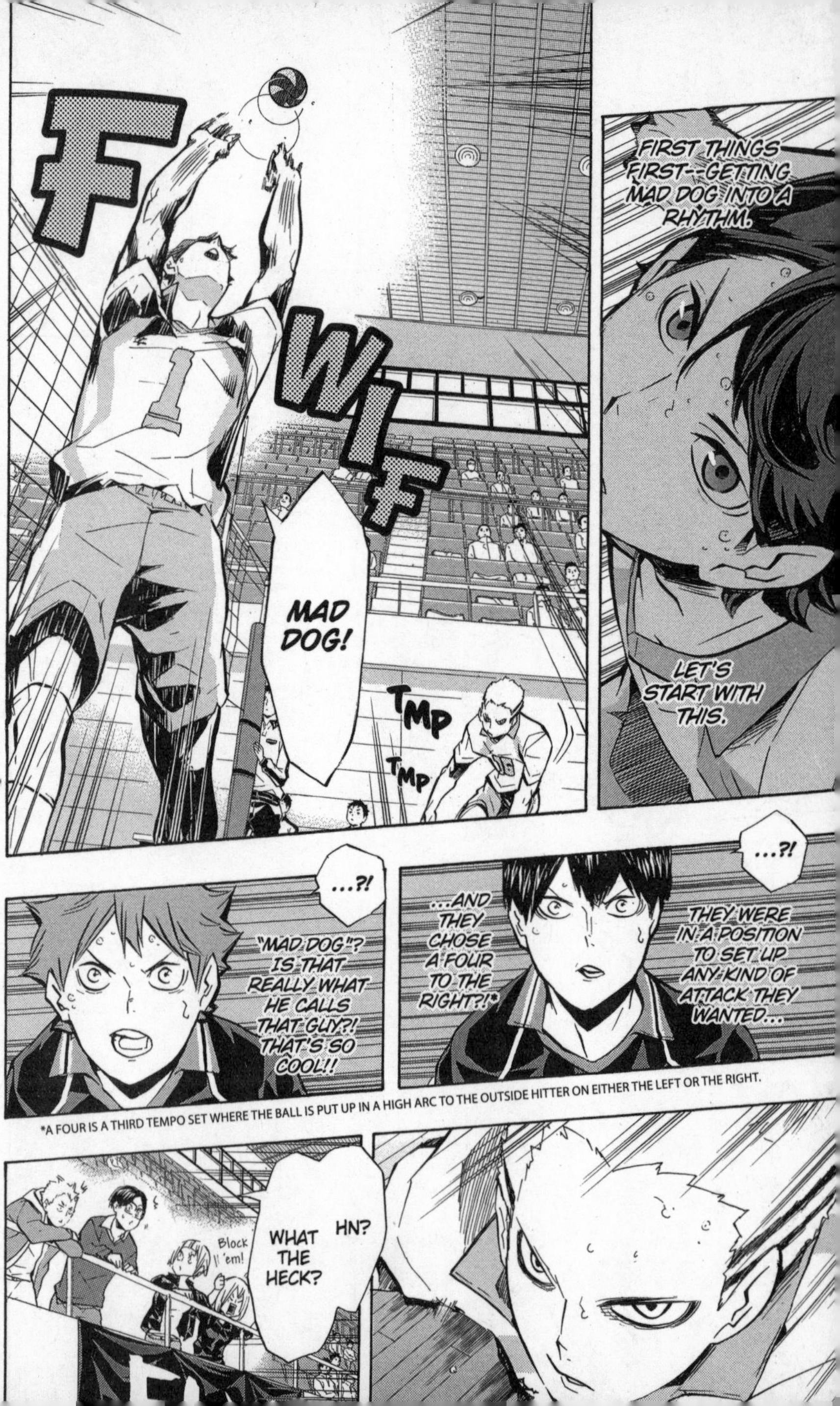
FIRST THINGS FIRST--GETTING MAD DOG INTO A RHYTHM.
LET'S START WITH THIS.
FWIF
MAD DOG!
TMP
TMP
...?!
THEY WERE IN A POSITION TO SET UP ANY KIND OF ATTACK THEY WANTED...
...AND THEY CHOSE A FOUR TO THE RIGHT?!*
...?!
"MAD DOG"? IS THAT REALLY WHAT HE CALLS THAT GUY?! THAT'S SO COOL!!
HN?
WHAT THE HECK?
Block 'em!
*A FOUR IS A THIRD TEMPO SET WHERE THE BALL IS PUT UP IN A HIGH ARC TO THE OUTSIDE HITTER ON EITHER THE LEFT OR THE RIGHT.

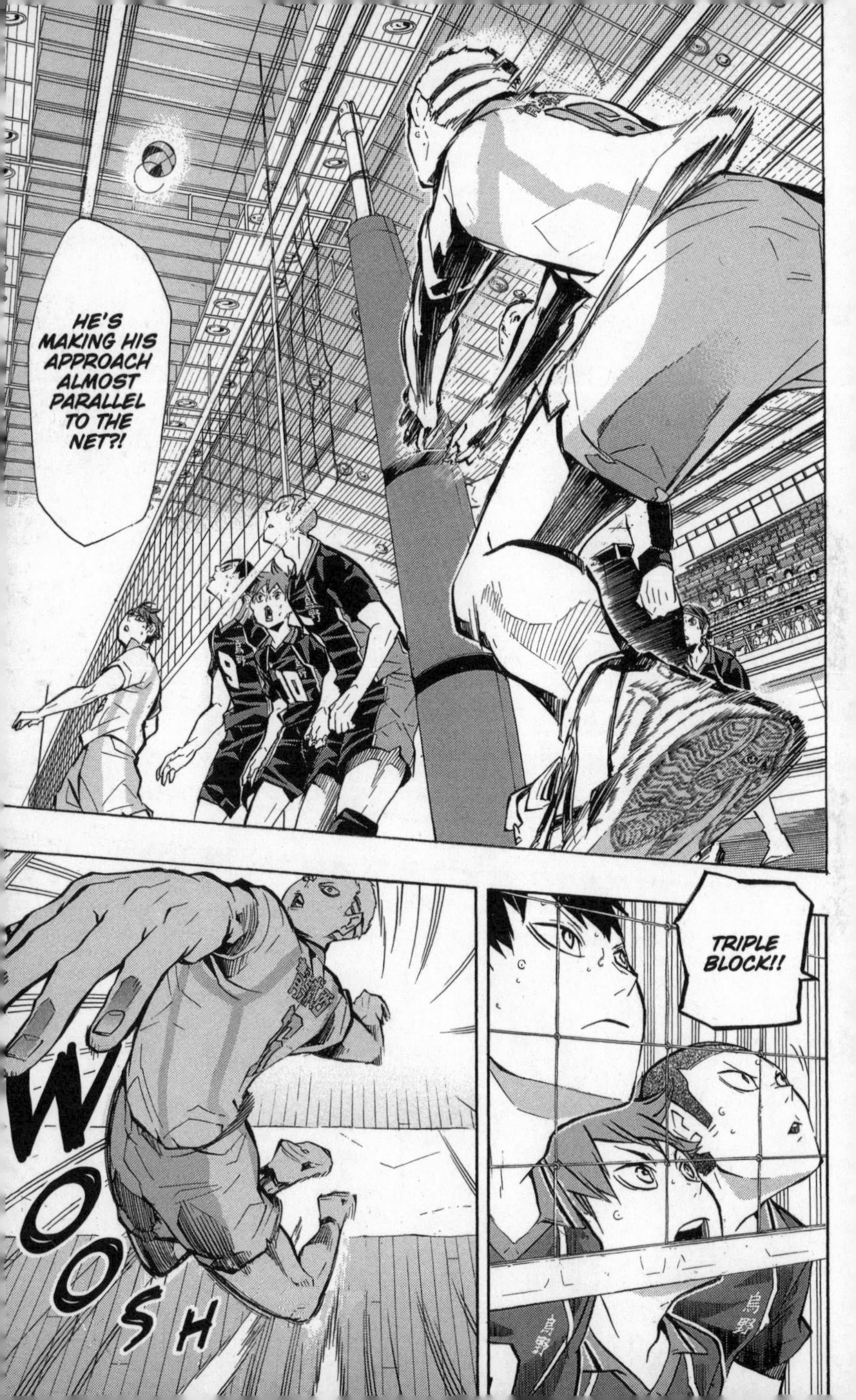
HE'S MAKING HIS APPROACH ALMOST PARALLEL TO THE NET?!
TRIPLE BLOCK!!
WOOOSH

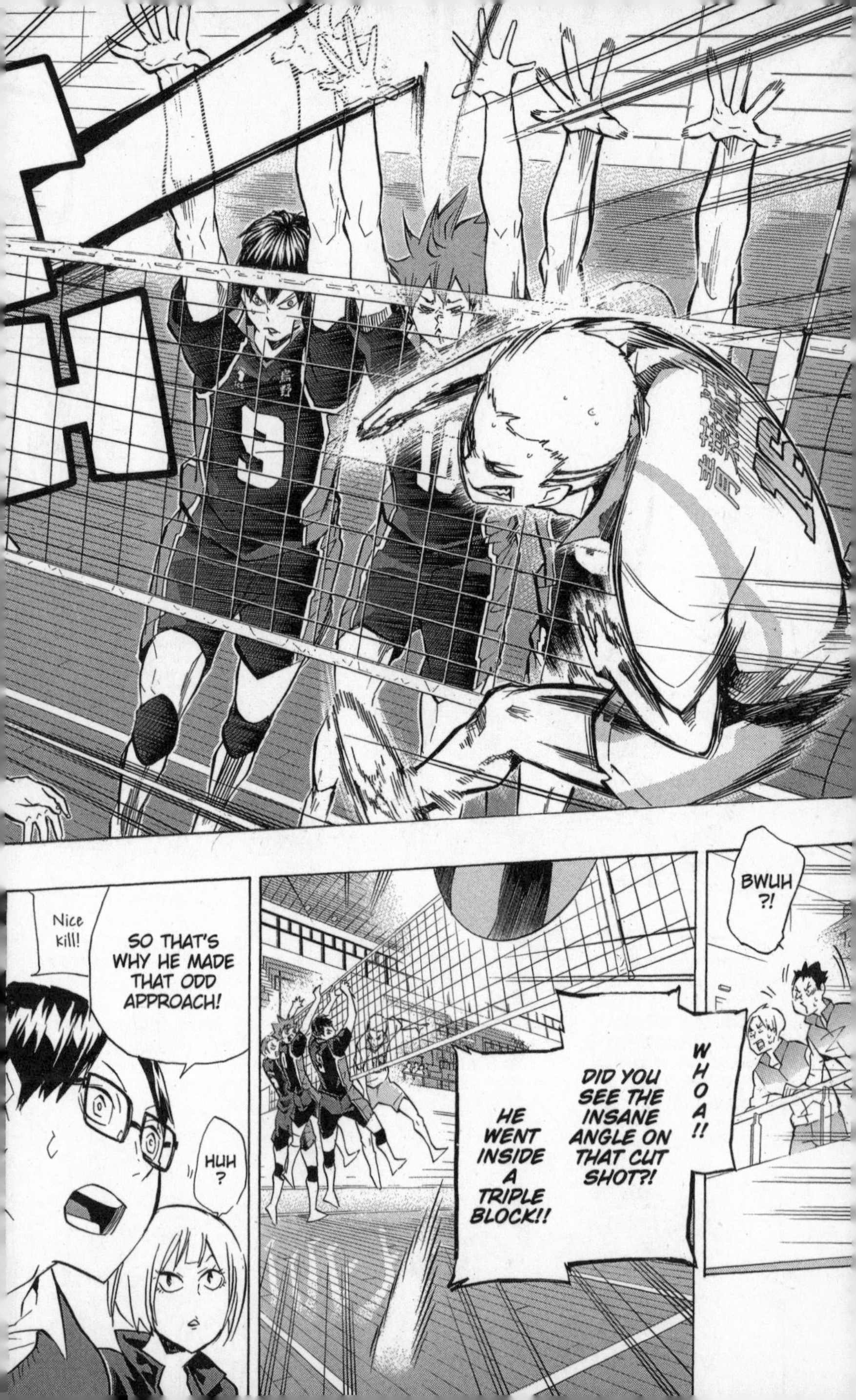
BWUH ?!
WHOA!!
DID YOU SEE THE INSANE ANGLE ON THAT CUT SHOT?!
HE WENT INSIDE A TRIPLE BLOCK!!
SO THAT'S WHY HE MADE THAT ODD APPROACH!
Nice kill!
HUH ?

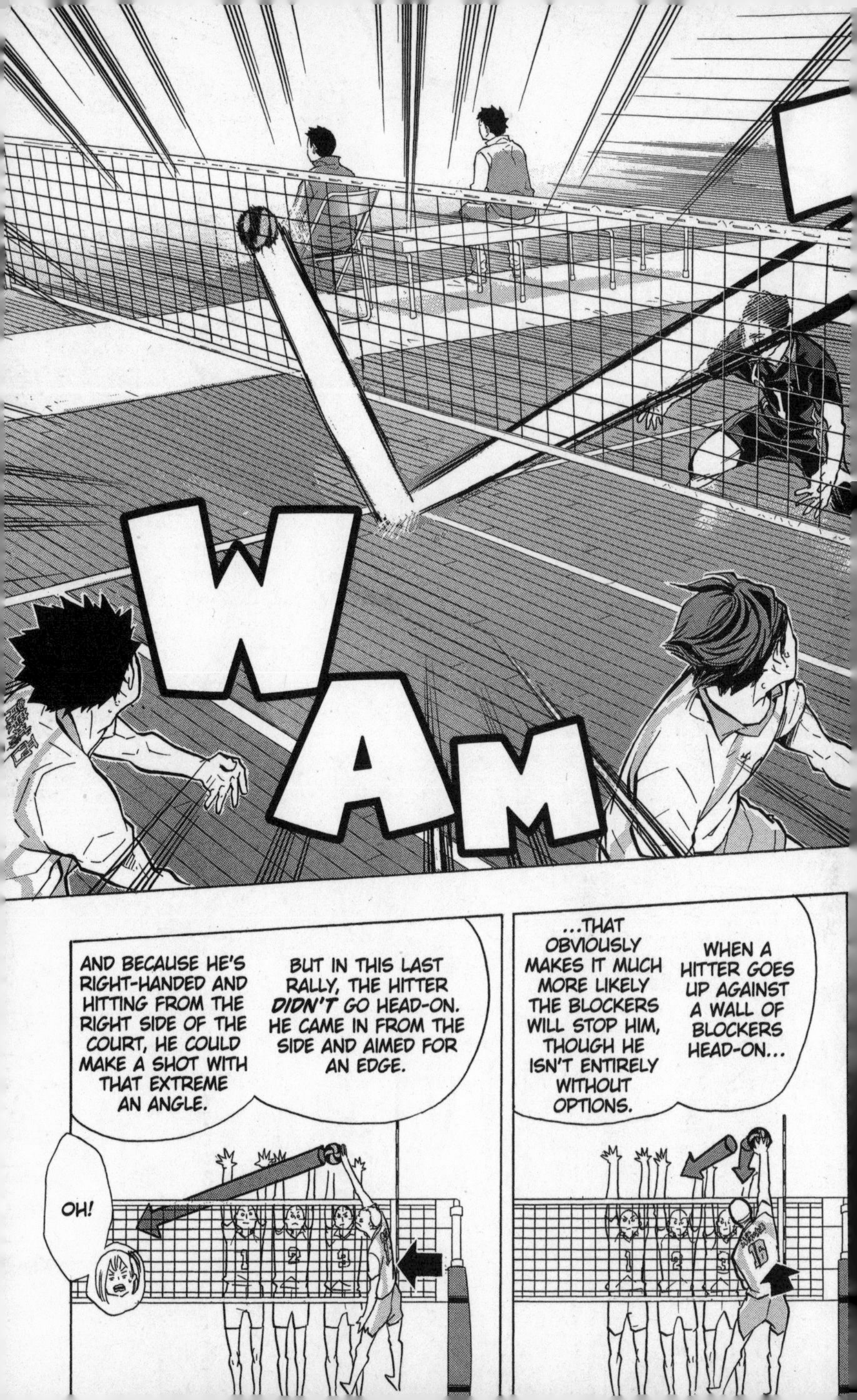
WAM
WHEN A HITTER GOES UP AGAINST A WALL OF BLOCKERS HEAD-ON...
...THAT OBVIOUSLY MAKES IT MUCH MORE LIKELY THE BLOCKERS WILL STOP HIM, THOUGH HE ISN'T ENTIRELY WITHOUT OPTIONS.
BUT IN THIS LAST RALLY, THE HITTER *DIDN'T* GO HEAD-ON. HE CAME IN FROM THE SIDE AND AIMED FOR AN EDGE.
AND BECAUSE HE'S RIGHT-HANDED AND HITTING FROM THE RIGHT SIDE OF THE COURT, HE COULD MAKE A SHOT WITH THAT EXTREME AN ANGLE.
OH!

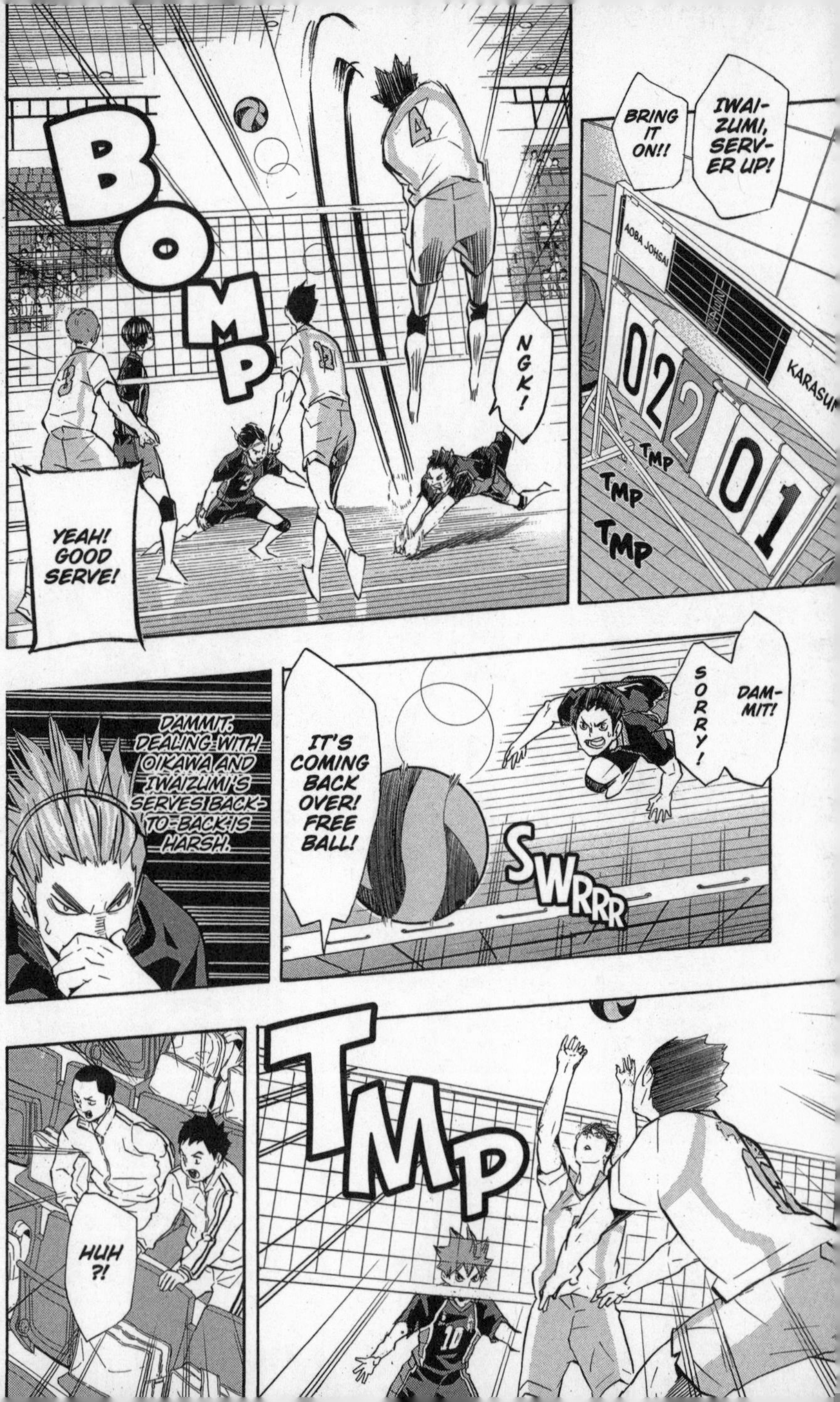
IWAIZUMI, SERVER UP!
BRING IT ON!!
AOBA JOHSAI
KARASU
TMP
TMP
TMP
BOMP
NGK!
YEAH! GOOD SERVE!
DAMMIT!
SORRY!
IT'S COMING BACK OVER! FREE BALL!
SWRRR
DAMMIT. DEALING WITH OIKAWA AND IWAIZUMI'S SERVES BACK-TO-BACK IS HARSH.
TMP
HUH?!

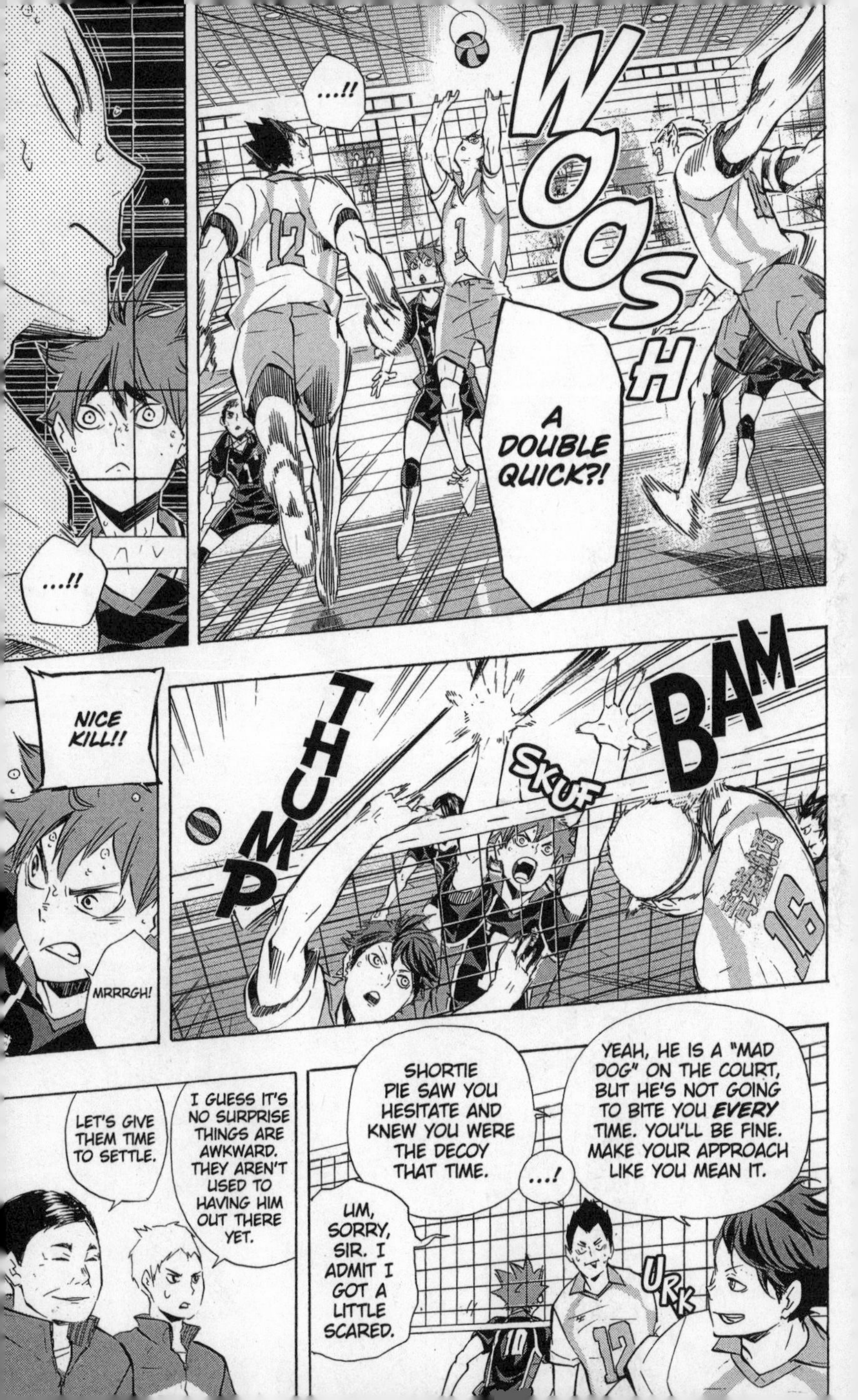

WOOSH
...!!
A DOUBLE QUICK?!
...!!
BAM
SKUF
THUMP
NICE KILL!!
MRRRGH!
YEAH, HE IS A "MAD DOG" ON THE COURT, BUT HE'S NOT GOING TO BITE YOU EVERY TIME. YOU'LL BE FINE. MAKE YOUR APPROACH LIKE YOU MEAN IT.
SHORTIE PIE SAW YOU HESITATE AND KNEW YOU WERE THE DECOY THAT TIME.
...!
UM, SORRY, SIR. I ADMIT I GOT A LITTLE SCARED.
URK
I GUESS IT'S NO SURPRISE THINGS ARE AWKWARD. THEY AREN'T USED TO HAVING HIM OUT THERE YET.
LET'S GIVE THEM TIME TO SETTLE.

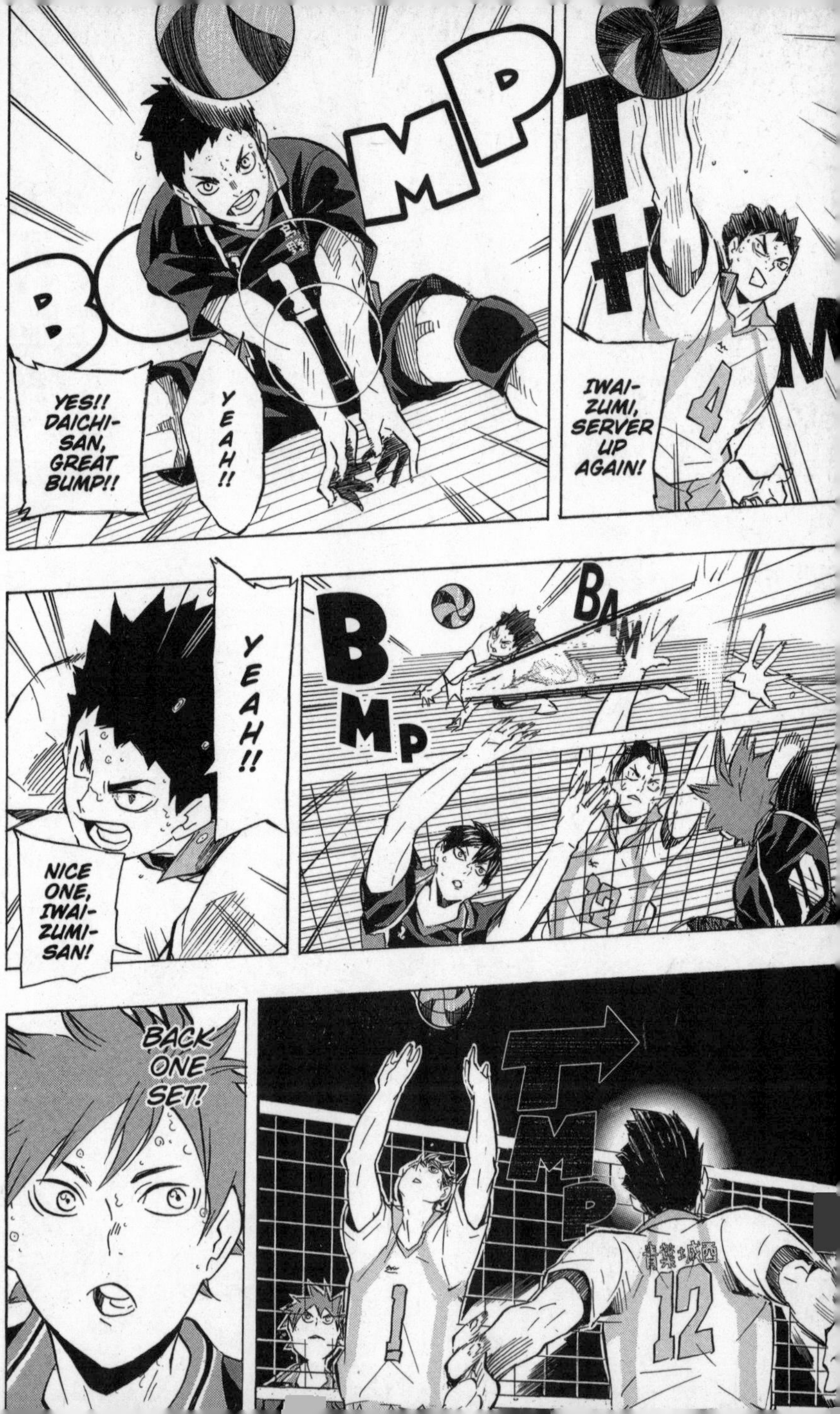
IWAIZUMI, SERVER UP AGAIN!
BUMP
YEAH!!
YES!! DAICHI-SAN, GREAT BUMP!!
BAM
BUMP
YEAH!!
NICE ONE, IWAIZUMI-SAN!
TMP
BACK ONE SET!

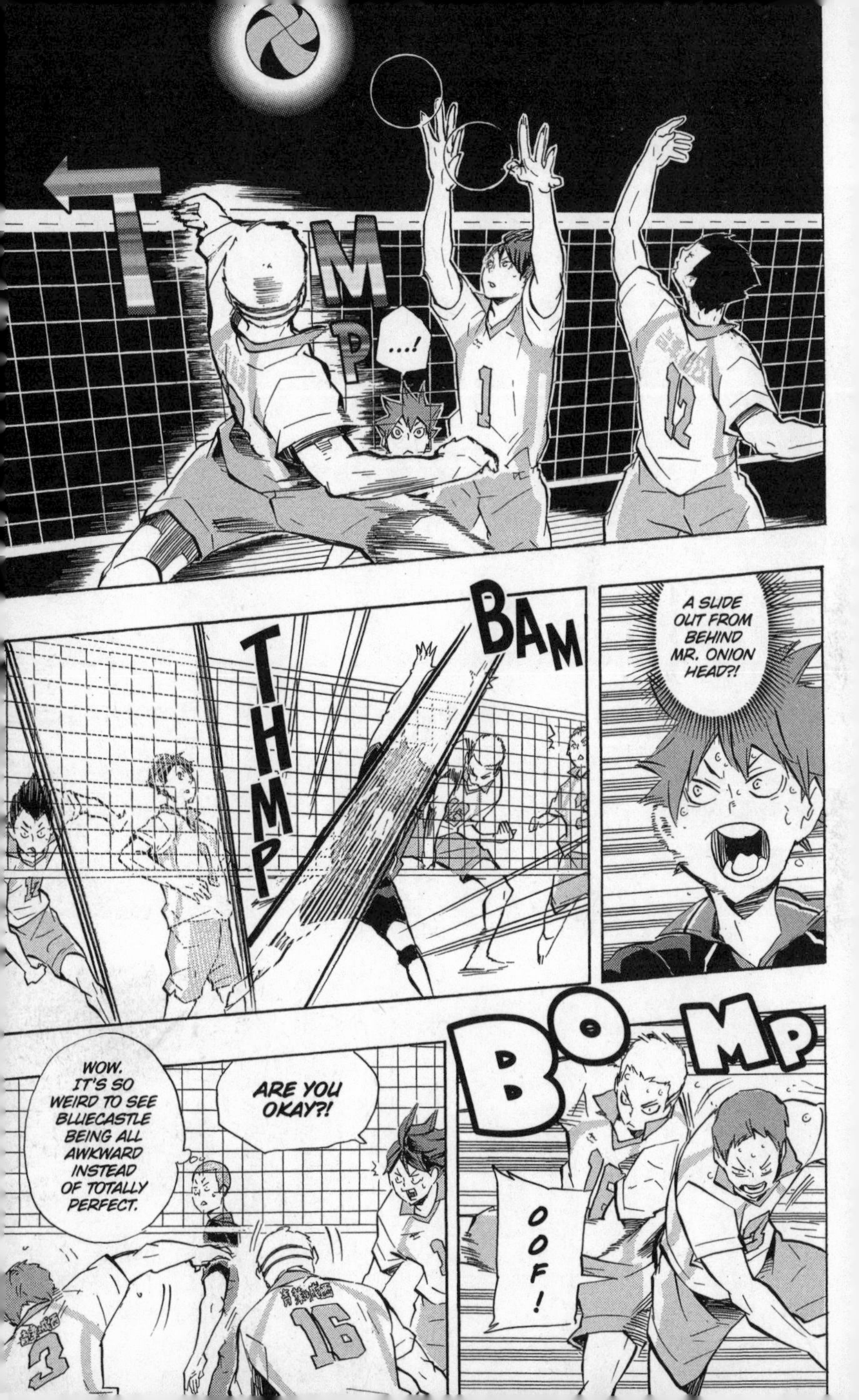
TMP
...!
A SLIDE OUT FROM BEHIND MR. ONION HEAD?!
BAM
THMP
BOMP
OOF!
ARE YOU OKAY?!
WOW. IT'S SO WEIRD TO SEE BLUECASTLE BEING ALL AWKWARD INSTEAD OF TOTALLY PERFECT.

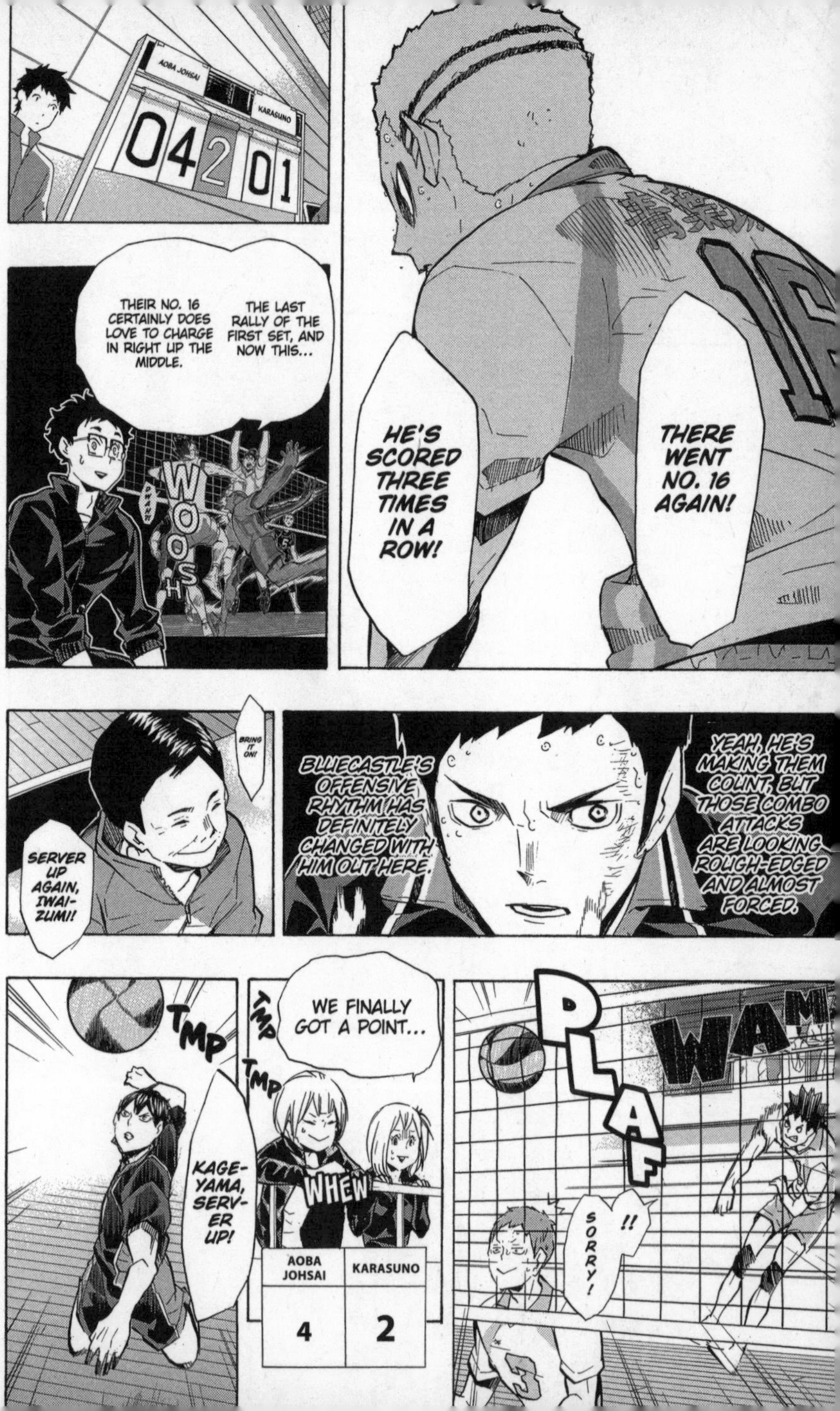
THERE WENT NO. 16 AGAIN!
HE'S SCORED THREE TIMES IN A ROW!
AOBA JOHSAI
KARASUNO
04 2 01
THE LAST RALLY OF THE FIRST SET, AND NOW THIS...
THEIR NO. 16 CERTAINLY DOES LOVE TO CHARGE IN RIGHT UP THE MIDDLE.
WOOSH
YEAH, HE'S MAKING THEM COUNT, BUT THOSE COMBO ATTACKS ARE LOOKING ROUGH-EDGED AND ALMOST FORCED.
BLUECASTLE'S OFFENSIVE RHYTHM HAS DEFINITELY CHANGED WITH HIM OUT HERE.
BRING IT ON!
SERVER UP AGAIN, IWAIZUMI!
WAM
PLAF
!!
SORRY!
WE FINALLY GOT A POINT...
TMP
TMP
WHEW
AOBA JOHSAI
KARASUNO
4
2
TMP
KAGEYAMA, SERVER UP!

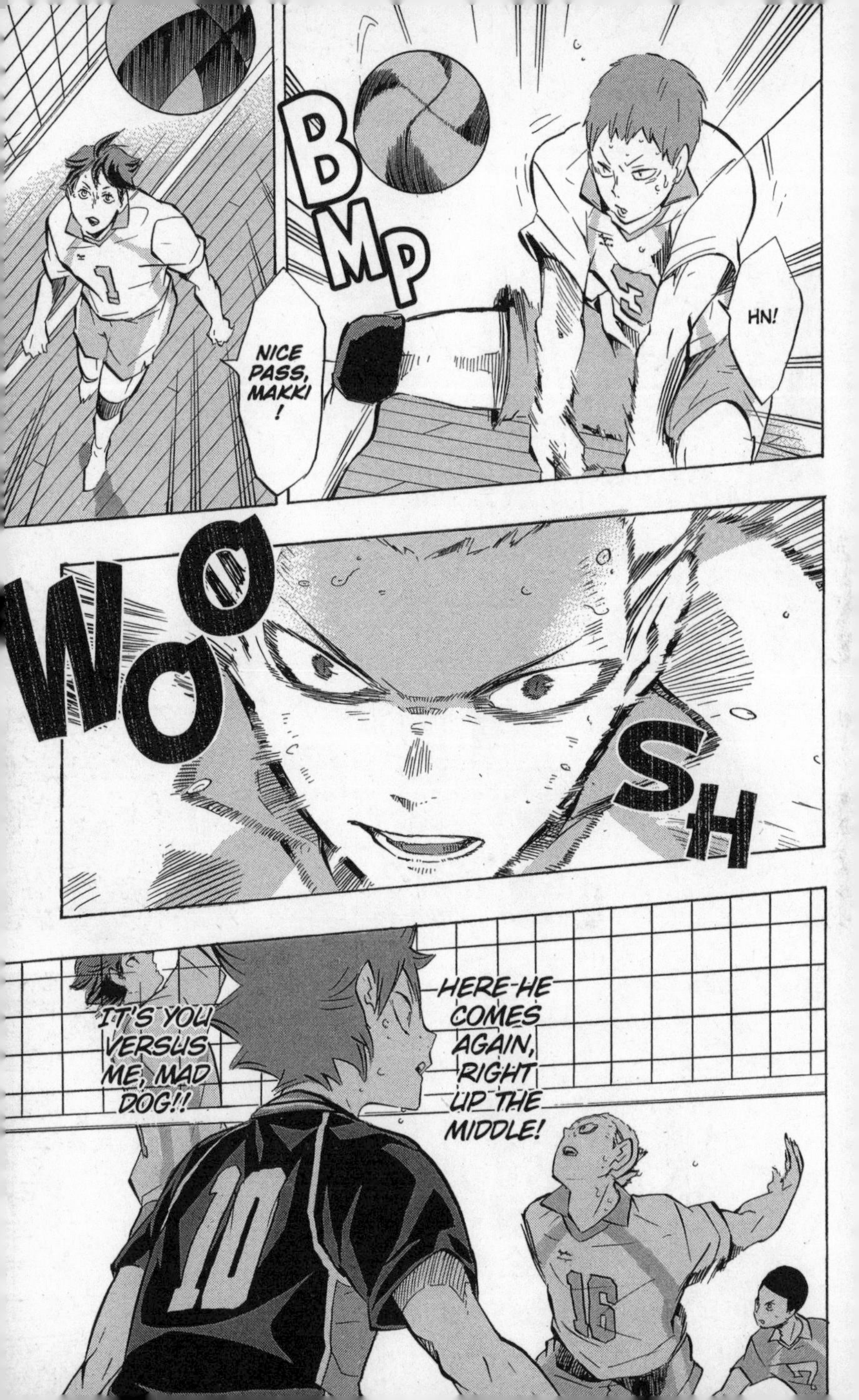
HN!
BOMP
NICE PASS, MAKKI!
WOOOSH
HERE HE COMES AGAIN, RIGHT UP THE MIDDLE!
IT'S YOU VERSUS ME, MAD DOG!!

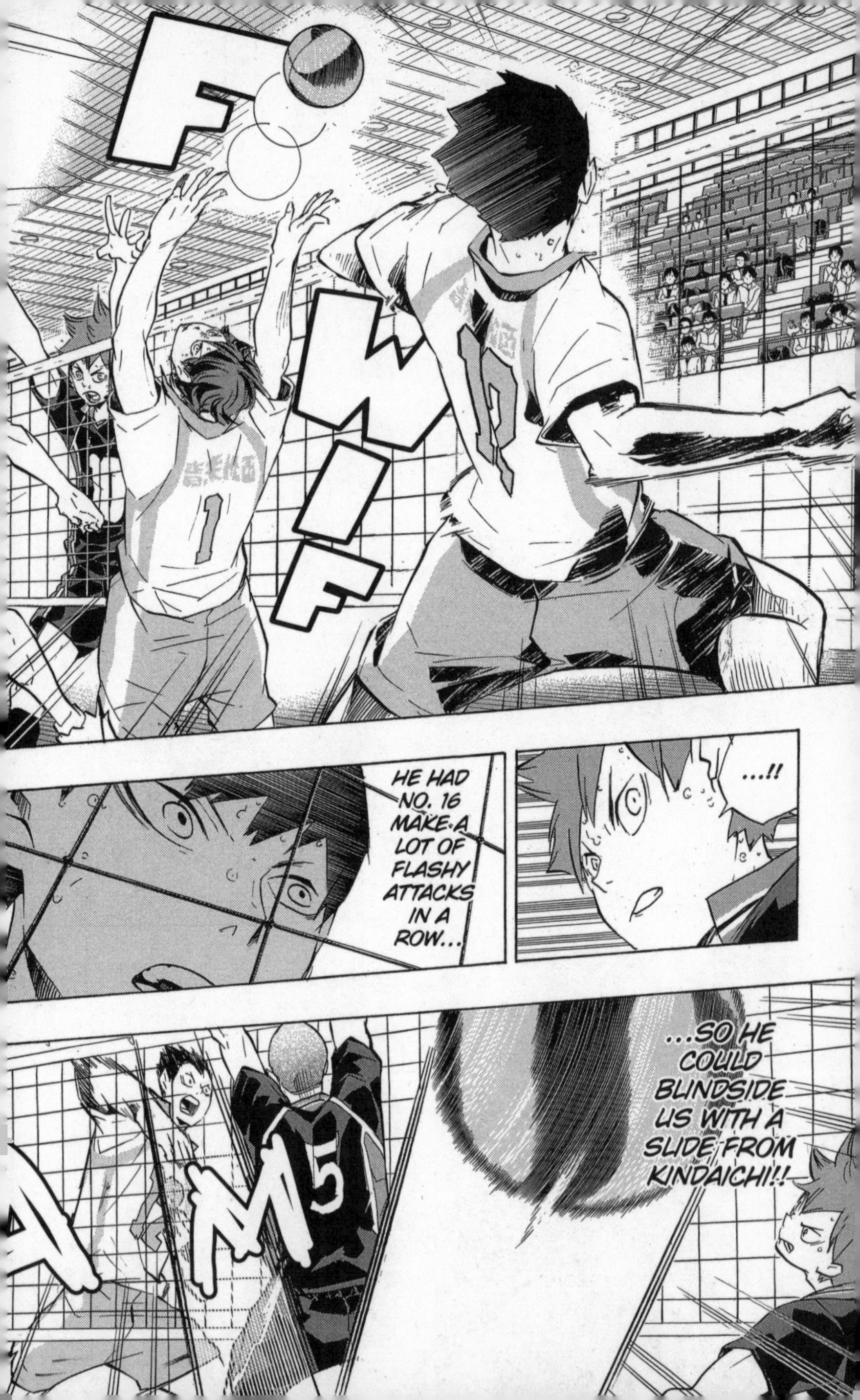
WHIFF
...!!
HE HAD NO. 16 MAKE A LOT OF FLASHY ATTACKS IN A ROW...
...SO HE COULD BLINDSIDE US WITH A SLIDE FROM KINDAICHI!!

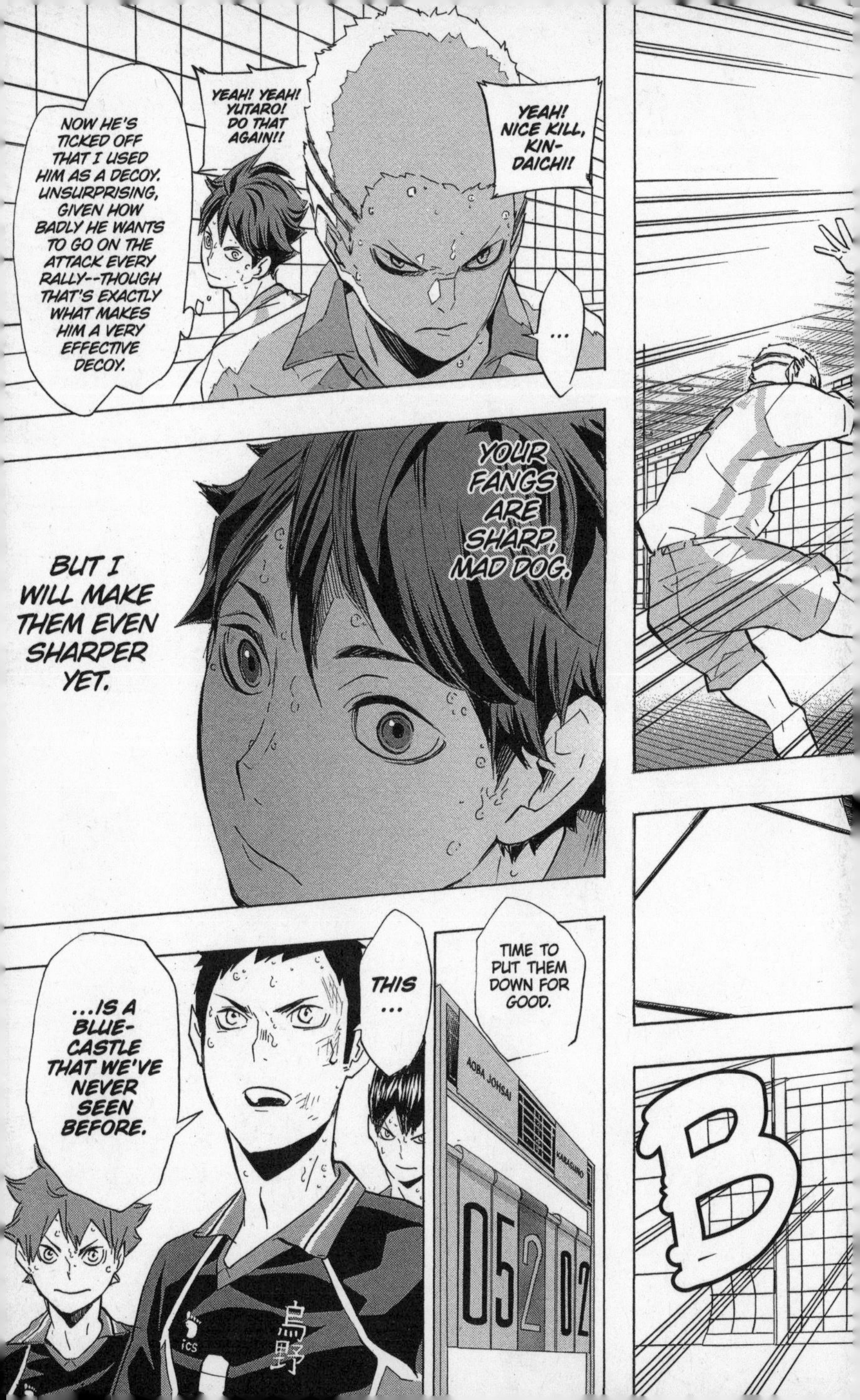
YEAH! NICE KILL, KIN-DAICHI!
YEAH! YEAH! YUTARO! DO THAT AGAIN!!
...
NOW HE'S TICKED OFF THAT I USED HIM AS A DECOY. UNSURPRISING, GIVEN HOW BADLY HE WANTS TO GO ON THE ATTACK EVERY RALLY--THOUGH THAT'S EXACTLY WHAT MAKES HIM A VERY EFFECTIVE DECOY.
YOUR FANGS ARE SHARP, MAD DOG.
BUT I WILL MAKE THEM EVEN SHARPER YET.
TIME TO PUT THEM DOWN FOR GOOD.
THIS...
...IS A BLUE-CASTLE THAT WE'VE NEVER SEEN BEFORE.
AOBA JOHSAI
KARASUNO
B

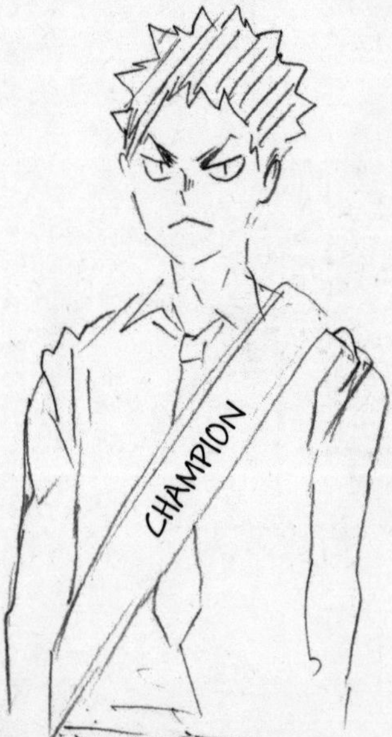
CHAMPION

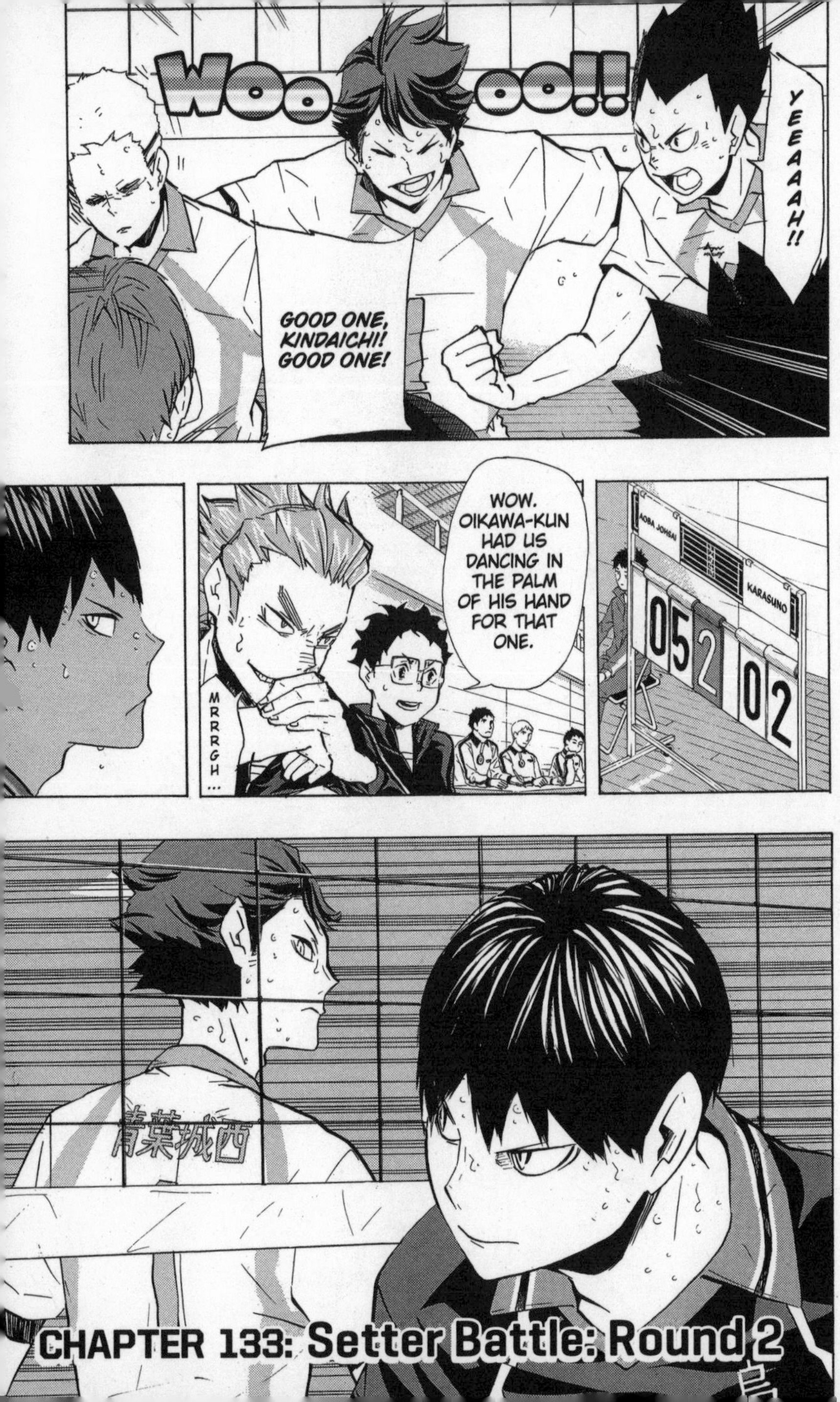
WOO...OO!!
YEEAAAAH!!
GOOD ONE, KINDAICHI! GOOD ONE!
AOBA JOHSAI
KARASUNO
05 2 02
WOW. OIKAWA-KUN HAD US DANCING IN THE PALM OF HIS HAND FOR THAT ONE.
MRRRGH...

CHAPTER 133: Setter Battle: Round 2

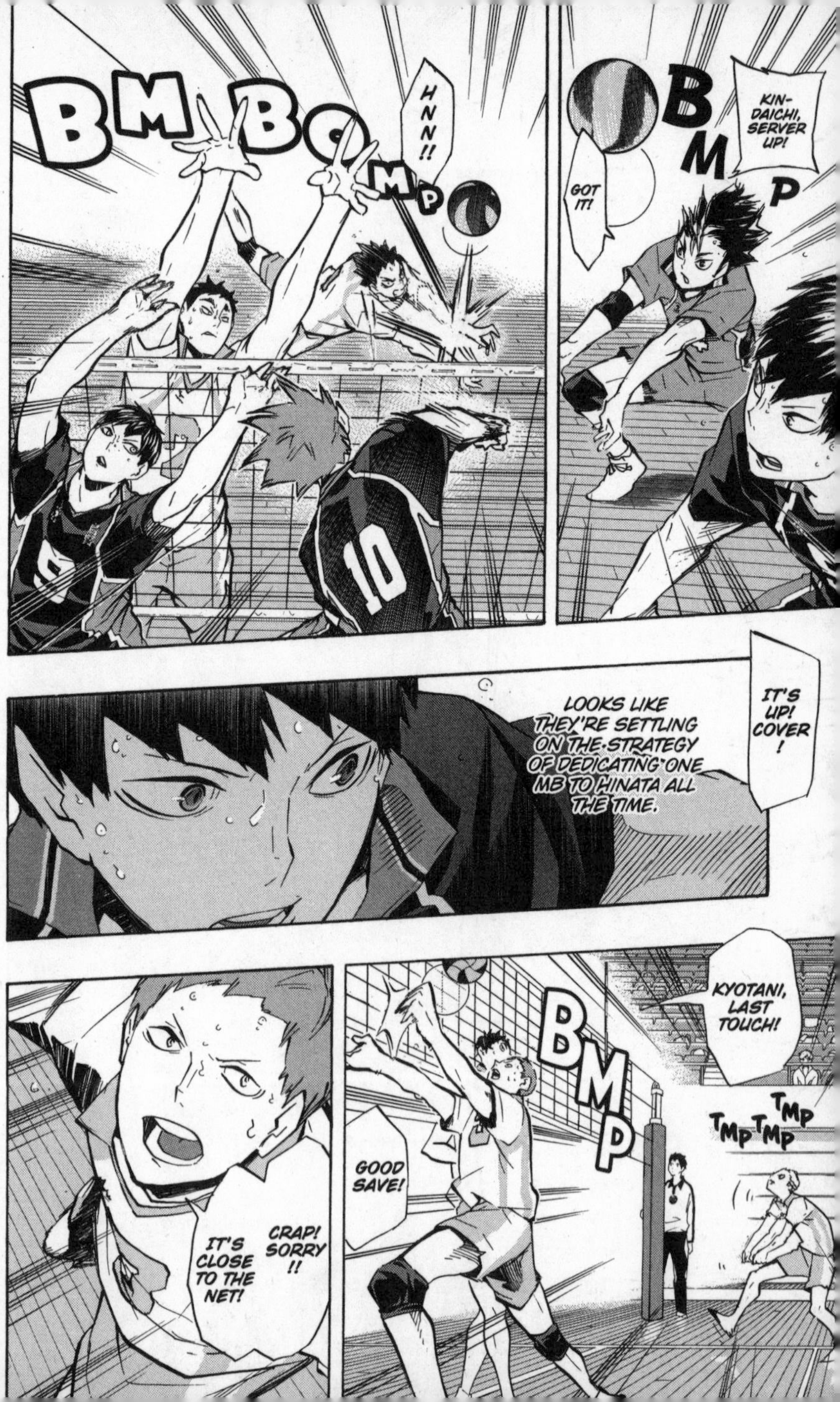
KIN-DAICHI, SERVER UP!
BMP
GOT IT!
HNNN!!
BOMP
BM
IT'S UP! COVER!
LOOKS LIKE THEY'RE SETTLING ON THE STRATEGY OF DEDICATING ONE MB TO HINATA ALL THE TIME.
KYOTANI, LAST TOUCH!
TMP TMP TMP
BMP
GOOD SAVE!
CRAP! SORRY!!
IT'S CLOSE TO THE NET!

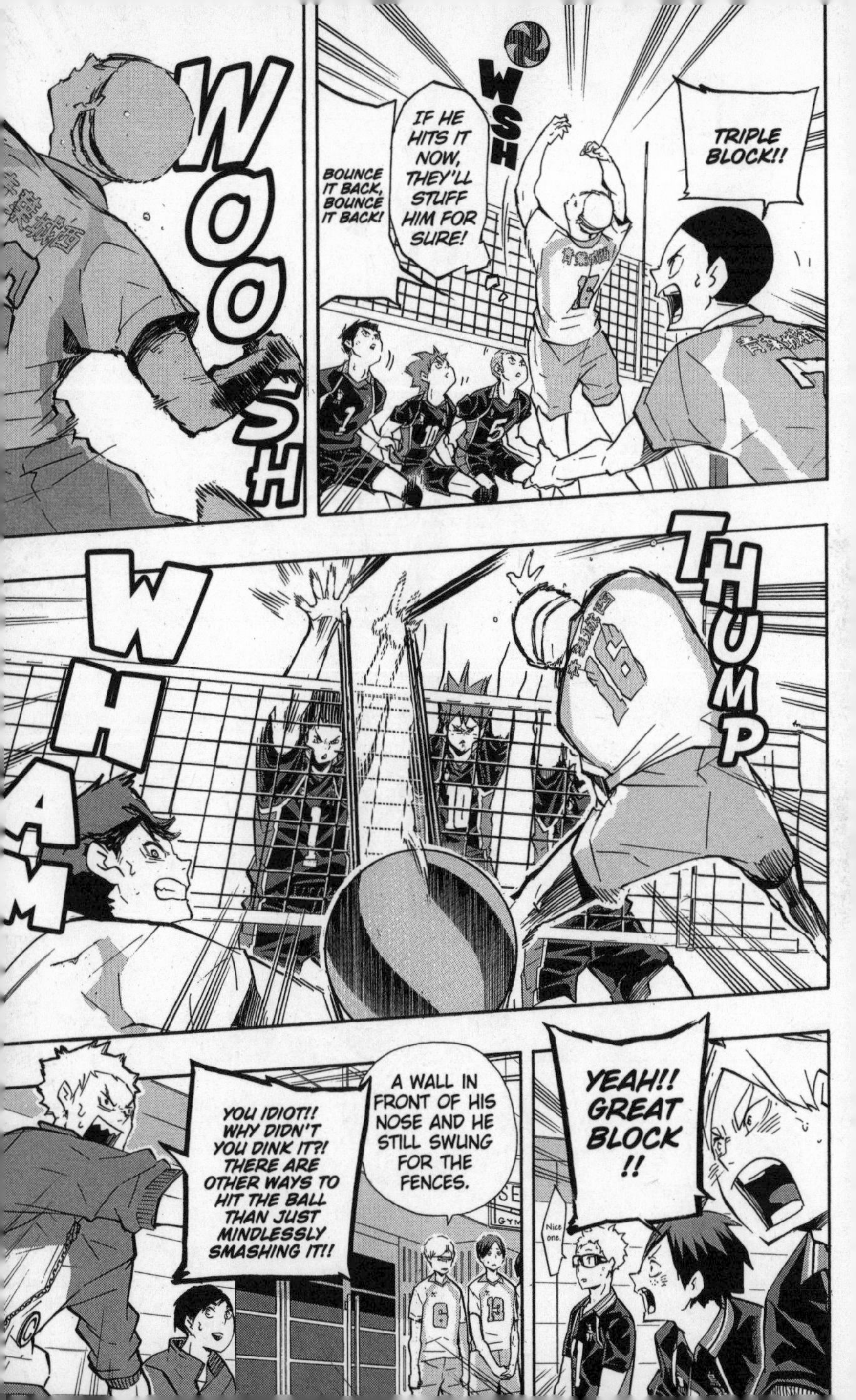
TRIPLE BLOCK!!
WSH
IF HE HITS IT NOW, THEY'LL STUFF HIM FOR SURE!
BOUNCE IT BACK, BOUNCE IT BACK!
WOOOSH
THUMP
WHAM
YEAH!! GREAT BLOCK!!
Nice one.
A WALL IN FRONT OF HIS NOSE AND HE STILL SWUNG FOR THE FENCES.
YOU IDIOT!! WHY DIDN'T YOU DINK IT?! THERE ARE OTHER WAYS TO HIT THE BALL THAN JUST MINDLESSLY SMASHING IT!!

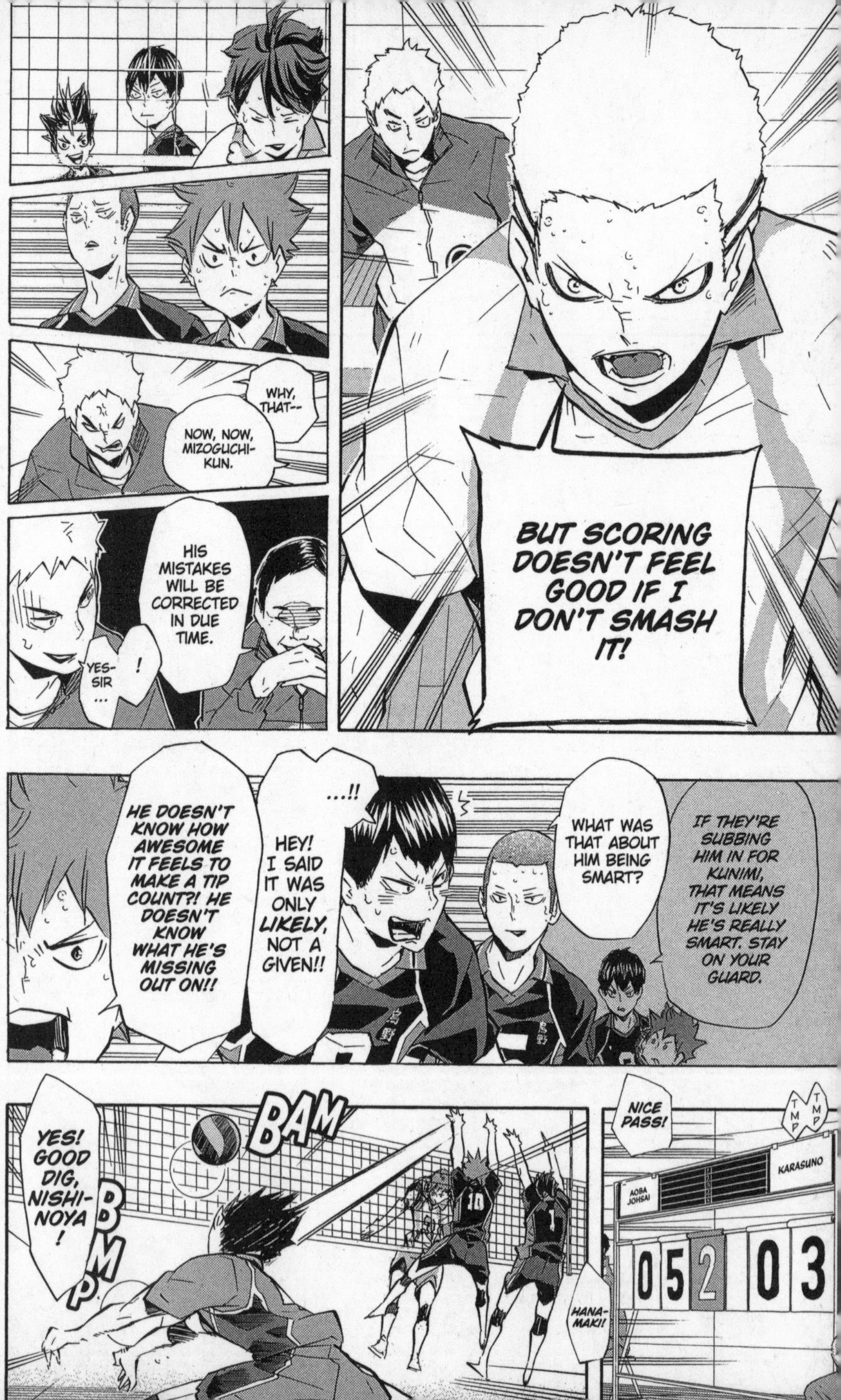
BUT SCORING DOESN'T FEEL GOOD IF I DON'T SMASH IT!
WHY, THAT--
NOW, NOW, MIZOGUCHI-KUN.
HIS MISTAKES WILL BE CORRECTED IN DUE TIME.
!
YES-SIR...
IF THEY'RE SUBBING HIM IN FOR KUNIMI, THAT MEANS IT'S LIKELY HE'S REALLY SMART. STAY ON YOUR GUARD.
WHAT WAS THAT ABOUT HIM BEING SMART?
...!!
HEY! I SAID IT WAS ONLY LIKELY, NOT A GIVEN!!
HE DOESN'T KNOW HOW AWESOME IT FEELS TO MAKE A TIP COUNT?! HE DOESN'T KNOW WHAT HE'S MISSING OUT ON!!
TMP TMP
NICE PASS!
KARASUNO
AOBA JOHSAI
05 2 03
HANAMAKI!
BAM
YES! GOOD DIG, NISHINOYA!
BUMP

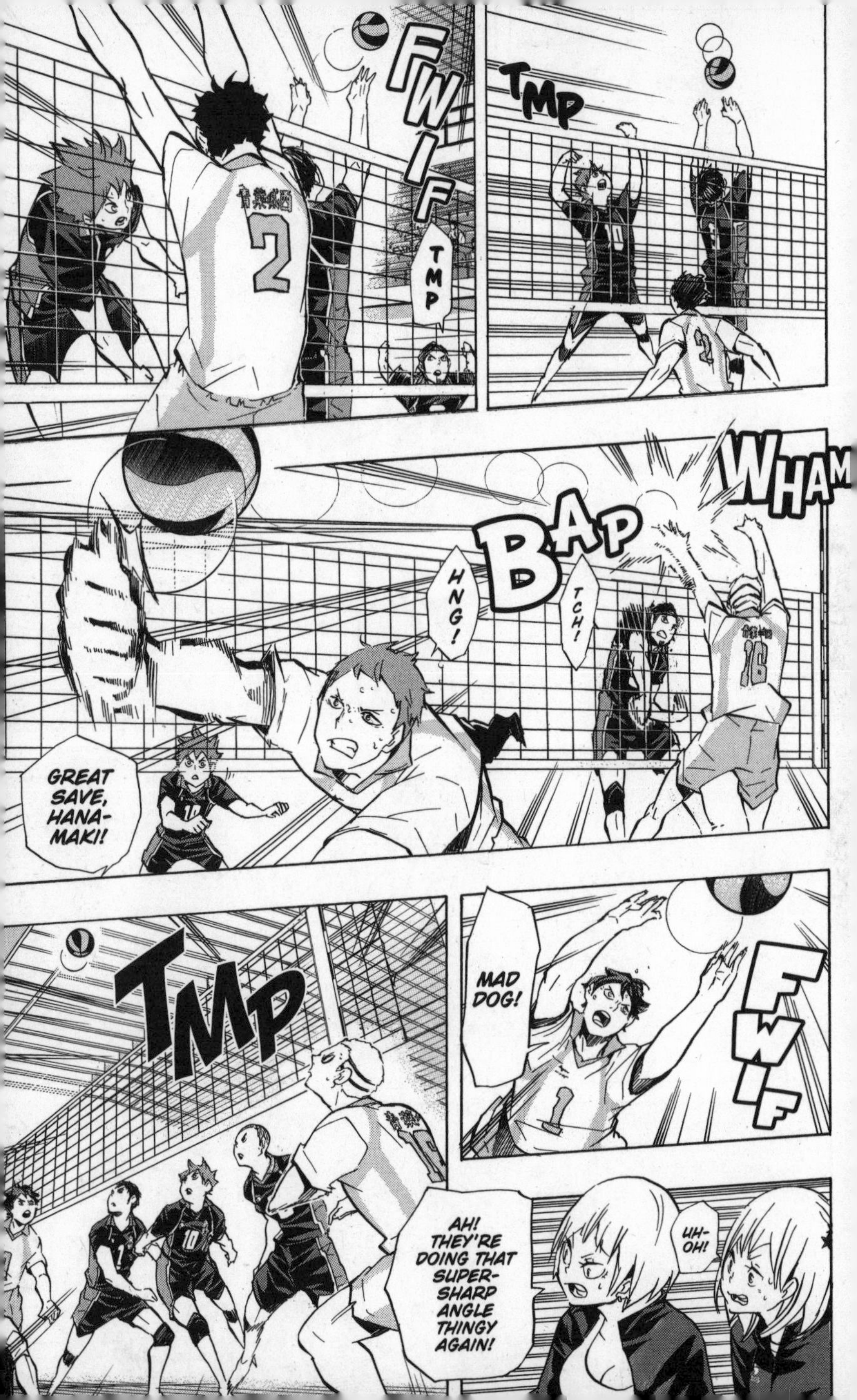
TMP
FWIF
TMP
WHAM
BAP
TCH!
HNG!
GREAT SAVE, HANA-MAKI!
FWIF
MAD DOG!
TMP
UH-OH!
AH! THEY'RE DOING THAT SUPER-SHARP ANGLE THINGY AGAIN!

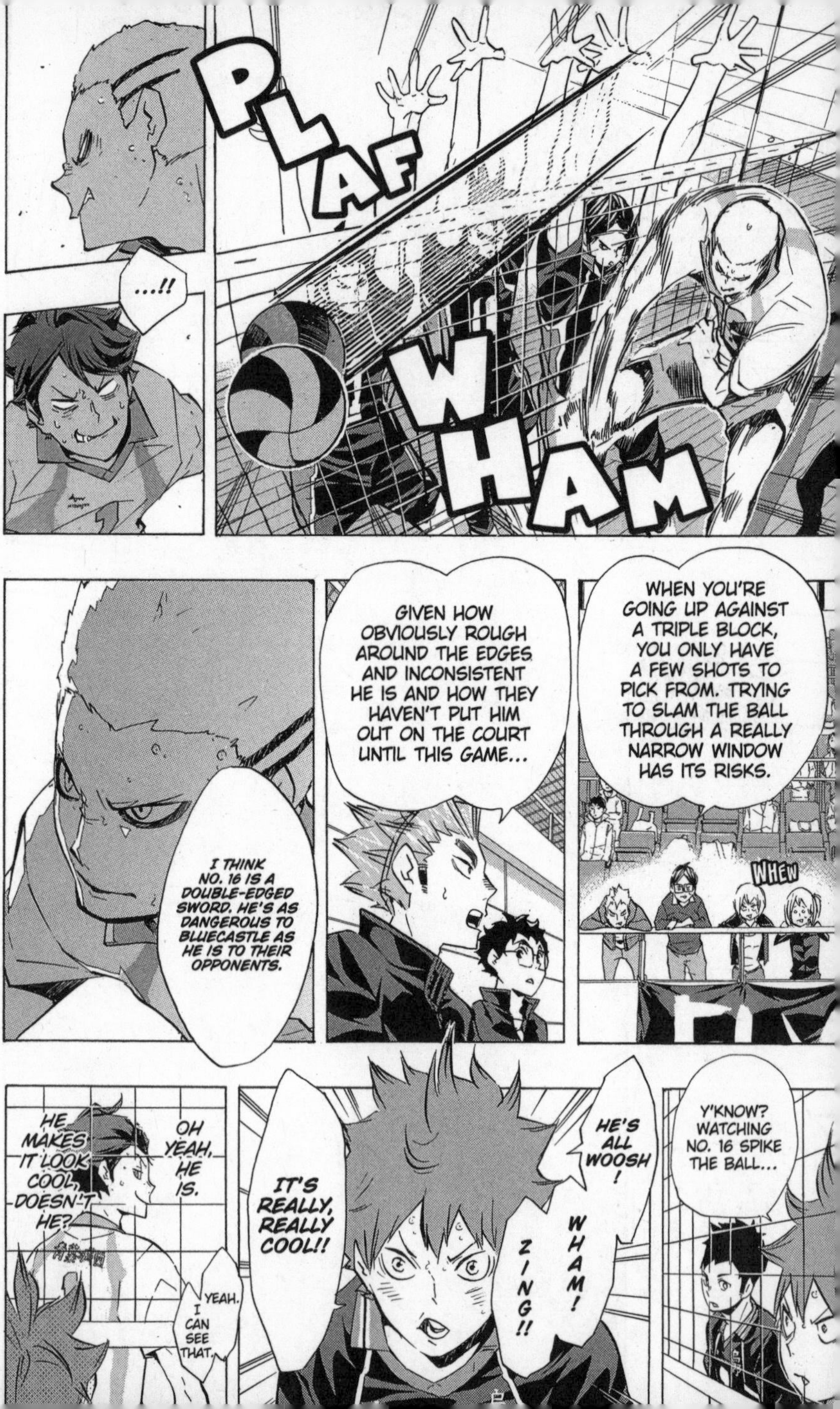
PLAF
WHAM
...!!
WHEN YOU'RE GOING UP AGAINST A TRIPLE BLOCK, YOU ONLY HAVE A FEW SHOTS TO PICK FROM. TRYING TO SLAM THE BALL THROUGH A REALLY NARROW WINDOW HAS ITS RISKS.
WHEW
GIVEN HOW OBVIOUSLY ROUGH AROUND THE EDGES AND INCONSISTENT HE IS AND HOW THEY HAVEN'T PUT HIM OUT ON THE COURT UNTIL THIS GAME...
I THINK NO. 16 IS A DOUBLE-EDGED SWORD. HE'S AS DANGEROUS TO BLUECASTLE AS HE IS TO THEIR OPPONENTS.
Y'KNOW? WATCHING NO. 16 SPIKE THE BALL...
HE'S ALL WOOSH!
WHAM!
ZING!!
IT'S REALLY, REALLY COOL!!
OH YEAH, HE IS.
HE MAKES IT LOOK COOL, DOESN'T HE?
YEAH. I CAN SEE THAT.

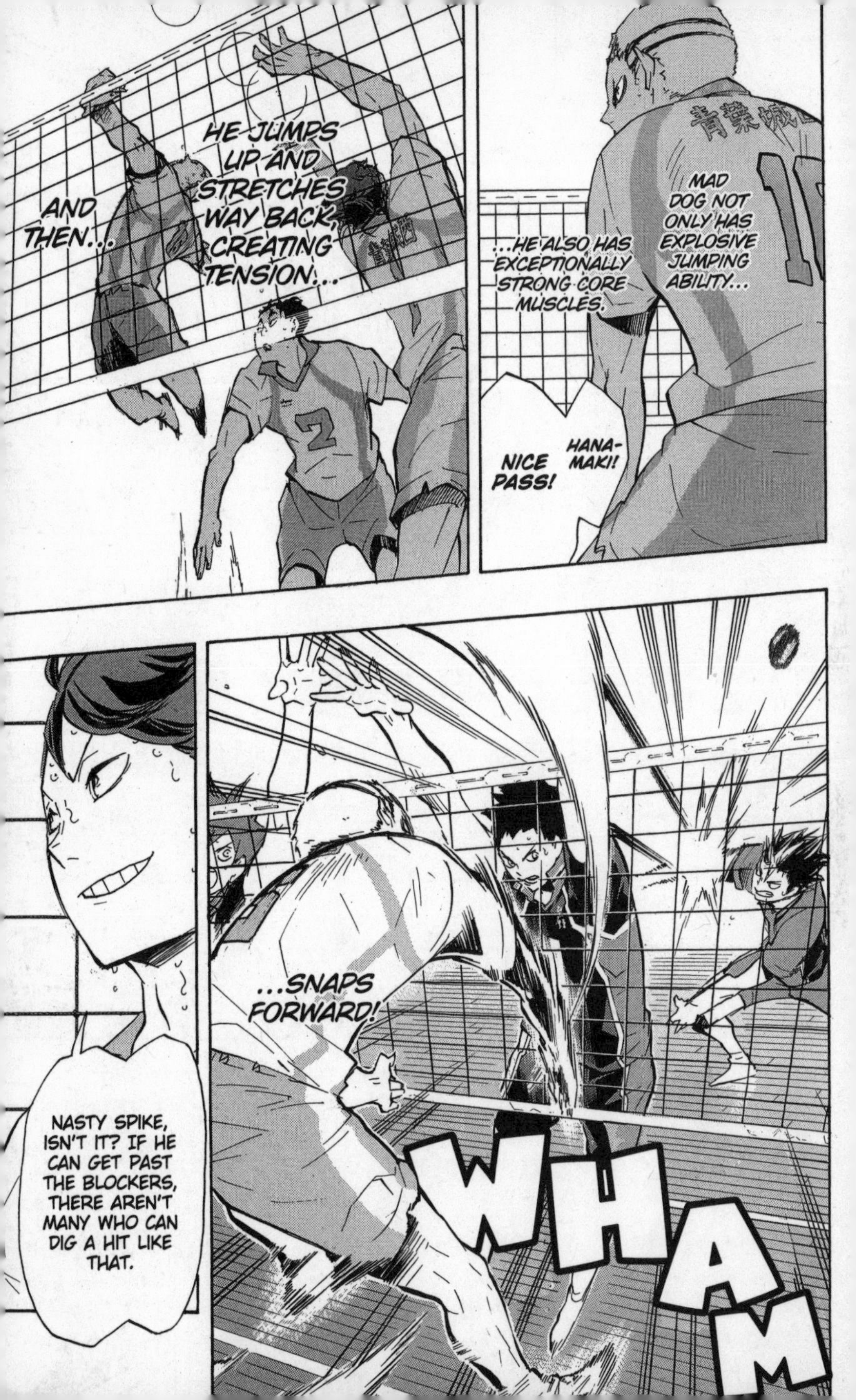
MAD DOG NOT ONLY HAS EXPLOSIVE JUMPING ABILITY...
...HE ALSO HAS EXCEPTIONALLY STRONG CORE MUSCLES.
HANA-MAKI!
NICE PASS!
HE JUMPS UP AND STRETCHES WAY BACK, CREATING TENSION...
AND THEN...
...SNAPS FORWARD!
WHAM
NASTY SPIKE, ISN'T IT? IF HE CAN GET PAST THE BLOCKERS, THERE AREN'T MANY WHO CAN DIG A HIT LIKE THAT.

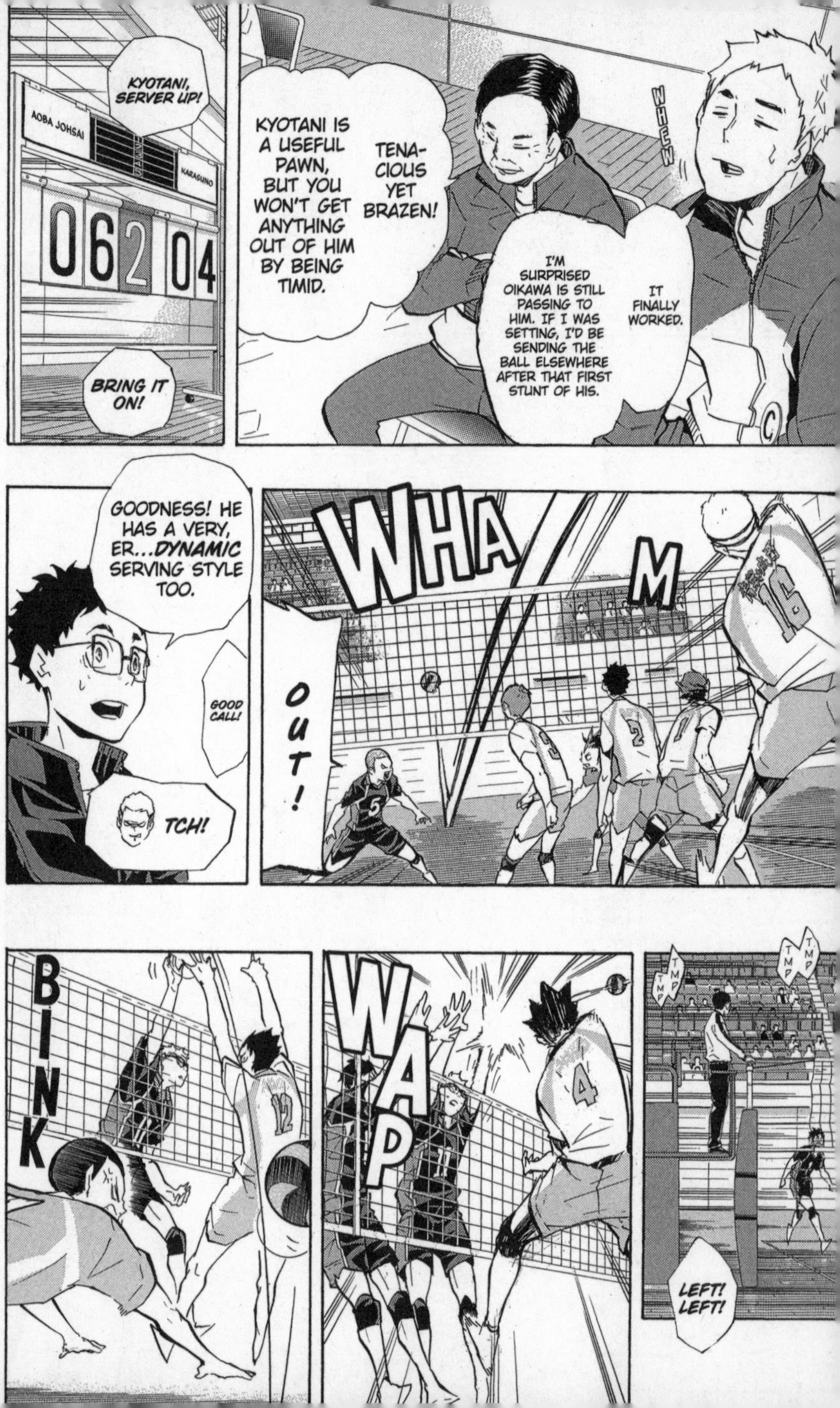
WHEW
IT FINALLY WORKED.
I'M SURPRISED OIKAWA IS STILL PASSING TO HIM. IF I WAS SETTING, I'D BE SENDING THE BALL ELSEWHERE AFTER THAT FIRST STUNT OF HIS.
TENACIOUS YET BRAZEN!
KYOTANI IS A USEFUL PAWN, BUT YOU WON'T GET ANYTHING OUT OF HIM BY BEING TIMID.
KYOTANI, SERVER UP!
AOBA JOHSAI
KARASUNO
06
2
04
BRING IT ON!
WHAM
OUT!
GOODNESS! HE HAS A VERY, ER...*DYNAMIC* SERVING STYLE TOO.
GOOD CALL!
TCH!
TMP TMP
TMP TMP
LEFT! LEFT!
WAP
BINK

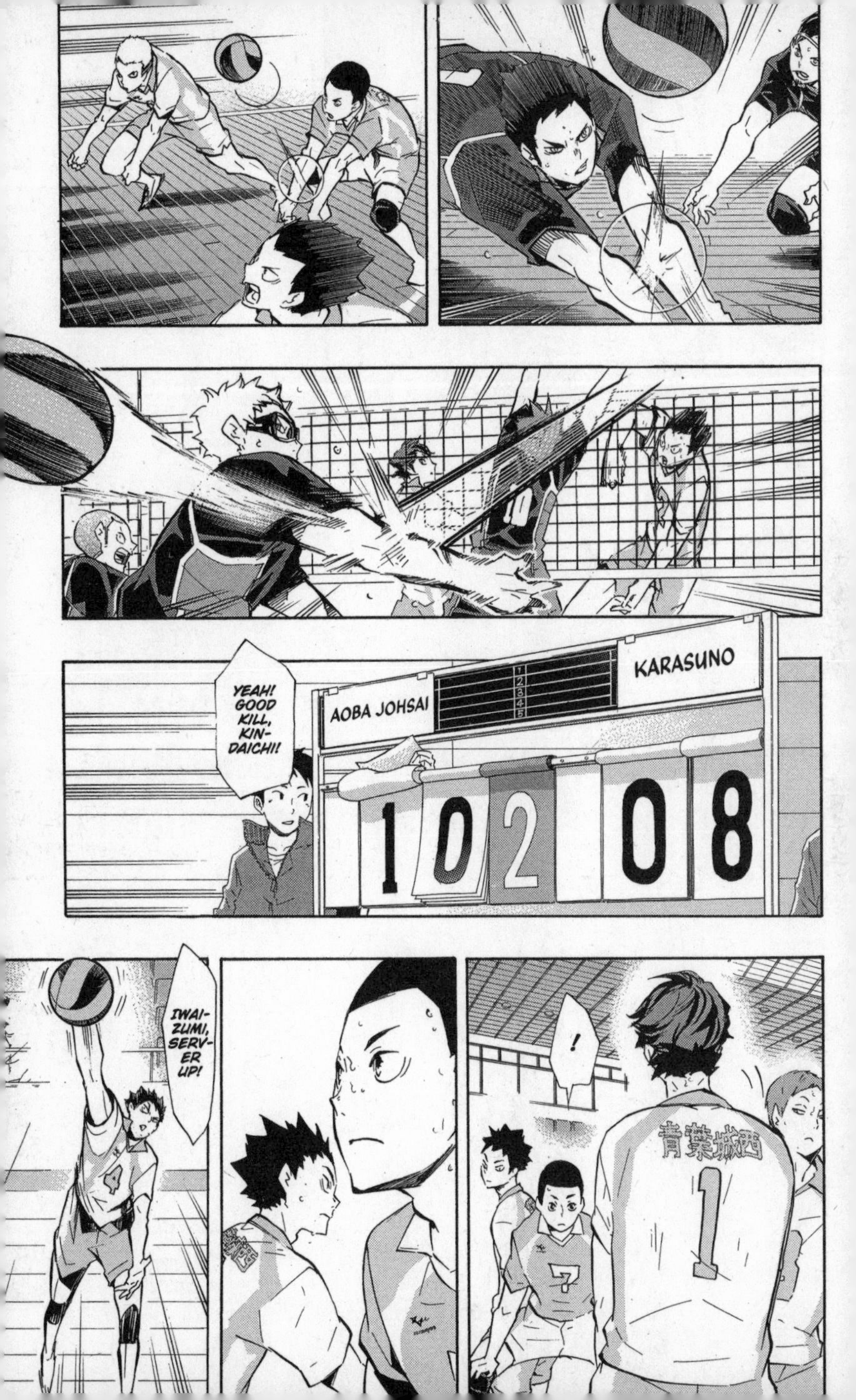
KARASUNO
YEAH! GOOD KILL, KIN-DAICHI!
AOBA JOHSAI
1 2 3 4 5
10 2 08
!
青葉城西
IWAI-ZUMI, SERV-ER UP!

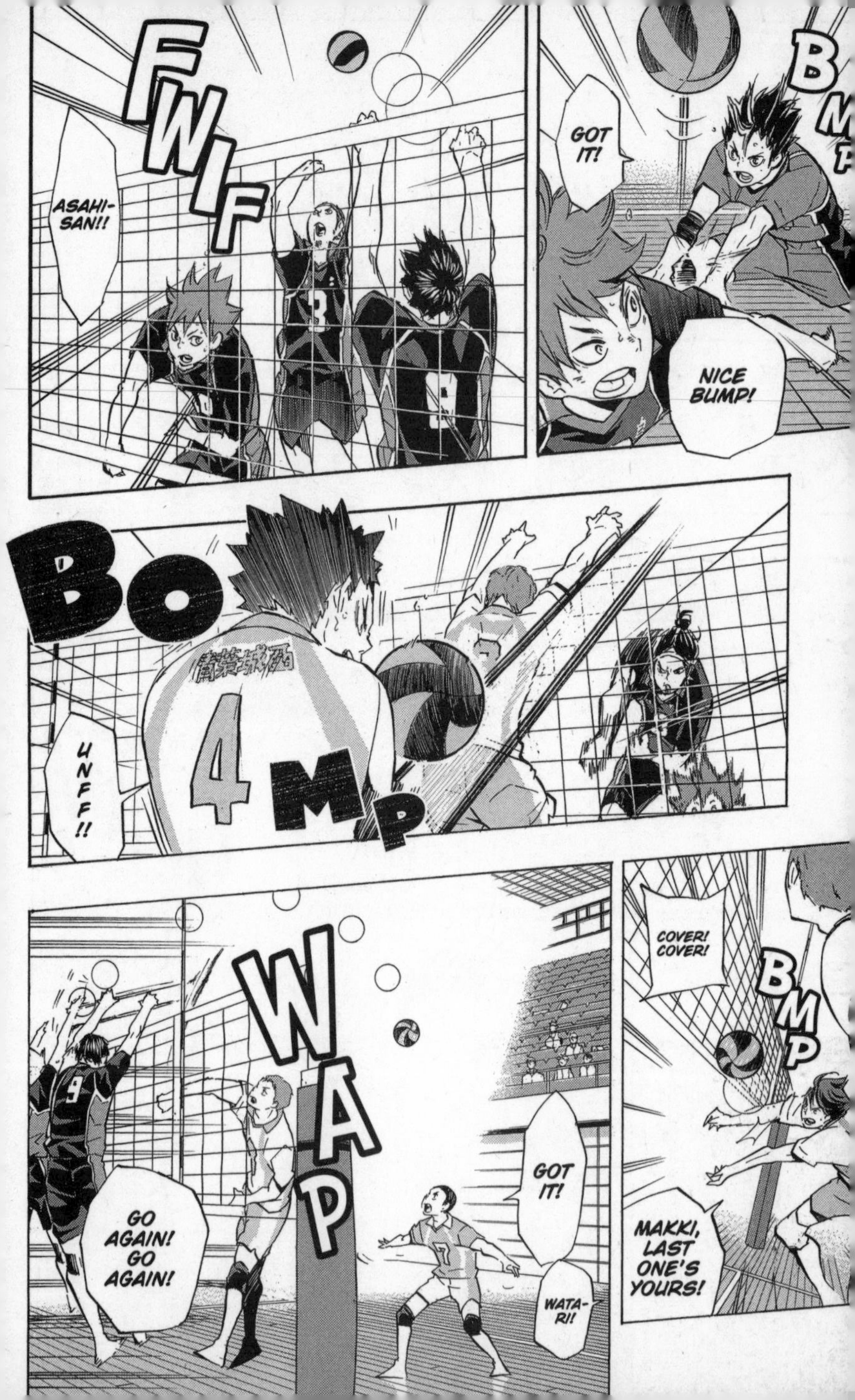
GOT IT!
BMP
NICE BUMP!
FWIF
ASAHI-SAN!!
BOMP
UNFF!!
COVER! COVER!
BMP
MAKKI, LAST ONE'S YOURS!
WAP
GOT IT!
WATA-RI!!
GO AGAIN! GO AGAIN!

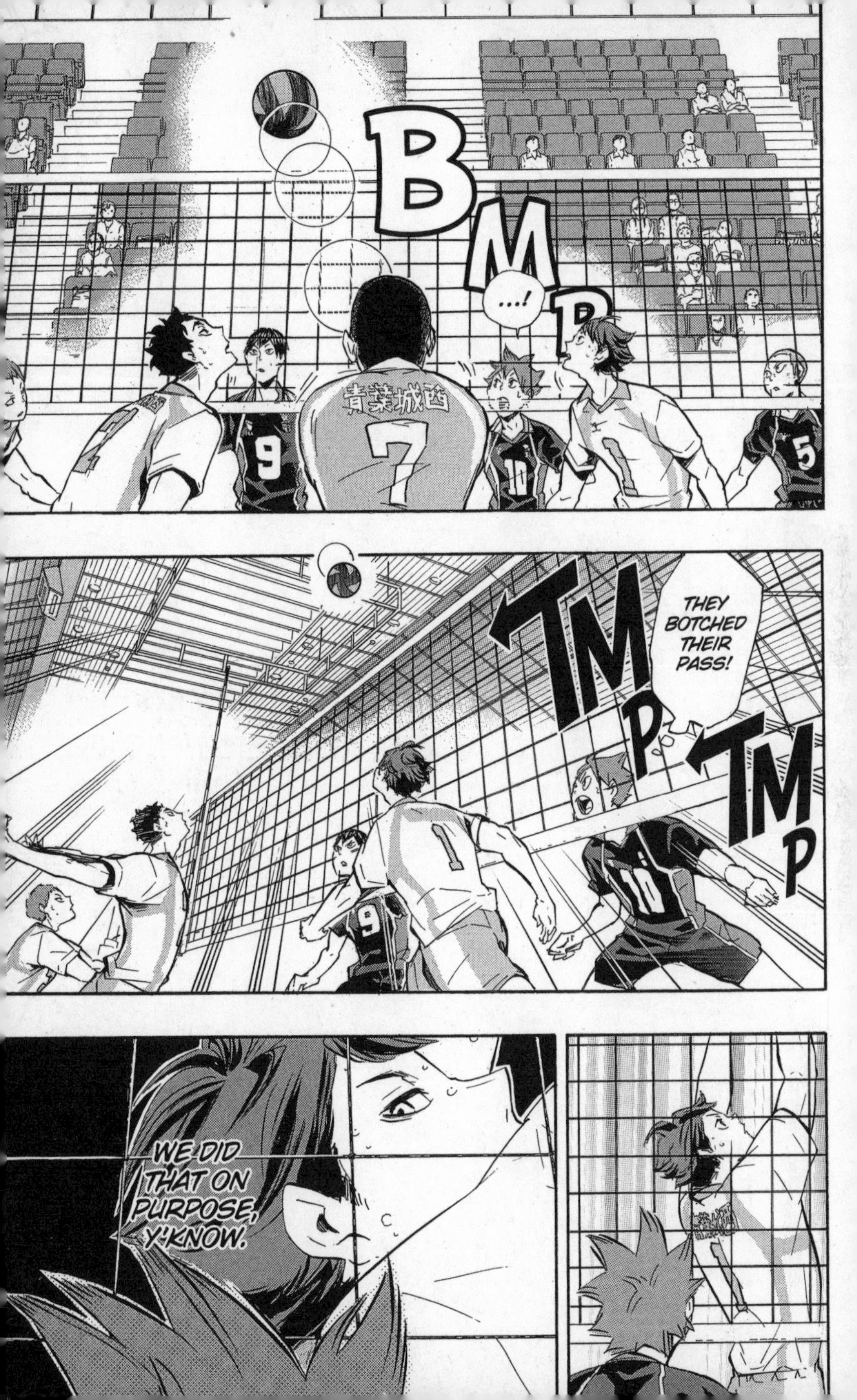
BMMP
...!
THEY BOTCHED THEIR PASS!
TMP TMP
WE DID THAT ON PURPOSE, Y'KNOW.

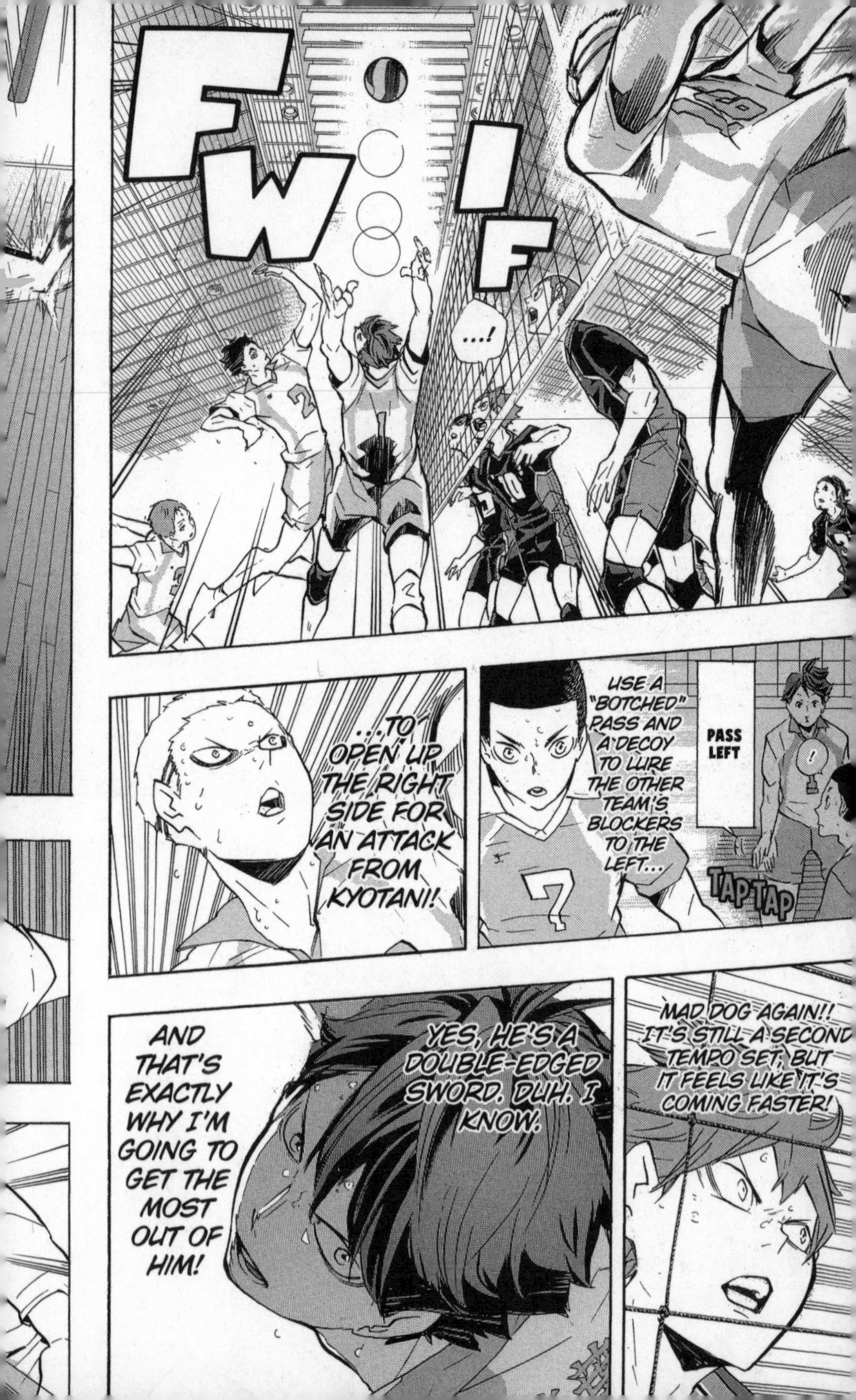
FWIF
....!
USE A "BOTCHED" PASS AND A DECOY TO LURE THE OTHER TEAM'S BLOCKERS TO THE LEFT...
PASS LEFT
!
TAP TAP
...TO OPEN UP THE RIGHT SIDE FOR AN ATTACK FROM KYOTANI!
MAD DOG AGAIN!! IT'S STILL A SECOND TEMPO SET, BUT IT FEELS LIKE IT'S COMING FASTER!
YES, HE'S A DOUBLE-EDGED SWORD. DUH. I KNOW.
AND THAT'S EXACTLY WHY I'M GOING TO GET THE MOST OUT OF HIM!

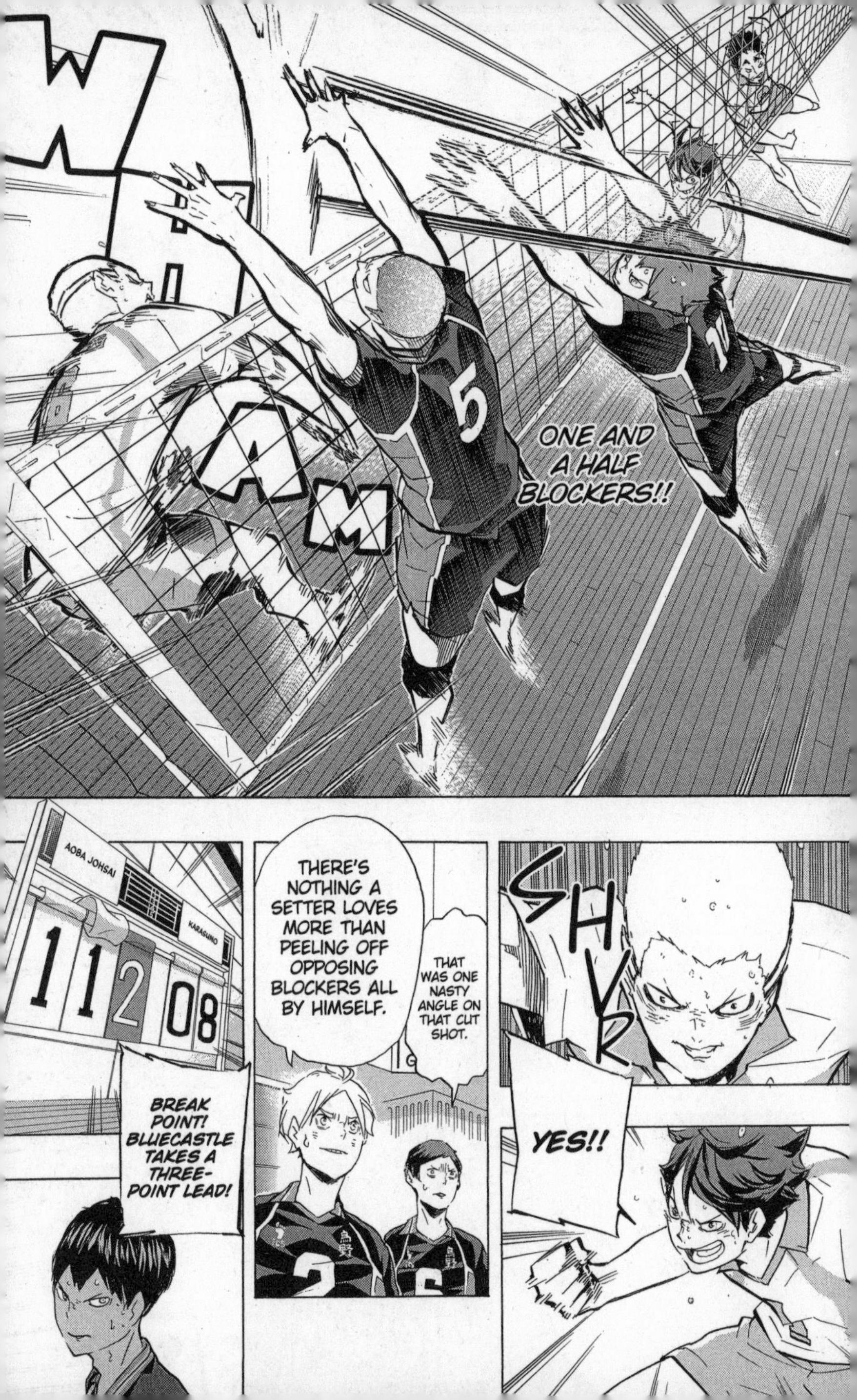
ONE AND A HALF BLOCKERS!!
YES!!
THAT WAS ONE NASTY ANGLE ON THAT CUT SHOT.
THERE'S NOTHING A SETTER LOVES MORE THAN PEELING OFF OPPOSING BLOCKERS ALL BY HIMSELF.
AOBA JOHSAI
KARASUNO
11 2 08
BREAK POINT! BLUECASTLE TAKES A THREE-POINT LEAD!

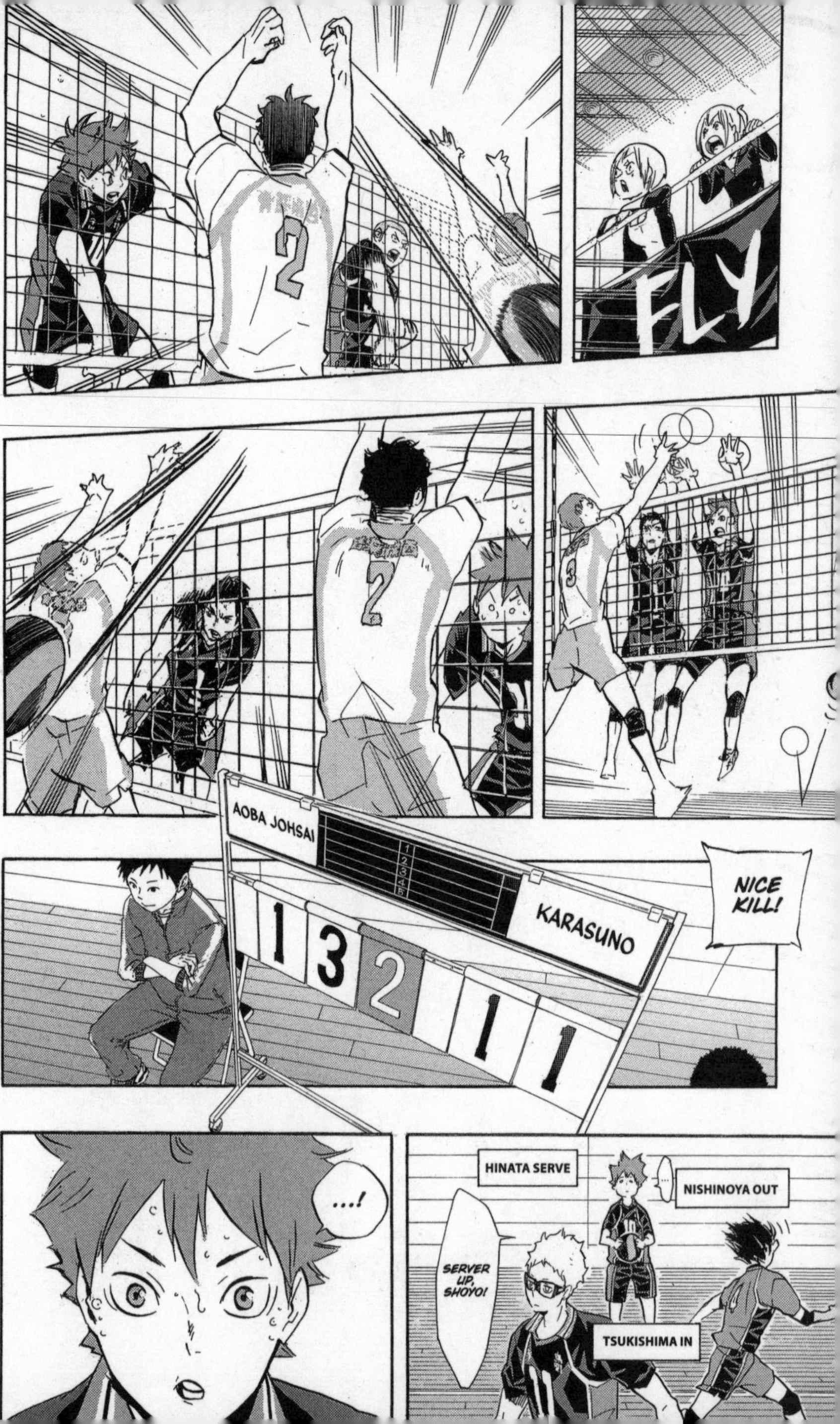
FLY
NICE KILL!
AOBA JOHSAI
13
2
11
KARASUNO
NISHINOYA OUT
...
HINATA SERVE
SERVER UP, SHOYO!
TSUKISHIMA IN
...!

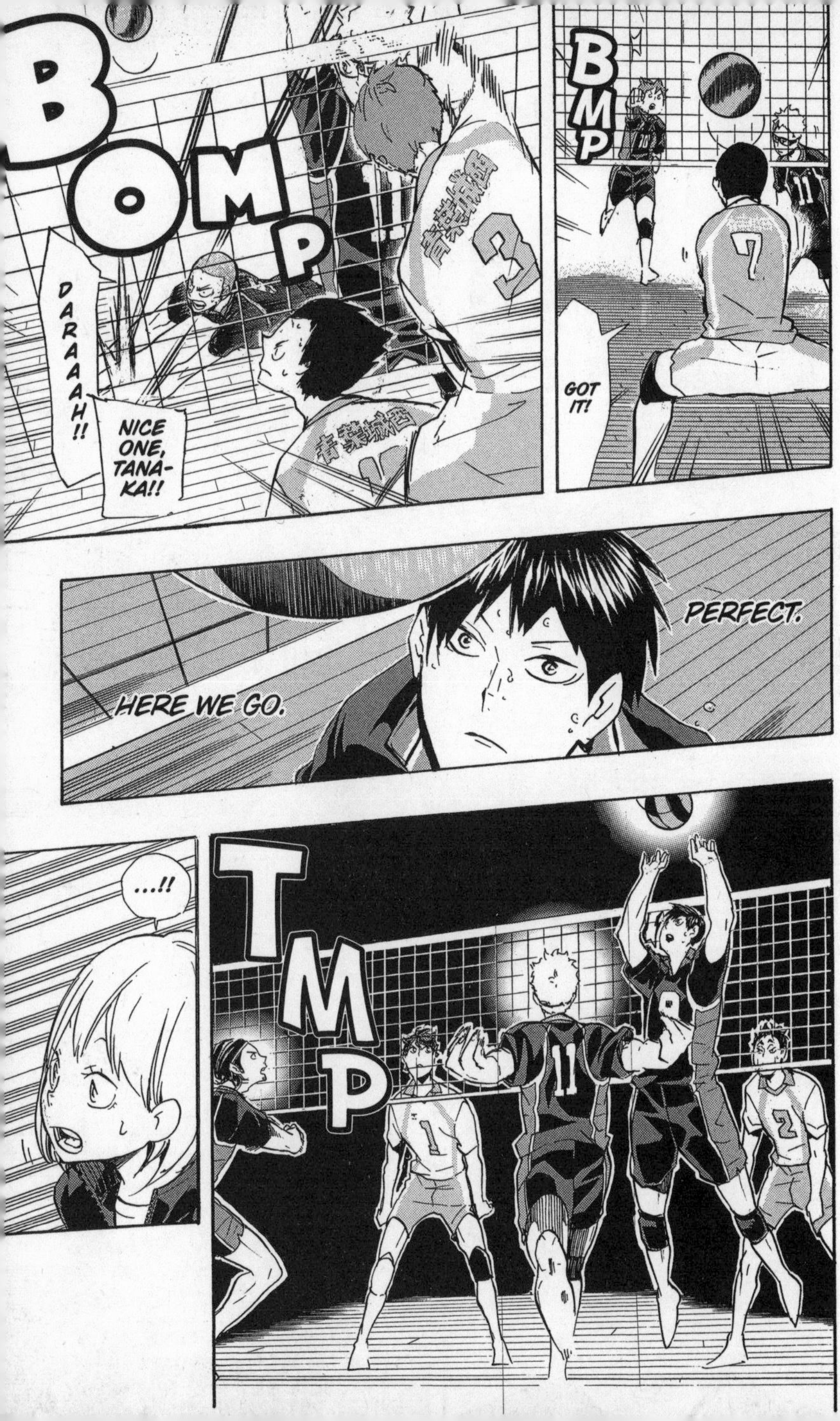
BMP
GOT IT!
BOMP
DARAAAAH!!
NICE ONE, TANAKA!!
PERFECT.
HERE WE GO.
TMP
...!!

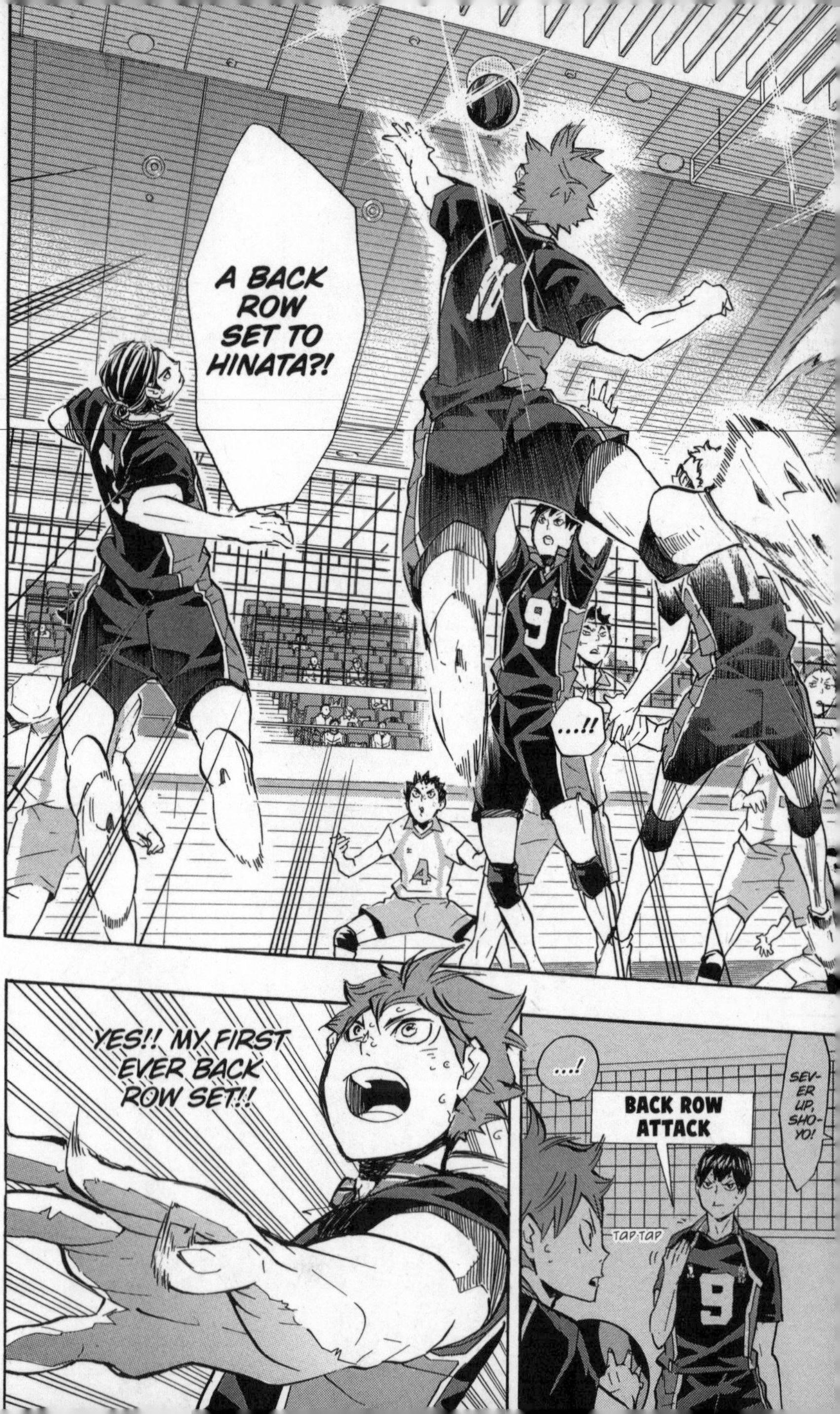
A BACK ROW SET TO HINATA?!
...!!
SEV-ER UP, SHO-YO!
...!
BACK ROW ATTACK
TAP TAP
YES!! MY FIRST EVER BACK ROW SET!!

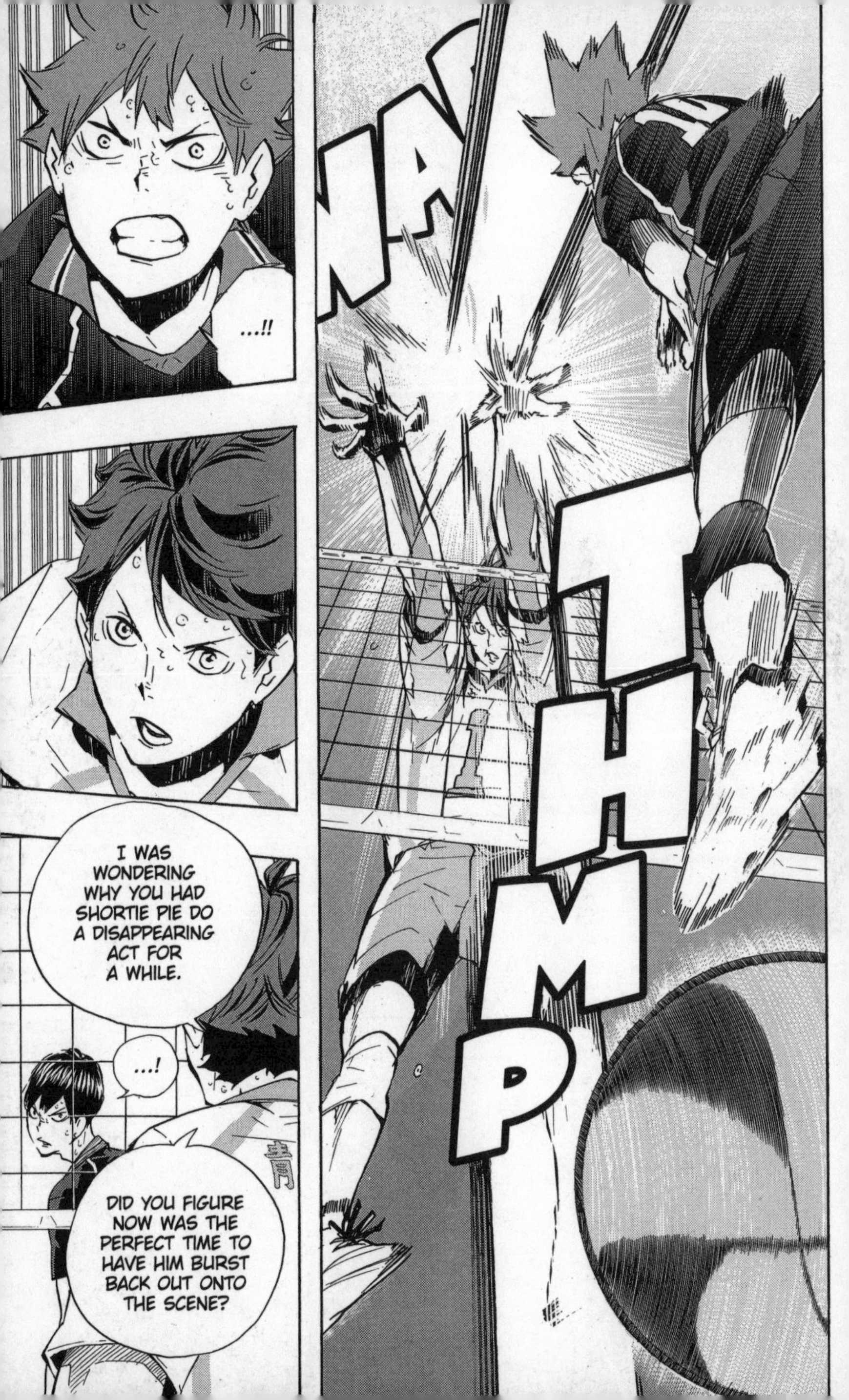

WA
THMP
...!!
I WAS WONDERING WHY YOU HAD SHORTIE PIE DO A DISAPPEARING ACT FOR A WHILE.
...!
DID YOU FIGURE NOW WAS THE PERFECT TIME TO HAVE HIM BURST BACK OUT ONTO THE SCENE?

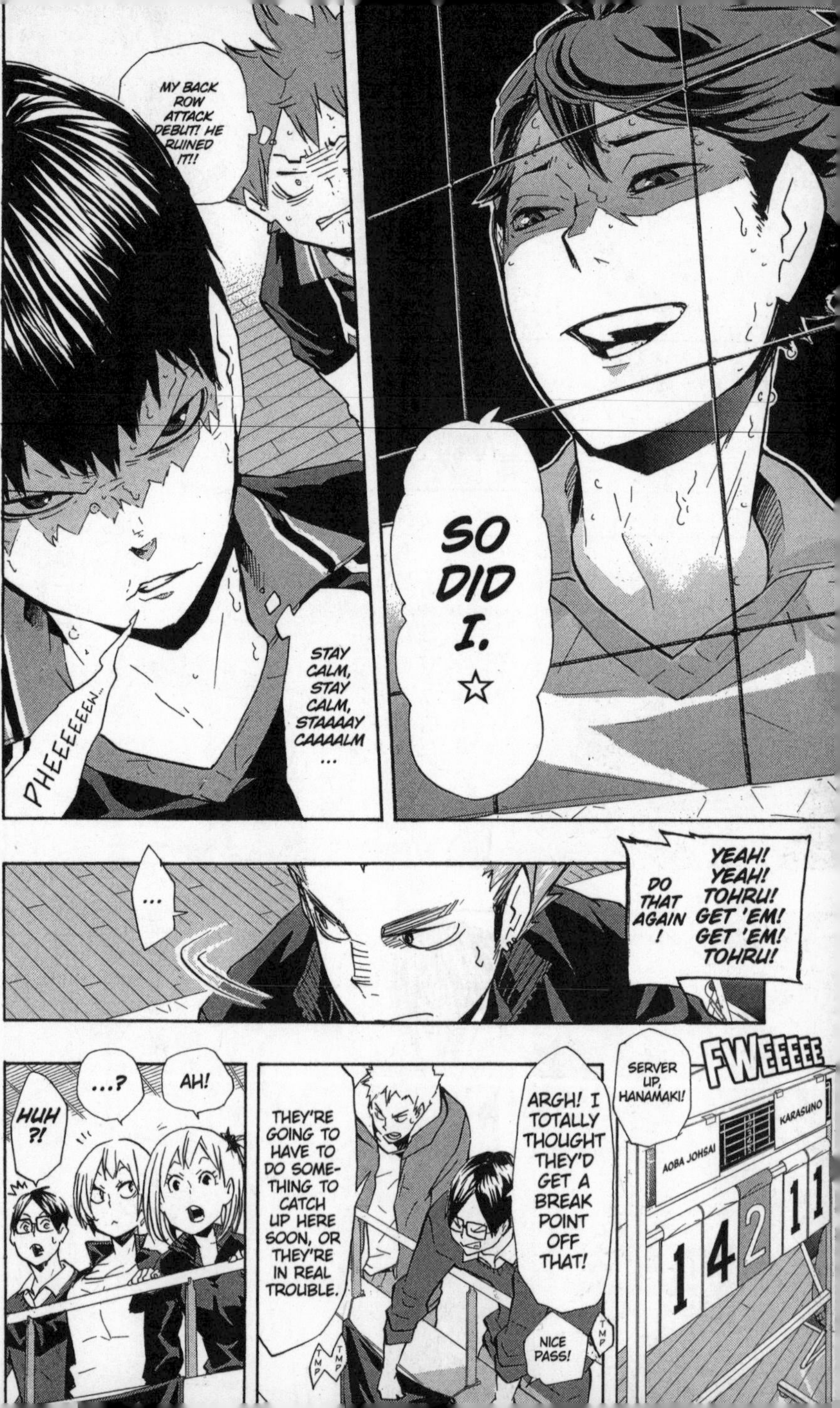

SO DID I. ☆
MY BACK ROW ATTACK DEBUT! HE RUINED IT!!
STAY CALM, STAY CALM, STAAAAY CAAAALM ...
PHEEEEEEW...
YEAH! YEAH! TOHRU! GET 'EM! GET 'EM! TOHRU!
DO THAT AGAIN!
...
FWEEEEE
SERVER UP, HANAMAKI!
KARASUNO
AOBA JOHSAI
14 2 11
ARGH! I TOTALLY THOUGHT THEY'D GET A BREAK POINT OFF THAT!
THEY'RE GOING TO HAVE TO DO SOMETHING TO CATCH UP HERE SOON, OR THEY'RE IN REAL TROUBLE.
TMP
NICE PASS!
TMP TMP
AH!
...?
HUH?!

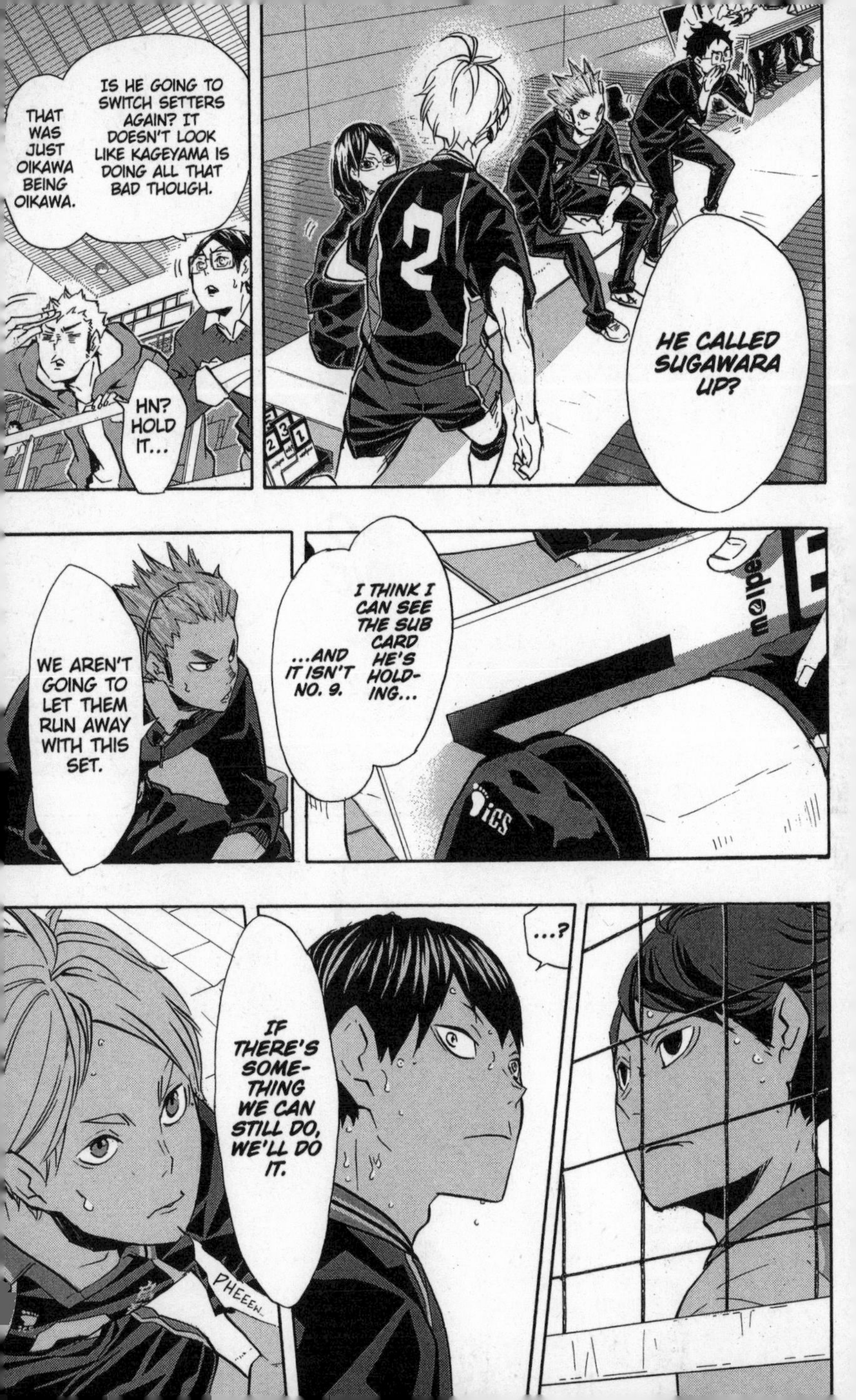
HE CALLED SUGAWARA UP?
IS HE GOING TO SWITCH SETTERS AGAIN? IT DOESN'T LOOK LIKE KAGEYAMA IS DOING ALL THAT BAD THOUGH.
THAT WAS JUST OIKAWA BEING OIKAWA.
HN? HOLD IT...
I THINK I CAN SEE THE SUB CARD HE'S HOLDING...
...AND IT ISN'T NO. 9.
WE AREN'T GOING TO LET THEM RUN AWAY WITH THIS SET.
...?
IF THERE'S SOMETHING WE CAN STILL DO, WE'LL DO IT.
PHEEEEN

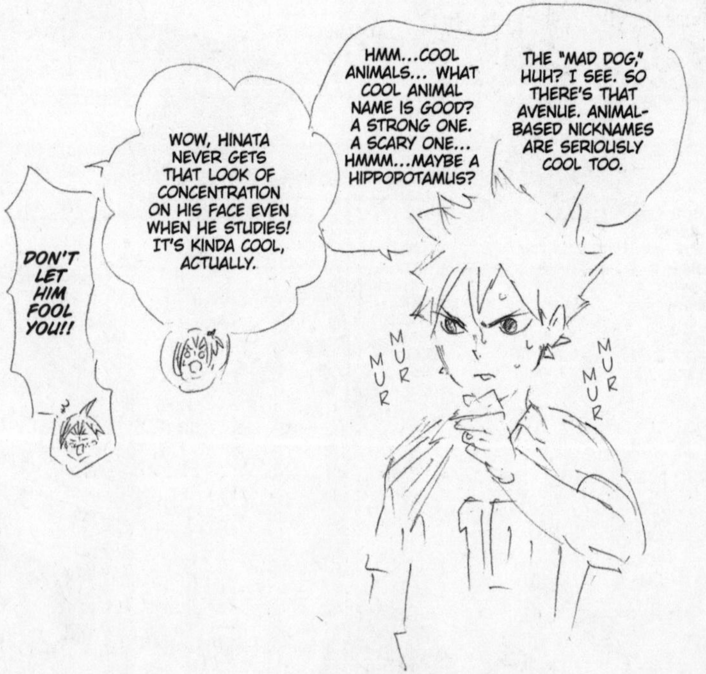
THE "MAD DOG," HUH? I SEE. SO THERE'S THAT AVENUE. ANIMAL-BASED NICKNAMES ARE SERIOUSLY COOL TOO.
HMM...COOL ANIMALS... WHAT COOL ANIMAL NAME IS GOOD? A STRONG ONE. A SCARY ONE... HMMM...MAYBE A HIPPOPOTAMUS?
MUR MUR
MUR MUR
WOW, HINATA NEVER GETS THAT LOOK OF CONCENTRATION ON HIS FACE EVEN WHEN HE STUDIES! IT'S KINDA COOL, ACTUALLY.
DON'T LET HIM FOOL YOU!!

CHAPTER 134: Both Teams

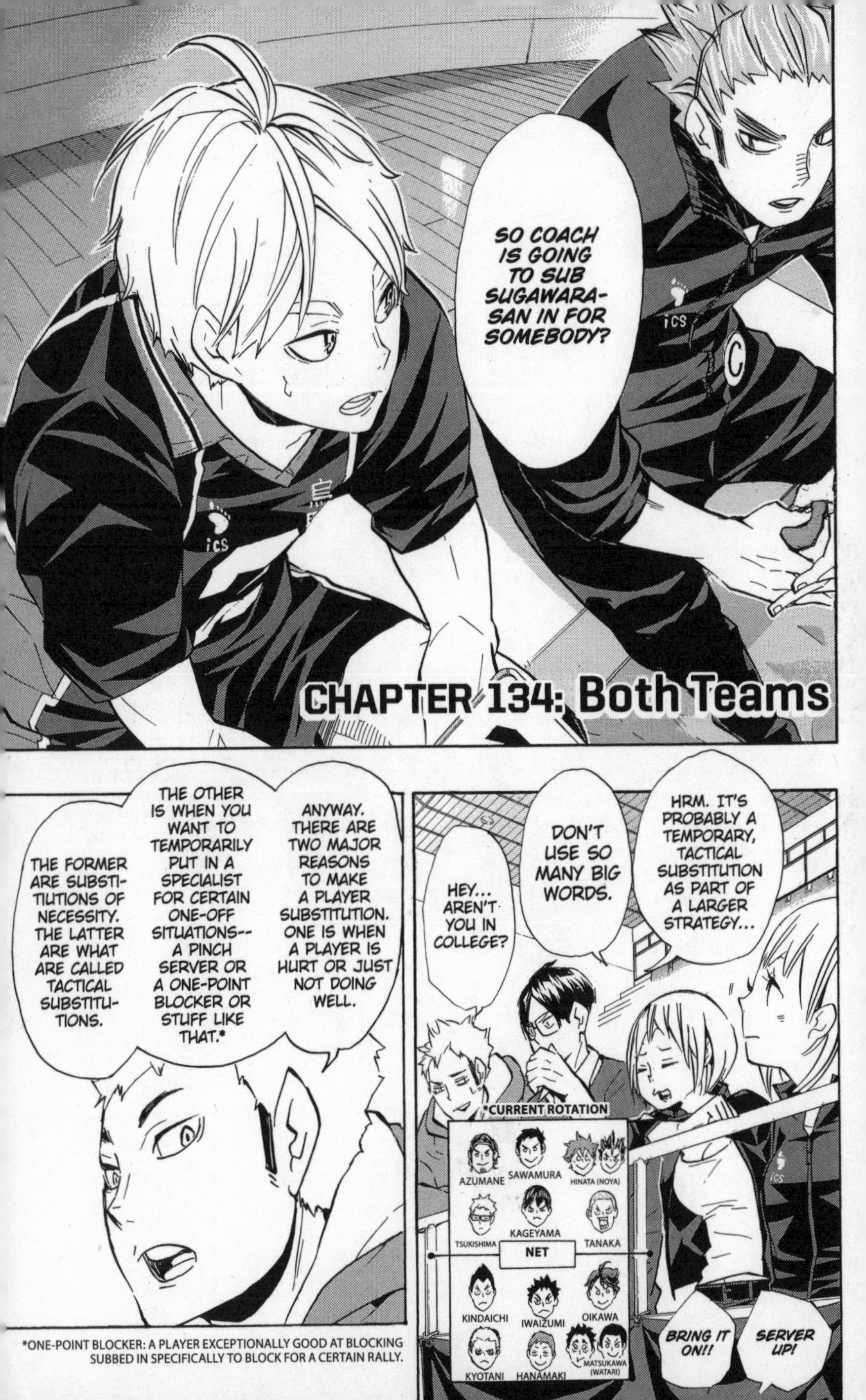
SO COACH IS GOING TO SUB SUGAWARA-SAN IN FOR SOMEBODY?
HRM. IT'S PROBABLY A TEMPORARY, TACTICAL SUBSTITUTION AS PART OF A LARGER STRATEGY...
DON'T USE SO MANY BIG WORDS.
HEY... AREN'T YOU IN COLLEGE?
*CURRENT ROTATION
AZUMANE
SAWAMURA
HINATA (NOYA)
TSUKISHIMA
KAGEYAMA
TANAKA
NET
KINDAICHI
IWAIZUMI
OIKAWA
KYOTANI
HANAMAKI
MATSUKAWA (WATARI)
SERVER UP!
BRING IT ON!!
ANYWAY. THERE ARE TWO MAJOR REASONS TO MAKE A PLAYER SUBSTITUTION. ONE IS WHEN A PLAYER IS HURT OR JUST NOT DOING WELL.
THE OTHER IS WHEN YOU WANT TO TEMPORARILY PUT IN A SPECIALIST FOR CERTAIN ONE-OFF SITUATIONS-- A PINCH SERVER OR A ONE-POINT BLOCKER OR STUFF LIKE THAT.*
THE FORMER ARE SUBSTI-TUTIONS OF NECESSITY. THE LATTER ARE WHAT ARE CALLED TACTICAL SUBSTITU-TIONS.

*ONE-POINT BLOCKER: A PLAYER EXCEPTIONALLY GOOD AT BLOCKING SUBBED IN SPECIFICALLY TO BLOCK FOR A CERTAIN RALLY.

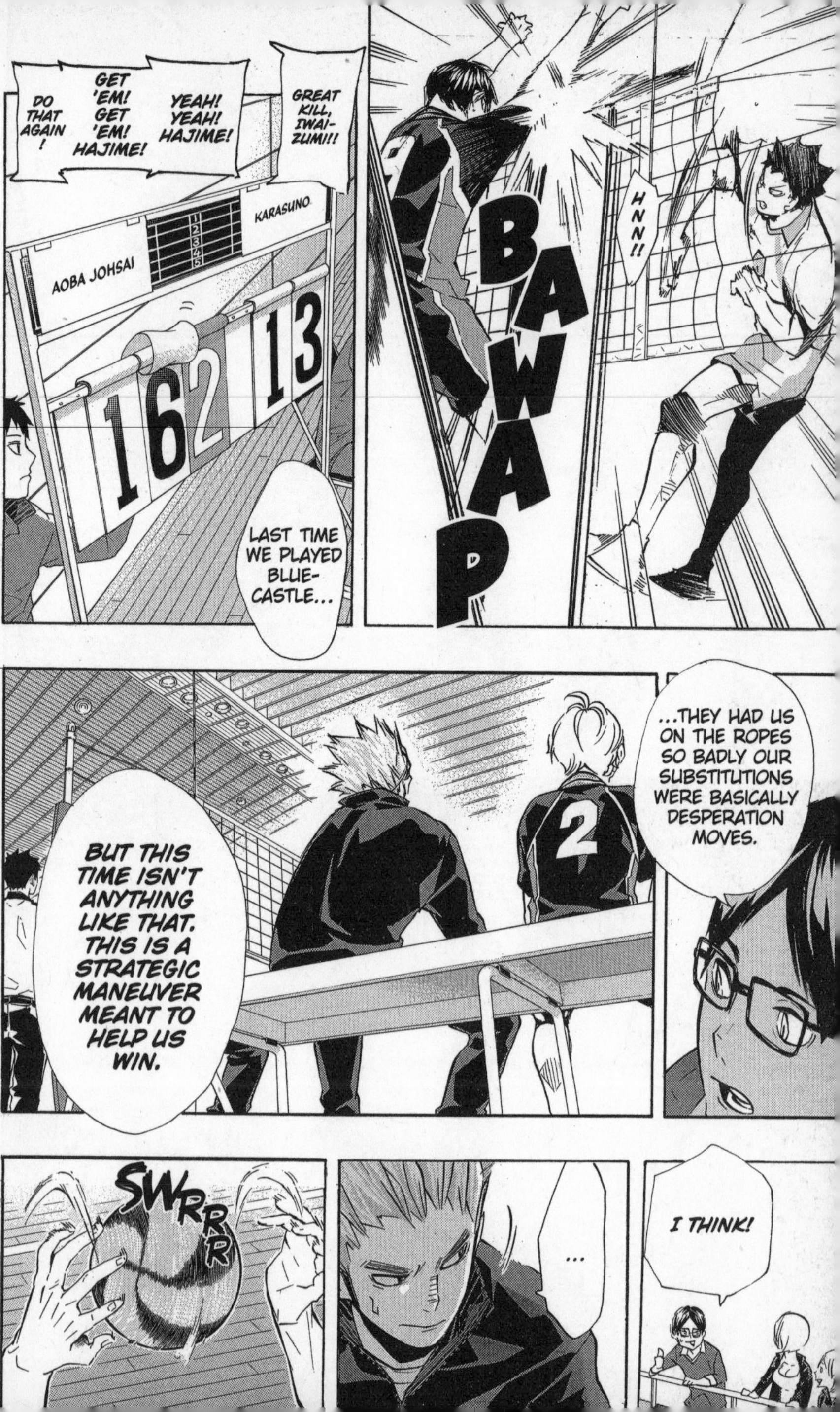

HNN!!
BAWAP
GREAT KILL, IWAI-ZUMI!!
YEAH! YEAH! HAJIME!
GET 'EM! GET 'EM! HAJIME!
DO THAT AGAIN!
KARASUNO
AOBA JOHSAI
1 2 3 4 5
16 2 13
LAST TIME WE PLAYED BLUE-CASTLE...
...THEY HAD US ON THE ROPES SO BADLY OUR SUBSTITUTIONS WERE BASICALLY DESPERATION MOVES.
BUT THIS TIME ISN'T ANYTHING LIKE THAT. THIS IS A STRATEGIC MANEUVER MEANT TO HELP US WIN.
I THINK!
...
SWRRR

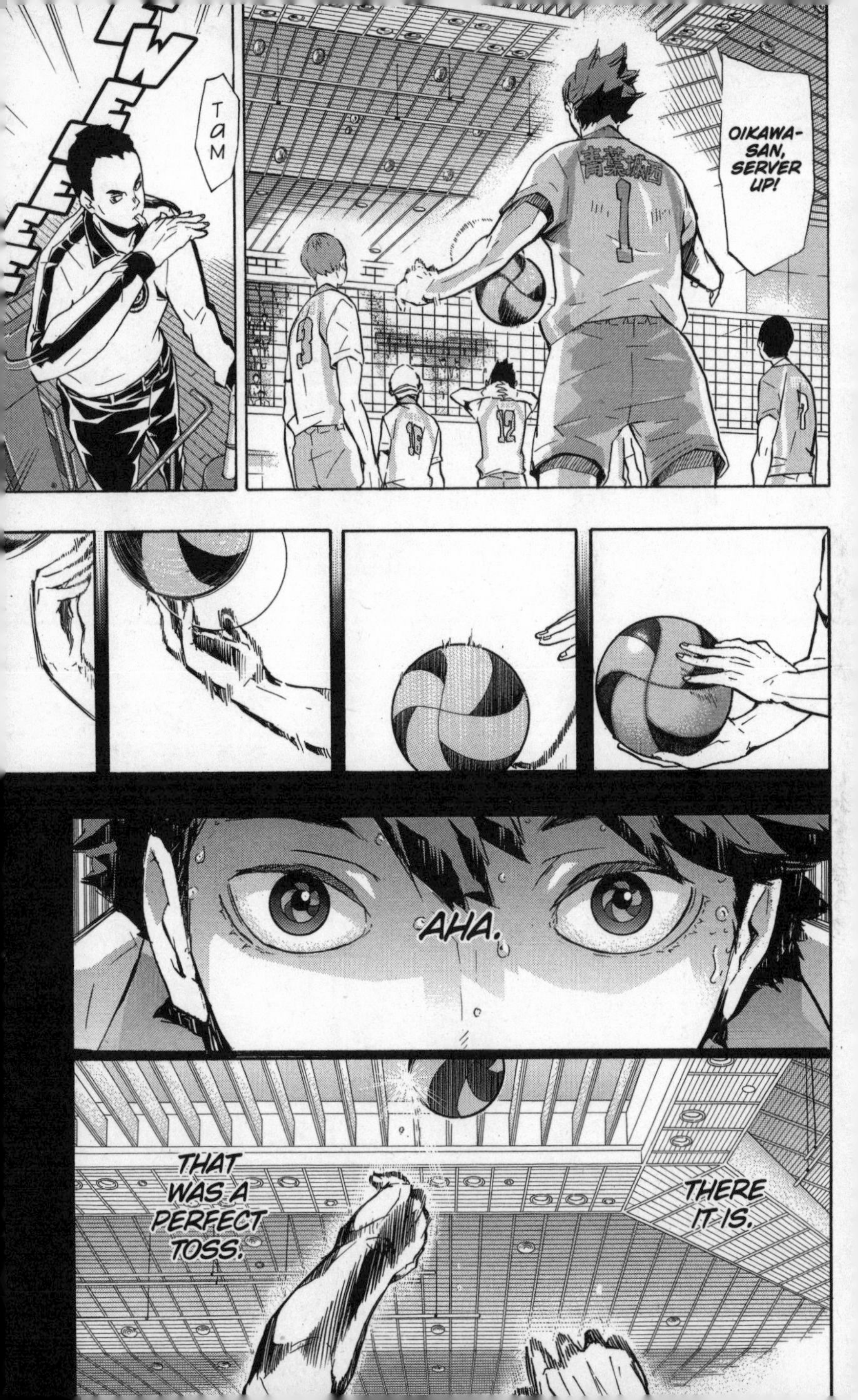
OIKAWA-SAN, SERVER UP!
Tam
AHA.
THERE IT IS.
THAT WAS A PERFECT TOSS.

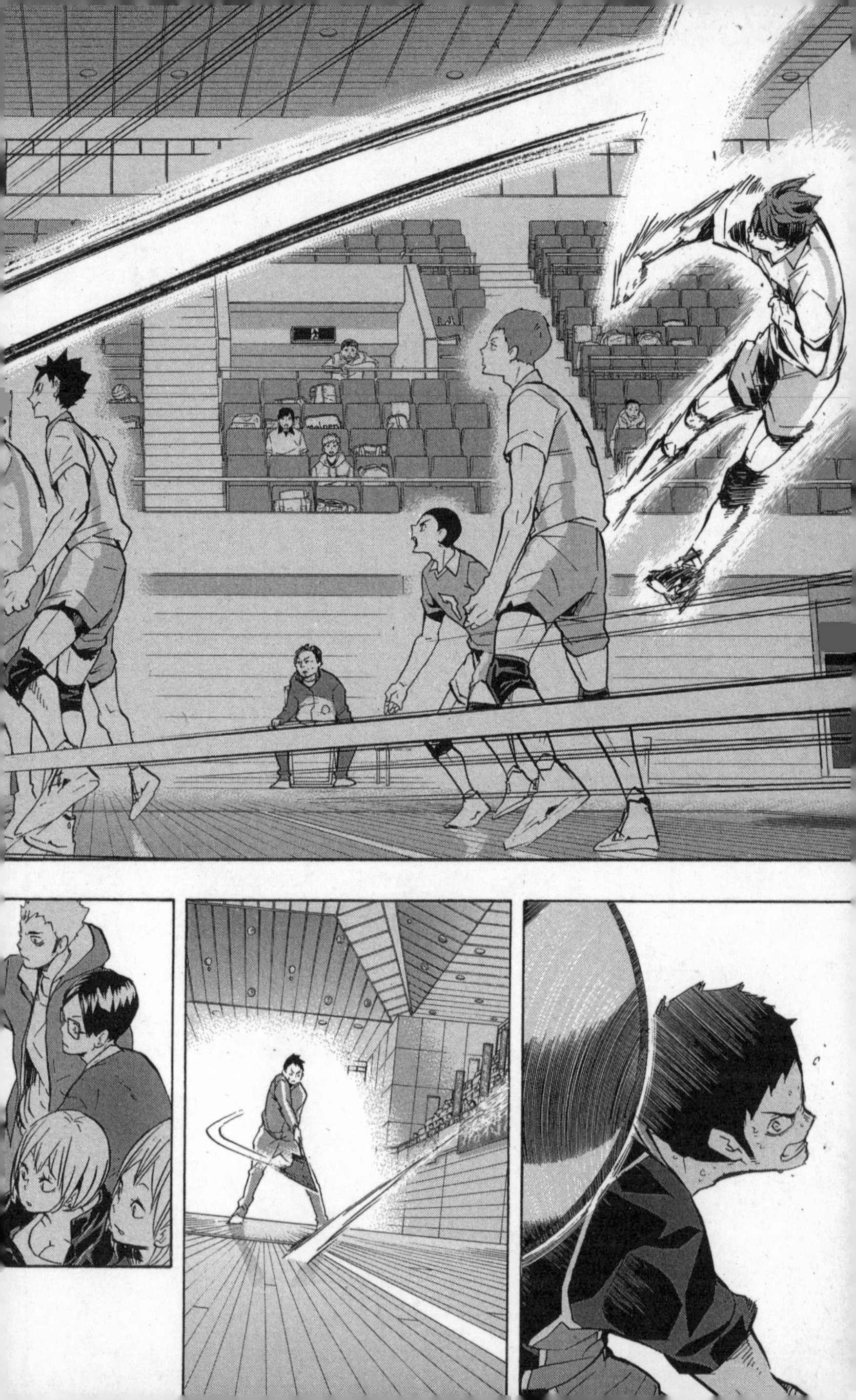

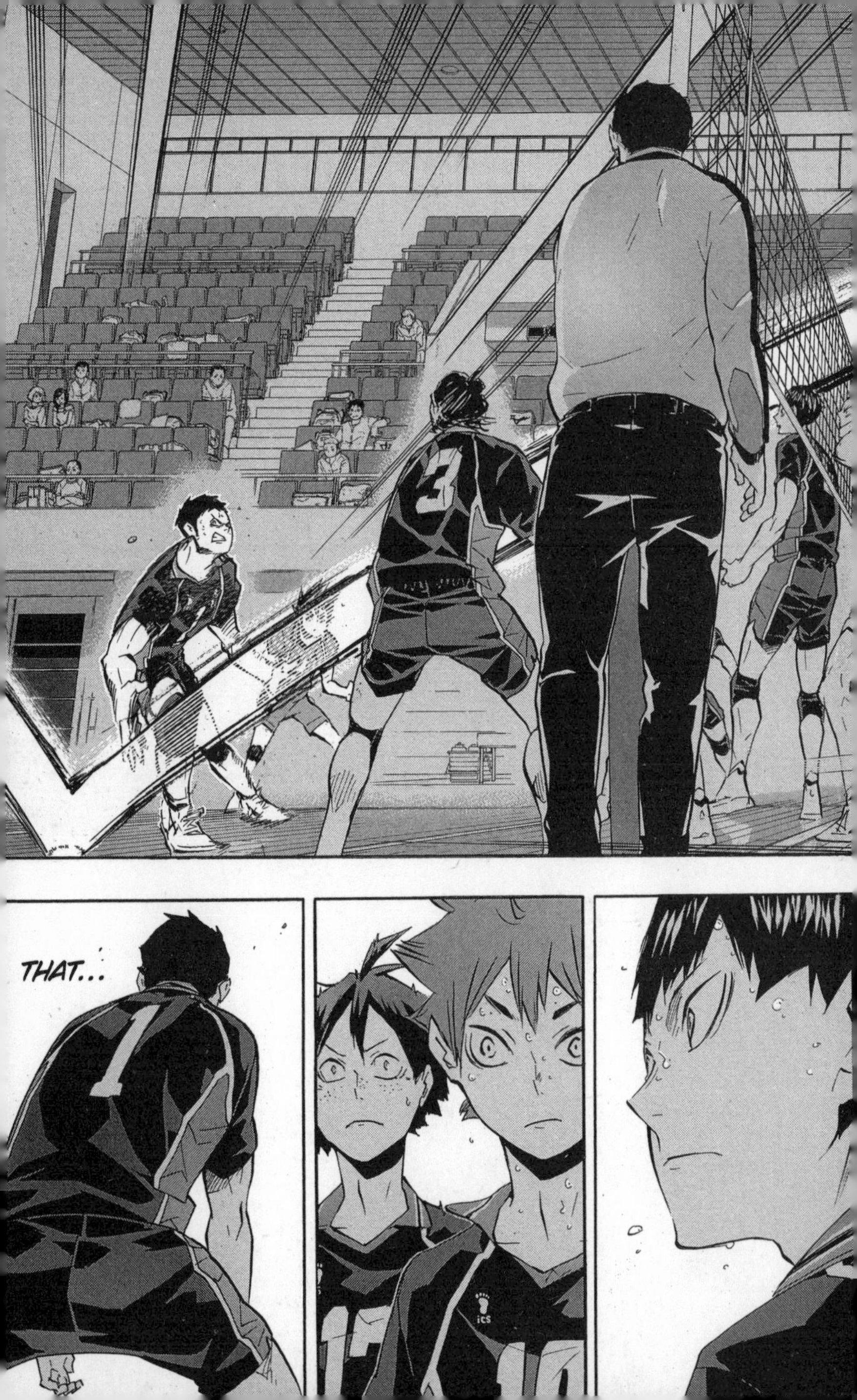
THAT...

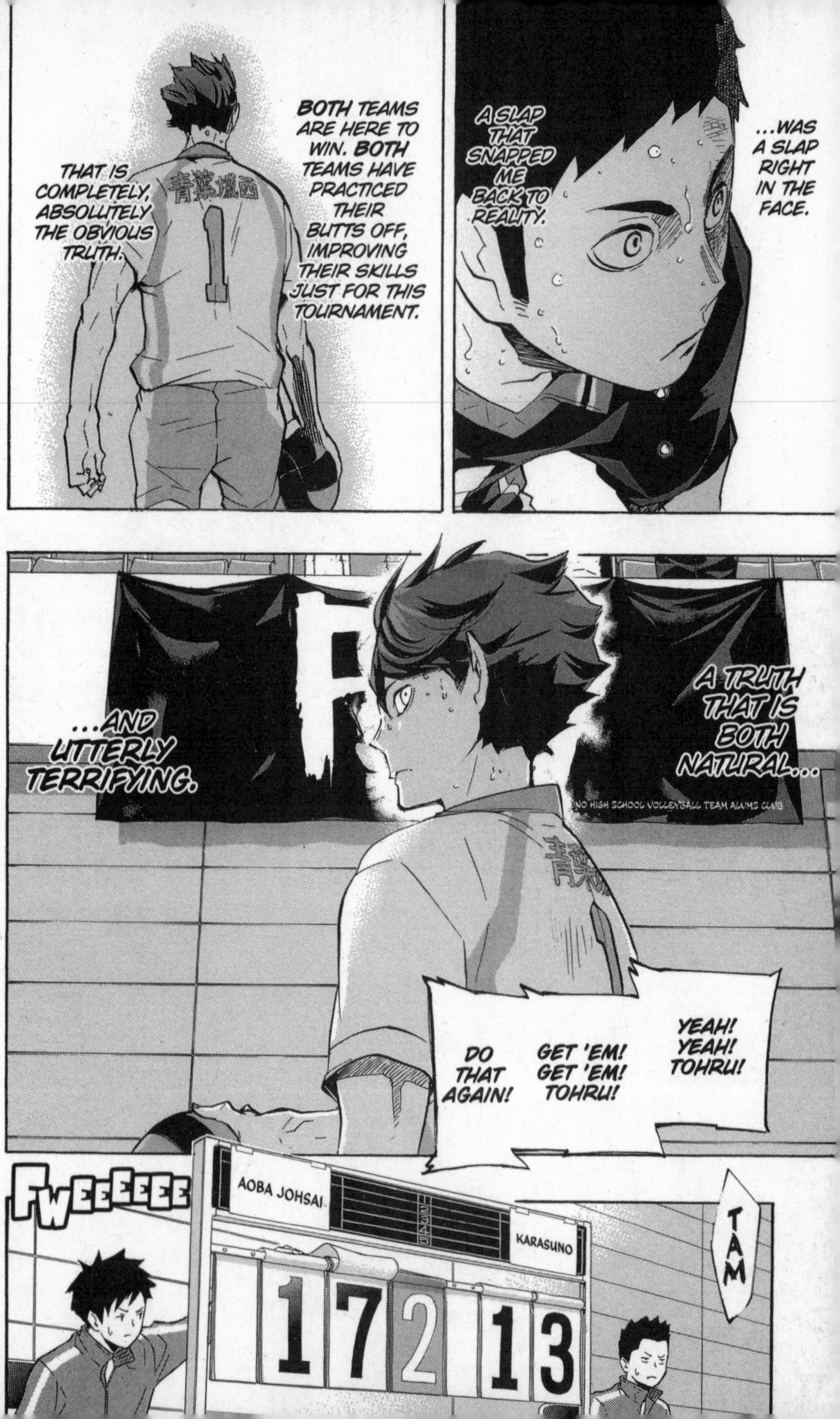
...WAS A SLAP RIGHT IN THE FACE.
A SLAP THAT SNAPPED ME BACK TO REALITY.
BOTH TEAMS ARE HERE TO WIN. BOTH TEAMS HAVE PRACTICED THEIR BUTTS OFF, IMPROVING THEIR SKILLS JUST FOR THIS TOURNAMENT.
THAT IS COMPLETELY, ABSOLUTELY THE OBVIOUS TRUTH.
青葉城西
1
A TRUTH THAT IS BOTH NATURAL...
NO HIGH SCHOOL VOLLEYBALL TEAM ALUMS CLUB
...AND UTTERLY TERRIFYING.
YEAH! YEAH! TOHRU!
GET 'EM! GET 'EM! TOHRU!
DO THAT AGAIN!
TAM
AOBA JOHSAI
KARASUNO
17 2 13
FWEEEEEE

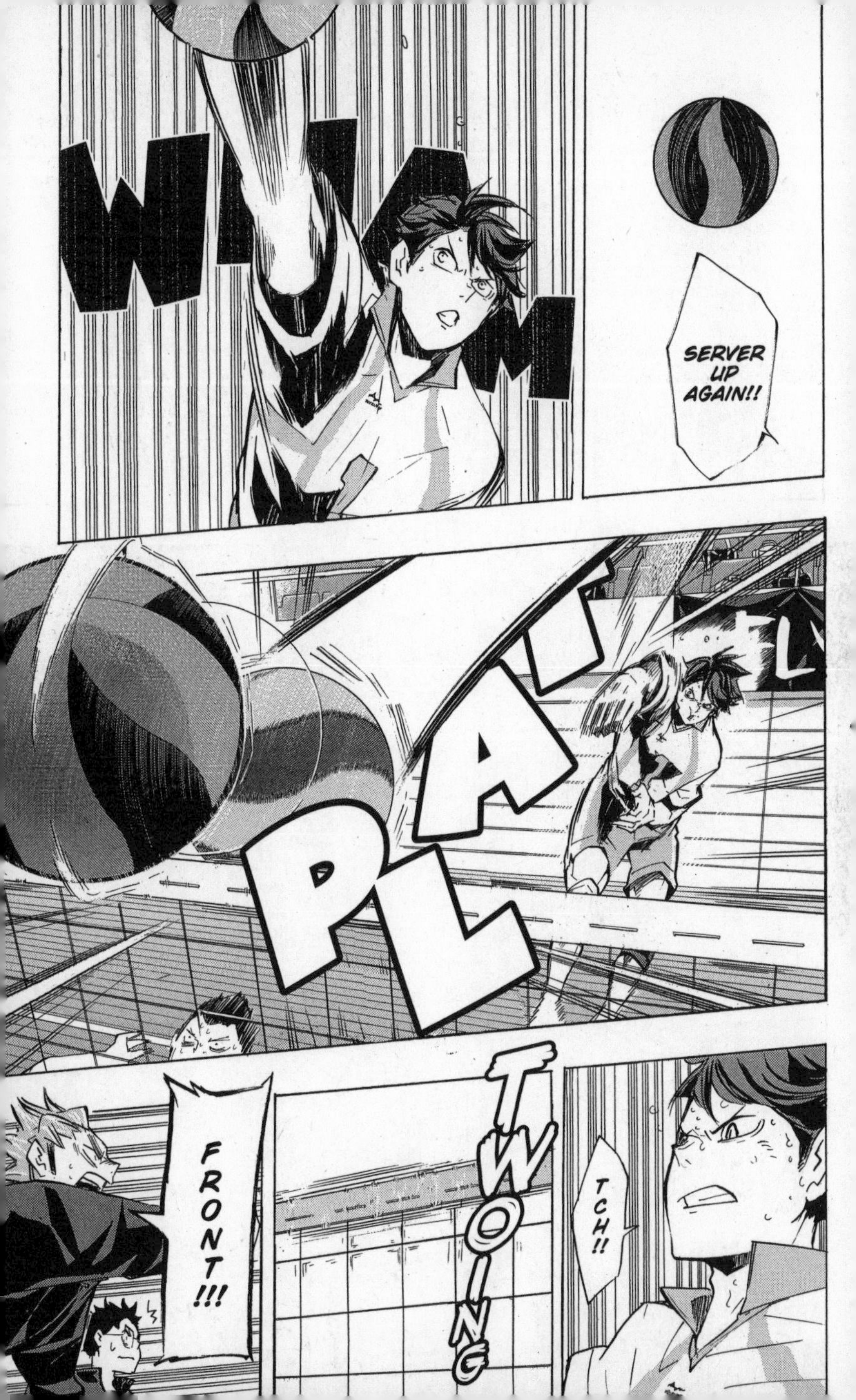
SERVER UP AGAIN!!
WHAM
PLAT
TCH!!
TWOING
FRONT!!!

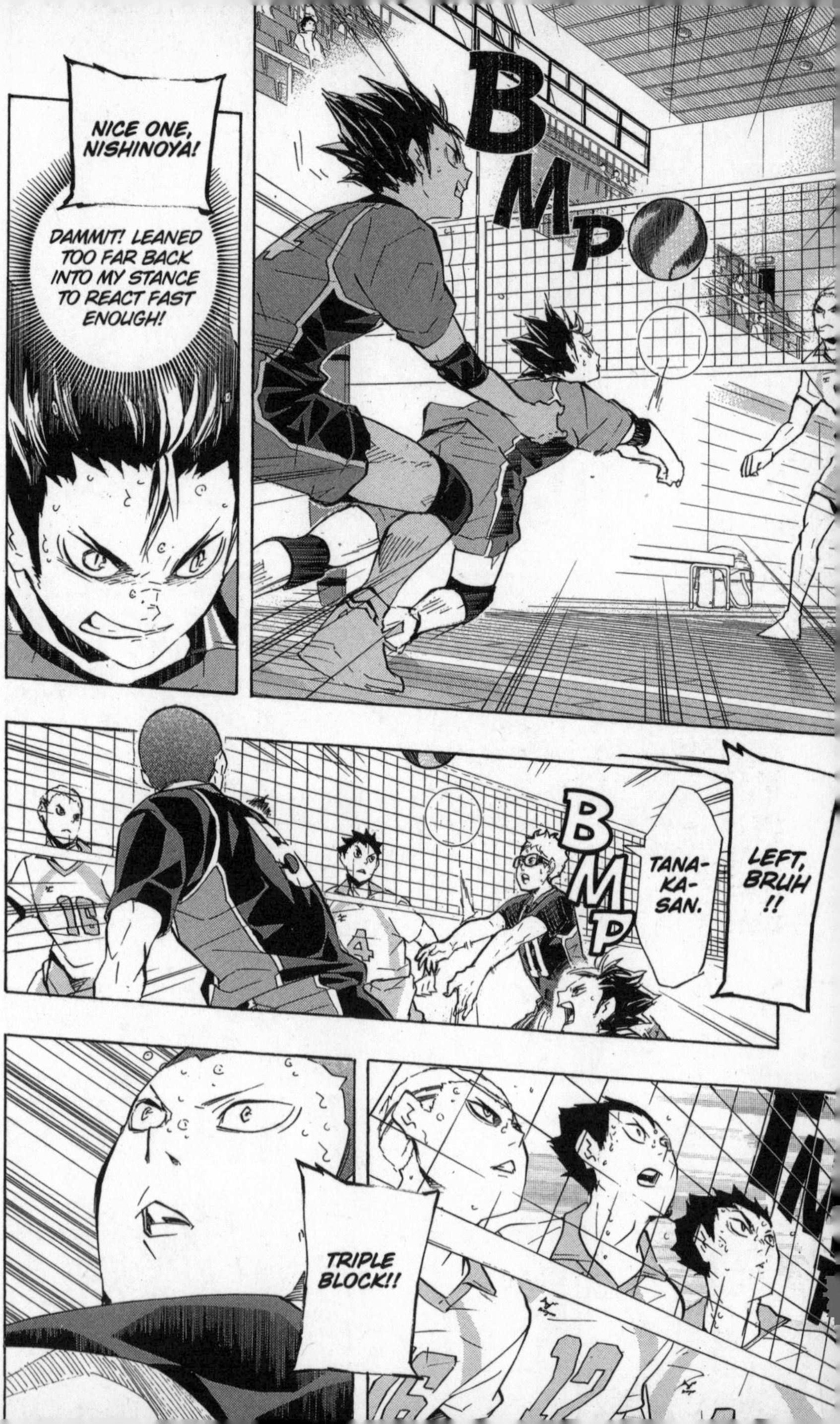
BMP
NICE ONE, NISHINOYA!
DAMMIT! LEANED TOO FAR BACK INTO MY STANCE TO REACT FAST ENOUGH!
LEFT, BRUH!!
TANA-KA-SAN.
BMP
TRIPLE BLOCK!!

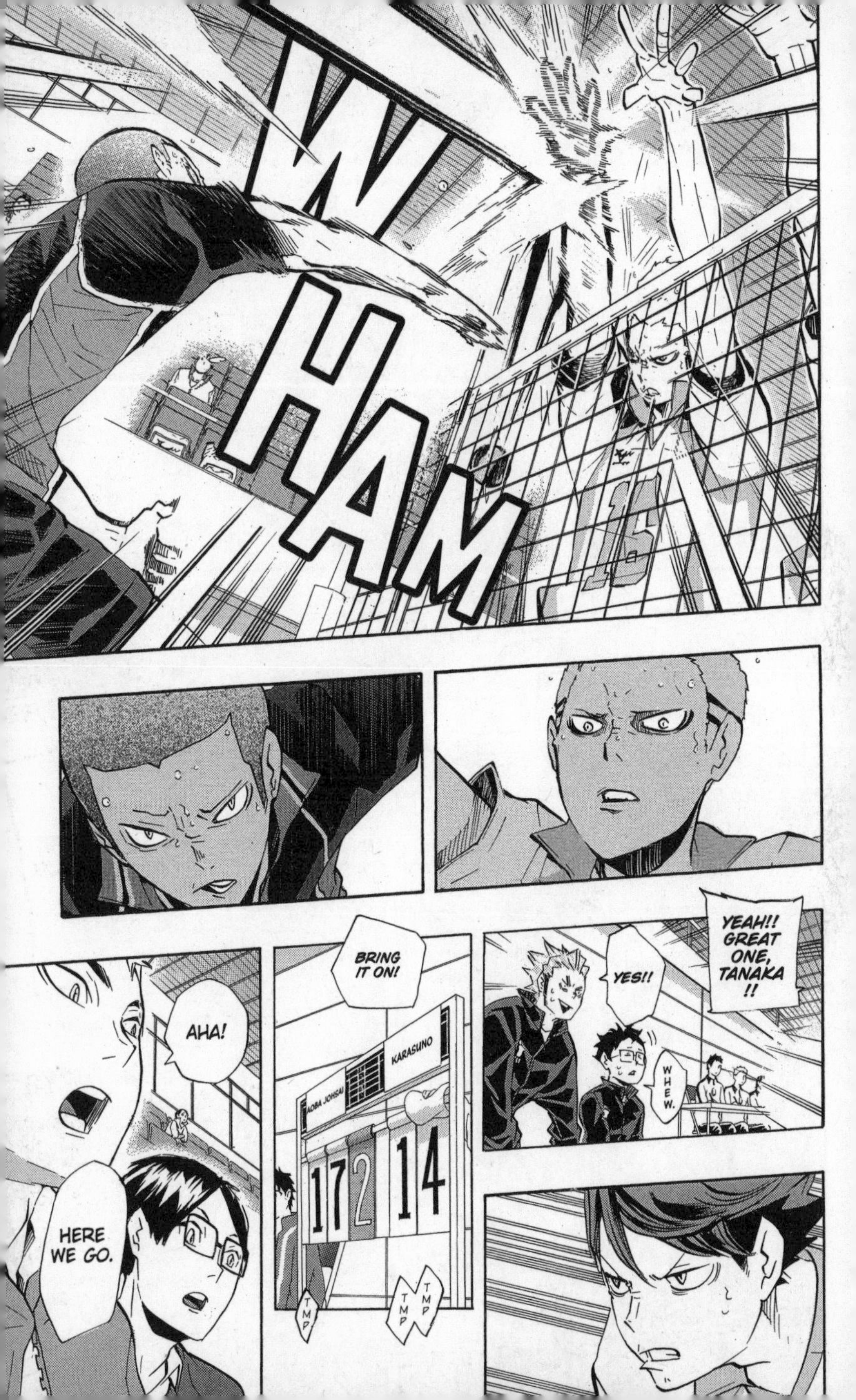
WHAM
YEAH!! GREAT ONE, TANAKA!!
YES!!
WHEW.
BRING IT ON!
KARASUNO
AOBA JOHSAI
17 2 14
TMP TMP
TMP
AHA!
HERE WE GO.

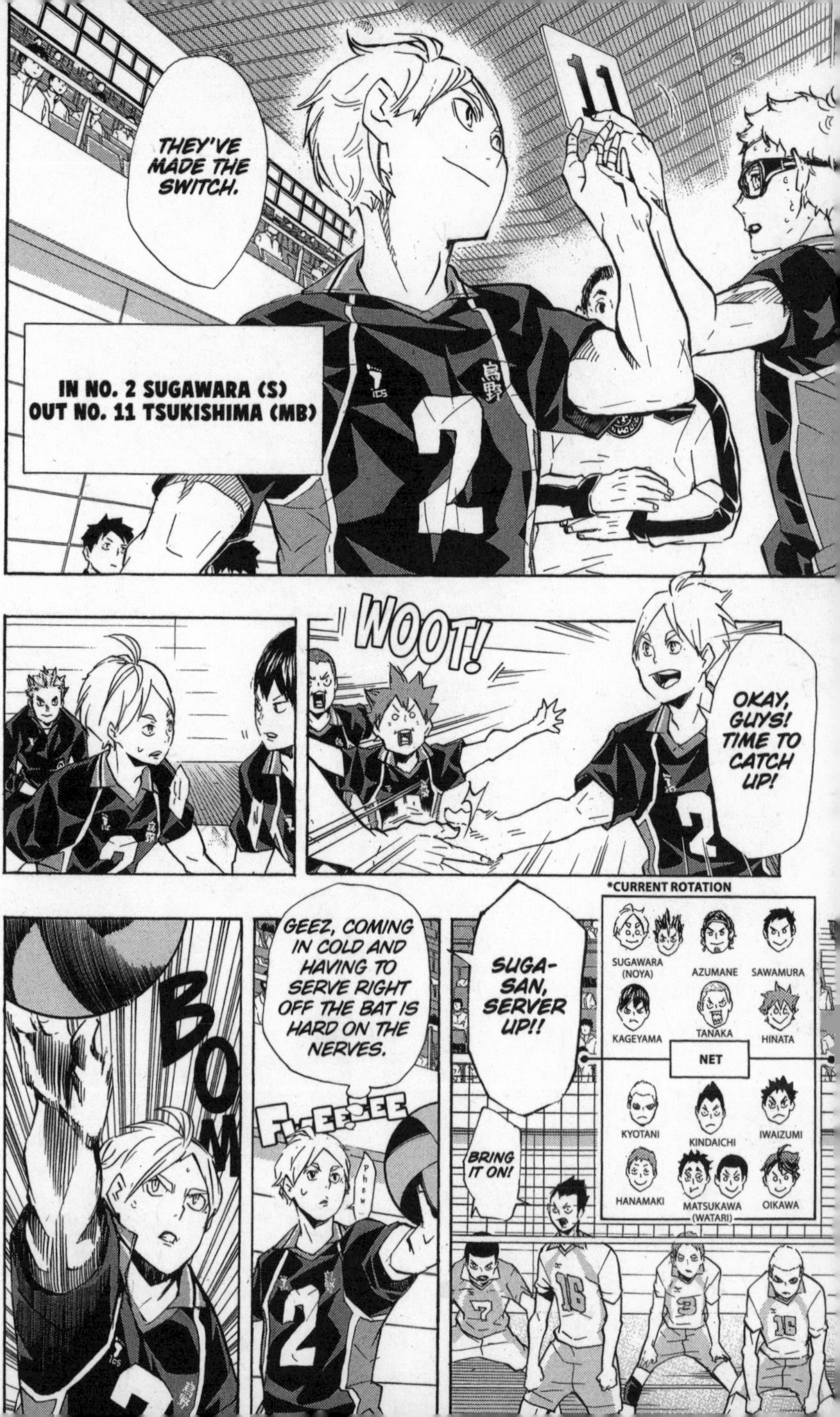
THEY'VE MADE THE SWITCH.
IN NO. 2 SUGAWARA (S)
OUT NO. 11 TSUKISHIMA (MB)
OKAY, GUYS! TIME TO CATCH UP!
WOOT!
*CURRENT ROTATION
SUGAWARA (NOYA)
AZUMANE
SAWAMURA
KAGEYAMA
TANAKA
HINATA
NET
KYOTANI
KINDAICHI
IWAIZUMI
HANAMAKI
MATSUKAWA (WATARI)
OIKAWA
SUGA-SAN, SERVER UP!!
BRING IT ON!
GEEZ, COMING IN COLD AND HAVING TO SERVE RIGHT OFF THE BAT IS HARD ON THE NERVES.
Phew...
BOM

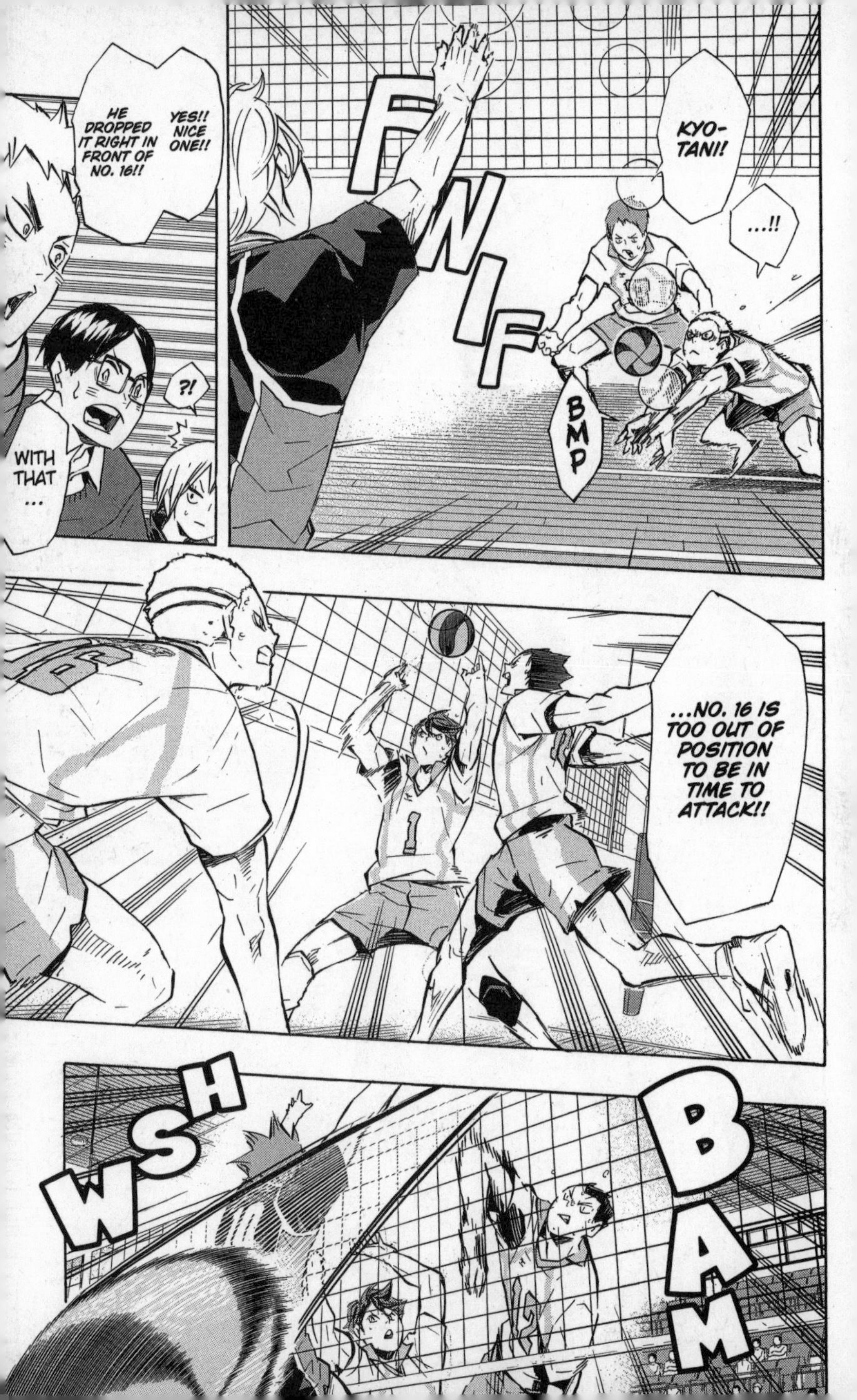
KYO-TANI!!
...!!
FNIF
BMP
YES!! NICE ONE!!
HE DROPPED IT RIGHT IN FRONT OF NO. 16!!
?!
WITH THAT ...
...NO. 16 IS TOO OUT OF POSITION TO BE IN TIME TO ATTACK!!
BAM
WSH

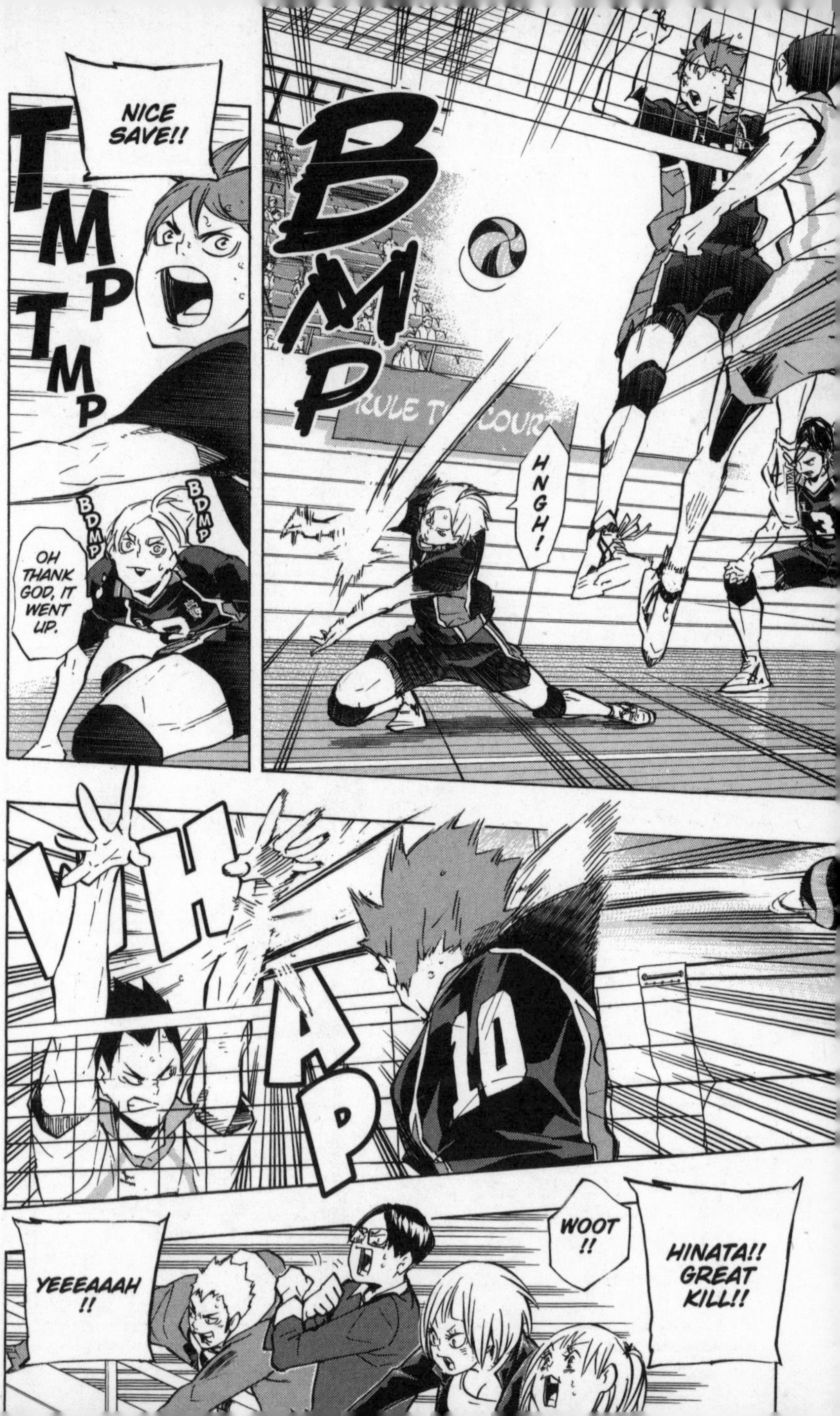
BMP
HNGH!
NICE SAVE!!
TMP TMP
BDMP
BDMP
OH THANK GOD, IT WENT UP.
WHAP
HINATA!! GREAT KILL!!
WOOT !!
YEEEAAAH !!

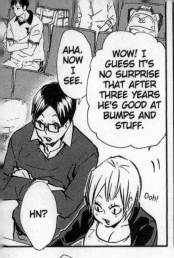

KARASUNO
AOBA JOHSAI
17 2 15
BREAK POINT !!
WOW! I GUESS IT'S NO SURPRISE THAT AFTER THREE YEARS HE'S GOOD AT BUMPS AND STUFF.
AHA. NOW I SEE.
Ooh!
HN?
PLAYERS ROTATING POSITIONS IS ONE OF THE BIGGEST, MOST VISIBLE RULES IN VOLLEYBALL.
SINCE EVERYBODY IS CONSTANTLY MOVING, THEY PLAY EVERY AREA OF THE COURT AND HAVE DIFFERENT RESPONSIBILI-TIES DEPENDING ON WHERE THEY ARE.
NET
SERVER
PLAYERS ROTATE ONE SPOT CLOCKWISE EVERY TIME THEY EARN THE RIGHT TO SERVE.
THAT MEANS A TEAM'S STRENGTHS AND STRATEGIES WILL CHANGE DEPENDING ON WHAT POINT IN THE ROTATION THEY'RE IN.
FOR EXAMPLE ...
...WHEN KAGEYAMA IS IN THE BACK ROW AND HINATA IS IN THE FRONT...
...THAT'S WHEN KARASUNO IS AT ITS PEAK OFFENSIVE POWER.
NET
3 HITTERS IN FRONT ROW
SAWAMURA
HINATA
TANAKA
GREATEST DECOY
AZUMANE
NOYA (TSUKKI)
KAGEYAMA
SETTER IN THE BACK ROW
CON-VERSELY ...
WHEN THE SIX-FOOTERS--TSUKISHIMA, AZUMANE AND KAGEYAMA--ARE ALL IN THE FRONT ROW, WITH RECEIVING EXPERTS NISHINOYA AND SAWAMURA IN THE BACK ROW...
...THAT'S WHEN OUR DEFENSE IS AT ITS MOST ROBUST.
NET
TALL GUYS BLOCKING
KAGEYAMA
TSUKISHIMA
AZUMANE
TANAKA
NISHINOYA (HINATA)
SAWAMURA
NISHINOYA/SAWAMURA IN POSITION TO RECEIVE

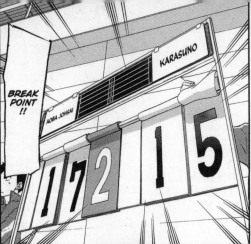

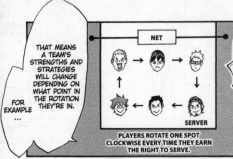

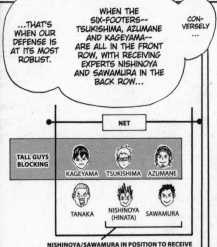

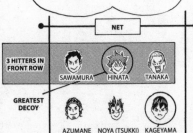

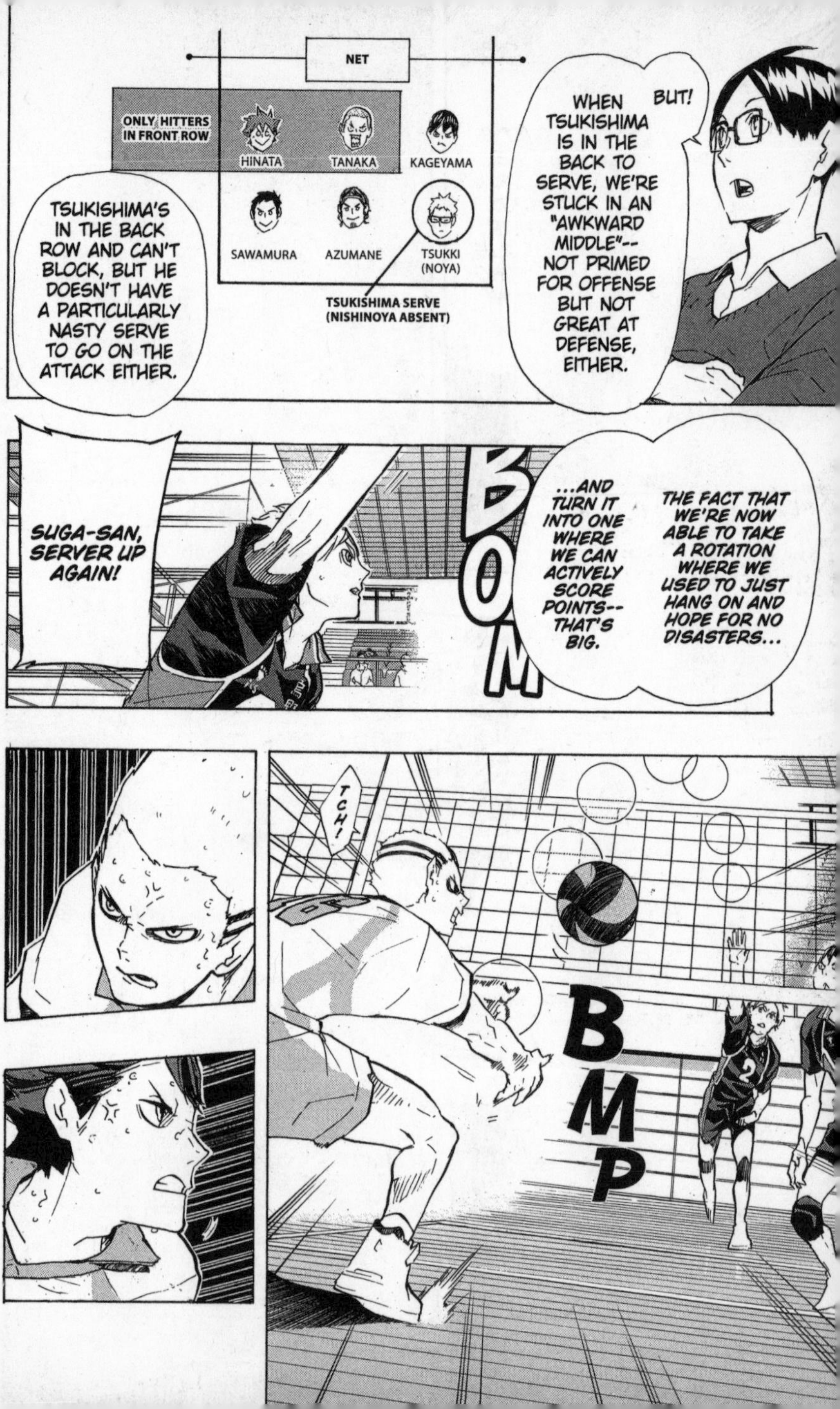
BUT!
WHEN TSUKISHIMA IS IN THE BACK TO SERVE, WE'RE STUCK IN AN "AWKWARD MIDDLE"-- NOT PRIMED FOR OFFENSE BUT NOT GREAT AT DEFENSE, EITHER.
NET
ONLY HITTERS IN FRONT ROW
HINATA
TANAKA
KAGEYAMA
SAWAMURA
AZUMANE
TSUKKI (NOYA)
TSUKISHIMA SERVE (NISHINOYA ABSENT)
TSUKISHIMA'S IN THE BACK ROW AND CAN'T BLOCK, BUT HE DOESN'T HAVE A PARTICULARLY NASTY SERVE TO GO ON THE ATTACK EITHER.
THE FACT THAT WE'RE NOW ABLE TO TAKE A ROTATION WHERE WE USED TO JUST HANG ON AND HOPE FOR NO DISASTERS...
...AND TURN IT INTO ONE WHERE WE CAN ACTIVELY SCORE POINTS-- THAT'S BIG.
BOOM
SUGA-SAN, SERVER UP AGAIN!
TCH!
BMP

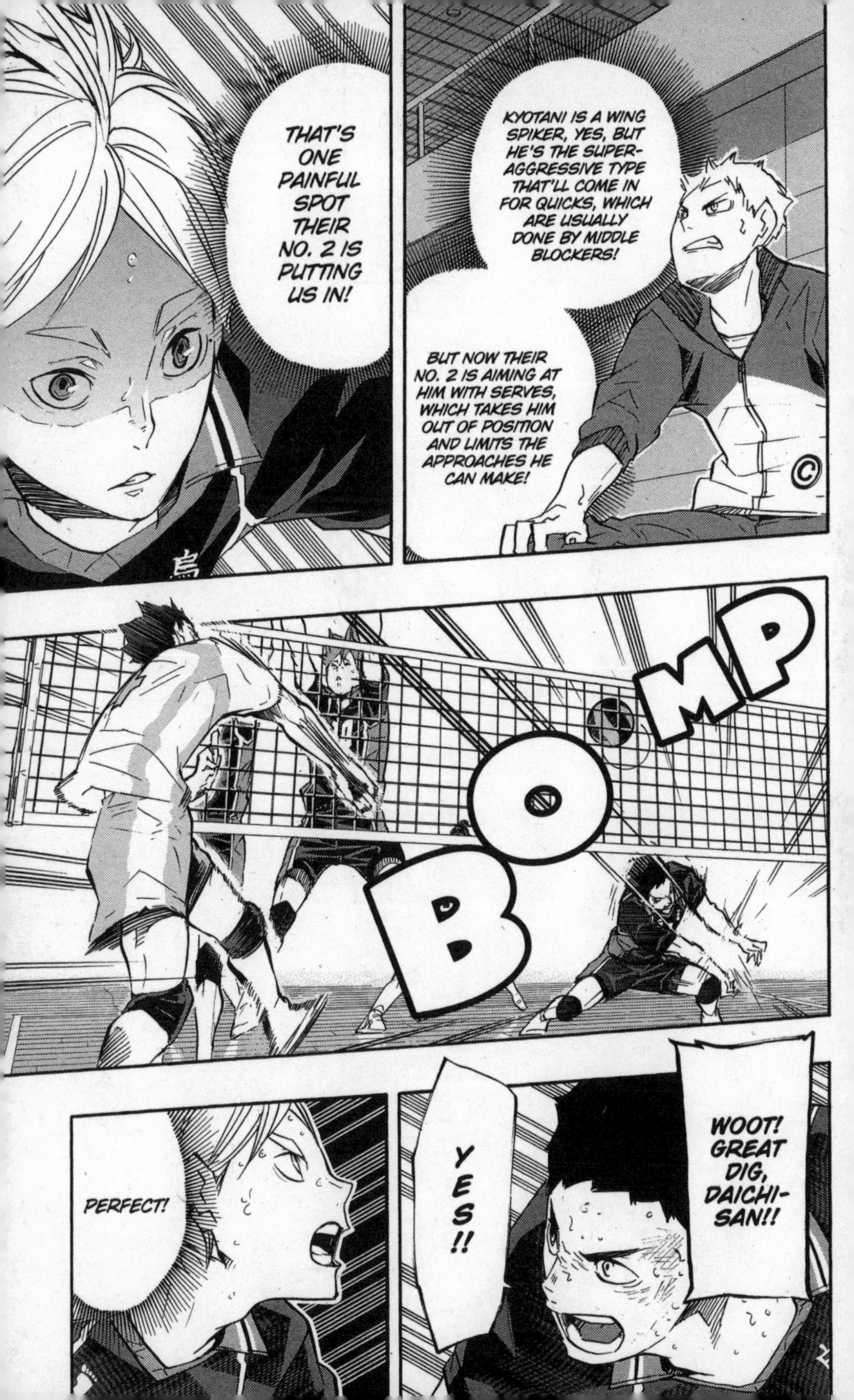
KYOTANI IS A WING SPIKER, YES, BUT HE'S THE SUPER-AGGRESSIVE TYPE THAT'LL COME IN FOR QUICKS, WHICH ARE USUALLY DONE BY MIDDLE BLOCKERS!
BUT NOW THEIR NO. 2 IS AIMING AT HIM WITH SERVES, WHICH TAKES HIM OUT OF POSITION AND LIMITS THE APPROACHES HE CAN MAKE!
THAT'S ONE PAINFUL SPOT THEIR NO. 2 IS PUTTING US IN!
BOOMP
WOOT! GREAT DIG, DAICHI-SAN!!
YES!!
PERFECT!

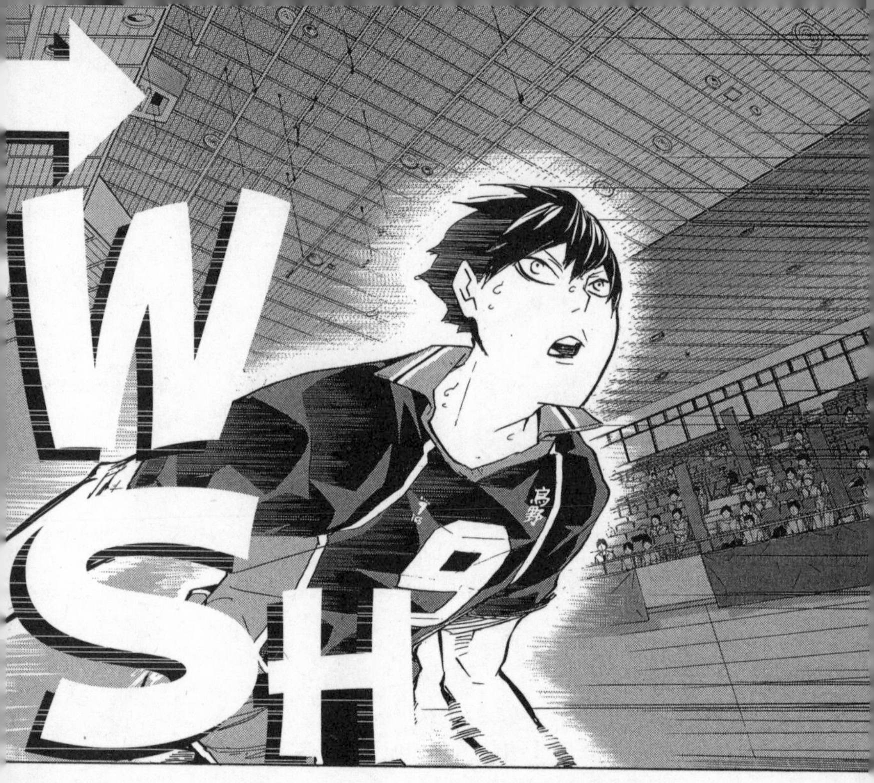
WSH

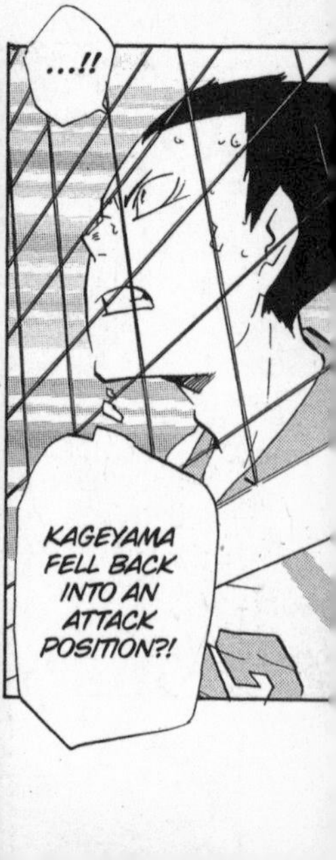
...!!
KAGEYAMA FELL BACK INTO AN ATTACK POSITION?!

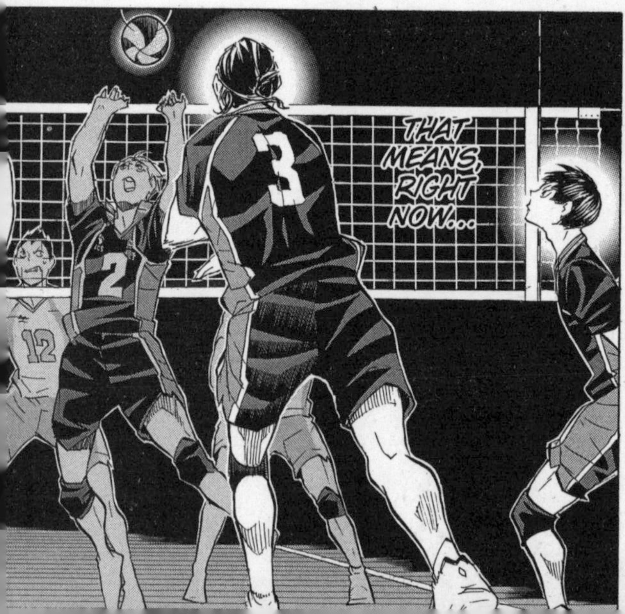
THAT MEANS, RIGHT NOW...

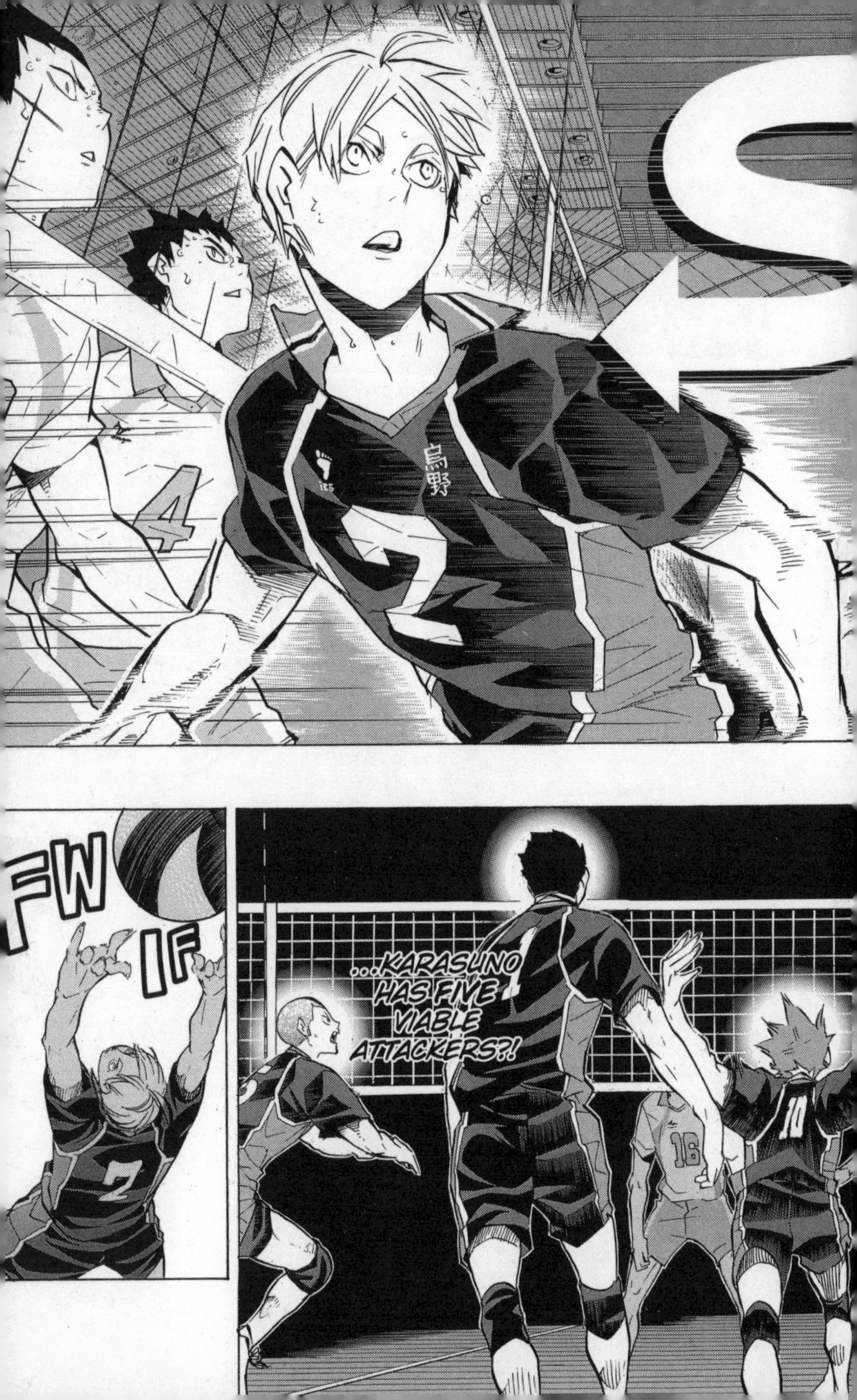
S
...KARASUNO HAS FIVE VIABLE ATTACKERS?!
FWIF

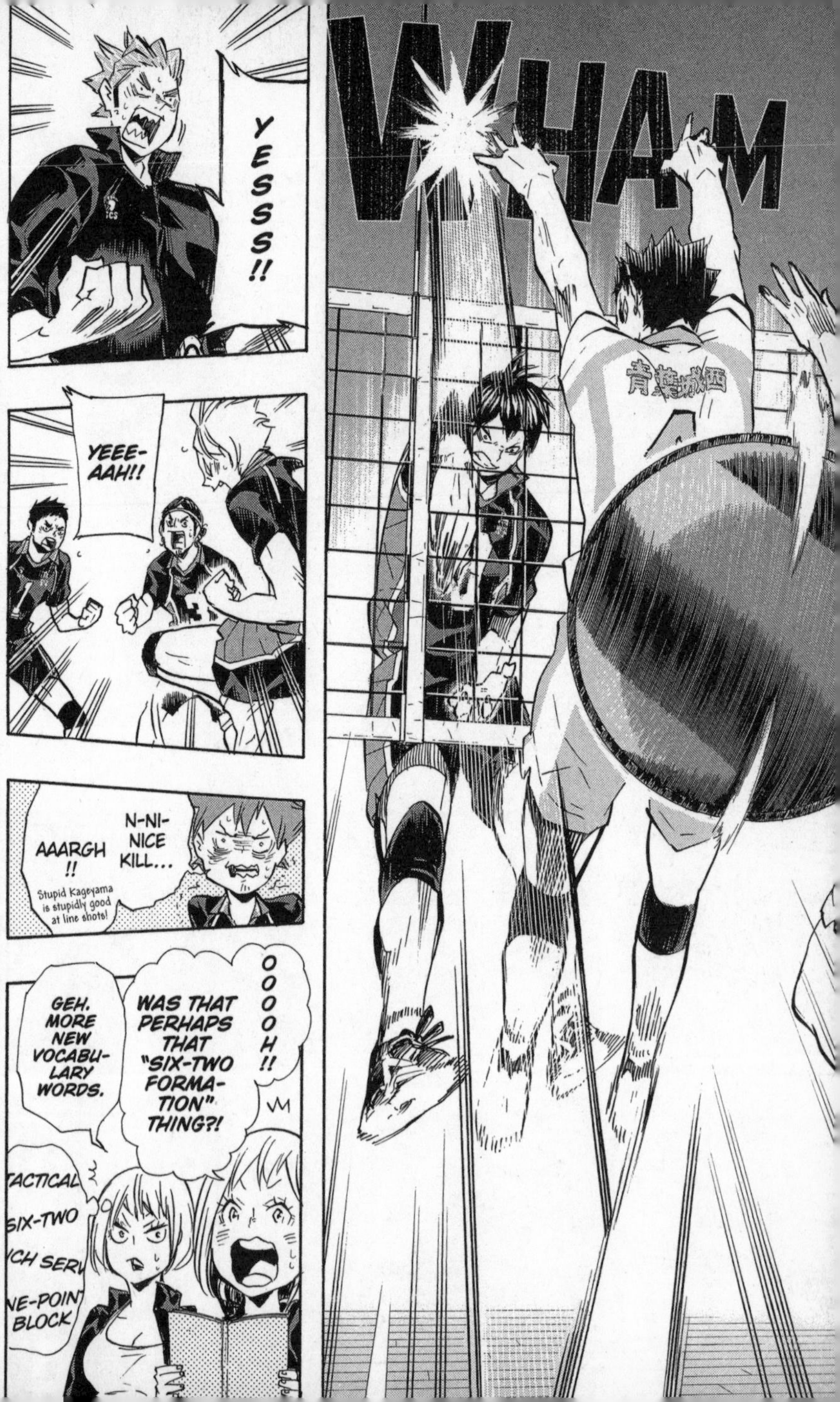
WHAM
YESSS!!
YEEE-AAH!!
N-NI-NICE KILL...
AAARGH!!
Stupid Kageyama is stupidly good at line shots!
OOOOOH!!
WAS THAT PERHAPS THAT "SIX-TWO FORMATION" THING?!
GEH. MORE NEW VOCABULARY WORDS.
TACTICAL
SIX-TWO
ICH SERV
NE-POINT BLOCK

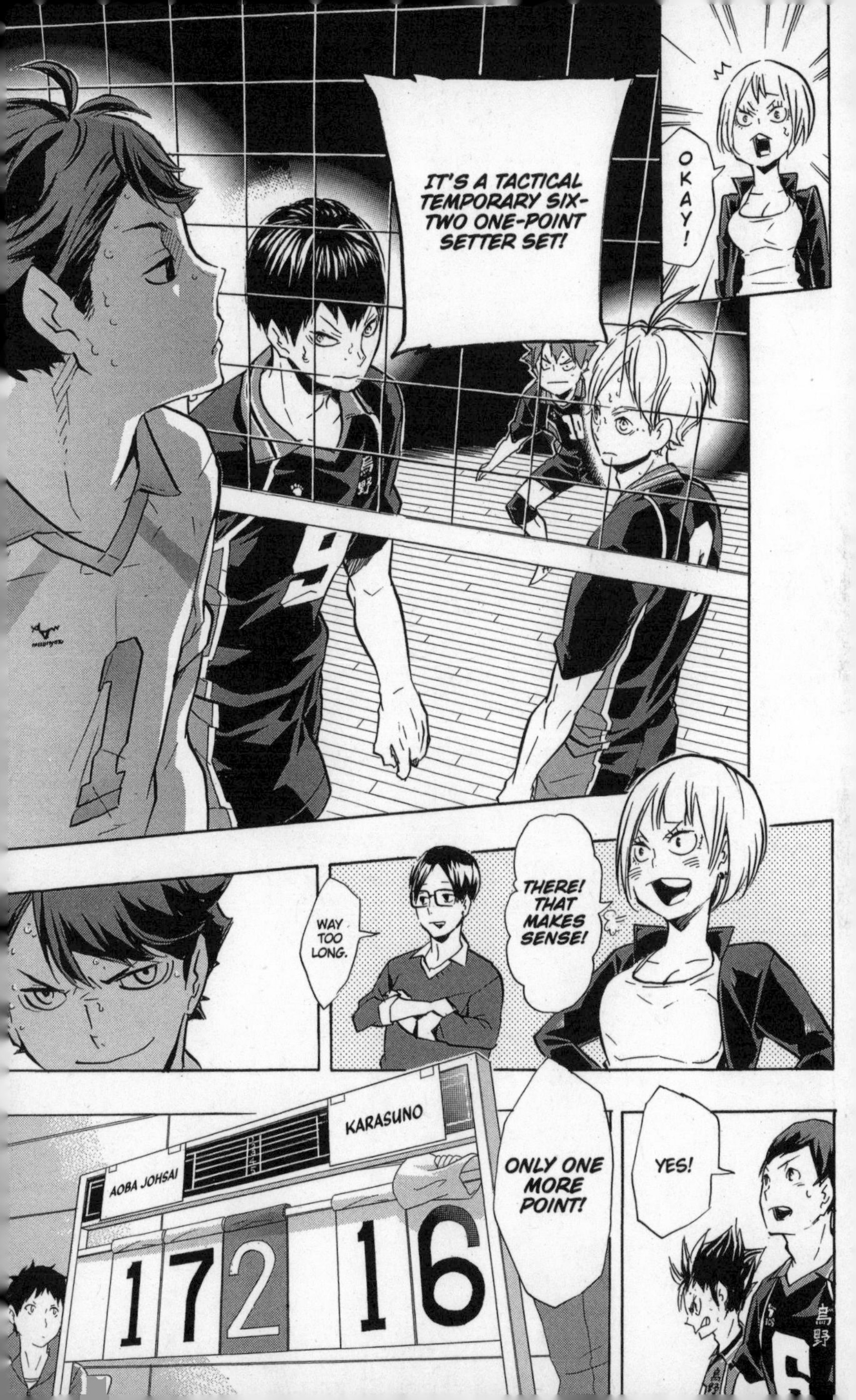
OKAY!
IT'S A TACTICAL TEMPORARY SIX-TWO ONE-POINT SETTER SET!
THERE! THAT MAKES SENSE!
WAY TOO LONG.
YES!
KARASUNO
ONLY ONE MORE POINT!
AOBA JOHSAI
17
2
16

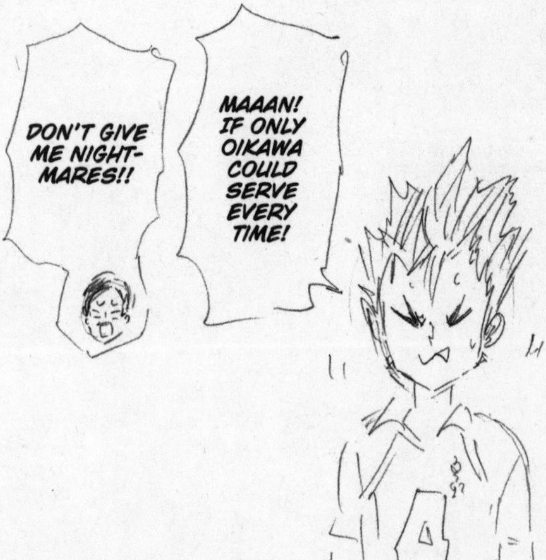
MAAAN! IF ONLY OIKAWA COULD SERVE EVERY TIME!
DON'T GIVE ME NIGHT-MARES!!

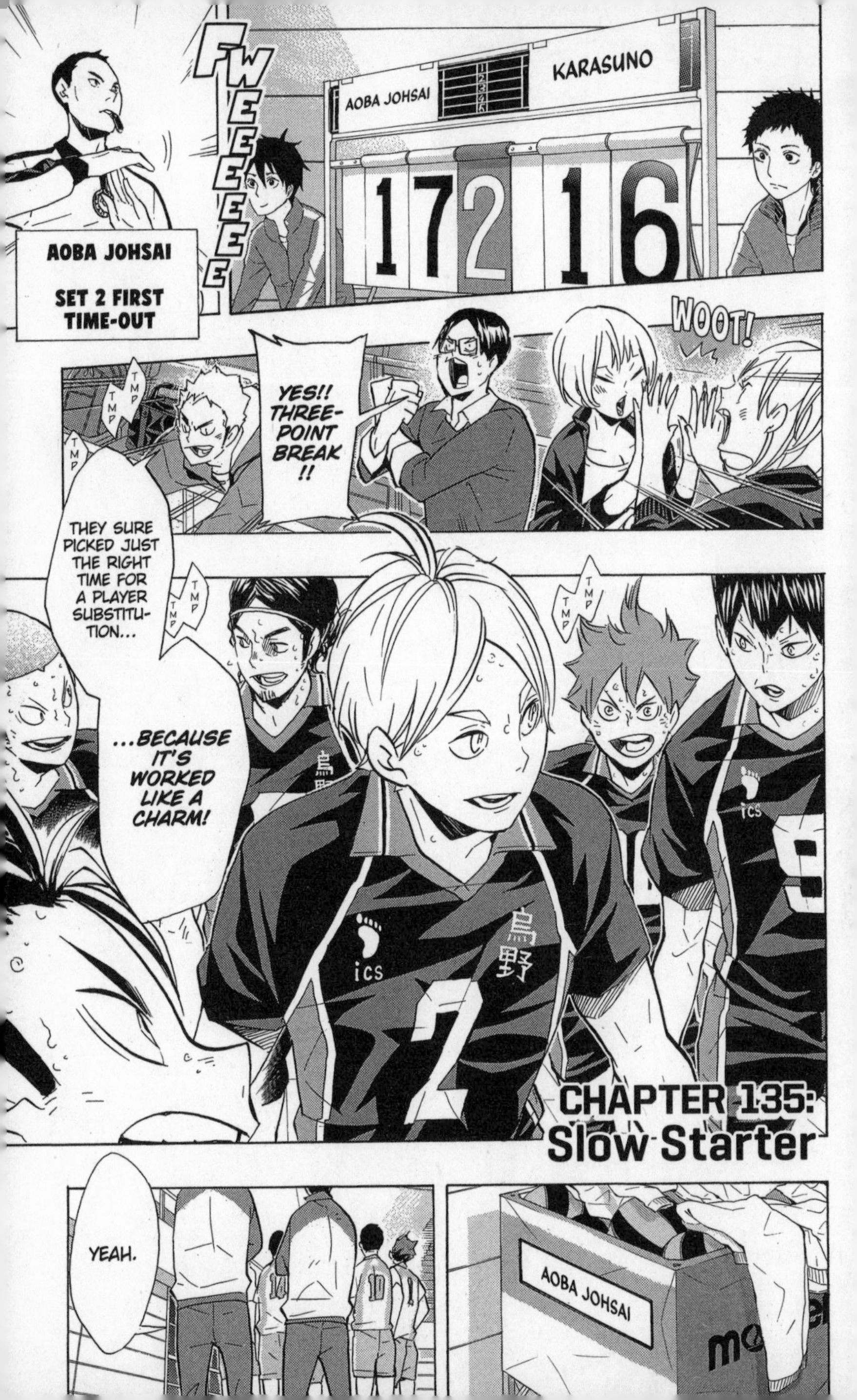
KARASUNO
AOBA JOHSAI
17 2 16
FWEEEEEE
AOBA JOHSAI
SET 2 FIRST TIME-OUT
WOOT!
YES!! THREE-POINT BREAK!!
TMP TMP TMP
TMP TMP TMP
THEY SURE PICKED JUST THE RIGHT TIME FOR A PLAYER SUBSTITUTION...
...BECAUSE IT'S WORKED LIKE A CHARM!
CHAPTER 135: Slow Starter
AOBA JOHSAI
YEAH.

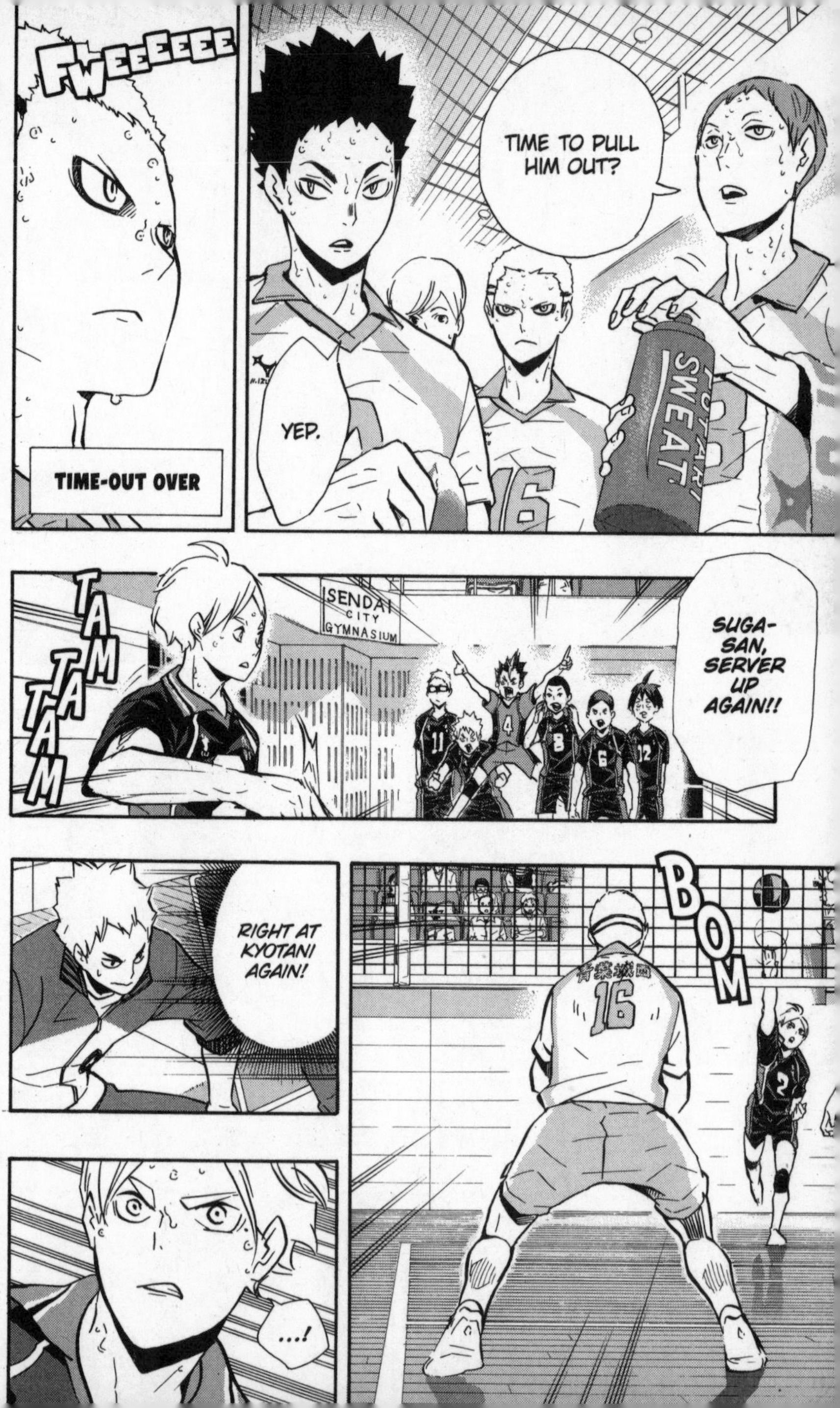
TIME TO PULL HIM OUT?
SWEAT
YEP.
FWEEEEEE
TIME-OUT OVER
SUGA-SAN, SERVER UP AGAIN!!
SENDAI CITY GYMNASIUM
TAM TA TAM
BOM
RIGHT AT KYOTANI AGAIN!
...!

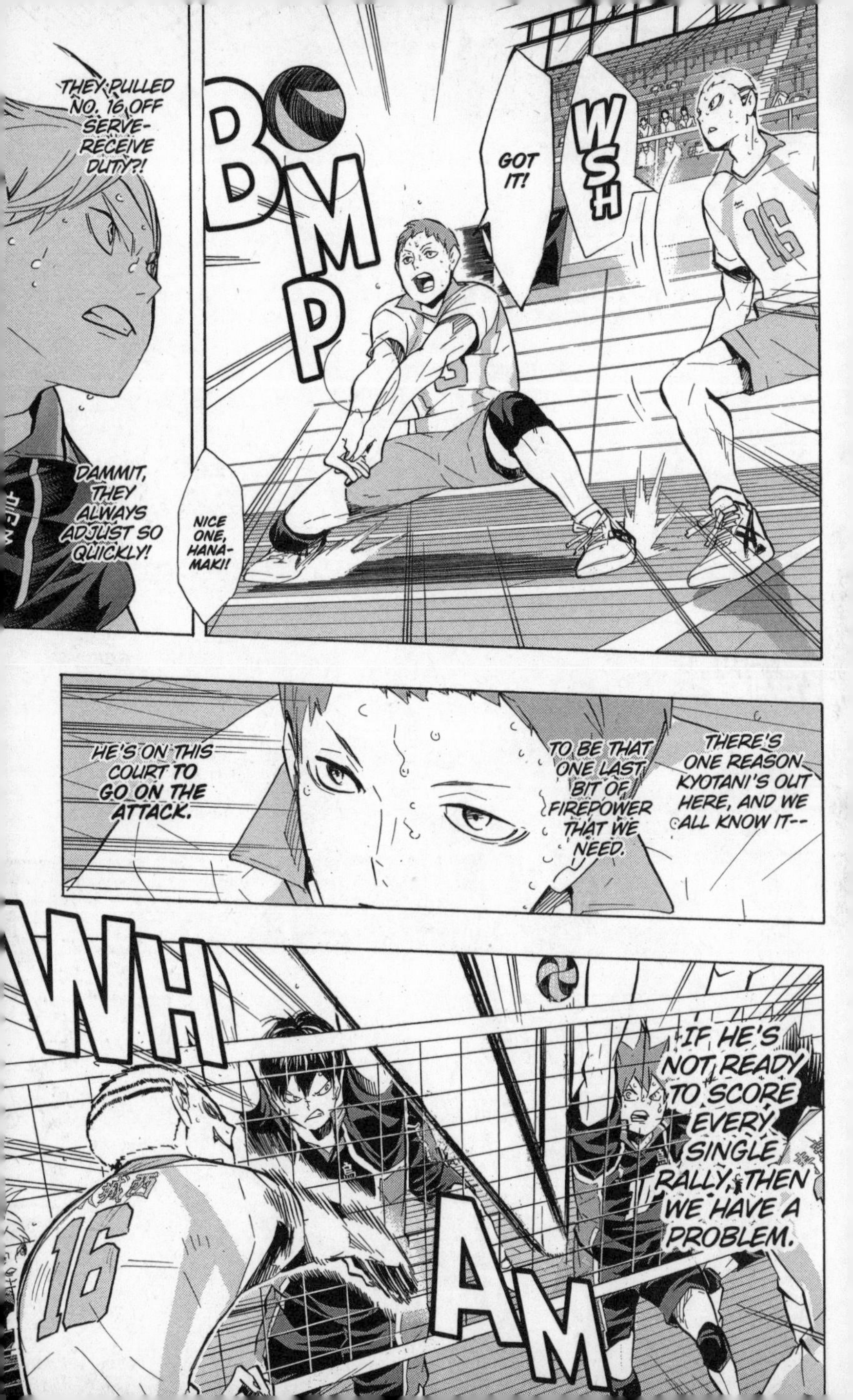
WSH
GOT IT!
BMP
NICE ONE, HANA-MAKI!
THEY PULLED NO. 16 OFF SERVE-RECEIVE DUTY?!
DAMMIT, THEY ALWAYS ADJUST SO QUICKLY!
THERE'S ONE REASON KYOTANI'S OUT HERE, AND WE ALL KNOW IT--
TO BE THAT ONE LAST BIT OF FIREPOWER THAT WE NEED.
HE'S ON THIS COURT TO GO ON THE ATTACK.
IF HE'S NOT READY TO SCORE EVERY SINGLE RALLY, THEN WE HAVE A PROBLEM.
WH
AM

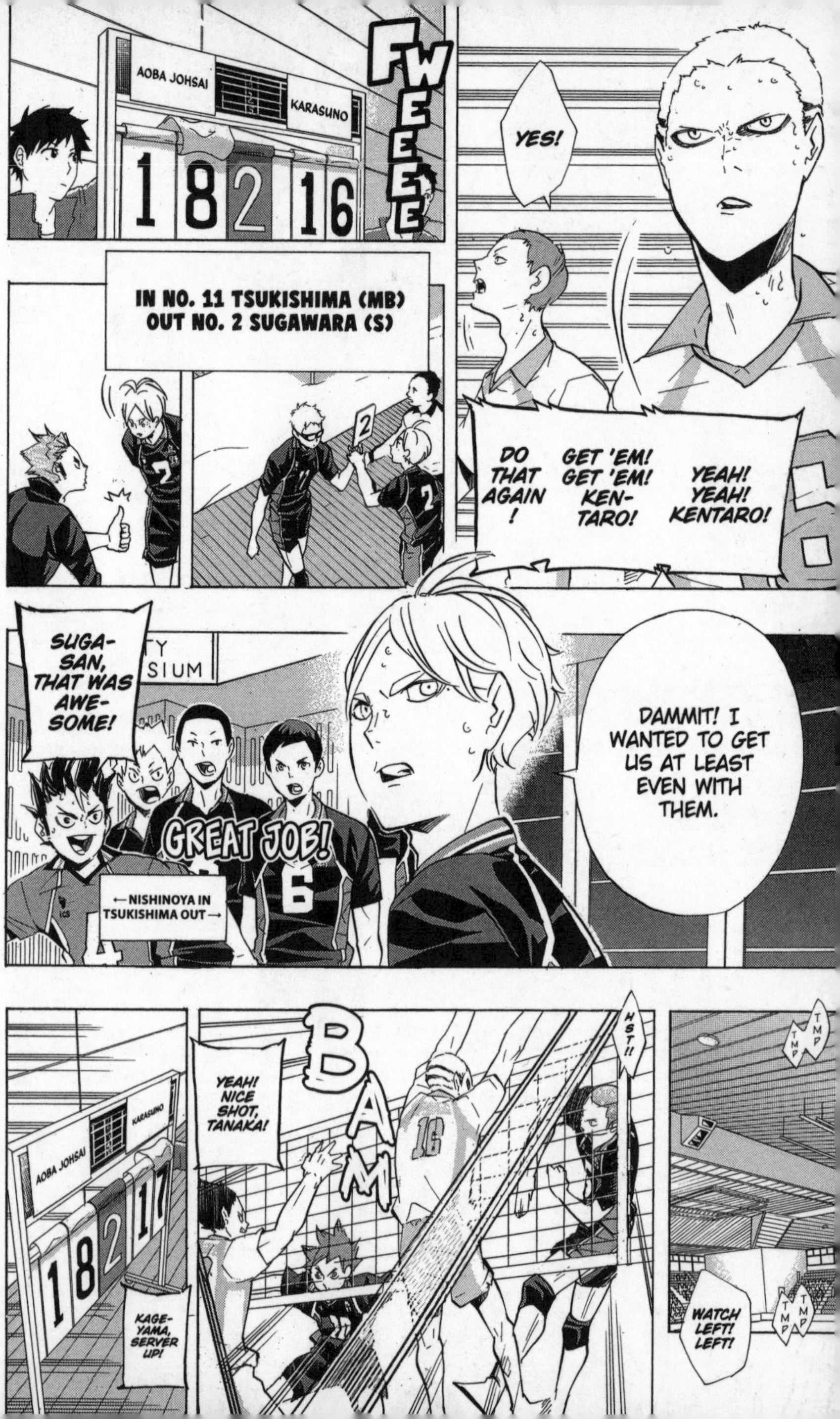
YES!
YEAH! YEAH! KENTARO!
GET 'EM! GET 'EM! KEN-TARO!
DO THAT AGAIN!
FWEEEE
AOBA JOHSAI
KARASUNO
18 2 16
IN NO. 11 TSUKISHIMA (MB)
OUT NO. 2 SUGAWARA (S)
DAMMIT! I WANTED TO GET US AT LEAST EVEN WITH THEM.
SUGA-SAN, THAT WAS AWE-SOME!
GREAT JOB!
←NISHINOYA IN
TSUKISHIMA OUT→
TMP TMP
TMP TMP
WATCH LEFT! LEFT!
HST!!
BAM
YEAH! NICE SHOT, TANAKA!
KAGE-YAMA, SERVER UP!
AOBA JOHSAI
KARASUNO
18 2 17

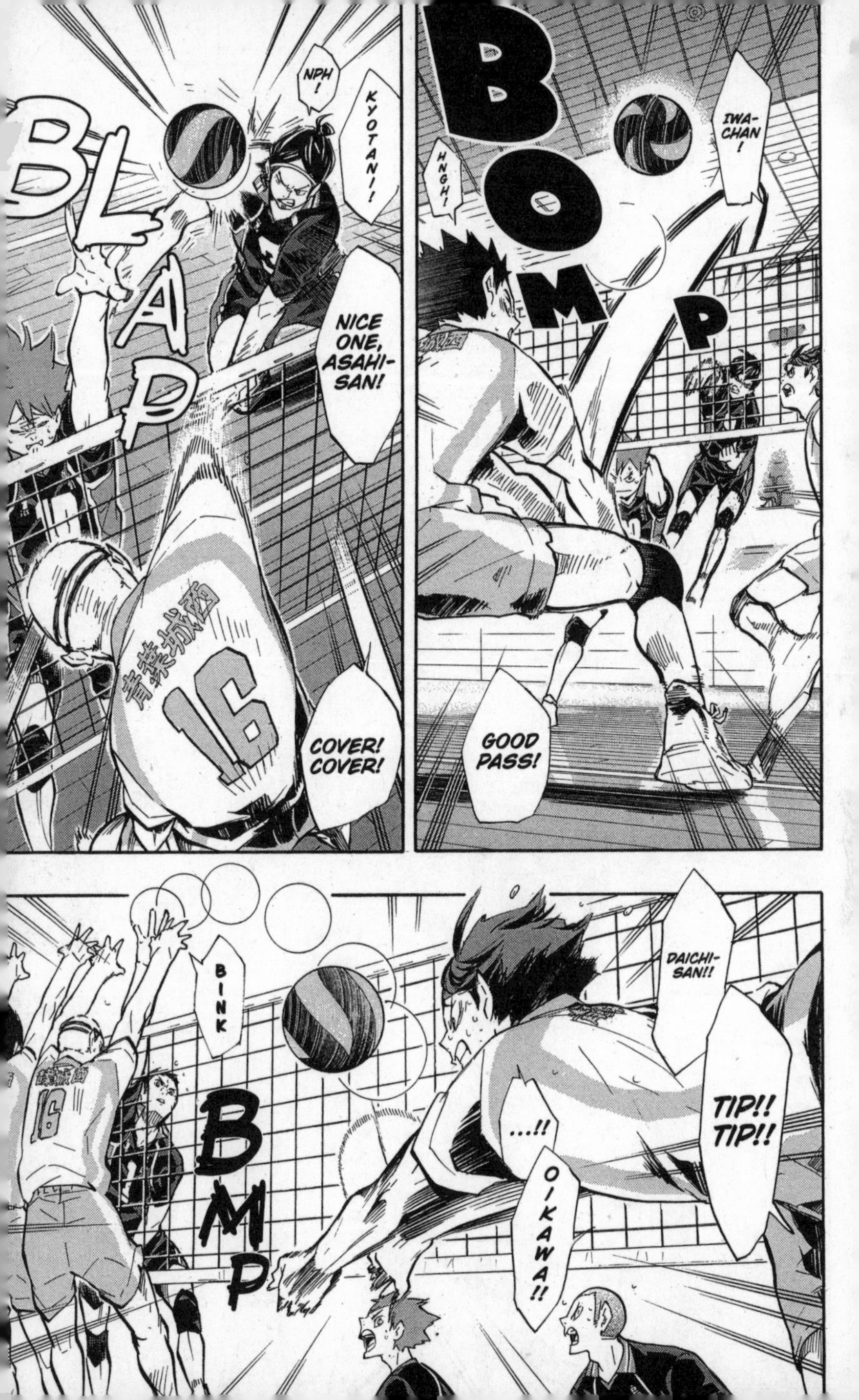
IWA-CHAN!
BOOMP
HNGH!
GOOD PASS!
KYOTANI!!
NPH!
BLAP
NICE ONE, ASAHI-SAN!
青葉城西
16
COVER! COVER!
DAICHI-SAN!!
TIP!! TIP!!
...!!
OIKAWA!!
BINK
BMP

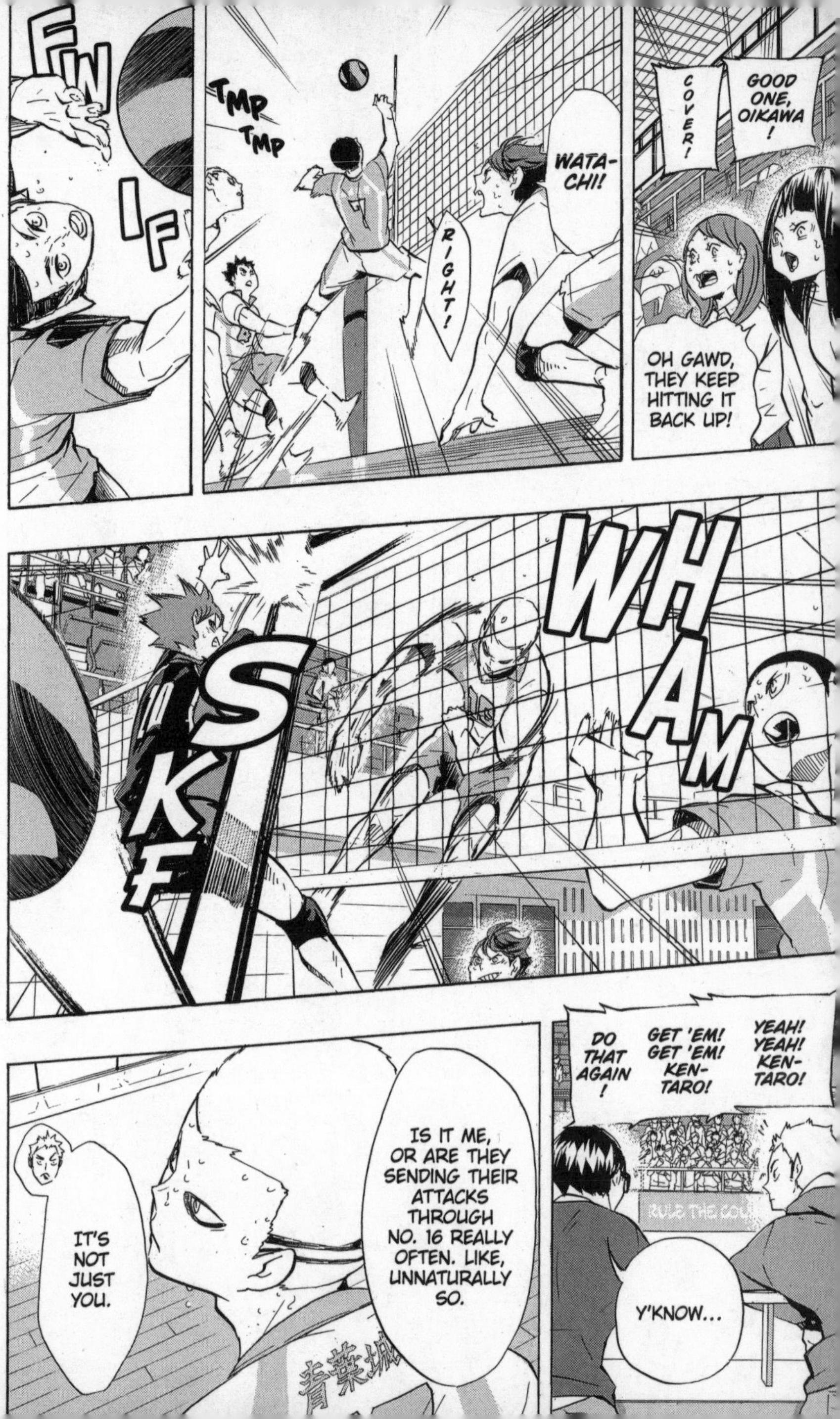
GOOD ONE, OIKAWA!
COVER!
OH GAWD, THEY KEEP HITTING IT BACK UP!
WATA-CHI!
RIGHT!
TMP TMP
FWIF
WHAM
SKF
YEAH! YEAH! KEN-TARO!
GET 'EM! GET 'EM! KEN-TARO!
DO THAT AGAIN!
Y'KNOW...
IS IT ME, OR ARE THEY SENDING THEIR ATTACKS THROUGH NO. 16 REALLY OFTEN. LIKE, UNNATURALLY SO.
IT'S NOT JUST YOU.

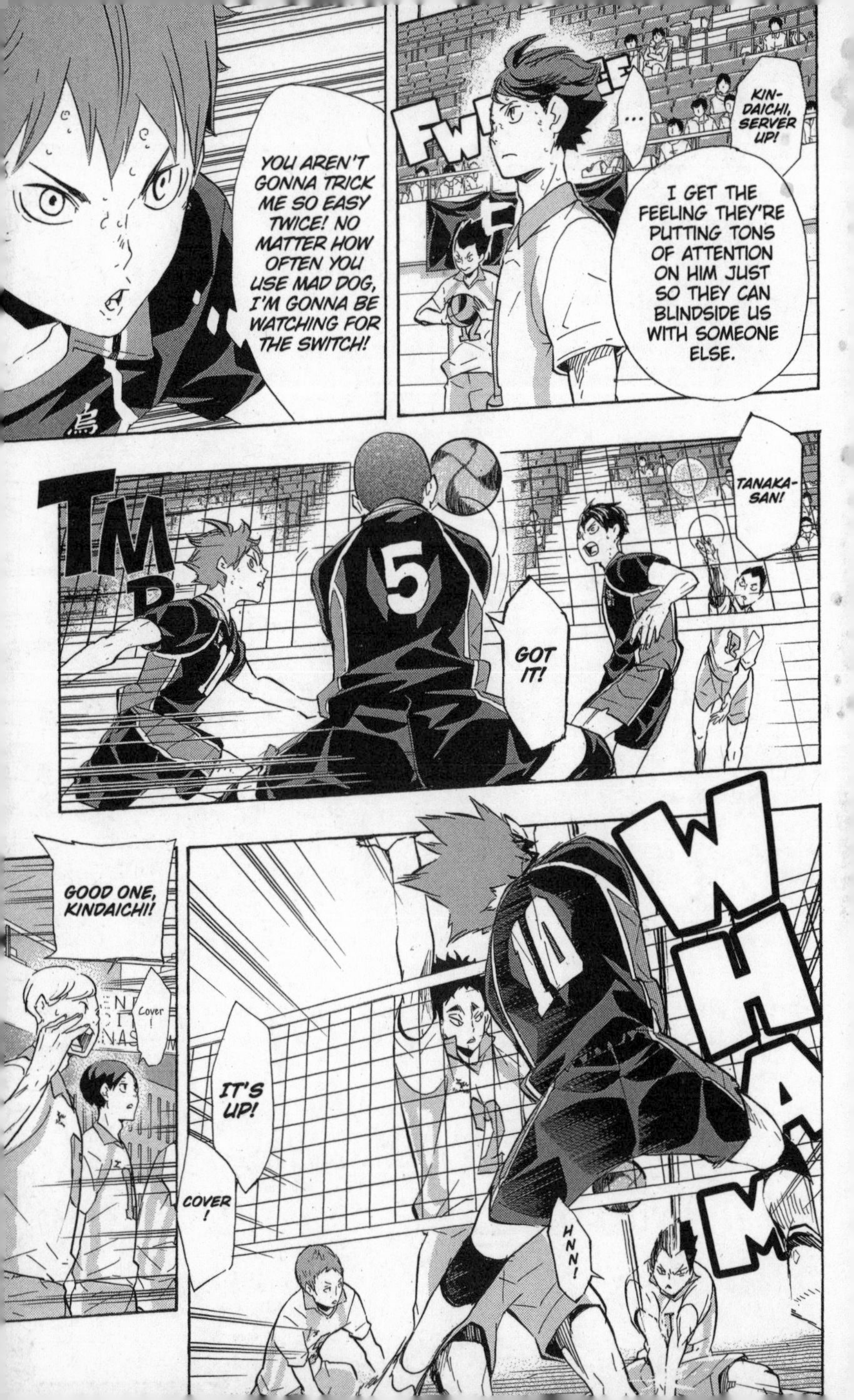
KIN-DAICHI, SERVER UP!
...
I GET THE FEELING THEY'RE PUTTING TONS OF ATTENTION ON HIM JUST SO THEY CAN BLINDSIDE US WITH SOMEONE ELSE.
YOU AREN'T GONNA TRICK ME SO EASY TWICE! NO MATTER HOW OFTEN YOU USE MAD DOG, I'M GONNA BE WATCHING FOR THE SWITCH!
TANAKA-SAN!
GOT IT!
TMP
WHAM
IT'S UP!
COVER!
HNN!
GOOD ONE, KINDAICHI!
Cover!

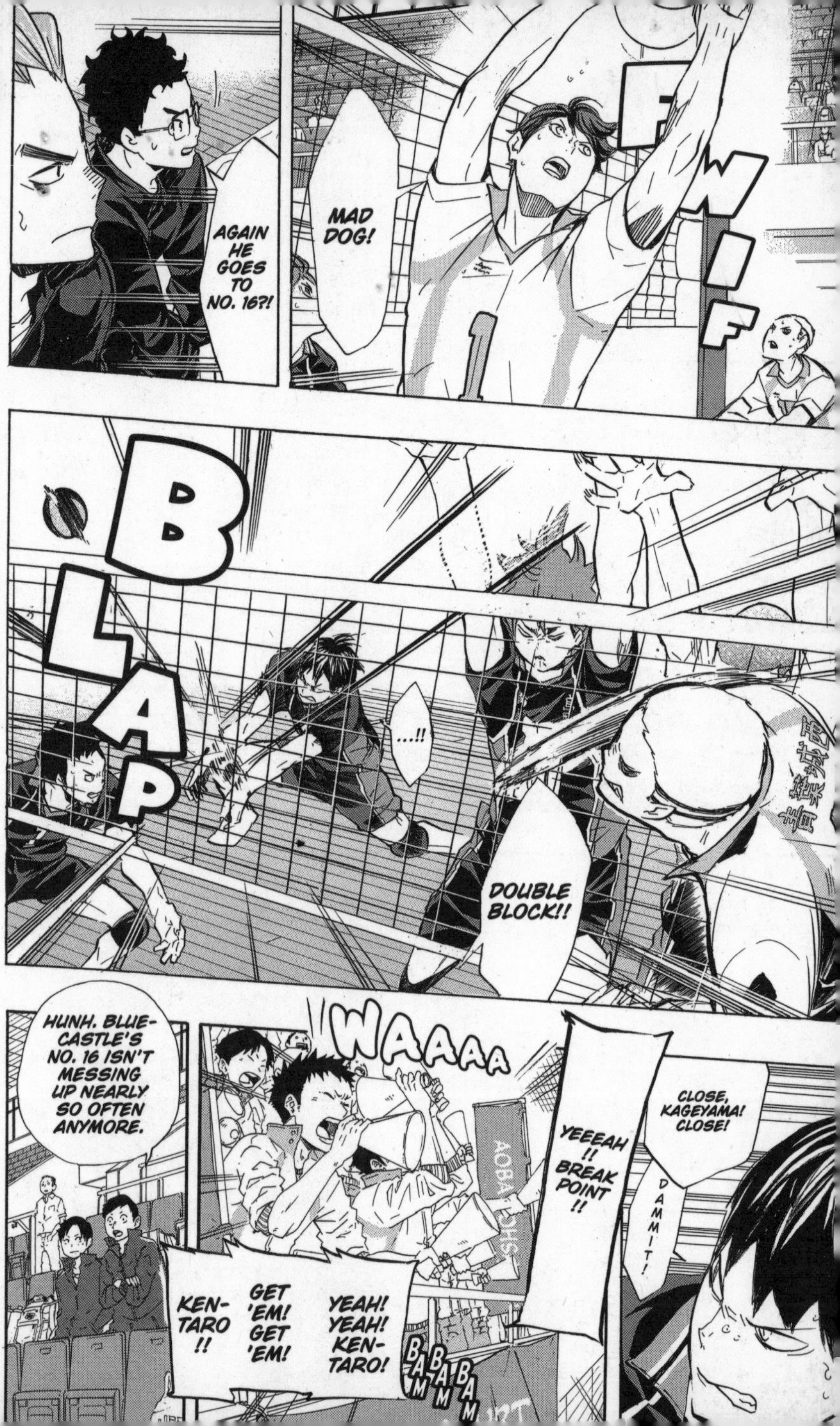
FWIF
MAD DOG!
AGAIN HE GOES TO NO. 16?!
BLAP
...!!
DOUBLE BLOCK!!
CLOSE, KAGEYAMA! CLOSE!
DAMMIT!
WAAAAA
YEEEAH!! BREAK POINT!!
YEAH! YEAH! KENTARO!
GET 'EM! GET 'EM!
KENTARO!!
BAM BAM BAM
HUNH. BLUE-CASTLE'S NO. 16 ISN'T MESSING UP NEARLY SO OFTEN ANYMORE.

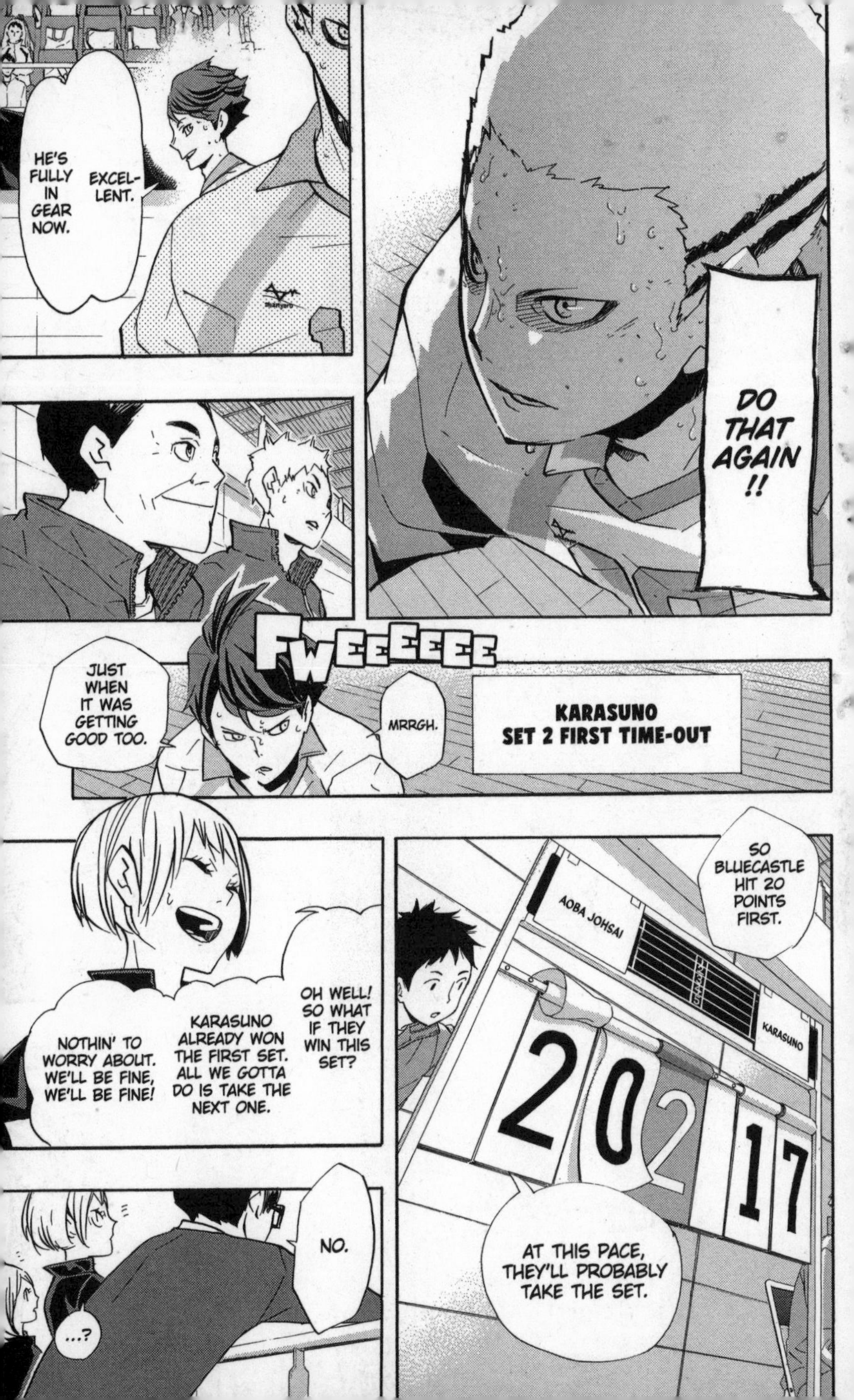
DO THAT AGAIN!!
EXCEL-LENT.
HE'S FULLY IN GEAR NOW.
FWEEEEEE
KARASUNO SET 2 FIRST TIME-OUT
MRRGH.
JUST WHEN IT WAS GETTING GOOD TOO.
SO BLUECASTLE HIT 20 POINTS FIRST.
AOBA JOHSAI
KARASUNO
20
17
AT THIS PACE, THEY'LL PROBABLY TAKE THE SET.
OH WELL! SO WHAT IF THEY WIN THIS SET?
KARASUNO ALREADY WON THE FIRST SET. ALL WE GOTTA DO IS TAKE THE NEXT ONE.
NOTHIN' TO WORRY ABOUT. WE'LL BE FINE, WE'LL BE FINE!
NO.
...?

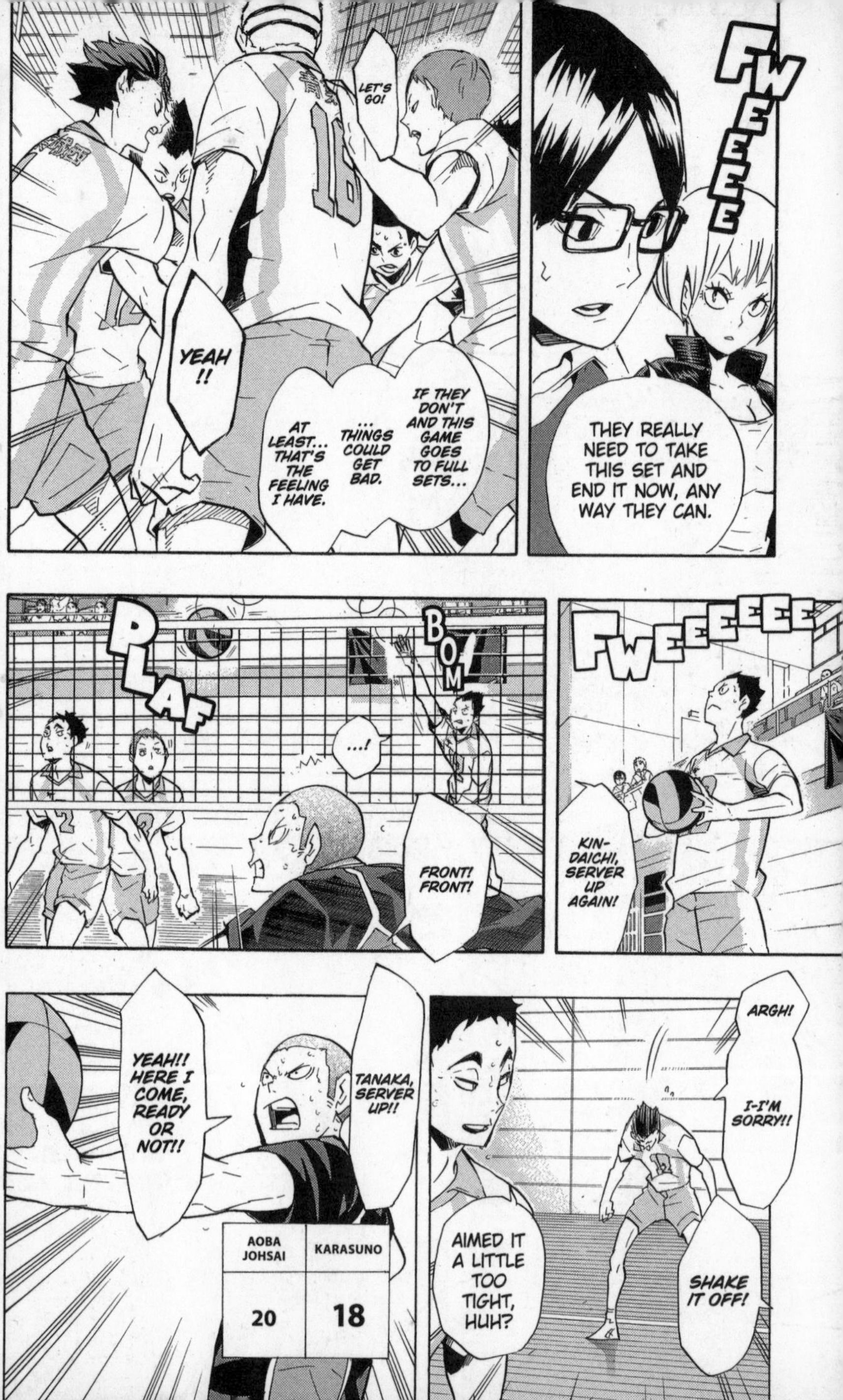
FWEEEE
THEY REALLY NEED TO TAKE THIS SET AND END IT NOW, ANY WAY THEY CAN.
LET'S GO!
YEAH!!
IF THEY DON'T AND THIS GAME GOES TO FULL SETS...
...THINGS COULD GET BAD.
AT LEAST... THAT'S THE FEELING I HAVE.
FWEEEEEE
KIN-DAICHI, SERVER UP AGAIN!
PLAF
BOM!
...!
FRONT! FRONT!
ARGH!
I-I'M SORRY!!
AIMED IT A LITTLE TOO TIGHT, HUH?
SHAKE IT OFF!
TANAKA, SERVER UP!!
YEAH!! HERE I COME, READY OR NOT!!
AOBA JOHSAI 20
KARASUNO 18

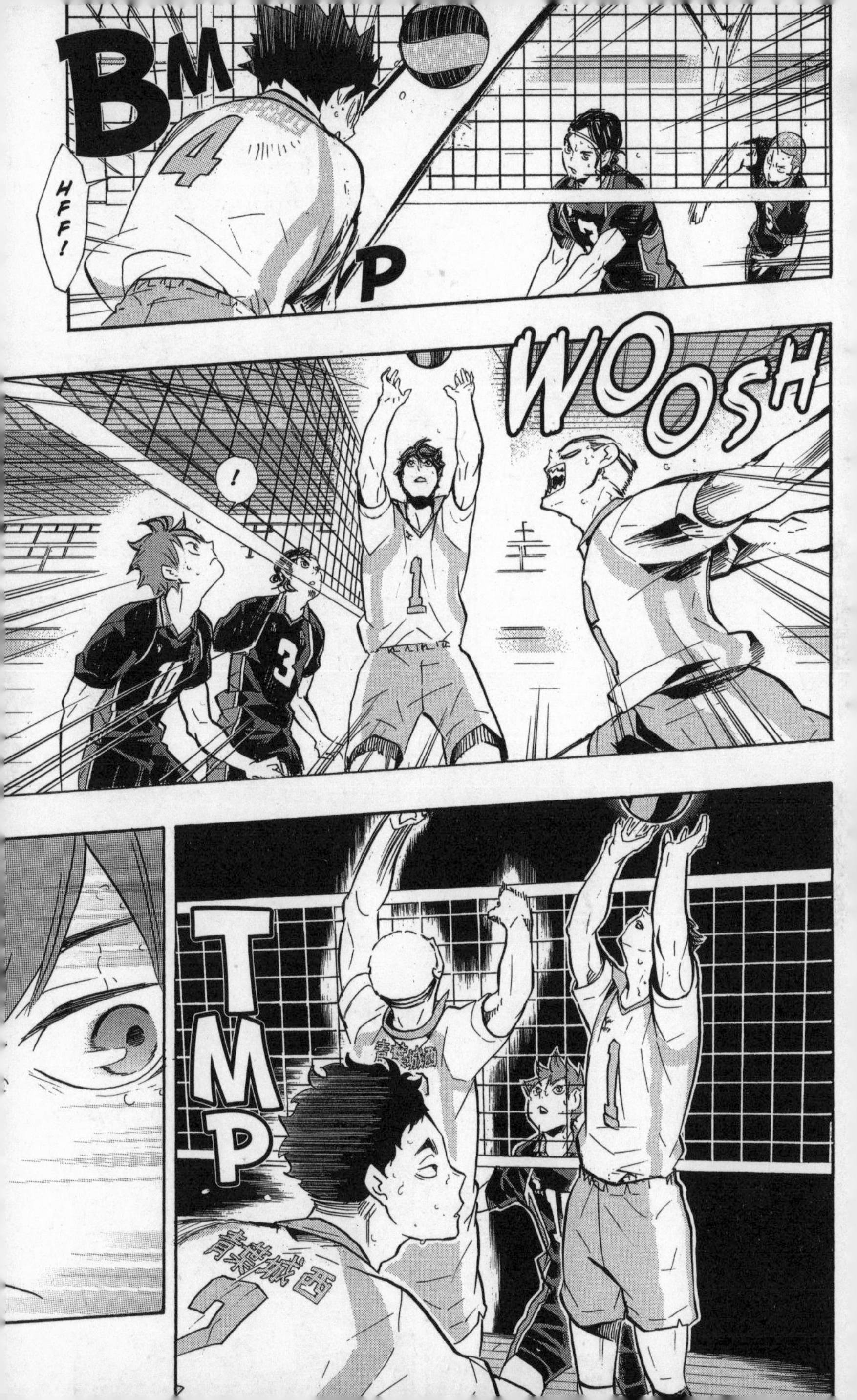
BMP
HFF!
WOOSH
!
TMP

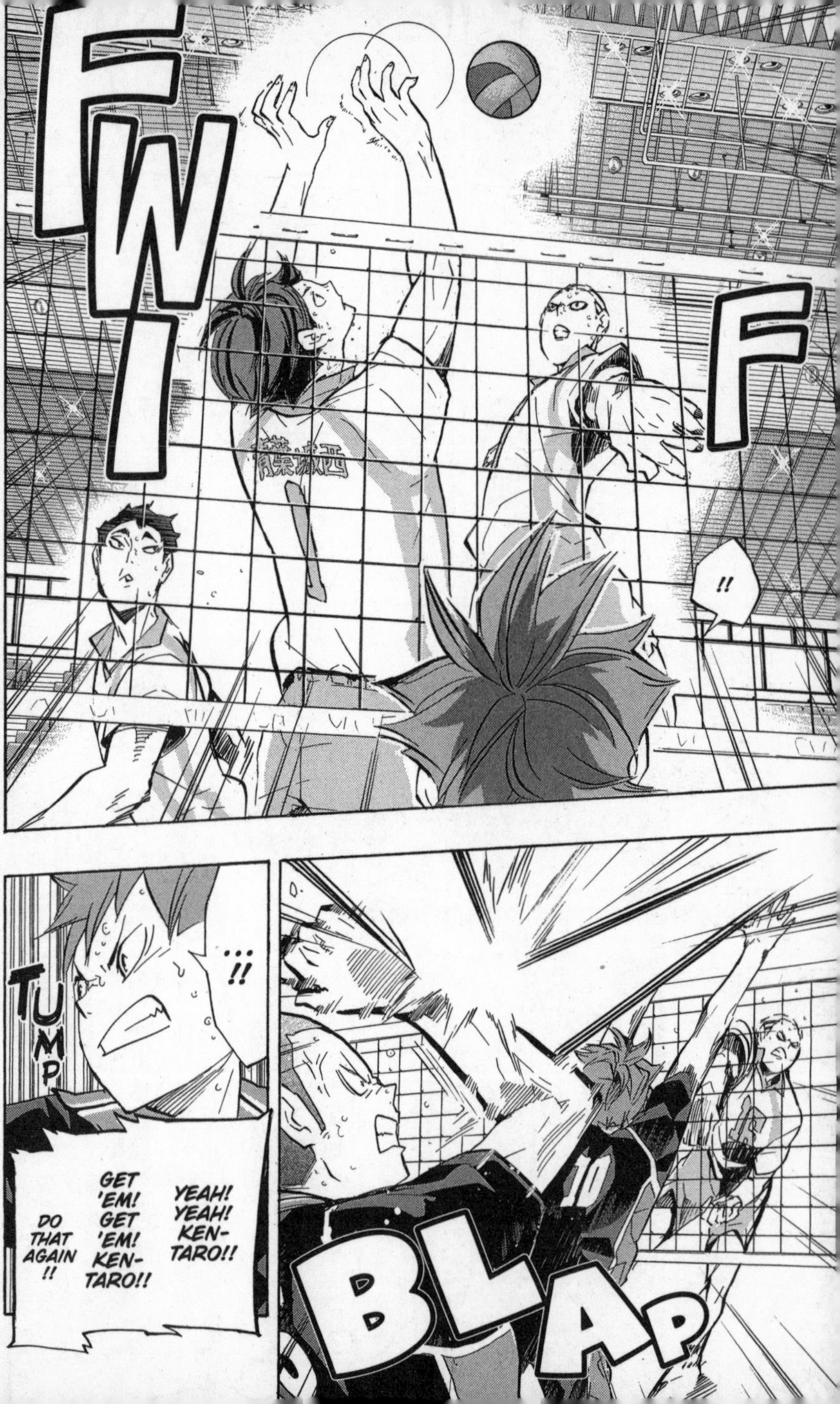
FWI
F
!!
BLAP
...!!
TUMP
YEAH! YEAH! KEN-TARO!!
GET 'EM! GET 'EM! KEN-TARO!!
DO THAT AGAIN!!

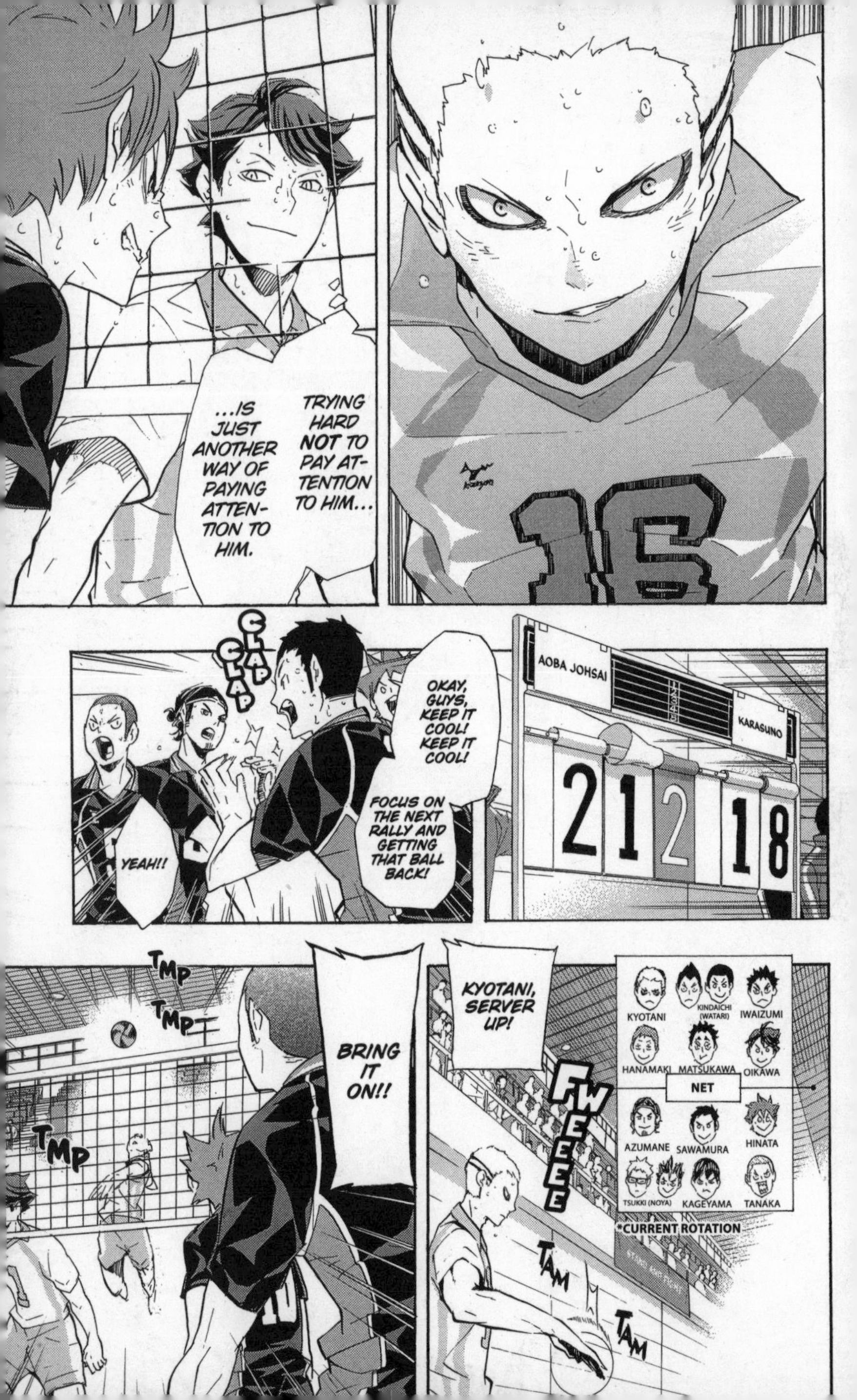
TRYING HARD NOT TO PAY ATTENTION TO HIM...
...IS JUST ANOTHER WAY OF PAYING ATTENTION TO HIM.
AOBA JOHSAI
KARASUNO
21
2
18
CLAP
CLAP
CLAP
OKAY, GUYS, KEEP IT COOL! KEEP IT COOL!
FOCUS ON THE NEXT RALLY AND GETTING THAT BALL BACK!
YEAH!!
KYOTANI, SERVER UP!
FWEEEE
KYOTANI
KINDAICHI (WATARI)
IWAIZUMI
HANAMAKI
MATSUKAWA
OIKAWA
NET
AZUMANE
SAWAMURA
HINATA
TSUKKI (NOYA)
KAGEYAMA
TANAKA
*CURRENT ROTATION
TAM
TAM
BRING IT ON!!
TMP
TMP
TMP

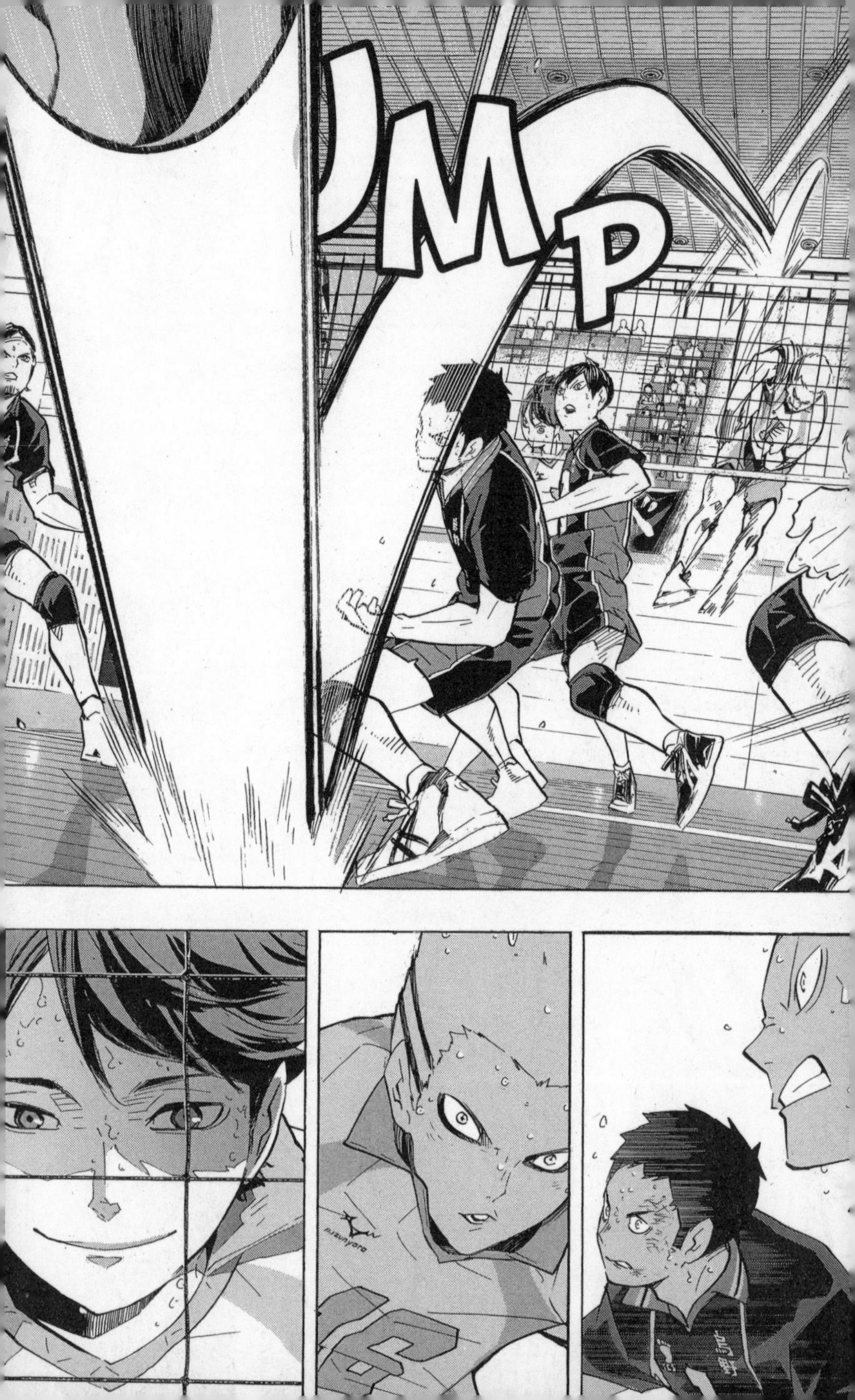
UMP

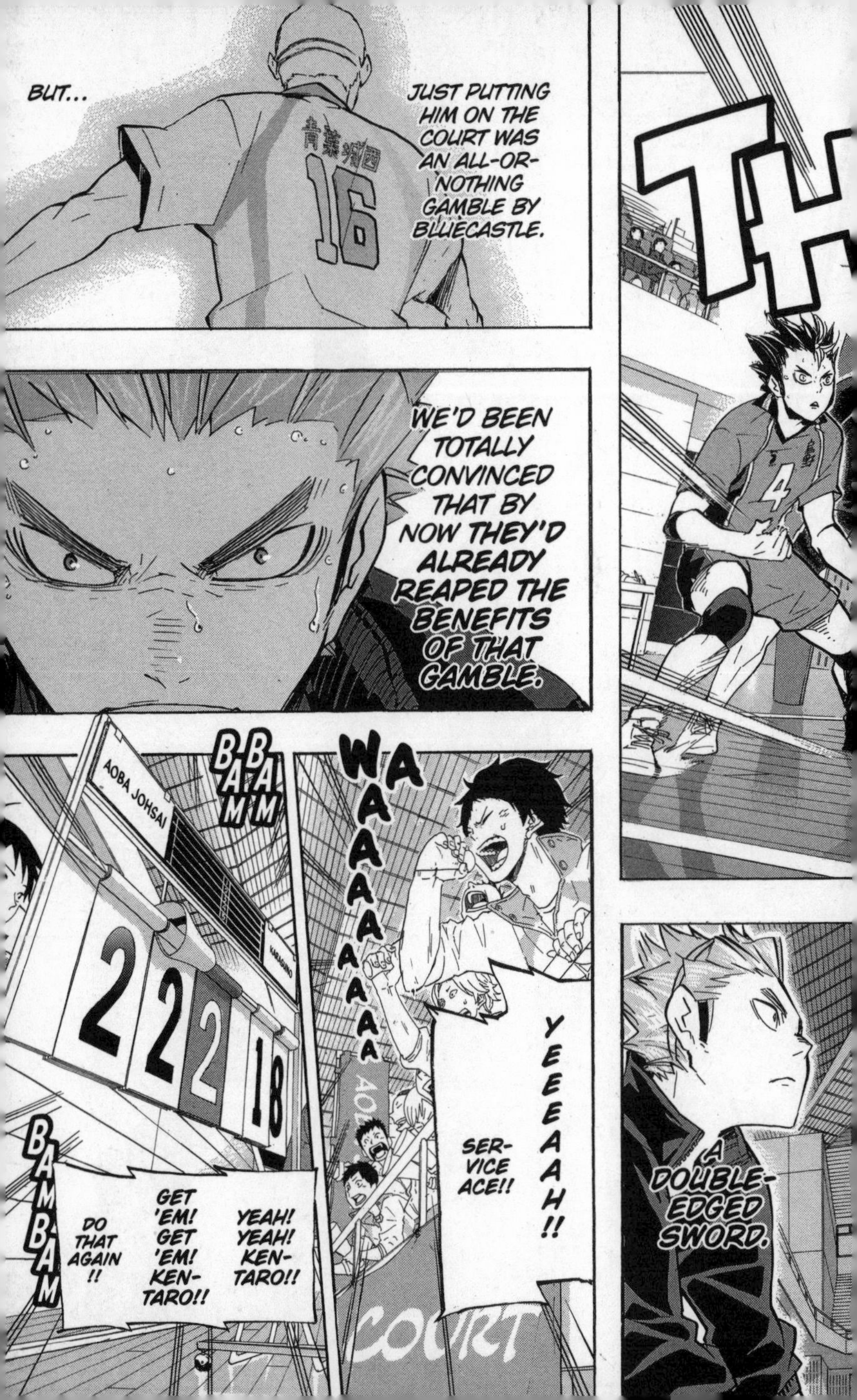
TH
BUT...
JUST PUTTING HIM ON THE COURT WAS AN ALL-OR-NOTHING GAMBLE BY BLUECASTLE.
WE'D BEEN TOTALLY CONVINCED THAT BY NOW THEY'D ALREADY REAPED THE BENEFITS OF THAT GAMBLE.
WAAAAAAAAAA
YEEEEAAAH!!
SER-VICE ACE!!
YEAH! YEAH! KEN-TARO!!
GET 'EM! GET 'EM! KEN-TARO!!
DO THAT AGAIN!!
COURT
BA-BAMM
BA-BAMM
AOBA JOHSAI
KARASUNO
22
18
BAM-BAM
A DOUBLE-EDGED SWORD.

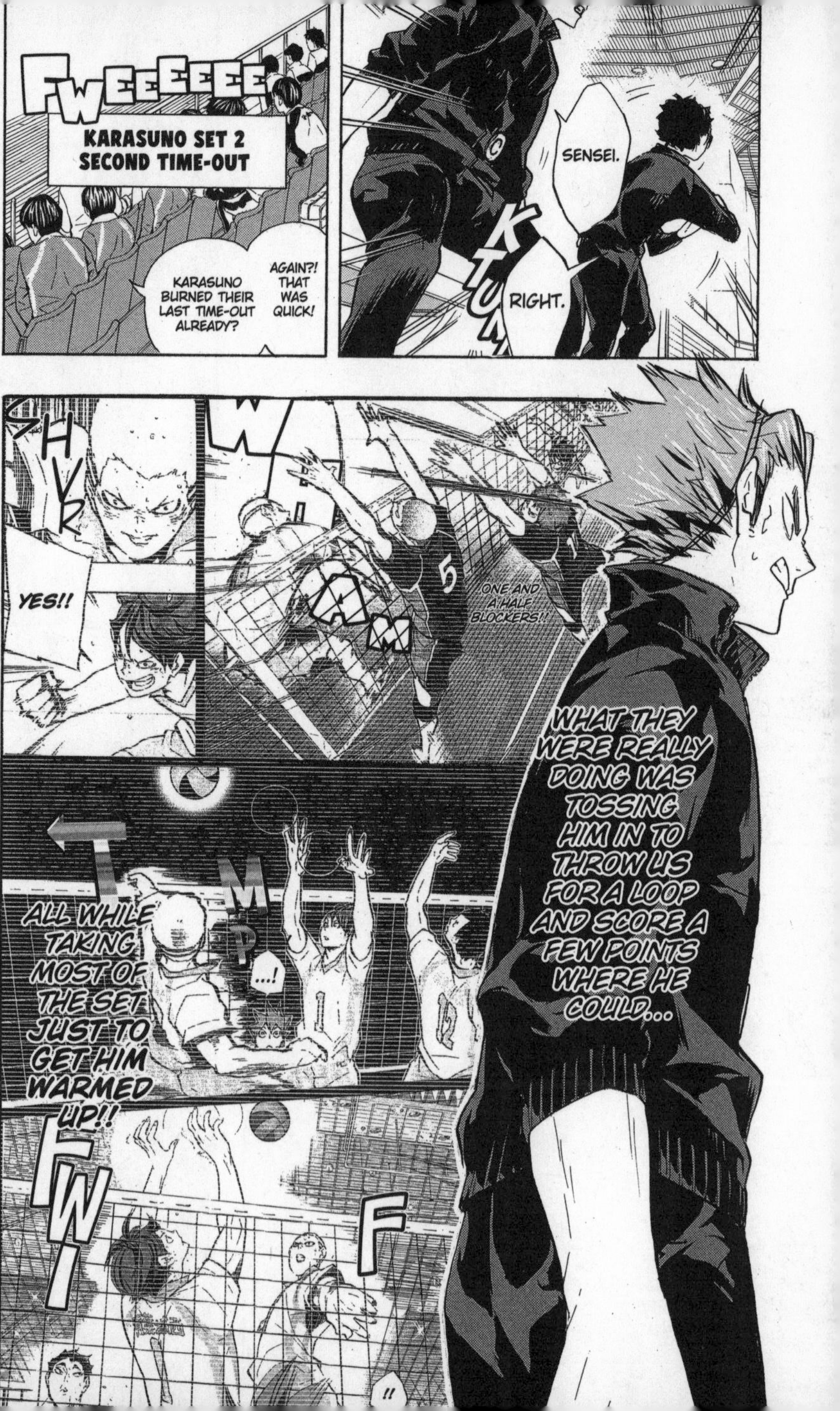
SENSEI.
RIGHT.
FWEEEEEE
KARASUNO SET 2
SECOND TIME-OUT
AGAIN?! THAT WAS QUICK!
KARASUNO BURNED THEIR LAST TIME-OUT ALREADY?
WHAT THEY WERE REALLY DOING WAS TOSSING HIM IN TO THROW US FOR A LOOP AND SCORE A FEW POINTS WHERE HE COULD...
ONE AND A HALF BLOCKERS!!
YES!!
...!
ALL WHILE TAKING MOST OF THE SET JUST TO GET HIM WARMED UP!!
!!

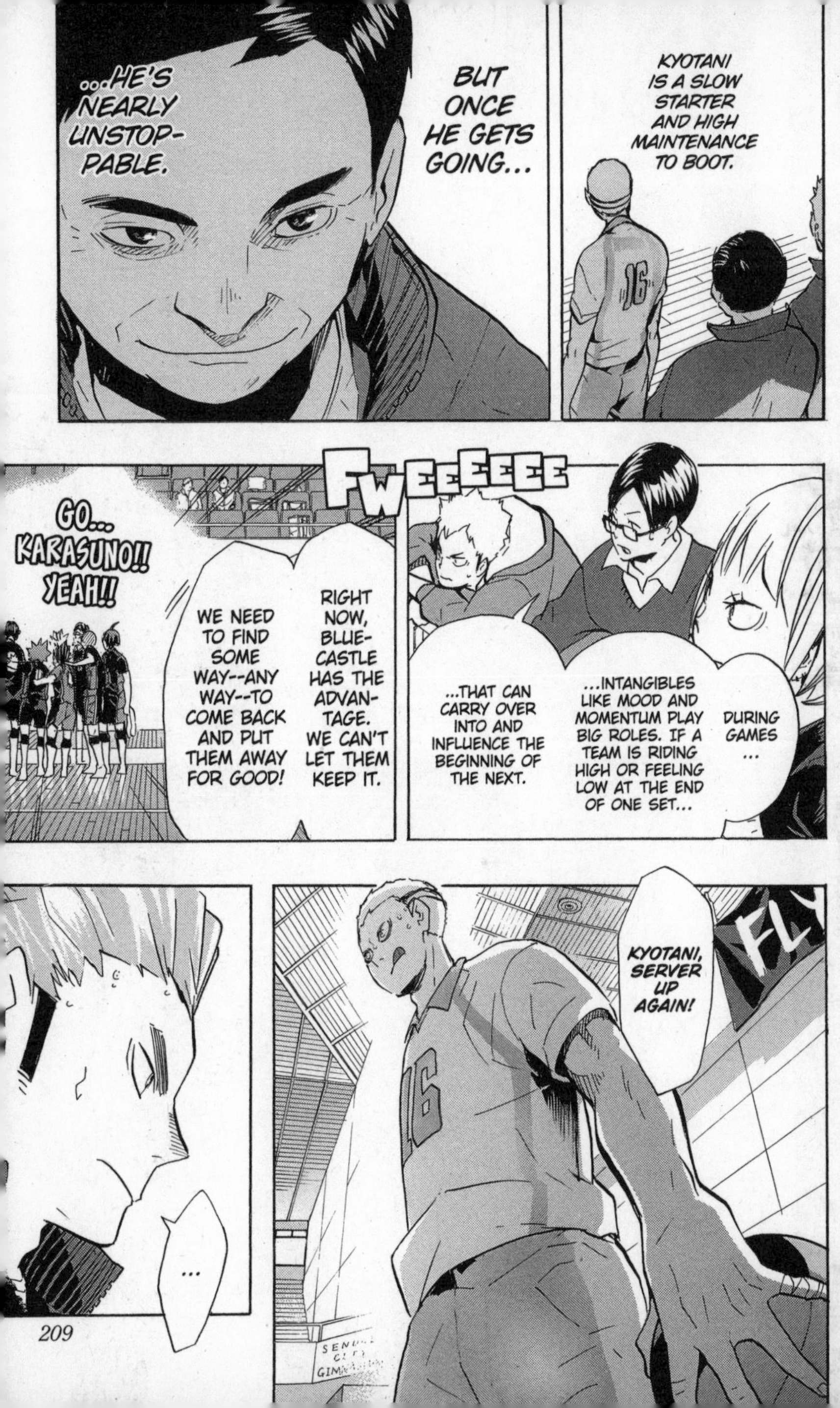
KYOTANI IS A SLOW STARTER AND HIGH MAINTENANCE TO BOOT.
BUT ONCE HE GETS GOING...
...HE'S NEARLY UNSTOP-PABLE.
FWEEEEEE
DURING GAMES ...
...INTANGIBLES LIKE MOOD AND MOMENTUM PLAY BIG ROLES. IF A TEAM IS RIDING HIGH OR FEELING LOW AT THE END OF ONE SET...
...THAT CAN CARRY OVER INTO AND INFLUENCE THE BEGINNING OF THE NEXT.
RIGHT NOW, BLUE-CASTLE HAS THE ADVAN-TAGE. WE CAN'T LET THEM KEEP IT.
WE NEED TO FIND SOME WAY--ANY WAY--TO COME BACK AND PUT THEM AWAY FOR GOOD!
GO... KARASUNO!! YEAH!!
KYOTANI, SERVER UP AGAIN!
FLY
...

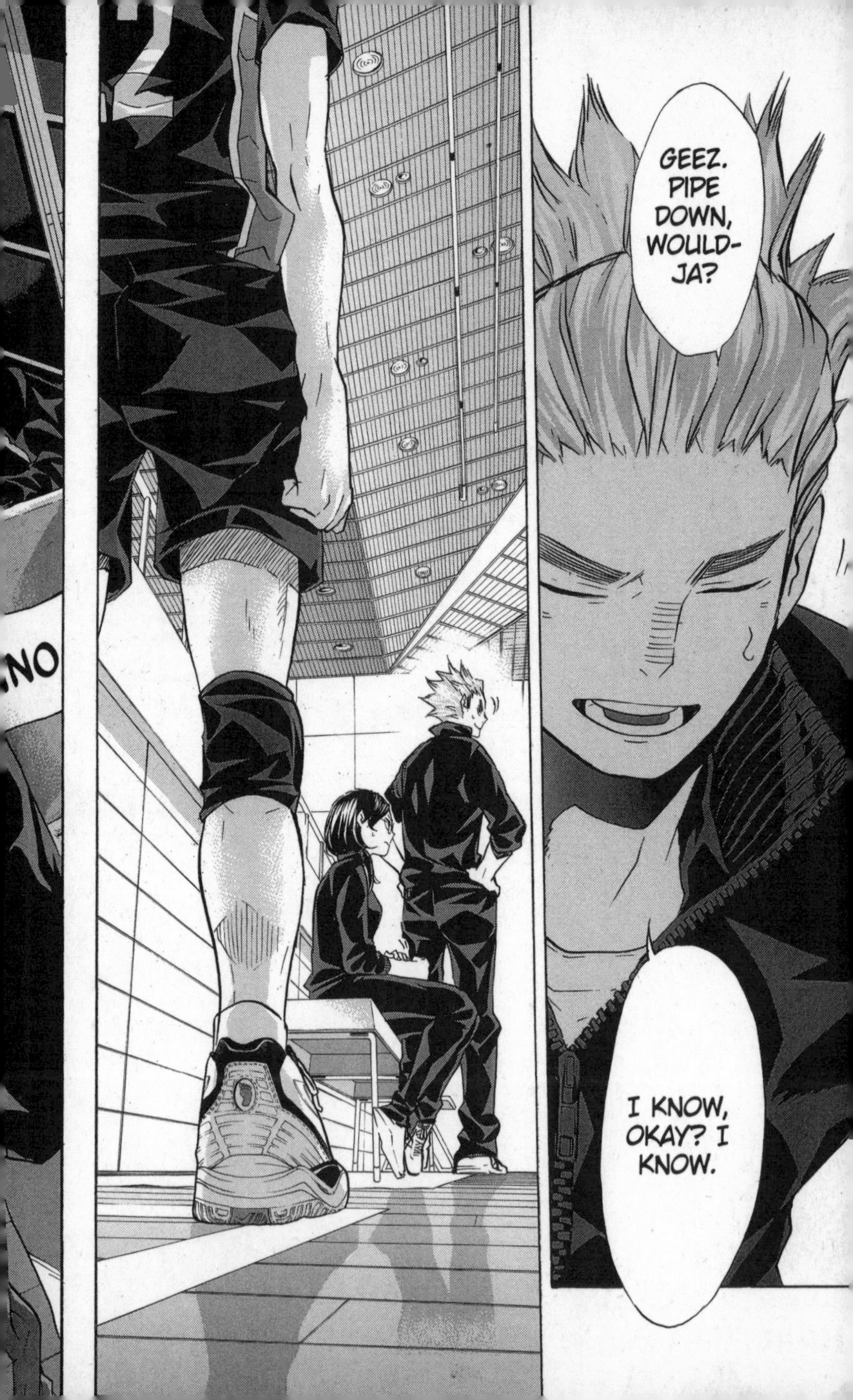
GEEZ. PIPE DOWN, WOULD-JA?
I KNOW, OKAY? I KNOW.

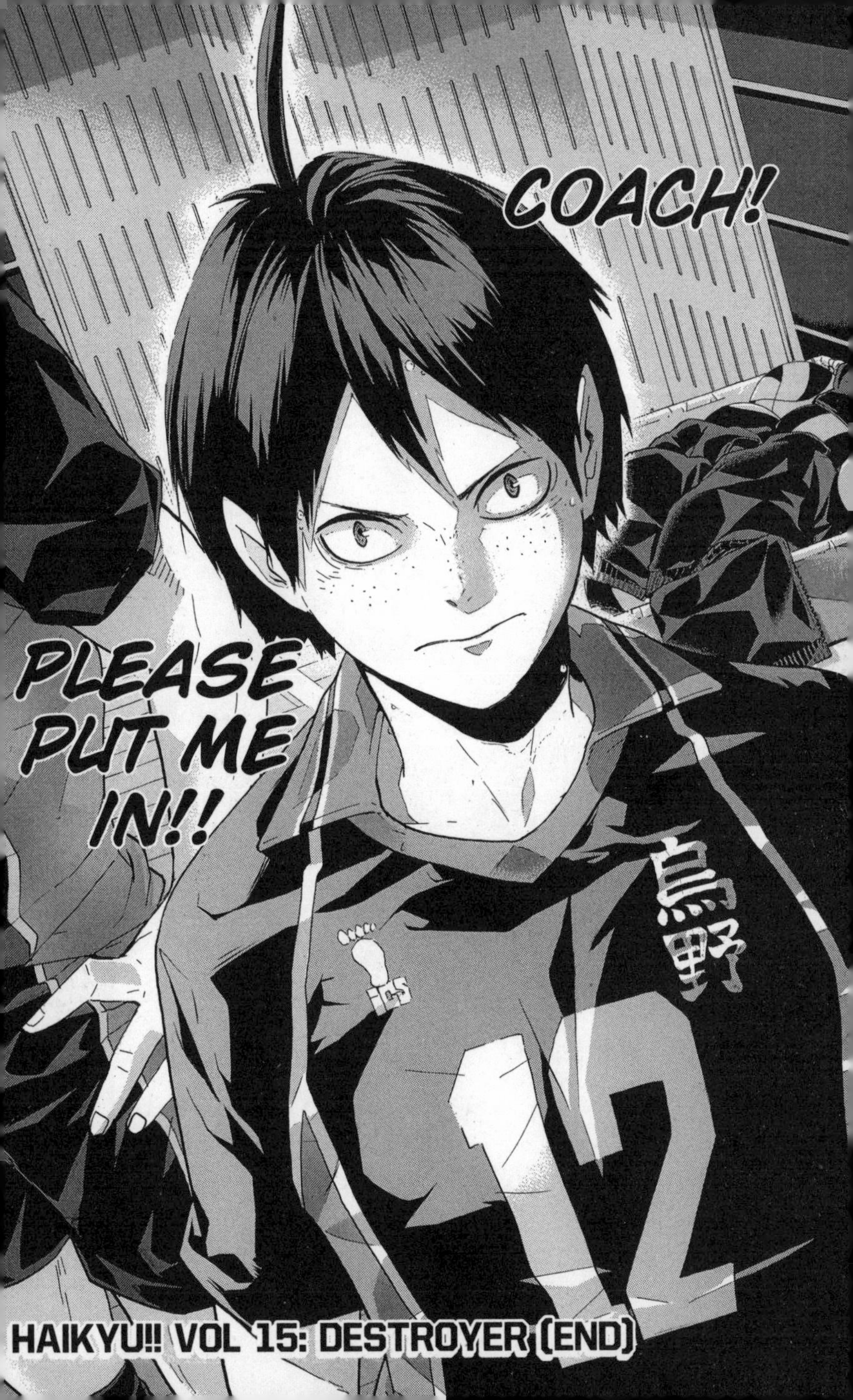
COACH!
PLEASE PUT ME IN!!
烏野
12
HAIKYU!! VOL 15: DESTROYER (END)

CHAPTER 127+

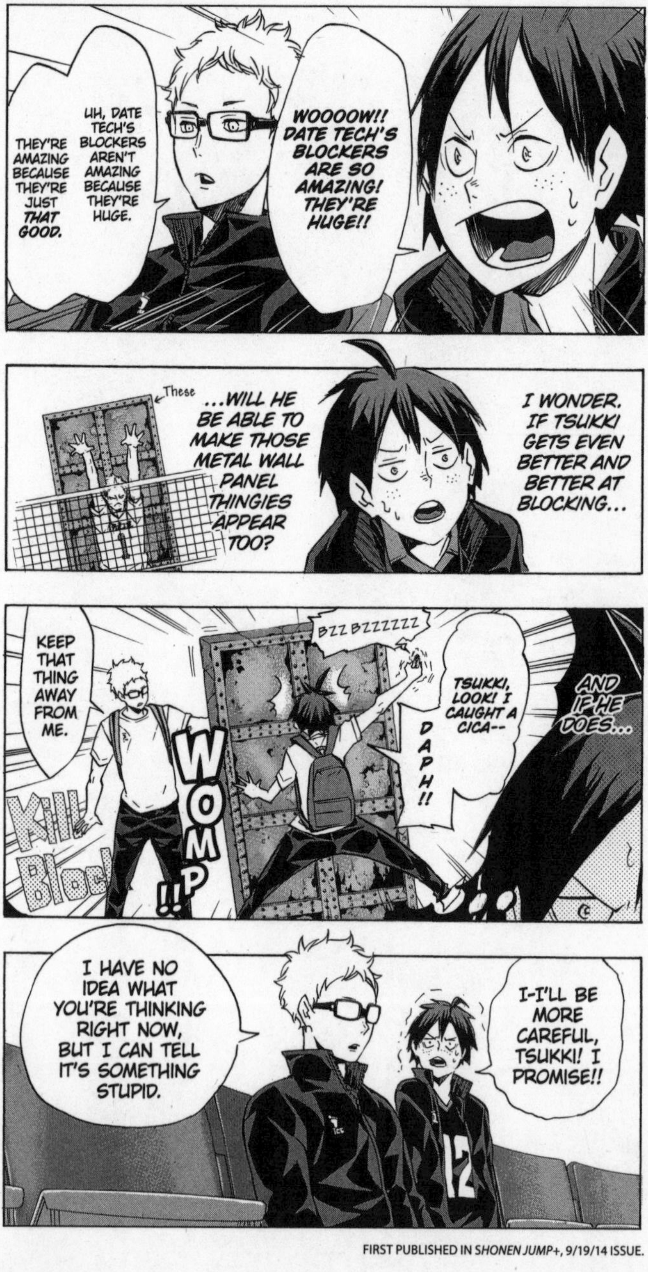
WOOOOW!! DATE TECH'S BLOCKERS ARE SO AMAZING! THEY'RE HUGE!!
UH, DATE TECH'S BLOCKERS AREN'T AMAZING BECAUSE THEY'RE HUGE.
THEY'RE AMAZING BECAUSE THEY'RE JUST *THAT* GOOD.
I WONDER. IF TSUKKI GETS EVEN BETTER AND BETTER AT BLOCKING...
...WILL HE BE ABLE TO MAKE THOSE METAL WALL PANEL THINGIES APPEAR TOO?
These
AND IF HE DOES...
TSUKKI, LOOK! I CAUGHT A CICA--
DAPH!!
BZZ BZZZZZZ
WOMP!!
KEEP THAT THING AWAY FROM ME.
Kill Block!
I-I'LL BE MORE CAREFUL, TSUKKI! I PROMISE!!
I HAVE NO IDEA WHAT YOU'RE THINKING RIGHT NOW, BUT I CAN TELL IT'S SOMETHING STUPID.

FIRST PUBLISHED IN *SHONEN JUMP+*, 9/19/14 ISSUE.

← STARTING ON THE NEXT PAGE IS THE "JOKE MOVIE POSTER" THAT RAN IN *JUMP NEXT!!* AND A LITTLE BONUS STORY RELATED TO IT. I HAD SO MUCH FUN DRAWING SOMETHING LIKE THIS THAT I THINK I'LL DO IT AGAIN WHEN I CAN FIND THE TIME.

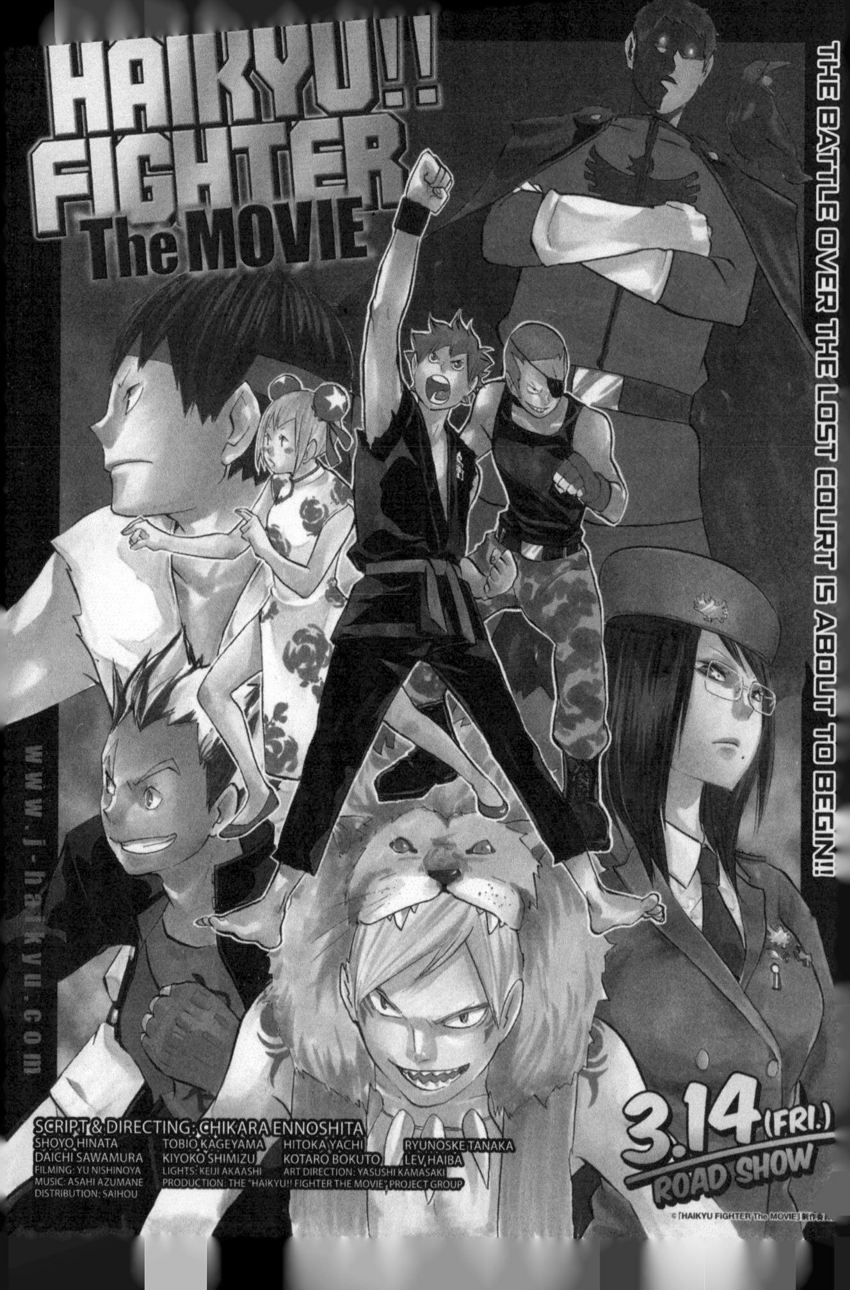
HAIKYU!! FIGHTER The MOVIE
THE BATTLE OVER THE LOST COURT IS ABOUT TO BEGIN!!
www.j-haikyu.com
SCRIPT & DIRECTING: CHIKARA ENNOSHITA
SHOYO HINATA
TOBIO KAGEYAMA
HITOKA YACHI
RYUNOSKE TANAKA
DAICHI SAWAMURA
KIYOKO SHIMIZU
KOTARO BOKUTO
LEV HAIBA
FILMING: YU NISHINOYA
LIGHTS: KEIJI AKAASHI
ART DIRECTION: YASUSHI KAMASAKI
MUSIC: ASAHI AZUMANE
PRODUCTION: THE "HAIKYU!! FIGHTER THE MOVIE" PROJECT GROUP
DISTRIBUTION: SAIHOU
3.14 (FRI.)
ROAD SHOW
©「HAIKYU FIGHTER The MOVIE」

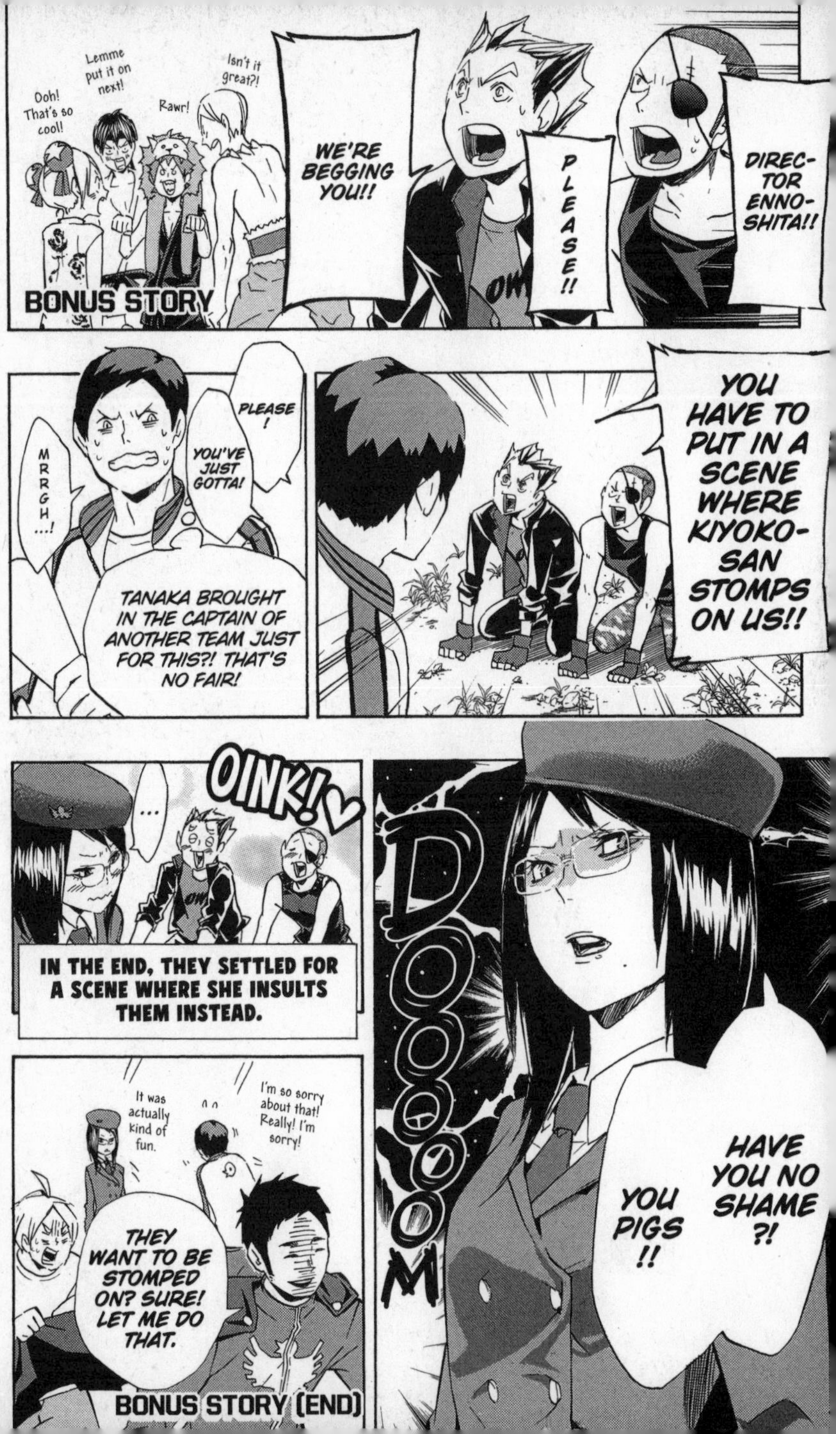
DIRECTOR ENNOSHITA!!
PLEASE!!
WE'RE BEGGING YOU!!
Isn't it great?!
Rawr!
Lemme put it on next!
Ooh! That's so cool!
BONUS STORY
YOU HAVE TO PUT IN A SCENE WHERE KIYOKO-SAN STOMPS ON US!!
PLEASE!
YOU'VE JUST GOTTA!
MRRGH...!
TANAKA BROUGHT IN THE CAPTAIN OF ANOTHER TEAM JUST FOR THIS?! THAT'S NO FAIR!
DOOOOOOM
HAVE YOU NO SHAME?!
YOU PIGS!!
OINK!♥
...
IN THE END, THEY SETTLED FOR A SCENE WHERE SHE INSULTS THEM INSTEAD.
I'm so sorry about that! Really! I'm sorry!
It was actually kind of fun.
THEY WANT TO BE STOMPED ON? SURE! LET ME DO THAT.
BONUS STORY (END)

EDITOR'S NOTES

The English edition of Haikyu!! maintains the honorifics used in the original Japanese version. For those of you who are new to these terms, here's a brief explanation to help with your reading experience!

When saying someone's name in Japanese, a suffix is often attached to indicate how familiar the speaker is with the person. Some are more polite and respectful, while others are endearing.

1. ***-kun*** is often used for young men or boys, usually someone you are familiar with.

2. ***-chan*** is used for young children and can be used as a term of endearment.

3. ***-san*** is used for someone you respect or are not close to, or to be polite.

4. ***Senpai*** is used for someone who is older than you or in a higher position or grade in school.

5. ***Kohai*** is used for someone who is younger than you or in a lower position or grade in school.

6. ***Sensei*** means teacher.

7. ***Bluecastle*** is a nickname for Aoba Johsai. It is a combination of *Ao* [blue] and *Joh* [castle].

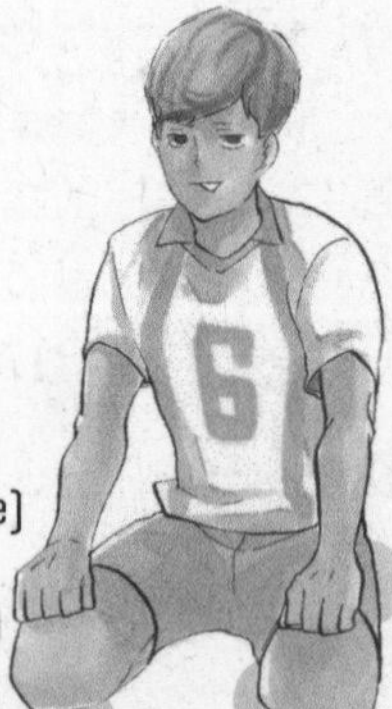
6

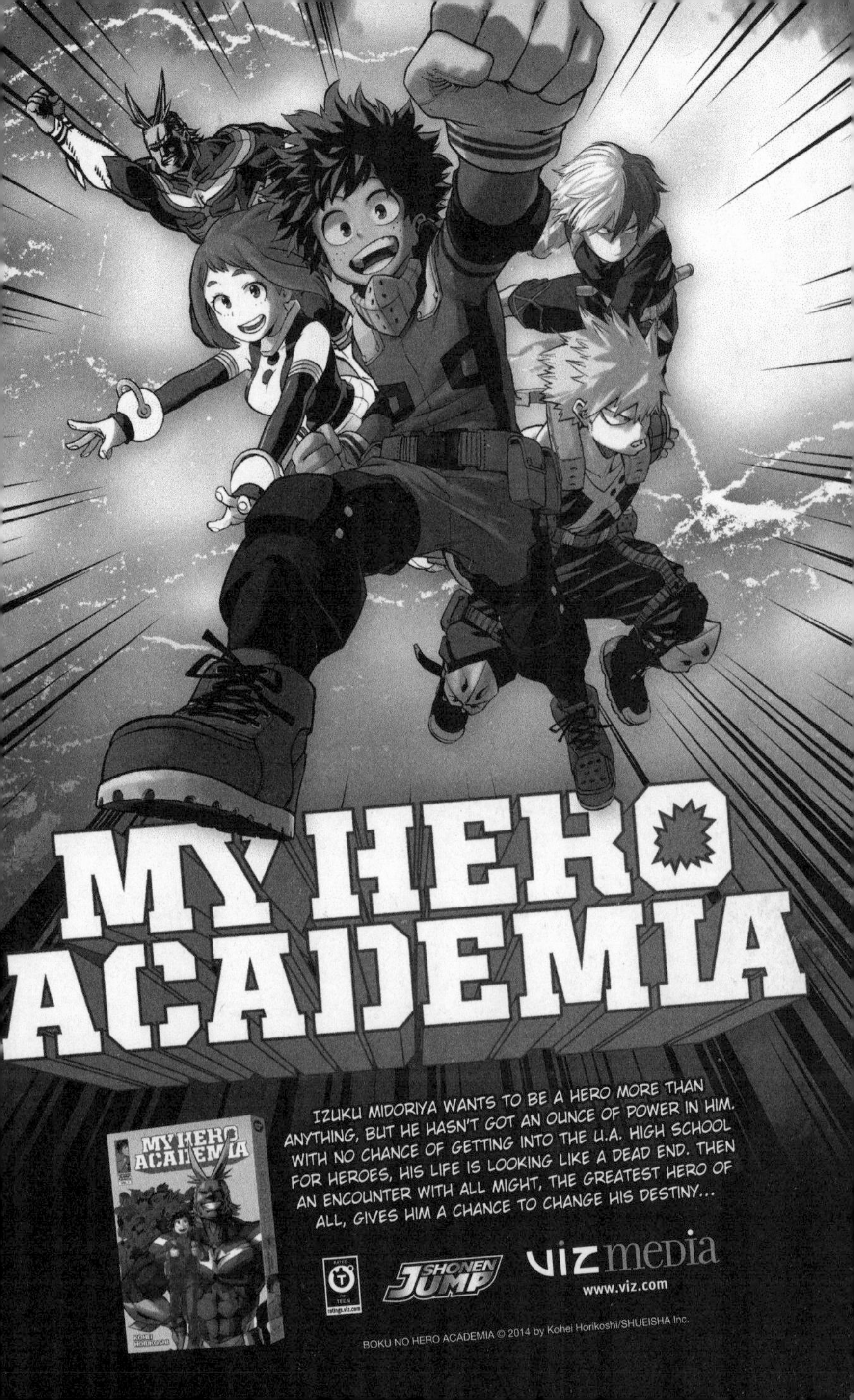
MY HERO ACADEMIA
IZUKU MIDORIYA WANTS TO BE A HERO MORE THAN ANYTHING, BUT HE HASN'T GOT AN OUNCE OF POWER IN HIM. WITH NO CHANCE OF GETTING INTO THE U.A. HIGH SCHOOL FOR HEROES, HIS LIFE IS LOOKING LIKE A DEAD END. THEN AN ENCOUNTER WITH ALL MIGHT, THE GREATEST HERO OF ALL, GIVES HIM A CHANCE TO CHANGE HIS DESTINY...
MY HERO ACADEMIA
KOHEI HORIKOSHI
RATED T TEEN
ratings.viz.com
SHONEN JUMP
viz media
www.viz.com
BOKU NO HERO ACADEMIA © 2014 by Kohei Horikoshi/SHUEISHA Inc.

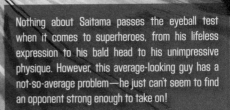

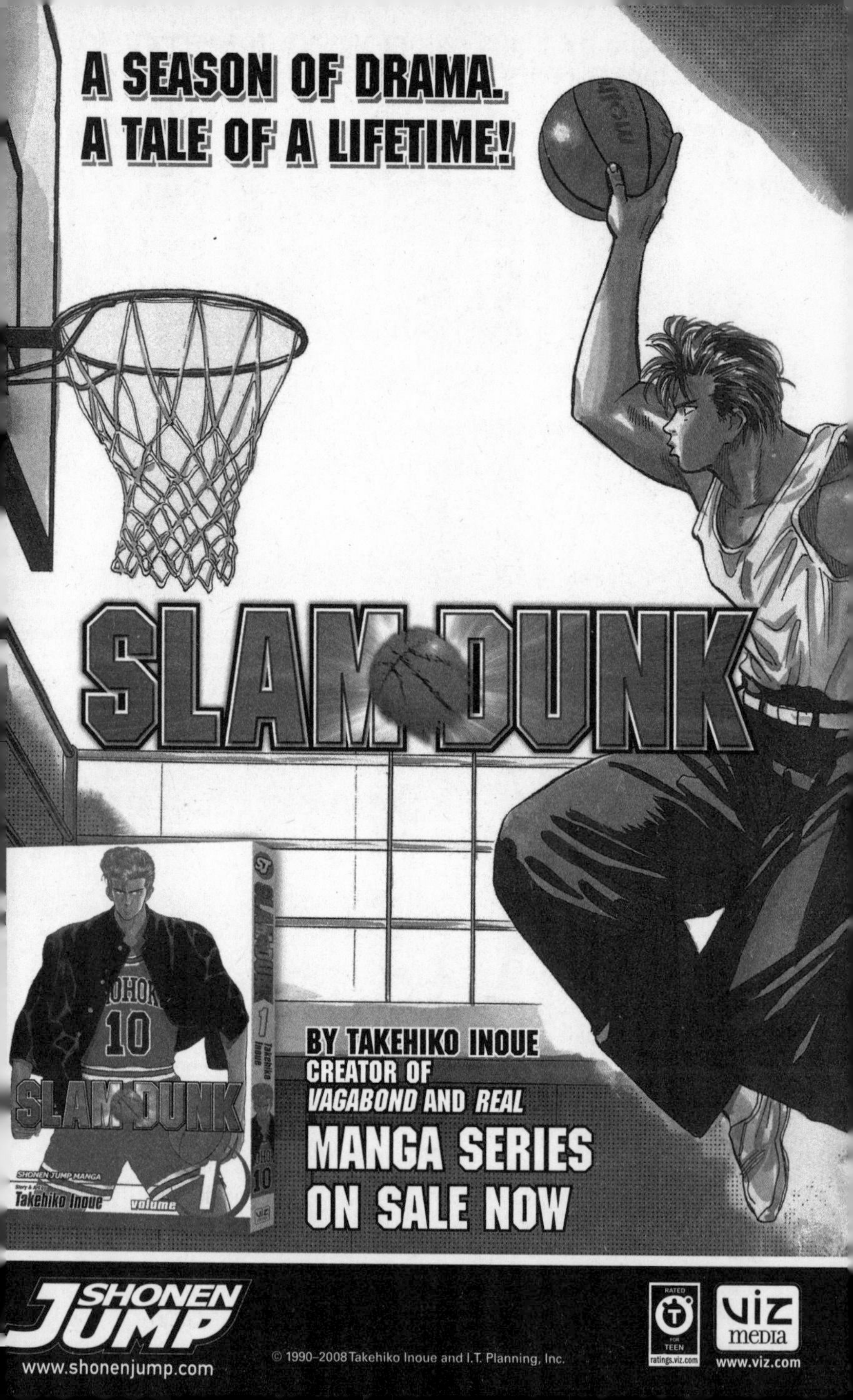
A SEASON OF DRAMA.
A TALE OF A LIFETIME!
SLAM DUNK
SLAM DUNK
SHONEN JUMP MANGA
Takehiko Inoue
volume 1
BY TAKEHIKO INOUE
CREATOR OF
VAGABOND AND REAL
MANGA SERIES
ON SALE NOW
SHONEN JUMP
www.shonenjump.com
© 1990–2008 Takehiko Inoue and I.T. Planning, Inc.
RATED T FOR TEEN
ratings.viz.com
viz media
www.viz.com

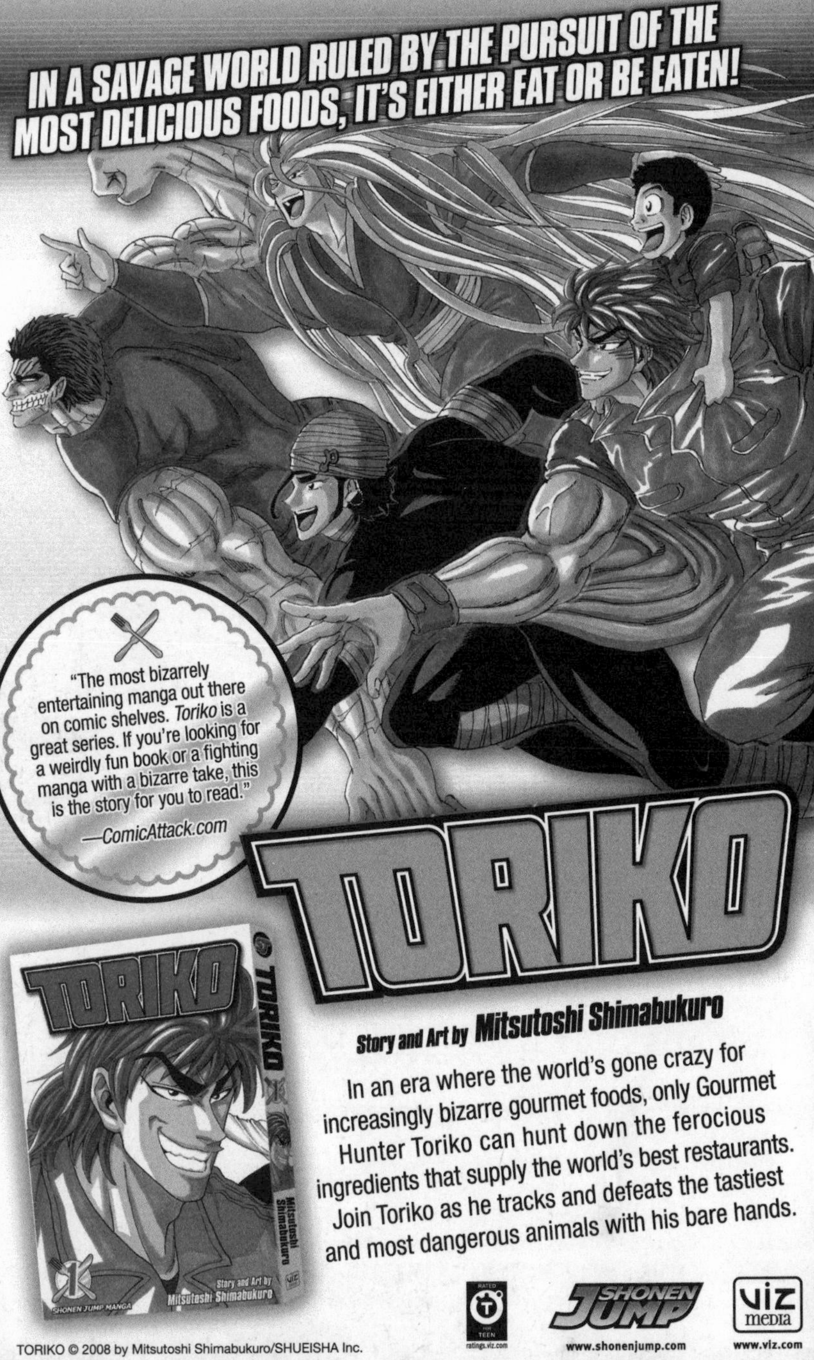
IN A SAVAGE WORLD RULED BY THE PURSUIT OF THE MOST DELICIOUS FOODS, IT'S EITHER EAT OR BE EATEN!
"The most bizarrely entertaining manga out there on comic shelves. Toriko is a great series. If you're looking for a weirdly fun book or a fighting manga with a bizarre take, this is the story for you to read."
—ComicAttack.com
TORIKO
Story and Art by Mitsutoshi Shimabukuro
In an era where the world's gone crazy for increasingly bizarre gourmet foods, only Gourmet Hunter Toriko can hunt down the ferocious ingredients that supply the world's best restaurants. Join Toriko as he tracks and defeats the tastiest and most dangerous animals with his bare hands.
RATED T TEEN
ratings.viz.com
SHONEN JUMP
www.shonenjump.com
VIZ media
www.viz.com

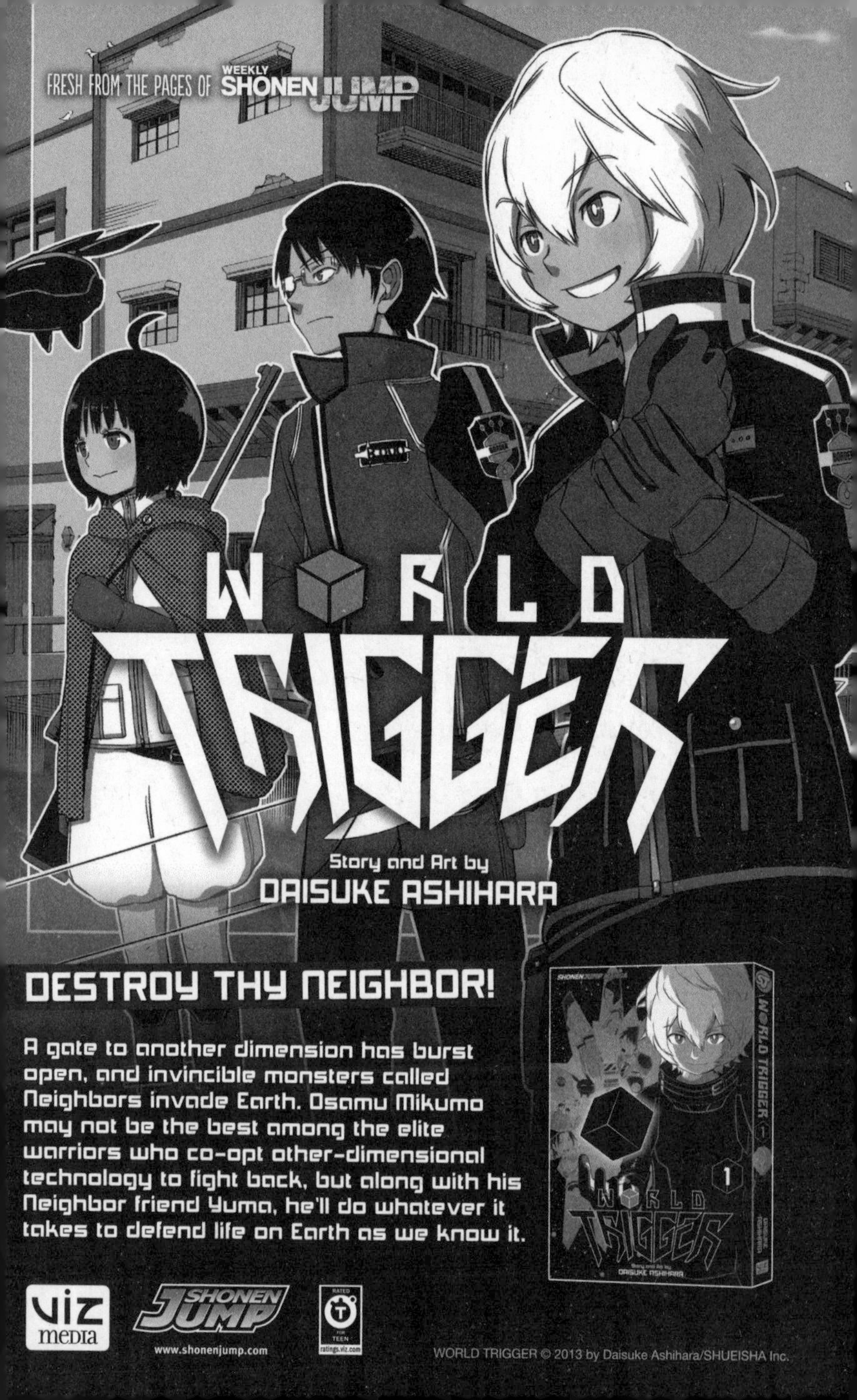

FRESH FROM THE PAGES OF WEEKLY SHONEN JUMP
WORLD TRIGGER
Story and Art by
DAISUKE ASHIHARA
DESTROY THY NEIGHBOR!
A gate to another dimension has burst open, and invincible monsters called Neighbors invade Earth. Osamu Mikumo may not be the best among the elite warriors who co-opt other-dimensional technology to fight back, but along with his Neighbor friend Yuma, he'll do whatever it takes to defend life on Earth as we know it.
viz media
SHONEN JUMP
www.shonenjump.com
RATED T FOR TEEN
ratings.viz.com
WORLD TRIGGER © 2013 by Daisuke Ashihara/SHUEISHA Inc.

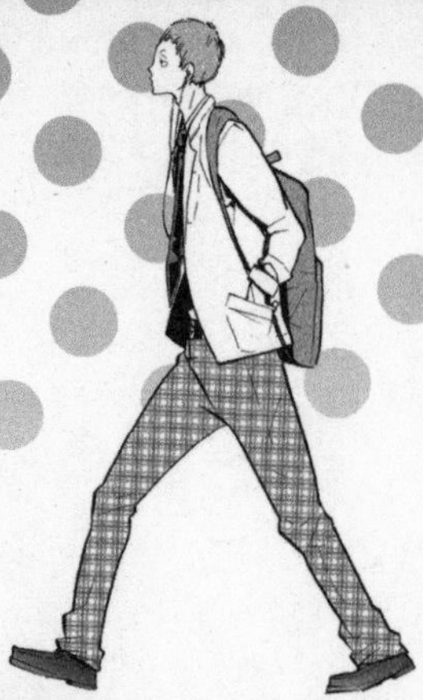

You're Reading the **WRONG WAY!**

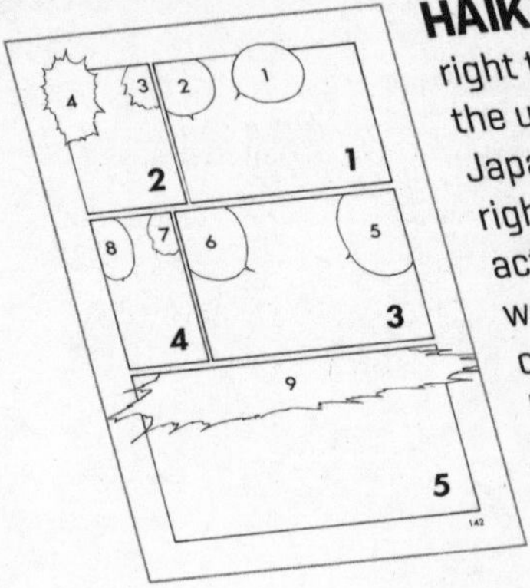
1
2
3
4
1
2
5
6
7
8
3
4
9
5
142

HAIKYU!! reads from right to left, starting in the upper-right corner. Japanese is read from right to left, meaning that action, sound effects and word-balloon order are completely reversed from English order.

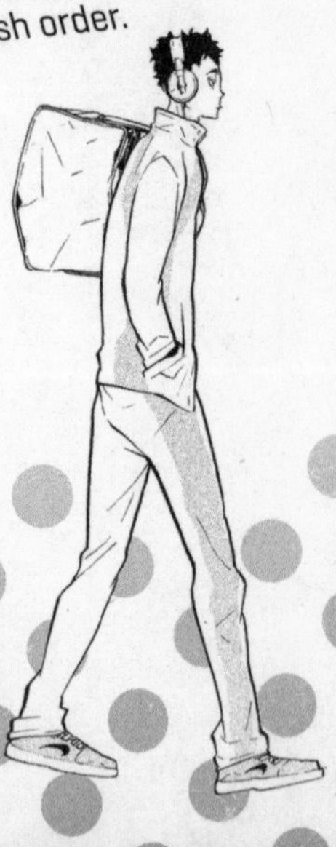